AN INTRODUCTION
TO THE
OLD TESTAMENT PROPHETS

AN INTRODUCTION
TO THE
OLD TESTAMENT
PROPHETS

by

HOBART E. FREEMAN

MOODY PRESS

CHICAGO

To My Wife
June

ISBN: 0-8024-4145-9

Library of Congress Catalog Card Number: 68-26412

A MOODY PRESS BOOK

Eleventh Printing, 1977

Manufactured in the United States of America

CONTENTS

PART II

THE BOOKS OF THE PROPHETS

PREFACE

THE MOTIVATION for this volume is twofold. First, while there is a profusion of commentaries on the Prophets, there is little available to the Old Testament student which provides an adequate conservative *introduction* to each of the books of the Prophets. Such a text would need to deal sufficiently with the historical background of each prophecy, the general nature of each book, an analysis of the prophet's message, a consideration of the prophet himself, a precise treatment of the questions of date and authorship, and the major critical problems of each book. The writer, who has taught in this area of Old Testament studies, has often wished for such an up-to-date source book of information. The present work is an outgrowth of the author's syllabus notes prepared for use in his classes.

Second, there is also a growing need today for a restatement of the biblical view of prophecy (or prophetism) in an era characterized by theological extremes, new orthodoxies and the unbiblical presuppositions of negative criticism.

Thus, the writer has set forth in the first section of the book a study in *prophetism*, that is, a survey of the nature of Old Testament prophecy and the prophetic institution in Israel. Then an introduction is provided to each book of the Prophets.

The writer wishes to express his appreciation to those who have encouraged completion of the manuscript. Acknowledgment is also due Dr. J. Barton Payne, Wheaton College, for the helpful suggestions concerning certain problems of chronology in Isaiah, and Dr. Robert D. Culver, Trinity Evangelical Divinity School, for his constructive evaluation of the manuscript on the book of Daniel. The writer is especially indebted to his wife, his faithful companion in the final preparation and typing of the manuscript. Biblical quotations are from the American Standard Version with the covenant name of God corrected from Jehovah to the Hebrew Yahweh throughout.

HOBART E. FREEMAN

PREFACE

THE MOTIVATION for this volume is twofold. First, while there is a profusion of commentaries on the Prophets, there is little available to the Old Testament student which provides an adequate conservative *introduction* to each of the books of the Prophets. Such a text would need to deal sufficiently with the historical background of each prophecy, the general nature of each book, an analysis of the prophet's message, a consideration of the prophet himself, a precise treatment of the questions of date and authorship, and the major critical problems of each book. The writer, who has taught in this area of Old Testament studies, has often wished for such an up-to-date source book of information. The present work is an outgrowth of the author's syllabus notes prepared for use in his classes.

Second, there is also a growing need today for a restatement of the biblical view of prophecy (or prophetism) in an era characterized by theological extremes, new orthodoxies and the unbiblical presuppositions of negative criticism.

Thus, the writer has set forth in the first section of the book a study in *prophetism*, that is, a survey of the nature of Old Testament prophecy and the prophetic institution in Israel. Then an introduction is provided to each book of the Prophets.

The writer wishes to express his appreciation to those who have encouraged completion of the manuscript. Acknowledgment is also due Dr. J. Barton Payne, Wheaton College, for the helpful suggestions concerning certain problems of chronology in Isaiah, and Dr. Robert D. Culver, Trinity Evangelical Divinity School, for his constructive evaluation of the manuscript on the book of Daniel. The writer is especially indebted to his wife, his faithful companion in the final preparation and typing of the manuscript. Biblical quotations are from the American Standard Version with the covenant name of God corrected from Jehovah to the Hebrew Yahweh throughout.

HOBART E. FREEMAN

7

PART I
PROPHETISM

INTRODUCTION

Nature of Old Testament Prophecy

THE RELIGION AND HISTORY of Israel are fundamentally prophetic. The Old Testament revelation was, according to Hebrews 1:1, a revelation through the prophets. In the Old Testament, *history* and *prophecy* are closely related, inasmuch as the great events of Israel's history (e.g., the call of Abraham, the exodus, the establishment of the Davidic kingdom, the destruction of Jerusalem, and the Babylonian exile) called forth the prophetic messages and revelations. Prophecy, by divine inspiration, arose from Israel's historical experiences and was to find its fulfillment in history. Israel's religion, unlike that of her contemporaries, was grounded in a revelation through historical events, rather than in metaphysical speculation, superstition or philosophical reasoning. This helps to explain why the Historical Books of Joshua, Judges, Samuel and Kings are designated the "Former Prophets" in the Hebrew canon. The authors of these books, like the later prophets, saw that the history of Israel was, in itself, a revelation of God. When a writer recorded Old Testament history, he was not interested simply in writing history as history, but in recording the revelation of God in and through that history.[1] Prophecy and providence run side by side in the Scriptures.

Hence, the Word of God consists in just this; it is the prophetic testimony to what God has said and done, and what He will yet do in history. Prophetic thought, therefore, includes a philosophy of history which interprets its course and predicts its ultimate outcome. Furthermore, not only the history of Israel but also the history of all nations is under God's sovereign control. All history is an arena for the demonstration of His wisdom, power and glory. This is clearly indicated, for example, in Amos 9:7 where God declares to sinful Israel:

[1]C. von Orelli also contends for this concept: "Even the historians, who illumined the foretime with the light of revelation, wrote prophetically, because they made known God's ways in the past" (*Old Testament Prophecy*, p. 7).

11

Are ye not as the children of the Ethiopians unto me, O children of Israel? saith Yahweh. Have not I brought up Israel out of the land of Egypt, and the Philistines from Caphtor, and the Syrians from Kir?

The significance of God's statement is first of all for Israel to make a proper evaluation of her history, since she was self-confidently resting in a false sense of security and exemption from judgment purely on the basis of the exodus and her deliverance from Egypt. Thus God reminds Israel that her exodus, apart from faithful obedience, gives her no prerogatives, for the Philistines and Syrians are, in one sense, exodus peoples also.[2] In addition to this fact, this text unequivocally declares that the God of Israel is also the omnipotent Master of the destinies of all men, nations and events, and is, in a word, the Lord of history. God's judgments upon the Gentile nations, as well as upon Israel, are evidence of this lordship over history. There are numerous prophecies of such judgments in the prophetic writings. Edom, Moab, Ammon, Philistia, Aram, Tyre and Sidon all were to be judged, together with the world empires of Assyria, Egypt, Babylon and others. In fact, the prophets pronounced judgments against all peoples (Isa. 34; Joel 3; Zech. 12-14; Jer. 25:15-29; Isa. 24-27; Micah 7:11 ff.; Zeph. 1-3).

However, the divine *purpose* of God in history most clearly delineates its prophetic character. In Hebrew thought in general, and the prophetic writers in particular, one finds a uniqueness in the concept of history that differs from the secular philosophy of history. This difference lies in the prophetic awareness of the overruling divine providence directing all events of history toward one central purpose. The purpose of God's providential workings in the arena of history, such as the raising up of Cyrus, is not only for Israel's sake, but it has an ultimate universal end in view: "That they may know from the rising of the sun, and from the west, that there is none besides me: I am Yahweh, and there is none else" (Isa. 45:6). Thus, Old Testament history is not just history, but history that is purposeful, and that purpose is redemptive. The purpose of God in the history of Israel is, to the eye of faith, the clue to the history of mankind. This is the theological emphasis of the prophets—that God, as the Lord of history and providence, was controlling the issues and movements of history for a purpose. With one voice the prophets declare that this purpose, toward which all history is being directed,

[2]G. C. Berkouwer, *The Providence of God,* p. 190.

is the establishment of the *kingdom of God*—the sovereign reign and rule of God upon earth:

> And Yahweh shall be King over all the earth: in that day shall Yahweh be one, and his name one (Zech. 14:9).

Prophecy and history, therefore, are seen to be inseparably related. But biblical prophecy is not, as many higher critics contend, merely the recital of history in the sense that "the meaning of the present was taken primarily from the understanding and interpretation of the past."[3] The modern critical hypothesis, relative to biblical prophecy, assumes that prediction of the distant future is impossible and, therefore, the predictive element in prophecy must either be rejected entirely or reduced to the absolute minimum. A. B. Davidson says of prophecy that "prediction is the least element in it. I do not know that it is an essential element in it at all."[4] And again he writes: "All thoughtful men have in them something of the prophetic gift. By observing what has been, they can come pretty near what will be."[5] Hence, the prophets are to be thought of simply as keen observers of their day. On the basis of their unique moral insight into history, and their ethical sensitivity to contemporary events, they were able to make reasonably accurate predictions. Certainly Oswald T. Allis is correct when, in criticism of this viewpoint, he concludes: "But so understood the prophet is practically transformed into a moral philosopher, whose predictions become little more than maxims. . . ."[6] Such a low view of prophecy, as proposed by negative criticism, cannot explain, for instance, how Ezekiel, exiled in Babylon, could by logical reasoning from the events of history predict the precise fate of King Zedekiah in Jerusalem, how that while trying to escape the besieged city, he would have his eyes put out and be carried captive to Babylon (Ezek. 12:8 ff.). Nor could he have known, as a mere interpreter of history, from his isolation in Babylon the exact day when the siege of Jerusalem began (Ezek. 24:2). Likewise Jeremiah's prediction of the death of Hananiah cannot be explained by the critical view of predictive prophecy (Jer. 28:16-17). The same may be said of Amos' prediction of the fall of Israel (Amos 5:27); Micaiah's prediction of the violent death of Ahab (I Kings 22); Isaiah's forecast of Jerusalem's unique deliverance from Sen-

---

[3]B. D. Napier, "Prophet, Prophetism," *The Interpreter's Dictionary of the Bible,* ed. George A. Buttrick, III, 911.
[4]A. B. Davidson, *Old Testament Prophecy,* p. 11.
[5]Davidson, p. 92.
[6]Oswald T. Allis, *The Unity of Isaiah,* p. 21.

nacherib (Isa. 37:26-36); his naming of Cyrus long before his birth (45:1); Jeremiah's prediction of the seventy years' captivity and return (Jer. 25:11-12); and Micah's naming of the birthplace of the Messiah (Micah 5:2).

These predictions cannot be explained as mere conclusions deduced by keen insight into contemporary moral and political conditions, inasmuch as the material and political prosperity of Israel in the time of Amos, and that of Judah in the time of Jeremiah, would not suggest to these prophets the extreme pessimistic outlook which characterizes their prophecies. There can be no satisfactory explanation apart from divine revelation. Moreover, unlike the heathen soothsayers, the Hebrew prophets never predict the future simply to satisfy idle curiosity, nor merely to draw attention to themselves. Prophecy of the future is never an isolated utterance, but is to find meaning in its bearing upon the future kingdom of God and the Messiah.

On the other hand, it is not the biblical view to suppose that prophecy is to be limited to the disclosure of the future. "That which is given by the Spirit to the prophet can refer to the past and to the present as well as to the future."[7] The prophets themselves were inspired preachers. To their contemporaries they were, in a real sense, *the moral and ethical preachers of spiritual religion.* Hence, Amos declares God's word of rebuke to those Israelites who had come to believe that mere outward conformity to sacrificial ritual and ceremony could atone for their sins:

> I hate, I despise your feasts, and I will take no delight in your solemn assemblies. Yea, though ye offer me your burnt-offerings and meal-offerings, I will not accept them. . . . But let justice roll down as waters, and righteousness as a mighty stream (Amos 5:21-24; cf. Isa. 1).

The prophets boldly rebuked vice, denounced political corruption, oppression, idolatry and moral degeneracy. They were preachers of righteousness, reformers, and revivalists of spiritual religion, as well as prophets of future judgment or blessing. They were raised up in times of crisis to instruct, rebuke, warn and comfort Israel, but interwoven with their ethical and moral teaching are to be found numerous predictions of future events concerning Israel, the nations, and the Messianic kingdom.

Hebrew prophecy is not something that can be carelessly defined

---

[7]James Orr (ed.), *The International Standard Bible Encyclopaedia,* IV, 2464.

and reduced to a simple pattern and thus dismissed merely as a part of a phenomenon common to Near Eastern cultures. On the contrary, it is absolutely imperative for a proper understanding of the nature of Old Testament prophecy to realize that the source of the prophetic message, while it often was related to the historical circumstances in which the prophet lived, was nevertheless supernatural in its origin. It was derived from neither observation, reason, speculation, innate sagacity nor the imagination, but was the result of divine revelation. There is sufficient evidence to demonstrate the divine origin and uniqueness of the prophetic institution in Israel. Whatever resemblance it might bear outwardly to the practices of other religions can be shown to be superficial and nonessential. In Deuteronomy 18 we are told that from the very beginning of the prophetic institution in Israel a clear distinction was to be made between Hebrew prophecy and the current practices of Israel's pagan neighbors.

Considerable light has been brought to bear on the Old Testament by the achievements of archaeology and the results of textual studies during the nineteenth and twentieth centuries. The cultural, political, economic, social and religious histories of Israel and her border neighbors, as well as the history of the Mesopotamian world, have now been illuminated to such a degree that knowledge of the world of Israel's day is quite extensive. Thus present understanding of the cultural and religious milieu in which Israel developed and the prophets preached not only facilitates interpretation of their message but also increases our appreciation of the *uniqueness* of the prophetic institution in Israel.

Chapter 1

ORIGIN AND DEVELOPMENT
OF OLD TESTAMENT
PROPHECY

Problem of Origin

The uniqueness of Israel's prophetic institution is apparent when analogous phenomena among the heathen nations are observed. Critical scholarship, however, contends that Israel borrowed her religious ideas and institutions from her Near Eastern neighbors, largely Canaan, who already had an established prophetic and institutional life. The early Hebrew prophets are depicted, in this view, as the crude, nonmoral, ecstatic type who had much in common with the prophets of Baal encountered by Elijah on Mount Carmel, who were using primitive methods of divination and self-torture. This is the view of H. Wheeler Robinson,[1] Hölscher, Jepsen, and W. O. E. Oesterley and Theodore Robinson. The latter, writing with regard to the

[1]H. Wheeler Robinson is representative of this extreme viewpoint. He writes: "The institutions of Israelite worship, its religious festivals, and sacrificial customs, appear to have been drawn largely from the practices of Canaan. The holy places of the land, each with its sacred stone and wooden post, passed over to the victorious invaders, and became the sanctuaries of Yahweh. The same relation holds of the three great festivals of the Jewish year. The Feast of Unleavened Bread, the Feast of Weeks, and the Feast of Booths are all shown by the details of their observance to be agricultural in character—i.e. they could not have belonged to a period prior to settlement in Canaan, and were most probably adopted from the Canaanites. Even the prophets themselves . . . are genetically related to an older non-moral type Nebi'im, who are, perhaps, like the holy places and festivals, and the general details of sacrifice, a contribution of Canaan to Israel's development" (*The Religious Ideas of the Old Testament* [2d ed., rev.], pp. 17-18).

17

origin of Hebrew religion, state categorically: "Israel inherited both the Law and the Prophets from her predecessors in Palestine."[2] However, this view ignores the fact that Israel possessed its prophetic institution, together with injunctions against adopting the priestly and prophetic practices of Canaan, *before* its entrance into Palestine.

Others seek to trace the origin of Israel's prophetic institution to other cultures outside Canaan. Cornill holds that Arabia was the home of prophetism. He seeks to support his theory by pointing to the fact that the basic root form of the verb corresponding to the term "prophet" (*nābhi'*) does not occur in Hebrew; hence, the word cannot be Israelitish, but must have been transplanted to Israel before the historical period. Since the root does occur in Arabic, a cognate language, he concludes that Arabia is the home of prophecy. Furthermore, the visionary and ecstatic elements characteristic of prophesying savor somewhat of the desert.[3] Jacobi, on the other hand, conjectured that prophecy of the type found in Israel took its rise in Asia Minor.[4] Hölscher and Jepsen trace the peculiar ecstatic phenomenon, said to be characteristic of Hebrew prophecy, to the Syria-Asia Minor region, whereas it is not found among the early Arabs, Babylonians and Assyrians.[5] Gottwald disassociates Israelite prophecy from Canaanite forms, the nation having derived it, he contends, from its early contacts with trans-Jordan peoples.[6] Others suggest that prophetism was a common phenomenon in the ancient Near East among all Semites including the Babylonians and Assyrians. Thus H. H. Rowley states that "it is . . . quite impossible to treat Hebrew prophecy as an isolated phenomenon. It grew out of a background of ancient Near Eastern prophecy, going back very far and spreading widely."[7] T. J. Meek, however, suggests another approach to the problem and traces the rise of the prophetic institution to Palestine itself as a result of the Philistine conquest and oppression of Israel. The movement was thus political as well as religious. Under the crisis of the Philistine threat, the prophets, as zealous champions of Yahwism, roused the

[2]W. O. E. Oesterley and Theodore H. Robinson, *Hebrew Religion: Its Origin and Development* (2d ed., rev.), p. 200.

[3]Carl Heinrich Cornill, *The Prophets of Israel*, pp. 8-12.

[4]H. H. Rowley, *The Re-discovery of the Old Testament*, p. 135.

[5]H. H. Rowley (ed.), *The Old Testament and Modern Study*, p. 135.

[6]Norman K. Gottwald, *All the Kingdoms of the Earth*, pp. 47-49.

[7]H. H. Rowley, "Ritual and the Hebrew Prophets," *Journal of Semitic Studies*, I, No. 4 (October, 1956), 340-41.

people to action by preaching a politico-religious crusade against
the heathen.[8]

Hence, the question which needs to be examined, in view of all
this, is: Was there to be found in other nations a phenomenon
precisely analogous to biblical prophecy in Israel which may account
for its rise among the Hebrews? Criticism contends that Hebrew
prophecy is associated with kindred developments among non-
Israelitish peoples and that it rises in the human desire to know the
divine will for mankind. It is this desire that has produced among all
nations the numerous forms of soothsaying and divination of which
prophecy is a part.[9]

The Old Testament text itself shows that the art of soothsaying
and divination was extensively practiced in Canaan (Deut. 18:9-14).
Nor was the phenomenon limited to Palestine; it was to be found in
all nations including Egypt (Gen. 41:8; cf. 44:5;[10] Exodus 7:11),
Babylonia (Ezek. 21:21-22), as well as throughout the Near East.
Balaam (Num. 22-24) is a biblical example of a heathen soothsayer
or clairvoyant who was a contemporary of Moses. Moreover, the
ecstatic prophets of Baal were a product of Canaan.

However, the existence of the practices of soothsaying and divination among the heathen nations, rather than being evidence of a
phenomenon identical with biblical prophecy, on the contrary, only
tends to emphasize the uniqueness of the institution in Israel. Against
the background of these pagan practices the moral and spiritual
superiority of Old Testament prophecy stands in bold contrast. In
fact these very practices of the heathen which are cited by the liberal
scholars as evidence of practices among the heathen analogous to
Israel's prophets are prohibited in Israel upon penalty of death!
(See Lev. 19:26, 31; 20:6, 27; Deut. 18:9-22.)

What then of the claim by some critical writers that outside
Canaan and the prophets of Baal there were also to be found in the
ancient Near East individuals of prophetic character comparable to

---

[8]Theophile James Meek, *Hebrew Origins,* pp. 156-57.

[9]Melancthon W. Jacobus (ed.), *A Standard Bible Dictionary,* p. 704.

[10]This interesting and somewhat perplexing reference to Joseph's "divining" cup does not necessarily imply that he used the cup in divining, but more
likely indicates the Egyptians, who believed him a magician and interpreter of
dreams, so thought. For our purposes this mention does indicate a knowledge
of the practice in Egypt.

the prophets of Israel?[11] That is, in addition to the recognized practices of divination and soothsaying among the heathen, there were to be found throughout the Near East actual *prophets* analogous to the Hebrew prophets.[12]

It is true that prophetic phenomena, in the form of certain aspects of external behavior and religious psychology, were to be found in other cultures outside Israel throughout various periods. The general characteristics of all religions with respect to certain beliefs and practices show some superficial similarities. However, it is the divine source of Israel's prophecy and the unique characteristics of her prophetic institution that confirm the fact that mere external similarities do not prove relationship.

For instance, the primitive shaman of northern Asia, typical of witch doctors, medicine men and sorcerers, works himself up to a frenzy of demonic spirit-possession and trance in order to elicit secrets from the spirits whereby he can divine oracles, cure sicknesses and bewitch others. He has nothing in common with genuine prophecy merely because revelations are received and oracles delivered. The same is true of the dervishes of Islam who through self-induced religious ecstasy often experience visions and exhibit powers of divination and other psychical phenomena. Muhammad was an ecstatic visionary who looked upon himself as a prophet of Allah and a recipient of revelations he held to be of greater authority than the Hebrew-Christian Scriptures. Zarathustra, often called the Iranian prophet, was another ecstatic given to visions and revelations. There are many references in Greek literature concerning a form of prophetic endowment. Plato calls Pythia in Delphi a "prophetess." The gift of prophetic inspiration is attributed to Sybil and others, who, in an ecstatic state of mind, imparted oracles allegedly received from the gods.

[11]According to the Talmud there were prophets among the heathen before the time of Moses. Seven prophets prophesied to the heathen: Balaam and his father, Job, Eliphaz the Temanite, Bildad the Shuhite, Zophar the Naamathite, and Elihu the Buzite. Although Balaam prophesied after this, the Midrash explains this by saying he prophesied for the good of Israel. After the erection of the tabernacle, according to this tradition, prophecy ceased from the heathen because Moses prayed that the divine presence would no longer rest upon them, the Scripture proof being Exodus 33:16. See John Bowman, "Prophets and Prophecy in Talmud and Midrash," *Evangelical Quarterly*, XXII, No. 2 (April, 1950), 107-8.

[12]For a more exhaustive study of this problem see the article by E. König in *Encyclopaedia of Religion and Ethics*, X (1928), 392 ff.; also E. J. Young, *My Servants the Prophets*, Appendix, pp. 193-205; C. von Orelli, *Old Testament Prophecy*, pp. 13-24.

Thus while it is evident that prophetic phenomena are not limited to particular countries and religions "it is not accurate," as Lindblom notes, "to say that ecstasy or prophecy in itself is commonly borrowed by one people from another. These phenomena have arisen in different regions quite independently."[13]

There have been attempts to find a personality of the prophetic type in Hammurabi (eighteenth century B.C.), who is depicted on a stela, inscribed with a code of laws, as receiving the scepter and ring from Shamash, the sun-god.[14] Advocates of this viewpoint contend that this scene allegedly depicts King Hammurabi in the role of a prophet, receiving from the god his laws which are to be proclaimed by Hammurabi as his representative. However, as König has observed, we are not to infer from this scene that Hammurabi is the prophet of the deity, but rather his *counterpart;*[15] for we read in the prologue of the inscription:

> . . . at that time Anum and Enlil named me to promote the welfare of the people, me, Hammurabi, the devout, god-fearing prince, to cause justice to prevail in the land, to destroy the wicked and the evil, that the strong might not oppress the weak, to rise like the sun. . . and to light up the land.[16]

Obviously the language portrays Hammurabi as more than a mere representative or prophet of the sun-god. Furthermore, the particular laws of the code which follows are as often ascribed to Hammurabi as to the sun-god Shamash. Hammurabi claims of himself (unlike Moses) in the epilogue:

> The laws of justice, which Hammurabi, the efficient king, set up. . . .[17]

> I, Hammurabi, the perfect king, . . . I caused light to rise on them.[18]

> I wrote my precious words on my stela.[19]

He, unlike the prophets of Israel, speaks of "my" law, "my" words, and "my" statutes:

> If that man heeded my words which I wrote on my stela, and did

[13]J. Lindblom, *Prophecy in Ancient Israel,* p. 32.
[14]D. Winton Thomas (ed.), *Documents from Old Testament Times,* p. 27.
[15]James Hastings (ed.), *Encyclopaedia of Religion and Ethics,* X, 392.
[16]James B. Pritchard (ed.), *Ancient Near Eastern Texts,* p. 164.
[17]*Ibid.,* p. 177.
[18]*Ibid.*
[19]*Ibid.,* p. 178.

not scorn my law, did not distort my words, did not alter my statutes. . . .[20]

Several texts have been found in excavations from the eighteenth century B.C. kingdom of Mari (a West Semitic kingdom on the middle Euphrates) exhibiting mantic phenomena which some have compared to Israelite prophecy. In some of these texts messengers are sent to the king of Mari, Zimri-Lim, from the god Dagan concerning delinquency in making certain reports and offerings, and in building a city gate. It has been suggested that these are prophetlike persons functioning a thousand years before the canonical prophets of the Old Testament. Yehezkel Kaufmann observes, however, that the idea of a divine messenger is somewhat commonplace in paganism and mythology, but in pagan manticism the idea of *commission*, unlike Israel's prophets, is of minor importance. An external, merely formal resemblance to this or that element in paganism does not indicate identity.[21] There is a marked difference in function and message content between the Mari messengers and the prophets of Israel.[22] "At Mari, it deals with cult and political matters of very limited importance."[23] The Hebrew prophetic literature occupies itself with the great moral and ethical issues of eternal consequence and questions of universal scope. Except for the Mari documents there is scant material from Mesopotamia which could be considered as analogous to Old Testament prophecy. Robert H. Pfeiffer has translated certain oracles concerning Esarhaddon in Pritchard's *Ancient Near Eastern Texts*, but they bear no relation to the Israelite institution.[24]

Others, including E. Meyer in *Die Israeliten und ihre Nachbarstamme*, contend that Hebrew prophecy was derived from Egypt where we find analogous phenomena. The "Admonitions of Ipu-wer" contains the oracles of an Egyptian sage, Ipu-wer, who portrays the terrible conditions existing in the land because of the negligence of the ruling house (cf. Isa. 1:7: "Your country is desolate; your cities

---

[20]*Ibid.*

[21]Kaufmann writes that "Noth's estimate of the Mari material . . . [cf. Martin Noth, 'Geschichte und Gotteswort im Alten Testament,' *Gesammelte Studien zum Alten Testament*, Munich, 1957, pp. 230-47] as leveling the qualitative difference between the Bible and its historical milieu in an essential point is greatly exaggerated" (*The Religion of Israel*, trans. and abridged by Moshe Greenberg, p. 215, n.).

[22]So also contends Th. C. Vriezen, *An Outline of Old Testament Theology*, pp. 257, 259.

[23]B. D. Napier, "Prophet, Prophetism," *The Interpreter's Dictionary of the Bible*, ed. George A. Buttrick, III, 901.

[24]See Pritchard, pp. 450 f.; also Young, pp. 198-200.

are burned with fire; your land, strangers devour it. . .''), and hopes for the appearance of an ideal king who will be "the shepherd of all men."[25] "Such is one of the earliest expressions of the Messianic hope in history," writes Finegan.[26] However, as E. J. Young has observed, similarity of language is to be expected in describing a chaotic land.[27] Moreover, there is little resemblance between this ideal ruler, who is depicted as a herdsman, and the clear prediction of the true Shepherd of Israel who, according to Zechariah, is God Himself.[28] A comparison of the prophetism of Israel and that of the sage, soothsayer and diviner of other religions clearly emphasizes the differences and reveals the similarities as superficial. The prophetism of Israel is not in a continuum with that of the Near East.

Somewhat later is the so-called prophecy of Nefer-rehu (or Nefer-rohu) which Albright designates as the oldest certain example of a *vaticinium ex eventu* ("a prediction of an event") since it purports to date from the Fourth Dynasty, but describes in some detail events of the Twelfth Dynasty, six centuries later.[29] But as Young points out, Nefer-rehu does not claim to be a prophet and, in fact, states that he cannot foretell the future: " 'I cannot foretell what has not [yet] come.' "[30] The message, by the speaker's own admission, is not by revelation, but is mere speculation.

Finally, the story of Wen-amon from the eleventh century B.C. describes the account of Wen-amon sent by Ramses XII to get cedar from the king of Byblos. The king of Byblos would not receive him until a man at the court who was seized by an ecstatic trance demanded that he be received. This ecstasy has been called by some a "prophetic frenzy"[31] and equated with the so-called ecstatic behavior of the early Hebrew prophets.[32] But we have here no genuine prophecy, and it is interesting that the king of Byblos was little

[25]According to John A. Wilson, translator of "The Admonitions of Ipu-wer," "the following text is 'prophetic' in a biblical sense. The 'prophet' is not foretelling the future but is standing before a pharaoh and condemning the past and present administration of Egypt. . . ." The text reveals that "Egypt had suffered a breakdown of government, accompanied by social and economic chaos" (Pritchard, p. 441).

[26]Jack Finegan, *Light from the Ancient Past,* p. 79.

[27]Young, p. 201.

[28]The text of Ipu-wer reads: "Men shall say: 'He is the herdsmen of all men. Evil is not in his heart. Though his herds may be small, still he has spent the day caring for them' " (Pritchard, p. 443).

[29]William F. Albright, *From the Stone Age to Christianity,* p. 186.

[30]Young, p. 203.

[31]Millar Burrows, *What Mean These Stones?* p. 98.

[32]Robert H. Pfeiffer, *Introduction to the Old Testament,* p. 32.

impressed by this ecstatic performance, which is revealed by the fact that he, denying any obligation to Egypt, would not supply the lumber until Wen-amon had sent to Egypt for additional money. The actions of this courtier are doubtless another case of pathological behavior or self-imposed ecstasy similar to the frenzied behavior of the prophets of Baal. C. von Orelli insists that these so-called "prophetical texts" of Egypt may show external similarity to the prophecies of Israel, "but they lack the spiritual and religious depth and the strictly ethical dignity of the prophets of the Scriptures."[33]

In contrast to the heathen soothsayers and diviners the Hebrew prophets were men with the sense of a special call to the prophetic ministry. They were men of consecration and lofty character, courageous critics of the social, political, moral and religious wrongs of their day. Accuracy of prediction, confirmed by fulfillment on the historical plane, characterized their ministry. Hence, the assumption of a uniform religious phenomenology over the entire ancient East is basically fallacious and is now rejected by an increasing number of critical scholars.[34] From the very beginning of Israel's national life, the Scriptures draw a clear distinction between true prophecy which is the result of divine revelation and the heathen methods of divination; for we are told in Numbers 23:23:

> Surely there is no enchantment with Jacob;
> Neither is there any divination with Israel:
> In due time it is said to Jacob and to Israel what God doth work.[35]

Origin of the Prophetic Institution in Israel

The divine origin of the prophetic institution is set forth by Moses himself in Deuteronomy 18:9-22. Moses, who never came into direct contact with the religious institutions of Canaan, declared in this passage that there was to be an institution of prophets raised up who

---

[33]James Orr, (ed.) *The International Standard Bible Encyclopaedia*, IV, 2466.

[34]This fact is borne out by the position of the latest critical dictionary on the Bible, published in 1962: "We must reject extreme positions which seek to clarify all possible uncertainties in OT prophetism by analogy with associations of cultic personnel in ancient Mesopotamia, the broader West Semitic area, and Arabia" (Napier, III, 900).

[35]Hebrew Masoretic text.

would declare the messages of God, and that this office would one day culminate in one great Prophet like unto himself.

The first thing to be noted from this passage is that it sets forth the reason and basis for the origin of Israel's prophetic institution. Verse 9 states: "When thou art come into the land which Yahweh thy God giveth thee, thou shalt not learn to do after the abominations of those nations." Then follows in verses 10 and 11 a list of terms including divination, augury and spiritism which describe the methods by which the heathen soothsayers sought to unveil hidden knowledge, ascertain future events and uncover secret wisdom, on which to base their counsels and prognostications. Verse 14, emphasizing the two most significant methods of heathen prediction, states: "For these nations, that thou shalt dispossess, hearken unto them that practise augury [soothsayers], and unto diviners; but as for thee, Yahweh thy God hath not suffered thee so to do." And then, in contrast to the methods employed by the heathen for discovering the will of the gods and uncovering the hidden secrets of the spiritual realm, God declares in verses 15-22 that Israel will learn the things that she needs to know, not by *discovery* through the methods of divination and occult practices, but by *revelation*.[36] Furthermore, the means of revelation, which would come unsought at the sovereign discretion of Yahweh, was to be by the word of His prophets through whom God would speak and make known His will. Finally, the method of distinguishing between true and false prophets is set forth in verses 21 and 22.

It should also be stressed that the passage is not to be limited to the establishment of the prophetic institution, as some interpreters have erroneously done, but verse 15 quite definitely speaks of God

---

[36]The modern-day spiritist medium, fortune-teller, astrologer, clairvoyant, hypnotist and magician all had their ancient heathen counterpart in the person with a familiar spirit (necromancer), the wizard, charmer, magician, soothsayer, diviner and enchanter. Sinful man has always been fascinated with the idea of uncovering hidden knowledge that belongs only to God (cf. Gen. 3). He has sought to learn his fate, determine the course of the future, obtain guidance, favor and special powers from the dead and the "spirits," thereby making himself independent of God. Satan has accommodated such men with substitutes for true religion and counterfeits for genuine revelation, thus deceiving the gullible. These practices are all alike condemned by God without reservation. (See Deut. 18:9-14; Exodus 22:18; Lev. 19:26, 31; Isa. 2:6; Ezek. 13:18; Acts 16:16 f.; 19:19; 8:9-24; 13:6-12.)

Thus critical scholarship is in error when it states, as does G. Ernest Wright (*The Old Testament Against Its Environment,* p. 88), that official Yahwism was not completely lacking in magical practices. It was forbidden from the outset, such prohibitions being contained in the law itself!

raising up *a* prophet (singular noun) like unto Moses. Verses 18-19 likewise use singular nouns, pronouns and verbal forms. Furthermore, the New Testament interprets this passage as a Messianic prophecy, according to Acts 3:22-23, and applies it to Christ.[37] Moses, in Deuteronomy 18, declares that God would establish the Hebrew prophetic institution, which as a type would one day culminate in the ideal Prophet, the antitype, Jesus Christ.[38] The prophetic institution was to be a type or "sign" of the God-anointed Prophet (Christ), after the same manner that the priesthood, or priests, were a sign of God's anointed Priest as depicted in Zechariah 3:8:

> Hear now, O Joshua the high priest, thou and thy fellows that sit before thee [i.e., the priesthood]; for they are men that are a sign: for, behold, I will bring forth my servant the Branch.

Therefore, the origin of the prophetic institution in Israel is not to be found in Canaan nor in other Near Eastern cultures, as negative criticism contends, but was itself established *for the specific purpose of guarding Israel against Canaan's superstitious practices, as well as those of her neighbors.*

After the death of Moses, Israel's leader of forty years who had talked with God "mouth to mouth" and received those revelations which He had given them,[39] the nation would be tempted to adopt the methods of divination used by their heathen neighbors in Palestine. Because of this, Moses announced the forming of the prophetic office for the purpose of continuing the divine revelation through the line of prophets.[40]

DEVELOPMENT OF THE PROPHETIC INSTITUTION IN ISRAEL

In the historical development of Old Testament prophecy two general periods appear: the era of the precanonical prophets and the era of the canonical prophets. The precanonical prophets were those

---

[37]Note that the N.T. writer carefully uses the singular in referring Deut. 18:15-19 to Christ in contrast to the plural "prophets" in Acts 3:24.

[38]Certainly this is the classic conservative understanding of this passage. See J. Barton Payne, *The Theology of the Older Testament,* p. 49; Merrill F. Unger, *Unger's Bible Dictionary,* pp. 890-91; Young, pp. 29-35.

[39]It is interesting to note that this is precisely the way the sinful and terrified Israelites wished God's word to be mediated to them, i. e., through an intermediary (prophet). Cf. Deut. 18:15-19 with Exodus 20:18-21. The office of prophet was to replace direct theophany.

[40]Robert D. Culver, "The Difficulty of Interpreting Old Testament Prophecy," *Bibliotheca Sacra,* CXIV, No. 455 (July, 1957), 202-3.

who came, for the most part, before the ninth century B.C. and left no written records of their prophetic messages.[41]

PRECANONICAL PROPHETS

This period may itself be separated into several divisions.

Pre-Mosaic period. Prophecy itself began with the protevangelium in the Garden of Eden subsequent to the fall (Gen. 3:15). According to the testimony of Christ, the oral or nonliterary prophets have existed from the very beginning. Jesus declared this fact to the rebellious Jews in Luke 11:49-51:[42]

> Therefore also said the wisdom of God, I will send unto them prophets and apostles; and some of them they shall kill and persecute; that the blood of all the prophets, which was shed from the foundation of the world, may be required of this generation; from the blood of Abel unto the blood of Zachariah, who perished between the altar and the sanctuary: yea, I say unto you, it shall be required of this generation.

The Old Testament speaks of other ancient prophets after Abel and before Moses, for instance, Enoch who foretold the coming of the Lord with ten thousand of his saints (Jude 14). Noah prophesied concerning the approaching flood and, afterward, concerning the future destinies of his descendants (Heb. 11:7; I Peter 3:20; Gen. 9:25-27). Abraham, Isaac, Jacob, Joseph and perhaps other patriarchs generally are considered prophets of the Old Testament era (Gen. 20:7; Ps. 105:15).

Mosaic period. The work of Moses gave an entirely new emphasis to prophecy and the function of the prophet. Prediction is largely subordinated to preaching and teaching. His ministry was largely didactic; he was Israel's lawgiver with an emphasis upon ethical monotheism. The biblical foundation for the later prophetic organization was the work of Moses who, in a real sense, was the first great Hebrew prophet. Other prophetic voices were heard in this period: Miriam is called a prophetess (Exodus 15:20); Aaron, her brother, is also designated a prophet as well as priest (Exodus 7:1); in Judges 4:4 Deborah is called a prophetess who judged Israel; and Judges 6:8 indicates that God sent an anonymous prophet with a message to Israel.

---

[41]The term "precanonical" is being used here in its limited or technical sense in contradistinction to the "literary" or writing prophets. Certainly Moses as a pre-ninth century prophet wrote his revelations; and the historical books themselves are designated the "Former Prophets" in the Hebrew canon. Other prophets wrote, but their writings have not been preserved. (Cf. Nathan, II Chron. 9:29; Gad, I Chron. 29:29; Shemaiah, II Chron. 12:15, etc.)

[42]Cf. Luke 1:70; Acts 3:21.

Period of Samuel. From Moses to Samuel the voice of prophecy was rarely heard. The prophetic movement did not really become an *organized institution* until the time of Samuel and the rise of the Old Testament phenomenon known popularly as the "schools of the prophets," or as they are designated in the Scriptures, "the sons of the prophets." Thus Moses, as the mediator of the old covenant, was the founder of the prophetic institution which was to be formally organized later under Samuel. Before noting the other precanonical prophets continuing after Samuel, it will be necessary for an adequate understanding of Old Testament prophetism to examine in some detail that unique phenomenon which made its appearance in Israel in the time of Samuel, namely, *the sons of the prophets.*

SAMUEL AND THE PROPHETIC SCHOOLS

The development of Hebrew prophecy as an institution is varied and complex and is divided into two classes. In one class are outstanding individuals such as Samuel, Elijah, Amos, Isaiah and Jeremiah. The other group is composed of those who are called "sons of the prophets," whose work was undertaken primarily in bands or companies.

Origin. In the time of Samuel, in the eleventh century B.C., a new institution arose in Israel in connection with her spiritual and religious life. This is first noted in I Samuel 10:5-13, where Samuel directed the newly anointed Saul to return to his home, and advised him that on the way he would witness certain signs which would confirm his selection by God to the kingship of Israel. The subject under consideration is concerned with the third of these signs recorded in I Samuel 10:5:

> After that thou shalt come to the hill of God, where is the garrison of the Philistines: and it shall come to pass, when thou art come thither to the city, that thou shalt meet a band of prophets coming down from the high place with a psaltery, and a timbrel, and a pipe, and a harp, before them; and they will be prophesying.

This is the first mention of such a group of prophets in the Old Testament, and there is nowhere an explanation of their origin. Apparent similarity between this "band of prophets" and the Nazirites and Rechabites has led some to speculate that the latter may be the forerunners of the prophetic bands or guilds. These ancient groups, according to R. B. Y. Scott, may be considered as forerunners of the prophets. While they were not in any sense prophets of Israel, yet their religious ideals gave them true affinity with the prophetic tradition. They maintained a constant protest against the religion and culture of Canaan. The Rechabites, as seen from I Chronicles 2:55 and II Kings 10:1-28, were a Kenite clan who first appeared in the Old Testament as a group in protest in the ninth century B.C. when Jonadab, the son of Rechab, cooperated with Jehu in annihilating Ahab's household to eliminate Baal worship from Israel.[43] The Rechabites abstained from intoxicating wine and continued to live in tents as nomads after Israel had settled in houses and cities in Canaan. This continued nomadism was in protest against the corrupting influences of urban civilization. The Prophet Jeremiah commends the principles of the Rechabites (Jer. 35:6-10).

The Nazirites, according to Numbers 6, were also members of an ancient institution. The Nazirite was an individual who had taken special religious vows. He drank no wine; he scrupulously avoided unnatural defilement and touched no dead body. He was clean, undefiled and devoted to Yahweh's service. It is interesting to note that Samuel the prophet was also a Nazirite. Scott holds that the influence exerted by these two classes as "forerunners" of the prophets in the constant struggle to preserve the distinctive values and tenets of the Mosaic revelation in the midst of the Canaanite perils is obvious. The Prophet Amos, according to this view, would seem to link the Nazirites with the older prophets:[44]

> And I raised up of your sons for prophets, and of your young men for Nazirites. Is it not even thus, O ye children of Israel? saith Yahweh. But ye gave the Nazirites wine to drink, and commanded the prophets, saying, Prophesy not (Amos 2:11-12).

However, the passage from Amos cited by Scott, when taken together with Numbers 6 and Jeremiah 35:6-10, would seem rather to indicate that in ancient Israel there were three institutions similar in many respects: the Nazirites, the Rechabites and the prophetic order, instead of the two former groups being the earlier forerunners of the latter. The Nazirites and prophets seem to have existed side by side, for Amos said, "I raised up of your sons for prophets, and of your young men for Nazirites." The context of his declaration would indicate he referred to ancient Israel when they came up out of Egypt. Jeremiah likewise traced the prophetic institution back at least to the exodus:

> Since the day that your fathers came forth out of the land of Egypt unto this day, I have sent unto you all my servants the prophets, daily rising up early and sending them (Jer. 7:25).

[43]R. B. Y. Scott, *The Relevance of the Prophets,* p. 40.
[44]*Ibid.,* pp. 49-50.

It is worth noting that God declared through Jeremiah that He *daily* sent *them* (plural, i.e., "my servants the prophets"), which would seem to indicate that He not only referred to a group or order, but that they existed long before the day of Samuel. In fact, as previously noted, Christ traced the origin of the prophets to the beginning (Luke 11:49-51).

However, there is no indication in Scripture prior to I Samuel 10 as to when the organized bands or so-called "schools of the prophets" originated. Since it was, however, the custom of great prophets to gather disciples around them, the "schools of the prophets" may have originated in this way, as disciples of the Prophet Samuel. This practice was followed by Elijah and Elisha (II Kings 2-6). Isaiah and Jeremiah seem to have had disciples (Isa. 8:16; Jer. 45:1). John the Baptist and Christ gathered groups of disciples whom they trained in the Word for spiritual service. Moses was provided with seventy elders with whom he was to share the burdens of leading Israel. When this group of "disciples" was gathered, evidence that God had imparted His Spirit to them and established them in this office was seen in that they "prophesied" (Num. 11:25). From the time of Moses until Samuel, when these prophetic groups first appear in Scripture, there was no outstanding spiritual leader to train and direct Israel religiously, as can be seen from the spiritual declension recorded in the book of Judges and the early chapters of I Samuel.

Wellhausen and his school hold that prior to Samuel's time there was a host of *nebhî'îm* in Israel, and Samuel simply organized them and made himself their head. On the contrary, I Samuel 3:1 declares that "the child Samuel ministered unto Yahweh before Eli. And the word of Yahweh was precious in those days; there was no frequent vision." From this text it seems correct to assume that the bands of the prophets were not then in existence, that they arose in the lifetime of Samuel, and in all probability owe their origin to him, being raised up of God to stem the spiritual and moral declension and prevent further apostasy. Further evidence for viewing Samuel as their founder is seen in I Samuel 19:18-20, where he is pictured "standing as head over them" at Ramah. It is uncertain whether or not such groups existed besides the one at Ramah in his day. In I Samuel 10:5, 10 there was a band at Gibeah, coming down from the high place, but it is not stated that the prophets were located there. No further mention of these companies of prophets is made in the time of Samuel. They appear quite suddenly again in the time of Elijah and Elisha, where for the first time they are designated sons of the prophets (I Kings 20:35). At that time they lived in considerable numbers at Gilgal, Bethel and Jericho (II Kings 2:3, 5, 7, 15; 4:1, 38; 6:1; 9:1). According to II Kings 4:38, 42-43, approximately one hundred sons of the prophets sat before Elisha at Gilgal and ate their meals together. The number at Jericho was probably great since fifty of them went with Elijah and Elisha to the Jordan (II Kings 2:7, 16-17). They lived in a common house, as is noted from II Kings 6:1-2. The large number of prophets in existence in Elijah's and Elisha's time and their apparent organization is strong evidence for the uninterrupted continuance of these schools from the time of Samuel.

Meaning of the phrase "sons of the prophets." The bᵉnê-han-nebhî'îm, "sons of the prophets," are not to be considered the children, but rather the pupils or disciples of the prophets. For this usage of "son" see I Samuel 20:31; II Samuel 12:5, note; Matthew 23:15. The term does not necessarily imply extreme youth, since sometimes they were married (II Kings 4:1). That this is the proper interpretation is to be seen in the fact that as they were called sons, so their instructor or head was called father (II Kings 2:12), a term used in Proverbs to describe a similar relationship between teacher and pupil. Thus the term is not a hereditary designation, but indicates discipleship.

Characteristics of these groups. Although there is not a great amount of information in the Scriptures concerning these bands or sons of the prophets, there is sufficient mention of them to enable one to draw certain conclusions as to their means of livelihood, housing, behavior and function.

1. Means of support. The great number of these prophets raises the inquiry as to their support. Did they provide for themselves or were there other means of support? The passages where they are mentioned provide some information. The gift given to Samuel by Saul seems to suggest that it was an accepted custom to give offerings to the seers for their services (I Sam. 9:8). The messengers of Balak carried a fee to Balaam (Num. 22:7). Naaman intended to make a generous payment for the cure of his leprosy (II Kings 5:15). A gift to a prophet was an accepted practice, for when Benhadad sent Hazael to consult Elisha he naturally directed him to take a present in his hand (II Kings 8:8). Elijah, during the drought, was fed by a widow of Zarephath (I Kings 17:8 ff.). Elisha ate frequently at the home of the rich Shunammite, who had built a special room for his accommodation. A man of Baal-shalisha brought Elisha the firstfruits for himself and the sons of the prophets who were with him (II Kings 4:42 ff.). The company of prophets who

uttered their oracles in harmony with Ahab's will, were no doubt supported by the royal treasury. Obadiah, Ahab's steward, provided food for one hundred prophets he had hidden in a cave during Jezebel's persecution.[45] These prophets did not always have ample necessities of life. The widow of one of the prophets came to Elisha in great distress (II Kings 4:1). When they needed larger quarters they were obliged to build them, even being constrained to borrow the necessary tools. At a period of famine the sons of the prophets went out to gather herbs for food. Thus it appears that the maintenance of the sons of the prophets came from their private means and personal efforts and from the alms of the people.[46]

2.   Dwellings. If Samuel gathered a band of disciples at each of the cities on his circuit, that is, at Bethel, Gilgal, Mizpah and Ramah (I Sam. 7:15-17), then they no doubt lived in common dwellings in all these centers. Saul met a band of prophets coming down from the high place, which some believe is a technical term for a worship center,[47] although there is no evidence that this was the location of a school of the prophets. Samuel had built an altar at Ramah, his home, where he was the head of a company of prophets (I Sam. 19:18-20). Later other bands were stationed at Bethel, Gilgal and Jericho (II Kings 2). The term Naioth in I Samuel 19:18-19 means "dwellings," according to Schultz,[48] and some scholars have thus held that this signifies the huts or dwellings of a school or college of prophets over which Samuel presided.[49] Others contend, however, that there may have been only one group who worked under Samuel's direction, in loose organization, and would be with him whenever he needed them.[50]

After Samuel there is a gap of over one hundred and fifty years before the sons of the prophets appear upon the scene again. By that time the prophetic group seems to have become settled in communities. Community buildings were erected, common meals shared, and the groups were under the supervision of a master, such as Elijah and Elisha (II Kings 2-6). In some instances the sons of the prophets were married and maintained their own houses (II Kings 4:1-2).

[45]L. W. Batten, *The Hebrew Prophet,* pp. 65-67.
[46]*Ibid.,* pp. 67-68.
[47]*Ibid.,* p. 46.
[48]Hermann Schultz, *Old Testament Theology,* I, 241.
[49]James C. Gray and George M. Adams, *Gray and Adams Bible Commentary,* I, 747.
[50]Young, p. 91.

Likewise Samuel maintained his house at Ramah, and Elisha at Samaria.

3. Behavior. The question of the behavior of the sons of the prophets, since it is related to the problem of ecstasy and the prophetic movement as a whole, is discussed in chapter 3, "The Prophetic Consciousness."

Function and purpose. Some scholars assert that the sons of the prophets arose as a result of political conditions of the day and that their chief purpose was patriotic. They were bands of religious devotees moving throughout Palestine awakening the patriotism of the people.[51] The Philistine oppression in the time of Samuel gave rise to the prophetic institution. According to this concept, Saul's meeting the band of the prophets was for the purpose of permitting these enthusiasts to arouse his patriotic and religious spirit. It is true that due to the theocratic nature of the kingdom of Israel, nationalism was not an insignificant concept to the prophets; nevertheless the aim of the prophets was primarily religious and not political.

What then were the true function and purpose of the sons of the prophets? In attempting to answer this question it will be well to note their function in those passages where they are mentioned in Scripture: (1) They are depicted as residing together in common dwellings at religious centers like Gilgal, Bethel and Jericho, sitting before a great prophet. We are perhaps warranted in supposing that spiritual instruction was imparted to them (II Kings 4:38; 6:1; I Sam. 19:20). (2) Another of the spiritual functions of these groups was that of prophesying together (I Sam. 10:5 ff.). Just what this prophesying was and what form it took, has been the subject of much speculation. First Samuel 10 seems to indicate that a part of it was the singing and chanting of praises to God. The band of prophets was descending from the high place where they had participated in some form of religious observance, and they were prophesying accompanied by musical instruments. Evidence that this was an accepted method of prophetic expression is clear from I Chronicles 25:1-3. Thus the groups would not simply prophesy as individuals, but jointly in a body, or in a procession, at various places in public praise and worship. (3) They also acted as spiritual messengers in important matters pertaining to Israel. This is seen when Elisha sent one of the sons of the prophets to anoint Jehu king of Israel (II Kings 9:1), and again when God sent another as a messenger of judgment to

[51]Scott, p. 47.

speak His word of rebuke to King Ahab for his leniency in dealing with Ben-hadad (I Kings 20:35-43). In view of these facts, what then was the divine purpose in the appearance of these prophetic companies during the period of Samuel?

The actual situation in which these prophetic bodies arose is clearly indicated in the historical narratives. The early zeal and faithfulness so characteristic of the early conquest of Canaan had waned. The national and religious life of Israel had declined and the Philistines threatened the survival of the nation. Furthermore, even the high priestly family fell into a state of degeneracy previously unknown, as the record in I Samuel 1-4 all too clearly reveals. Later, in the time of Elijah, Baalism became a serious threat to Israel's very existence as a theocratic nation under Yahweh. In the midst of this situation it would appear that God raised up, under the leadership of Samuel, and then later Elijah and Elisha, the sons or disciples of the prophets to minister with them in the instruction of the people in the law of God and to promote religious and spiritual revival to the end that the nation might survive. They were raised up of God in these periods of spiritual crisis to stem the tide of religious and moral declension and to call the nation to repentance.

Period of the early monarchy. After the early word of Samuel, the prophetic institution continued in operation until Malachi in the fifth century B.C. During the period of the early monarchy under the reign of David is mentioned the prophetic ministry of the Prophet Nathan, who was both a prophet and royal adviser of David and Solomon (II Sam. 7:2-17; 12:1-22; I Kings 1:8-45), as well as Gad the prophet (I Sam. 22:5; I Chron. 21:9-19).

Period of the divided monarchy. In this period Ahijah the prophet prophesied with respect to Jeroboam and the division of Solomon's kingdom (I Kings 11), and in Judah, Shemaiah was sent with a message from God to Rehoboam (I Kings 12). Two unnamed prophets appear in I Kings 13, a young prophet who forecasts judgment upon Jeroboam's house, and an older prophet of Bethel. In I Kings 16 the Prophet Jehu denounced Baasha, king of Israel, for his sins. At this time Hanani the seer came to Asa, king of Judah, and rebuked his lack of faith. Micaiah ben Imlah, the Lord's prophet, denounced the proposed campaign of Ahab against Syria (I Kings 22), and finally Elijah and Elisha, constituting the last of the precanonical prophets, combated the idolatry which had arisen under the reign of Ahab and Jezebel (I Kings 17—II Kings 8).

CANONICAL PROPHETS

The canonical period begins with the Prophet Obadiah (*c.* 845 B.C.) in the reign of Jehoram of Judah. But it should be noted here that the lengthy period of the nonliterary Prophet Elisha, which began in 852 during the reign of Jehoshaphat, continued down to about 796, thus overlapping the ministries of both Obadiah and Joel (*c.* 835), and extending almost to the time of Jonah (*c.* 782).

The Prophetical Books in our English Bible are the sixteen books of the Old Testament from Isaiah to Malachi. They are further subdivided into the four Major Prophets (Isaiah, Jeremiah [Lamentations], Ezekiel, Daniel) and the twelve Minor Prophets. This arrangement, however, is not to be found in the Hebrew Bible which is divided into the Law, the Prophets and the Writings (Daniel being included in the latter division). The canonical or literary prophets are the subject of Part II of this volume.

THE PROPHETESS IN ISRAEL

Women were not altogether excluded from the functions of prophecy in the precanonical and canonical periods of the Old Testament dispensation. A few appear speaking or singing by inspiration and are designated by the term *nebhîâh*, "prophetess" (masc., *nābhî'*).

Miriam, the sister of Moses, is called a *nebhîâh* or prophetess in Exodus 15:20. So too is Deborah who judged Israel during an early period of its history. Her inspired song is considered one of the most beautiful compositions in the Scriptures (Judges 5:2-31). Hannah, the mother of the Prophet Samuel, while not called a prophetess, nevertheless uttered one of the most remarkable prophecies in the Old Testament (I Sam. 2:1-10). Isaiah's wife, who bore him a son whom God named Maher-shalal-hash-baz, is called a prophetess (Isa. 8:2-3). Huldah, the wife of Shallum, the keeper of the royal wardrobe, was a prophetess whose advice King Josiah sought (II Kings 22:14). Noadiah is named as a prophetess who lived during the restoration period and was with those who opposed Nehemiah (Neh. 6:14). In the time of Ezekiel there were certain false prophetesses, women who pretended to be divinely inspired (Ezek. 13:17-18).

In the New Testament the prophetess of Israel appears in the person of Anna, the daughter of Phanuel, of the tribe of Asher, who was a widow of great age and remained in the temple worshiping with fastings and supplications night and day. When Jesus' parents brought the Child to the temple for presentation, Anna prophesied concerning Jesus to all those looking for redemption in Israel (Luke 2:36-38). Elizabeth and Mary were inspired with poetic utterance (Luke 1:41-45; 46-55). The four daughters of Philip prophesied in Caesarea (Acts 21:9). We read also that the gift of prophecy was bestowed upon women in the Corinthian church where these gifts of the Holy Spirit were quite prevalent (I Cor. 11:5). Finally, a false prophetess, Jezebel, is mentioned in Revelation 2:20.

Chapter 2

FUNCTION OF THE PROPHET

Meaning of the Terms
"Prophet" and "Prophesy"

IN ORDER TO DETERMINE the precise function of the prophet in Israel it is necessary, first of all, to discover the basic or root meanings of the terms "prophet" and "prophesy."

PRIMARY TERM FOR PROPHET

The basic and common Hebrew word for prophet in the Old Testament is *nābhî'*. Many have attempted to ascertain the root meaning of this term on etymological grounds; but, as will be readily apparent, there is no common agreement among the scholars, whose views may be divided into four general groups.

The noun is from an Arabic root. Cornill, König, Eiselen[1] and G. A. Smith are proponents of this etymological view. The Arabic root *naba'a* means "to proclaim or announce," according to König.[2] Hence, the Hebrew noun *nābhî'*, "prophet," means literally a "spokesman" or "speaker."[3] Cornill contends that the Arabic root does not have simply the general sense of speaking, as in the Assyrian-Babylonian, but has the special sense of a deputed speaker. Thus the speaker discourses not of himself, but as an agent of another who has some special communication to deliver.[4]

The noun is from a Hebrew root. The advocates of this view are Gesenius, C. von Orelli, A. Kuenen, Girdlestone, Oehler and others. Gesenius in his Hebrew-English lexicon cites the Hebrew verb *nābhā'*, "to prophesy," as a softened form of the Hebrew verb *nābha'*, "to flow, boil up, bubble forth," hence, "to pour forth words," the 'ayin, in this case, being softened to an 'aleph. Gesenius writes: "The proph-

---

[1]Frederick Carl Eiselen, *Prophecy and the Prophets*, p. 23.
[2]James Hastings (ed.), *Encyclopaedia of Religion and Ethics*, X, 384.
[3]George Adam Smith, *The Book of the Twelve Prophets*, p. 19.
[4]Carl Heinrich Cornill, *The Prophets of Israel*, p. 10.

ets when under the power of inspiration, appear to have been greatly
agitated and to have exhibited writhings and spasmodic affections of
the body like delirious persons."[5] Orelli cites the Old Testament
usage of the near-related *nābha'* in the Hiphil stem with the meaning
"to make to gush or pour forth," sounds or words for the most part
forming the object as in Proverbs 15:28: "The mouth of the wicked
poureth out evil things" (cf. 15:2; Ps. 29:2; 119:171).[6] Oehler,
referring to the passive usage of *nābhā'*, "to prophesy," holds that a
nābhī' is one "who is the *speaker as the instrument of another*, viz.
God."[7]

The noun is from an Akkadian root. This is the view of Albright,
Meek, Rowley and Scott. Albright, rejecting the former view, says
that "the current explanation of the word *nābhī'* 'prophet,' as 'speaker, announcer,' is almost certainly false."[8] The correct etymological
meaning of this term is passive according to Albright, and means
"one who is called [by God], one who has a vocation [from God]."[9]
This is almost always the sense of the verb *nabū*, "to call," in
Akkadian. The king is styled a *nibītu* (the noun being derived from
the verb), meaning "the one called" by the gods. "The verbal adjective *nabi'* means 'called' in the Code of Hammurabi."[10] Since the
verbal forms in Hebrew are denominatives they give no clue as to the
root meaning of the noun. Thus, on analogy with the Akkadian, "the
prophet was a man who felt himself called by God for a special
mission."[11] This interpretation is followed by H. H. Rowley.[12]

Meek and Scott likewise trace the noun to the Akkadian root
nabū, "to call or speak," the noun meaning "speaker or spokesman"
(of God). Meek, however, takes the active force of the root and
rejects Albright's passive etymological meaning of the word as "one
who is called," since etymology alone is rarely a safe guide to the
meaning of a word and must be confirmed by usage.[13] Furthermore,
it should be noted that the majority of those who hold one of these
first three views interpret the term as signifying one who was pos-

[5]William Gesenius, *A Hebrew and English Lexicon of the Old Testament,* trans. Edward Robinson, pp. 638-39.

[6]C. von Orelli, *Old Testament Prophecy,* p. 11.

[7]Gustave Friedrich Oehler, *Theology of the Old Testament,* p. 363.

[8]William F. Albright, *From the Stone Age to Christianity,* p. 303.

[9]*Ibid.*

[10]*Ibid.*

[11]*Ibid.*

[12]H. H. Rowley, *Prophecy and Religion in Ancient China and Israel,*
p. 4.

sessed by religious ecstasy, which was supposedly demonstrated by the prophet's raving and violent behavior while prophesying.

The noun is from an unknown Semitic root. This view, which appears as the most likely, is supported by A. B. Davidson,[14] Koehler and Baumgartner,[15] Brown, Driver and Briggs,[16] E. J. Young[17] and Heinisch,[18] among others. The verbal root *nābhā'*, "to prophesy," used in the Old Testament, is unquestionably a denominative from the noun *nābhî'*, "prophet." Hence, it would be difficult, as Meek and Young note, to determine the precise meaning of the verb on philological grounds alone, since the root from which *nābhî'* is derived does not itself occur in the Old Testament. Usage alone, therefore, can determine the meaning of the term.

Fortunately, Old Testament usage does provide knowledge of the precise meaning of the term "prophet." The classic passage is Exodus 7:1-2, which clarifies the meaning of *nābhî'* as one who speaks for God:

> And Yahweh said unto Moses, See, I have made thee as God to Pharaoh; and Aaron thy brother shall be thy prophet. Thou shalt speak all that I command thee; and Aaron thy brother shall speak unto Pharaoh.

Here the function of the prophet is to speak forth the divine message. The same concept is taught in Exodus 4:16: "And he shall be thy spokesman unto the people; . . . he shall be to thee a mouth, and thou shalt be to him as God." Thus the prophet is a speaker, a mouthpiece or a spokesman for God. The Septuagint translators understood *nābhî'* to have this meaning, for they translated the word by the Greek *prophētēs*, a noun derived from the preposition *pro*, "for, on behalf of," and the verb *phēmi*, "to speak," hence, "to speak for another."

Numerous other passages in the Old Testament support this fact. In the call of Jeremiah to be a prophet, God tells him, "Whatsoever I shall command thee thou shalt speak" (Jer. 1:7). In 15:19 the

[13]Theophile James Meek, *Hebrew Origins*, p. 150.

[14]A. B. Davidson, *Old Testament Prophecy*, p. 85.

[15]Ludwig Koehler and Walter Baumgartner (eds.), *Lexicon in Veteris Testamenti Libros*, II, 586.

[16]Francis Brown, S. R. Driver and Charles A. Briggs, *A Hebrew and English Lexicon of the Old Testament*, 2d ed., rev., p. 612.

[17]Edward J. Young, *My Servants the Prophets*, p. 57.

[18]Apparently Heinisch has this viewpoint in mind also. See Paul Heinisch, *Theology of the Old Testament*, trans. William G. Heidt, p. 18.

prophet is described by the Lord as one who stands before Him and "shalt be as my mouth." The false prophets are described as they who speak out of their own heart and "not out of the mouth of Yahweh" (23:16). Isaiah's words were said to be from "the mouth of Yahweh" (Isa. 1:20). Zechariah states that all the former prophets spoke God's words: "the words which Yahweh of hosts had sent by his Spirit by the former prophets" (Zech. 7:12). Amos cries, "The Lord Yahweh hath spoken; who can but prophesy?" (Amos 3:8; cf. 7:16). These texts, as well as many other Old Testament passages, clearly indicate that the primary function of the prophet was to prophesy, that is, *to speak the message which God had revealed unto him.*

OTHER TERMS

Seer. Two other terms which appear to be synonyms for *nābhî'*, "prophet," are *rō'eh* and *ḥōzeh*, both translated as "seer." Their verbal roots mean "to see." First Samuel 9:9 indicates that the offices of prophet and seer were substantially identical:

> Beforetime in Israel, when a man went to inquire of God, thus he said, Come, and let us go to the seer; for he that is now called a Prophet [*nābhî'*] was beforetime called a Seer [*rō'eh*].

The other term, *ḥōzeh*, is more frequent. The Prophet Amos is called a *ḥōzeh* (seer) in 7:12. That the seer also prophesies is seen from this text: "O thou seer, go, flee thou away into the land of Judah. . . and prophesy there." In II Samuel 24:11 the Prophet Gad is called both prophet and seer: "the prophet [*nābhî'*] Gad, David's seer [*ḥōzeh*]." He is again called the king's seer in II Chronicles 29:25. In I Chronicles 29:29 all three terms are used together: "Now the acts of David the king. . . are written in the history of Samuel the seer [*rō'eh*], and in the history of Nathan the prophet [*nābhî'*], and in the history of Gad the seer [*ḥōzeh*]."

Since, quite obviously, the same individual can be designated by the three terms, what, if any, is the distinction between them? As has already been shown, the word *nābhî'*, prophet, stressed the *objective* or *active* work of the messenger of the Lord in speaking forth God's word. The terms *rō'eh* and *ḥōzeh*, translated "seer," on the other hand emphasized the *subjective* element, namely, the mode of receiving divine revelation, by "seeing." In Isaiah 30:10 the rebellious Israelites "say to the seers, See not." The term "prophet" emphasized the prophet's utterances, *rō'eh* and *ḥōzeh* indicated his method of receiving the divine communication. The terms for "seer" speak of the receptive aspect, whereas the term for "prophet" points up the communicative function.

Man of God. This was a common and general term for the prophet of Israel which emphasized his holy calling, moral character and divine ministry. The term is used quite early, for instance, of Moses, Samuel, Elijah and Elisha (Deut. 33:1; I Sam. 9:6; II Kings 4:9, etc.).

Servant of the Lord. This title stresses the close and holy relationship between God and His faithful messengers. It is used of the Prophet Ahijah in I Kings 14:18. God frequently speaks of "my servants the prophets" (cf. II Kings 9:7; 17:13; Jer. 7:25; Ezek. 38:17; Zech. 1:6, etc.).

Messenger of the Lord. The same Hebrew term (*mal'āk*) is used for both messenger and angel. As the angels of the Lord are His spiritual messengers, so too His prophets were the messengers of His revealed word. This term defines more exactly what the servant of the Lord was employed to do, namely, deliver the messages of God. Haggai, for instance, is called the Lord's messenger (Hag. 1:13). It is used of John the Baptist (Mal. 3:1) and the prophets generally (II Chron. 36:15-16; Isa. 44:26).

THE PROPHET AND HIS RELATION TO THE PRIESTHOOD IN ISRAEL

Having determined the general function of the prophet as that of a spokesman for God on the basis of the Old Testament usage of the term, we are now prepared to examine the prophet's function within the social and religious life of Israel.

EARLIER LIBERAL VIEWPOINT:
THE PROPHETS AS ANTAGONISTS OF THE PRIESTS

Until comparatively recent times the critical school advanced the theory that there was antagonism between the prophet and priestly ritual and sacrifice, allegedly found in such passages as I Samuel 15:22; Isaiah 1:10-15; Hosea 6:6; Micah 6:6-8; Amos 5:21-25; and the classic passages in Jeremiah 6:20 and 7:22-23. Oesterley and Robinson, representatives of this viewpoint, state that "the pre-exilic prophets, who represent. . . the older traditions of nomadic Israel, seem without a dissentient voice to deny that sacrifice was enjoined on Israel in the wilderness."[19] That this is not the biblical teaching may be seen from an examination of these passages.

[19] W. O. E. Oesterley and Theodore H. Robinson, *Hebrew Religion: Its Origin and Development* (2d ed., rev.), p. 165.

Higher critics have commonly assigned the so-called priestly legislation (P) with its laws of sacrifice and ritual not to Moses, but to the exilic period as a product of the priestly writers and as later introduced by Ezra. Amos 5:25 is often cited as evidence that the prophets knew nothing of the law of sacrifice, since, according to Amos, sacrifices were not offered during the forty years in the wilderness. The prophet declared God's rebuke to Israel by asking, "Did ye bring unto me sacrifices and offerings in the wilderness forty years, O house of Israel?" The fallacy of this criticism is seen, however, from an examination of the historical narrative of Numbers 14-26 which clearly indicates the apostate condition of Israel during the exilic period. This is confirmed by Exodus 32; Joshua 24:23; Ezekiel 20:7-26; and Amos 5:25-26 compared with Acts 7:42-43.

The obvious implication of God's inquiry of Israel in Amos 5:25, in view of what is stated in verse 26, together with the other passages mentioned, is that the Israelites offered Him no genuine worship in the wilderness, seeing that they carried their false gods with them, and mixed their idolatrous worship with, or substituted it for, the worship of Yahweh.

However, Jeremiah 7:22-23 is the classic passage which is appealed to by the critics to support the theory that the prophets were opposed to the sacrificial ritual:

> For I spake not unto your fathers, nor commanded them in the day that I brought them out of the land of Egypt, concerning burnt-offerings or sacrifices: but this thing I commanded them, saying, Hearken unto my voice, and I will be your God, and ye shall be my people; and walk ye in all the way that I commanded you, that it may be well with you.

In reply to the liberal contention, several facts may be noted. First, the critical view is *incompatible with the book of Jeremiah itself*. The Prophet Jeremiah, who allegedly denied the validity of sacrifice in chapters 6-7, nevertheless declares in 17:24-26 that God promises the Israelites, if they will obey Him (v. 24), that their *sacrifices* will be acceptable unto Him. Here we see the prophetic point of view demonstrated, that is, the inseparable relationship between obedience (v. 24) and acceptable worship (v. 26). Again, in Jeremiah 31:14 the restoration is depicted in which the priesthood is portrayed as being provided with abundance, which results from the people's sacrifices. Also in Jeremiah 33:17-24 sacrifices are said to be offered continually:

> For thus saith Yahweh: David shall never want a man to sit upon

the throne of the house of Israel; neither shall the priests and Levites want a man before me to offer burnt-offerings, and to burn meal-offerings, and to do sacrifice continually (Jer. 33:17-18).

There is no fundamental inconsistency between these passages and the earlier passage in 7:22-23. It is obvious that the prophet's denial in 7:22-23 is not absolute but relative, in view of the fact that God's chief concern was not with prescribed rules and ritual, but with moral obedience. The mere outward forms divorced from their inward meaning and from the practice of genuine piety were not the original divine intention. This is the word that He commanded them when He brought them out of Egypt (v. 23); the sacrifices, enjoined later at Sinai, were to be the outward form or *means of expressing their obedience.* They were not to be an end in themselves, as Israel had come to view them. God's commandments stressed the aspect of Israel's moral obedience, rather than the relatively unimportant ritual. Samuel's words in I Samuel 15:22 to disobedient Saul graphically illustrate where the divine emphasis lay with regard to sacrifice. When Saul sought to justify his disobedience to God on the ground that he took the forbidden animals as spoil to sacrifice to the Lord, Samuel rebuked him by saying:

Hath Yahweh as great delight in burnt-offerings and sacrifices, as in obeying the voice of Yahweh? Behold, to obey is better than sacrifice, and to hearken than the fat of rams.

Also it is interesting to note that Allis in his work *The Five Books of Moses* concurs in this interpretation and builds an excellent case for translating the Hebrew preposition *'al* in Jeremiah 7:22 "for the sake of" instead of "concerning." Hence, Jeremiah does not say that the Lord gave no commands to their fathers *concerning* sacrifice, but that He did not speak to them *for the sake of* sacrifices as if He needed them[20] (cf. 7:21; Ps. 50:8-14).

Furthermore, the critical view is *incongruous with history.* It is evident to all students of history that the Israelites were not the only people who had an established sacrificial system, priesthood and ceremonial ritual. The Old Testament itself has much to say about the heathen practices of Israel's neighbors with regard to sacrifice. The universal prevalence of sacrifice among the heathen nations is common knowledge. The obvious implication is that to admit the universality of sacrifice from earliest times in all cultures, and at the

---

[20]Oswald T. Allis, *The Five Books of Moses,* pp. 169-73.

same time to deny its existence in the religion of Israel until quite late in her history, is incongruous to say the least! This fact alone has led many critics to reject their earlier position and admit the existence of sacrifice quite early in Israel. Even Oesterley, quoted at the beginning of this subject as denying the presence of the sacrificial system in early Israel, later changed his viewpoint in the revised edition of his book *Hebrew Religion* on the basis of the prevalence of sacrificial ritual among other nomadic peoples, ancient and modern.[21] At no period in their history did the Israelites neglect the offering of sacrifices, which were the divinely appointed means of making atonement for their sins and for remaining in a harmonious relationship with God.

Finally, the critical concept of sacrificial ritual is based upon a *misunderstanding of the prophetic point of view*. It is a misunderstanding of the prophet's meaning to imply a contrast between the prophetic view of acceptable worship and the Levitical system. On the contrary, it is precisely because the subjective and spiritual element of Levitical worship and ritual had been ignored by the Israelites that the prophets were constrained to emphasize the true meaning of acceptable worship—it was inward and spiritual, not a mere outward and perfunctory conformity to Mosaic ritual. Although critical scholars formerly emphasized a strong distinction between the Levitical and prophetic elements in the Old Testament, and either condemned outright the former as crude and pagan, or minimized its spiritual significance, historically the Levitical element was as essential to the religious life and development of Israel as the prophetic. It formed the framework, as it were, without which the continuity of the religious life of the Jewish nation would have been impossible.

No valid distinction can be made between the priestly (or ceremonial) and the prophetic (or moral and ethical) elements of the Old Testament as if they were two different religions, since each was divinely instituted by the God of Israel to serve its proper purpose in the religious life of Israel. In fact biblical prophecy itself was grounded in the law and the prior revelation made to Moses.[22] Throughout

---

[21]H. H. Rowley, *The Re-discovery of the Old Testament*, p. 165.

[22]This is emphasized by J. Barton Payne, *The Theology of the Older Testament*, p. 49. He writes: "The attempt, therefore, that is made by liberalism to place prophecy in opposition to the law, or even anterior to it, runs counter to the testimony of Scripture itself. Biblical prophecy was based upon, and was a development out of, the law (Isa. 8:20; Dan. 9:11). God's revelation to Moses was, in fact, qualitatively superior to that granted to the prophets (Num. 12:7); and no subsequent prophet became Moses' equal (Deut. 34:10)."

the history of Israel the moral was taught *through* the ceremonial, the ceremonial being the necessary vehicle for the expression of the moral and ethical. The Jewish sacrifices were, by divine intention, to reflect the moral truths of obedience, self-sacrifice and dedication, love for and devotion to God, recognition of sin and guilt, repentance, and many other spiritual conceptions. Throughout the Old Testament the moral interprets the ritual, and the ceremonial gives meaning to the ethical. It is indeed a narrow view of Old Testament sacrifice and ceremony to fail to see in its institution moral, ethical and spiritual elements. Sacrifice was the divinely appointed, objective means of maintaining a right standing before God within the covenant community of Israel in the Mosaic dispensation.

Sacrifice, contrary to much popular opinion, was not to the Hebrew some crude, temporary and merely typical institution, nor simply a substitute for that dispensation until better things were to be provided later. *Sacrifice was then the only sufficient means of remaining in harmonious relation to God. No Hebrew dared neglect this obligation. It was adequate for the period in which God intended it should serve.* This is not the same as saying, however, that Levitical sacrifice was on an equal with the sacrifice of Christ, nor that the blood of bulls and goats could, from God's side, take away sins; but it is recognizing the reality of the divine institution of Mosaic worship, and looking, as too often Old Testament interpreters fail to do, at sacrifice and priestly ritual from the viewpoint of the Hebrew in the Old Testament dispensation. Sacrifice, to the pious Hebrew, was not something insignificant, nor simply a perfunctory ritual, but it was an important element in his *moral obedience to the revealed will of God.* Sacrifice was by its very nature, which involved faith and repentance on the part of the worshiper and the putting to death of his substitute victim, intensely personal, ethical, moral and spiritual, because it was intended to reflect the attitude of the heart and will toward God.

It is just at this point that the prophetic assaults upon the sacrificial ritual can find explanation. The Israelites had come to believe that punctilious attention to sacrificial ritual and ceremony could atone for their sins, however great. But this notion was a misconception of the very principle of the ceremonial system which was based upon moral and ethical conduct within the covenant. The prophets insisted that the people *unite* day-to-day moral conduct with their religious observances. This polemic against mere ceremonialism appears in many Old Testament passages (cf. Ps. 50:23; 40:6-10; 69:30; Isa. 1:11-15; Micah 6:6-8; Jer. 17:24-26). The two aspects of this problem are clearly seen in the words of the psalmist. He writes in Psalm 51:16-17:

> For thou delightest not in sacrifice; else would I give it: Thou hast no pleasure in burnt-offering. The sacrifices of God are a broken spirit: A broken and a contrite heart, O God, thou wilt not despise.

To the superficial observer this could appear as a rejection of animal sacrifice in view of the later higher moral concept of religion by the Hebrews. But verse 19 repudiates this view; it states that after the heart of the worshiper has turned in penitence toward God, his sacrifice will be fully acceptable:

> Then wilt thou delight in the sacrifices of righteousness, in burnt-offering and whole burnt-offering: Then will they offer bullocks upon thine altar.

Certain other factors also indicate that there was no inherent antagonism between prophet and priest. The Prophet Moses established the Levitical priesthood and its ritual. Samuel the prophet officiated in the sacrificial ritual at various places in Palestine and was officially connected with the tabernacle from his childhood. Jeremiah, Ezekiel and the postexilic Prophet Zechariah were from priestly families. In chapter 1 of his prophecy, Isaiah denounces not merely sacrifices (including festivals and ritual) but also prayer. Hence, if the condemnation of one is absolute, so is the other.[23] The prophets Micah and Jeremiah condemn the sins of not only the iniquitous priests but also the deceitful prophets (Micah 3:11; Jer. 23:9 ff.). Isaiah received his vision of the Lord while apparently at worship in the temple itself. Because of this evident accord and cooperation between the prophetical institution and the priestly cultus, later and more recent critical interpreters have postulated a new theory concerning the relationship that existed between these two bodies.

LATER CRITICAL THEORY:
THE PROPHETS AS TEMPLE PERSONNEL

As noted earlier, until recently it was common for scholars to set the prophets and priests against each other, the prophets repudiating practices of the priestly cultus as alien to the will of God. However,

---

[23]For a contemporary critical scholar's repudiation of the older liberal view see Rowley, *Prophecy and Religion...*, pp. 111-18.

Mowinckel in his work *Studies in the Psalms* represents the prophets as cultic officials or temple functionaries alongside the priests and contends that many of the psalms were composed by them. The view held by earlier scholars that the Psalter was the "hymnbook of the second temple" was set aside by Mowinckel who regards many of the psalms as preexilic, being the prophetic, ecstatic responses in the temple worship ritual.[24] Leslie calls these psalms "prophetic liturgies" in his book *The Psalms*. The prophet, as a cultic official, would speak in the first person on God's behalf to the worshiping congregation. Such oracles, at first spontaneous, gradually developed into a liturgical repertoire of the temple and were used over and over again in worship.[25]

Many writers believe that the prophets composed not only certain of the psalms (e.g., 50, 75, 81, 95) to accompany the ritual, but that liturgies are to be found also in the books of Joel, Nahum and Habakkuk composed under cultic influence.[26] A. C. Welch seeks to demonstrate how the functions of prophet and priest did not diverge as radically as the adherents of the Wellhausen school suggested.[27] A. R. Johnson would establish the view that the prophets and priests served together at the sanctuaries as cultic functionaries.[28] A. Haldar in his work *Associations of Cult Prophets among the Ancient Semites* has greatly influenced this new concept of the relation between the prophet and priest. However, Meek in *Hebrew Origins* thinks this was true only of the earlier prophets, but it is questionable whether or not many of the canonical or writing prophets were cult functionaries. To support this modified view he points to the frequent instances of hostility between the priests and canonical prophets and their severe criticism of the priestly cultus.[29] Roland de Vaux rejects altogether the theory of cultic prophets attached to the

---

[24]This is the current popular view as may be noted from the following quotation: "There is no reason to doubt that functionaries known as prophets were cultically institutionalized precisely as were the priests and other sanctuary personnel; nor is there any sufficient ground for rejecting the view that such prophets were attached to the temple in Jerusalem and that sometime before the time of the Chronicler (fourth or third century B.C.) the temple prophets became temple singers and merged with the other Levitical orders" (B. D. Napier, "Prophet, Prophetism," *The Interpreter's Dictionary of the Bible*, III, 900).

[25]H. H. Rowley (ed.), *Old Testament and Modern Study*, pp. 202-4.

[26]H. H. Rowley, *The Faith of Israel*, pp. 138-39.

[27]A. C. Welch, *Prophet and Priest in Old Israel*, pp. 130 ff.

[28]Aubrey R. Johnson, *The Cultic Prophet in Ancient Israel*, p. 122.

[29]Meek, pp. 178-80.

temple at Jerusalem.[30] However, there is no basic antagonism between the prophets and priests. "The prophets," he writes, "are
opposed to the formalism of exterior worship when it has no corresponding interior dispositions (Is. 29:13)."[31]

BIBLICAL VIEW OF THE
FUNCTION OF THE PROPHET

There is no evidence whatever that the prophets were some sort
of religious representatives of the priestly cultus, the so-called prophetic guilds being thus thought of (as Johnson contends) as a permanent element of the Jerusalem temple staff.[32] The prophets were
neither working in hostility to the priesthood, nor were they functioning as a part of the temple cultus. Both extremes are without
biblical warrant. What then was the true function of the prophet in
Israel? It was threefold.

First it must be kept in mind that the law itself provided for the
prophetic institution (Deut. 18); thus the ministry of the prophets
was not some later expedient developed to cope with the deficiencies
of the priesthood and the apostasy of Israel. On the contrary, the
prophets expounded and interpreted the Mosaic revelation to the
nation. Thus Calvin writes that we are "to trace the Prophets to the
Law, from which they derived their doctrine, like streams from a
fountain. . . so that they may be justly held. . . to be its interpreters. . . ."[33] He continues, "Thus when the Prophets inculcate moral
duties, they bring forward nothing new, but only explain those parts
of the Law which had been misunderstood."[34] The relation of the
Torah to prophecy, as conceived by the rabbis in the Talmud and
Midrash, subordinates the latter to the former. The Rabbinic view
was that the Prophets were a part of the Law and added nothing new,
nor contradicted the Law, which was summarized and epitomized by
them.[35]

Hence, the function of the prophets was first of all a practical
one—*they were the divinely appointed moral and ethical preachers
and teachers of true religion* as revealed to Israel:

[30]Roland de Vaux, *Ancient Israel: Its Life and Institutions,* trans. John
McHugh, pp. 384-86.
[31]*Ibid.,* pp. 454-55.
[32]Rowley, *The Old Testament and Modern Study,* p. 123.
[33]John Calvin, *Commentary on the Book of the Prophet Isaiah,* Vol. I of
Calvin's Commentaries, trans. William Pringle, p. xxvii.
[34]*Ibid.,* p. xxviii.
[35]John Bowman, "Prophets and Prophecy in Talmud and Midrash,"
The Evangelical Quarterly, XXII, No. 4 (October, 1950), 260-75.

It was their duty to admonish and reprove, to denounce prevailing sins, to threaten the people with the terrors of divine judgment and call them to repentance. They also brought the message of consolation and pardon (Is. xl. 1, 2).[36]

Thus the function of the prophet is seen most clearly in the Hebrew term and its usage in the Old Testament. Those passages where it is used indicate that the prophet's function was to speak the moral and ethical message God had revealed unto him. This function is quite prominent in all prophetic preaching. To their contemporaries they were the moral and ethical preachers of spiritual religion, calling the nation to obedience in conformity to the Mosaic legislation. They fearlessly rebuked vice, idolatry, infidelity, oppression, unfaithfulness, iniquity, and social, moral and political corruption wherever it was to be found. It was their calling to show the people "their transgression, and. . . the house of Jacob their sins" (Isa. 58:1). The last prophet of the Old Testament cried: "Remember ye the law of Moses my servant, which I commanded unto him in Horeb for all Israel, even statutes and ordinances" (Mal. 4:4).

But interwoven in their ethical preaching are to be found numerous *predictions of future events concerning the nation of Israel, the Gentiles and the Messianic age to come.* This is a second aspect of the prophetic function. Although the prophets spoke primarily to people of their own day, their divinely inspired messages often springing out of the historical situation in which they lived, there was, nevertheless, a predictive element pervading their messages. The prediction of the future was never merely to demonstrate that God knows the future, nor to satisfy man's curiosity, but there was always a definite, purposeful revelation in connection with the prophecy. Predictive prophecy was concerned with judgment, salvation, the Messiah and His kingdom.

The historical situation which brought the prophetic institution into prominence gives insight into the third aspect of its function and purpose. Although the prophet was not an unfamiliar figure in Israel from earliest times, the historical event that called forth the work of the prophets in a definite and uninterrupted ministry was the division of the kingdom and the consequent apostasy of the ten northern tribes under Jeroboam.[37] *They were watchmen standing upon the*

---

[36]John Peter Lange, *Minor Prophets, Lange's Commentary on the Holy Scriptures,* trans. Philip Schaff, XIV, 7.

[37]This fact is not to be confused with the critical theory respecting the cause of the origin of the prophetic institution in Israel. Meek, for example, contends that the pressures of the Philistine domination aroused a militant patriotic enthusiasm on behalf of Israel's religion which gave rise to the

walls of Zion to sound the trumpet against dangers of religious apostasy (Ezek. 3:17; 33:7). As a politico-religious measure to keep the two kingdoms separate, the northern kingdom, Israel, introduced calf worship under Jeroboam. During the reign of Ahab, Baal worship was also introduced and a temple and altar built in Samaria. Judah likewise fell into apostasy as a result of foreign alliances and intermarriage between the daughter of Ahab and Jezebel, and Jehoram, king of Judah, who "walked in the way of the kings of Israel, as did the house of Ahab; for he had the daughter of Ahab to wife: and he did that which was evil in the sight of Yahweh" (II Chron. 21:6). Furthermore, the priests, who were the religious teachers of the nation, instead of promoting reform in the face of this apostasy, fell into the moral and spiritual declension of the people. Into this spiritually degenerate situation the prophets were called. Their function or mission was to warn and turn the nation from its sin and idolatry as a result of the failure of the established priesthood. As in ancient Jerusalem, when the people of the city set a watchman on the walls to alert them to the approach of an enemy or threat of danger, so God set the prophets in Israel to be faithful watchmen over His heritage, Israel, to sound the alarm and warn of approaching spiritual peril to the nation.

prophetic schools. The close association of the inauguration of Saul as king and the companies of prophets in the historical narratives is said to emphasize this fact (Meek, pp. 156 ff.).

Chapter 3

THE PROPHETIC
CONSCIOUSNESS

THE PROPHETS OF ISRAEL claimed to be recipients of divine revelation, and they preached under the psychological conviction that the Lord had spoken His word to them and had commanded them to speak this word in turn to Israel. Amos declared:

> Surely the Lord Yahweh will do nothing, except he reveal his secret unto his servants the prophets. The lion hath roared; who will not fear? The Lord Yahweh hath spoken; who can but prophesy? (Amos 3:7-8).

Again we read in Amos 7:15-16 of this conviction on the part of the prophet: "Yahweh said unto me, Go, prophesy unto my people Israel. Now therefore hear thou the word of Yahweh." If the Old Testament is to be taken seriously, then a necessary prerequisite for a proper understanding of prophecy is a careful consideration of the conviction of the prophets themselves in their claims to be recipients of divine revelation. The unique nature of Old Testament prophecy stems from what might be called the *prophetic consciousness*—the unqualified conviction on the part of the prophets of a divine call and commission to proclaim the very words of God. This conviction, so clearly manifested in the declaration of Amos, is expressed countless times in the Old Testament by the prophetic formula "Thus saith the Lord," which always prefaced the prophet's message from God that followed. The prophets required no historical verification nor external evidence that the word they spoke was indeed the word of God. On the contrary, they spoke with the authority and conviction that the word of God carried its own seal of veracity, and that the force of its moral and spiritual integrity would impress itself upon the consciences of its hearers. This truth is graphically illustrated in God's charge to Ezekiel:

51

And he said unto me, Son of man, I send thee to the children of Israel, to nations that are rebellious, which have rebelled against me: they and their fathers have transgressed against me even unto this very day. And the children are impudent and stiff-hearted: I do send thee unto them; and thou shalt say unto them, Thus saith the Lord Yahweh. And they, whether they will hear, or whether they will forbear (for they are a rebellious house), yet shall know that there hath been a prophet among them (Ezek. 2:3-5).

The passage in Deuteronomy 18:9-22, which contrasts the heathen methods of divination of the other nations with supernatural revelation through the prophets of Israel, was the historical basis for this Old Testament phenomenon—the prophetic consciousness. The psychological conviction of the prophets that God had spoken to and through them is evident throughout the Old Testament in such statements as "Thus saith the Lord," "The word of the Lord came unto me," "Hear the word of the Lord," "And the Spirit entered into me when he spake unto me," "The Lord spake unto me," "The word of the Lord that came unto Hosea." These statements cannot be lightly dismissed as scribal glosses or a mere literary device used by the prophets. This is the significance of the statement of Amos. The word of the Lord came with such overwhelming certainty that Amos is constrained to speak: "The Lord Yahweh hath spoken; who can but prophesy?" (Amos 3:8). Isaiah declares, "For Yahweh spake thus to me with a strong hand" (Isa. 8:11). And Jeremiah cannot remain silent: "If I say, I will not make mention of him, nor speak any more in his name, then there is in my heart as it were a burning fire shut up in my bones, and I am weary with forbearing, and I cannot contain" (Jer. 20:9).

As concluded earlier, there was no phenomenon analogous to biblical prophecy outside Israel, for if Hebrew prophetism was simply a part of the characteristic practices common to the ancient Near East and an outgrowth of the religious institutions of Canaan, then there is little which is unique about Israel's prophetic institution. Pedersen claims that "the whole institution belonged to Canaan and was closely connected with Canaanite culture. . . . In the course of time Israel brought forth a specially Israelitish type of prophet, produced by the friction between the two cultures."[1] In this connection, the Old Testament critics stress that the prophets of Israel were *ecstatics*, as were the prophets of Canaan and those throughout the Near East. The ecstatic behavior of the prophets of Baal, who in frenzied

[1]Johannes Pedersen, *Israel: Its Life and Culture,* III-IV, 111.

dances cut and mutilated themselves on Mount Carmel, as well as the peculiar conduct of Saul, who stripped himself naked as he prophesied, and the unusual behavior of Balaam are usually cited as evidence of the characteristic abnormal behavior of the prophets of Israel when prophesying under the influence of the Spirit. To understand the nature of the prophetic consciousness, it will be necessary to examine two problems which have to do with the questions of ecstasy and inspiration respectively.

PROBLEM OF ECSTASY

Divine inspiration was, according to the early church Fathers, received by the prophets when in a state of mind expressed by the Greek term *ékstasis*, "ecstasy," that is, in a rapturous state in which rational self-consciousness was suspended. It is described as a state in which the mind of the prophet was said to have been freed from the limitations of the natural or physical and elevated to a sphere of mental exaltation and poetic inspiration. Ecstasy, according to a contemporary writer, is "a trancelike state of emotional rapture and mental exaltation in which the subject is so transported by emotion or so engrossed in some object of contemplation as to be extremely if not completely insensible to normal external stimuli."[2] Others would modify the meaning of prophetic ecstasy as an experience in which self-consciousness and spontaneity do not entirely disappear during the reception of revelation, although in prophecy spiritual states occur in which the prophet's mind is subjugated by the power of the divine Spirit.

The term "ecstasy" is used several times in the New Testament.[3] Here it signifies (1) a state of trance in which revelation is received (Acts 10:10; 11:5; 22:17); and (2) amazement (Mark 5:42; 16:8; Luke 5:26; Acts 3:10). In the verbal form (*éxistēmi*) it is translated with the sense "to be amazed, astounded," "to be beside oneself"[4] (Mark 2:12; 3:21; II Cor. 5:13). In II Corinthians 5:13 the Apostle Paul declares that his states of rapturous ecstasy (referring doubtless to his visions, revelations, fervent praise and joy, special anointings by the Holy Spirit, trances, manifestations of the spiritual gifts, e.g.,

[2]Vergilius Ferm (ed.), *An Encyclopedia of Religion*, p. 243.

[3]The Greek terms are used in the LXX to translate the Hebrew words "trembling," Gen. 27:33; Exodus 19:18; and "fear," II Chron. 14:14; Ruth 3:8, etc.

[4]The English translation "to be beside oneself" is not necessarily the most accurate rendition in every case, e.g., II Cor. 5:13, where it denotes a rapturous state of mental exaltation induced by the Spirit of God.

tongues, prophesyings, etc.) express a definite relationship to God. Hence, ecstasy, as several of these passages indicate, can be a spiritual state induced by the Spirit of God in connection with the reception of divine revelation, and can at times result in prophetic utterance, as is clearly evident, for example, in the message to Cornelius which resulted from Peter's ecstasy or trance (Acts 10:9-16, 28 f.).

The term "ecstasy" has become a catchword, however, in the vocabulary of the Old Testament critics to describe the abnormal behavior of the heathen prophets who practiced divination, sorcery and magic, and who, in their states of self-induced trances (ecstasy), were given to irrational utterances, raved, leaped about and often mutilated themselves. This so-called ecstatic state of mind, resulting in such abnormal behavior, is said to have been characteristic of the prophets of Israel also. "All prophecy," we are told, "at least until a comparatively late post-exilic period, was based on a peculiar psychological condition to which the name of ecstasy is often given. It was characteristic of the false prophet as well as the true."[5] Other critics, however, would limit such "ecstatic" behavior to the so-called $n^e bh\hat{\imath}'\hat{\imath}m$, or precanonical prophets, typical of which is said to be the "band" of prophets described in I Samuel 10:5-12, and the so-called "schools" of prophets in II Kings 2. The reform, or canonical, prophets, such as Isaiah and Hosea, do not exhibit such abnormal behavior. Two questions arise, therefore, with respect to prophetic consciousness and the problem of ecstasy. First, can such a distinction be made between the so-called $n^e bh\hat{\imath}'\hat{\imath}m$ and the canonical prophets? Second, were the Hebrew prophets ecstatics?

THE N^{E}BHÎ'ÎM

To answer the first question, we must first identify the so-called $n^e bh\hat{\imath}'\hat{\imath}m$. According to critical scholars, the early prophets were, like their pagan predecessors, of the dervish type, who, in their prophesying, lost normal consciousness and sense experience, raved, chanted, mutilated themselves and exhibited all kinds of abnormal behavior. These $n^e bh\hat{\imath}'\hat{\imath}m$ are to be identified with the prophets of Baal who exhibited such frenzied conduct on Mount Carmel (I Kings 18), the band of prophets under Samuel's leadership with whose spirit Saul was caught up and also began to prophesy (I Sam. 10), the schools of prophets under Elijah and Elisha (II Kings 2-6), and the band of four hundred prophets who were attached to King Ahab's court (I Kings 22). The early $n^e bh\hat{\imath}'\hat{\imath}m$, it is said, stand in

---

[5] W. O. E. Oesterley and Theodore H. Robinson, *An Introduction to the Books of the Old Testament*, p. 397.

sharp contrast with the later writing prophets who repudiated them
for their irrational behavior and identified them, as does Jeremiah,
with the false prophets and with those who associate themselves with
the royal court and prophesy words of "peace" for hire, as is seen in
the case of the group attached to Ahab's court.

R. B. Y. Scott takes this extreme view that these companies or
dervish-type prophets did not prophesy in intelligible speech, but
resembled those speaking with tongues in the book of Acts.[6] John B.
Noss contends that these early *nᵉbhî'îm* who appeared during the
time of the judges were the *predecessors* who prepared the way for
the later great prophets. They were ecstatics who, like the dancing
dervishes of the Orient today, were given to irrational utterance,
unintelligible even to themselves. Alongside of and perhaps associated with them, arose men of higher spiritual caliber, such as Nathan
and Gad, who were the predecessors of the later literary prophets.[7]
T. H. Robinson describes the alleged religious ecstasy of the prophets, common in the Near East, thus:

ECSTATIC

> It consisted of a fit or attack which affected the whole body.
> Sometimes the limbs were stimulated to violent action, and wild
> leaping and contortions resulted. These might be more or less
> rhythmical, and the phenomenon would present the appearance
> of a wild and frantic dance. At other times there was more or less
> complete constriction of the muscles, and the condition became
> almost cataleptic. The vocal organs were sometimes involved,
> noises and sounds were poured out which might be unrecognis-
> able as human speech. If definite words were uttered they were
> often unintelligible. Face and aspect were changed, and to all
> outward appearance the Ecstatic "became another man." An ad-
> ditional feature was insensibility to pain, and the extravagant
> activities of the Ecstatic frequently included violent slashing and
> cutting of his own body and limbs.[8]

According to Robinson, "men like Amos and Jeremiah were not
readily distinguishable by their contemporaries from the Ecstatics
whose symptoms resembled those of the epileptic or even the in-
sane."[9] Robinson holds that the Hebrew word for ecstatic is *nābhî'*,
that is, "prophet"![10] He thus identifies the two groups, regarding the
canonical prophets as ecstatics. He contends that even the prophetic

---

[6]R. B. Y. Scott, *Relevance of the Prophets,* pp. 45-46.

[7]John B. Noss, *Man's Religions,* pp. 483-84.

[8]Theodore H. Robinson, *Prophecy and the Prophets in Ancient Israel,* p.
31.

[9]*Ibid.,* p. 36.

[10]*Ibid.,* pp. 30-31.

formula "Thus saith the Lord" used to introduce a prophetic message suggests a past ecstatic experience.[11] Such an ecstatic experience was an indication that the "Spirit" had possessed him.

Mowinckel, however, makes a distinction between the reform, or
canonical, prophets and their predecessors, the so-called $n^e bh\hat{i}'\hat{i}m$, on
the basis of such passages as Jeremiah 5:13 and Micah 3:8.[12]
Mowinckel contends that only the early bands of prophets called the
$n^e bh\hat{i}'\hat{i}m$ were ecstatic as a result of the "Spirit" falling upon them,
whereas the canonical prophets were not ecstatics, but rational recipients of the "word" of the Lord. Hence, the primary distinction
between the two groups would be that the $n^e bh\hat{i}'\hat{i}m$ were ecstatics
who were Spirit-possessed and the canonical prophets were rational
religious thinkers who were stimulated by the "word" of the Lord
which came to them. There is, therefore, according to Mowinckel, a
distinction between the "Spirit" prophecy and the "word" prophecy.
The canonical prophets do not connect their ministry with the Spirit
($r\hat{u}ach$) of Yahweh, which was the source of the ecstatic behavior of
the $n^e bh\hat{i}'\hat{i}m$, but claimed to be recipients of the word ($d\bar{a}bh\bar{a}r$) of
Yahweh.[13] It was this possession by the Spirit of the Lord that is
said to have produced the ecstatic behavior in the early, precanonical
prophets, and because of this the later canonical prophets repudiate
them and deny Spirit-possession as the medium of inspiration.

However, is it valid to make such a distinction between the
precanonical and canonical prophets? We must reply in the negative,
since the later prophets nowhere repudiate the Spirit of God as the
medium of their inspiration. Although some of the canonical prophets
such as Amos, Isaiah and Jeremiah make no direct reference to the
Spirit of the Lord coming upon them, this is an argument from
silence and does not warrant the assumption that these prophets
actually repudiated the Spirit of God as their medium of inspiration.
Amos in fact speaks of his "visions" (8:1) and of "the words which
he saw" (1:1), as does Isaiah (1:1; 6:1), which clearly implies a
spiritual means of revelation and inspiration. The concept of being
"clothed" by the Spirit is by no means lacking in the book of Isaiah,
for we read of the Messiah, the greatest of the prophets, that "the
Spirit of Yahweh shall rest upon him, and the spirit of wisdom and
understanding" (11:2), and of Himself he said, "The Spirit of the

[11]*Ibid.,* pp. 43-44.
[12]See also A. Jepsen's *Nabi,* 1934.
[13]Sigmund Mowinckel, "The Spirit and the Word in Pre-exilic Reform
Prophets," *Journal of Biblical Literature,* LIII (1934), 199-227.

Lord Yahweh is upon me; because Yahweh hath anointed me to preach good tidings" (61:1). We note that in the first passage possession of the Spirit is equated with wisdom and understanding, and in the latter with preaching God's word. These are concepts which, quite obviously, are not in harmony with Mowinckel's low view of Spirit-possession by the $n^e bh\hat{i}\hat{i}m$. Jeremiah too, while he interprets his call by saying, "Now the word of Yahweh came unto me," nevertheless indicates in the verses which follow that he received these words in connection with a series of divine visions, thus again indicating revelation and inspiration through the Spirit.

In addition to these passages where revelation and inspiration by the Spirit are strongly implied are definite statements attesting to this fact by other canonical prophets. Ezekiel speaks of the Spirit "entering" into him (2:2; 3:24), the Spirit "lifting" him up and conveying him by vision to Jerusalem (8:3; 11:1) and to Chaldea "in the vision by the Spirit of God" (11:24). Alongside these claims by Ezekiel to be a recipient of the Spirit of the Lord, he also uses the so-called canonical terminology, speaking of the "word" of the Lord coming unto him (1:3; 12:1). Furthermore, in two passages Ezekiel describes his prophetic experience in terms of Isaiah's familiar phrase "the hand of the Lord," and speaks of the Spirit of the Lord being upon him (3:14; 37:1). Hence, contrary to critical scholarship, the "word" of the Lord, the "hand" of the Lord, and the "Spirit" of the Lord all serve to describe *the same type of experience*. Therefore, no artificial distinction can be made between the precanonical prophets' use of the phrase "the Spirit of the Lord" and the canonical prophets' use of the phrase "the word of the Lord," inasmuch as the literary prophets use both expressions. This unbiblical distinction is refuted in many passages by such statements from the canonical prophets as that of Micah who declared, "But as for me, I am full of power by the Spirit of Yahweh" (3:8). Other examples of canonical prophets who use the idea of the Spirit of the Lord falling upon them, inspiring them or possessing them, appear in such passages as Daniel 4:8; 5:12; 6:3; Zechariah 7:12; Isaiah 11:2; 32:15; 48:16; 61:1; Joel 2:28. In Ezekiel 13:3 we read: "Thus saith the Lord Yahweh, Woe unto the foolish prophets, that follow their own spirit, and have seen nothing!" The obvious implication here is that the true prophets are inspired by the Spirit of God, whereas the false prophets, whom the critics equate with the $n^e bh\hat{i}\hat{i}m$, prophesy by their own spirits. A New Testament reference from the pen of the Apostle Peter likewise confirms the fact that the prophets of Israel were men who were

clothed with the Holy Spirit: "For no prophecy ever came by the
will of man: but men spake from God, being moved by the Holy
Spirit" (II Peter 1:21).

On the other hand, the early precanonical prophets (*nᵉbhî'îm*) use
the so-called canonical prophetic formula "the word of the Lord." In
the days of Samuel's childhood it was said that "the word of Yahweh
was precious in those days; there was no frequent vision" (I Sam.
3:1), implying this to be the usual method of prophetic revelation,
that is, revelation of the "word" to the prophet. Later we read of the
Prophet Micaiah declaring "the word of Yahweh" to King Ahab
(I Kings 22:14, 19). The unnamed prophet of Judah was sent to
Jeroboam of Israel under authority of the word of the Lord: "And,
behold, there came a man of God out of Judah by the word of
Yahweh unto Bethel. . . . And he cried against the altar by the word
of Yahweh" (I Kings 13:1-2). The same is true with respect to revelations made to Moses, Nathan, Gad and other precanonical prophets
—they were recipients of the word of the Lord (cf. Exodus 7:1-2; II
Sam. 12:7).

From all this evidence it is quite apparent that the distinction
between the precanonical prophets and the canonical prophets, in
which the former are said to be ecstatic *nᵉbhî'îm* who were Spirit-
possessed, and the latter refined recipients of the word of the Lord, is
both arbitrary and artificial. The true prophets of Israel, whether
precanonical or canonical, possessed *both* the *word* and the *Spirit* of
the Lord.

WERE THE HEBREW PROPHETS ECSTATICS?

Having shown the fallacy of Mowinckel's contention that there
existed a deep gulf between the precanonical prophets, or so-called
ecstatic *nᵉbhî'îm*, and the later prophets, the second problem has to
do with whether or not the Hebrew prophets were "ecstatics" in the
extreme sense that the critics contend, or whether the prophets of
Israel were unique, both in their behavior and inspiration. As noted
earlier, some critics contend that the precanonical prophets were
comparable in behavior to the prophets of Baal on Mount Carmel
shouting, leaping and dancing, and placing themselves through self-
induced means in heightened psychical, ecstatic states.

Meek, however, would modify this extreme critical hypothesis.
The early prophets were ecstatics, corresponding in a way to the
maḫḫû of the Babylonians, but their behavior was seldom, if ever, of

the frenzied type.[14] H. H. Rowley also contends that if Israel's prophets were essentially ecstatics, then the Hebrew verb "to prophesy," a denominative from the noun "prophet," would not have come to mean merely "to behave like a prophet," but "to act as one beside himself."[15] Yehezkel Kaufmann suggests that ecstasy is consequent on the word of God; that is, in the Hebrew conception, ecstasy does not induce prophecy, as the pagans believed, but, on the contrary, the divine word may cause ecstasy.[16]

Lindblom seeks to differentiate between two different kinds of ecstasy which are termed "absorption" ecstasy and "concentration" ecstasy.[17] Only the latter type, according to Lindblom, can be applied to the Old Testament prophets. In "absorption" ecstasy the personality of the individual is mystically fused into that of the divine Being, whereas "concentration" ecstasy maintains the distinction between the individual and Deity. Here, as a result of profound concentration upon a specific idea or feeling, there are a suspension of normal consciousness and a temporary interruption of the ordinary senses. If the term "ecstasy" is to be applied to the Old Testament prophets, Lindblom holds that it is only in this sense of concentration ecstasy and not that of absorption, where the personality of the prophet is merged and lost in union with God.[18] Were then the Hebrew prophets ecstatics, either in the extreme sense as proposed by such Old Testament critics as Robinson or Hölscher, or in the more moderate sense as suggested by Meek and others? Or were they ecstatics in any sense? To the solution of this question we now turn.

Superficially considered, there may at times be discerned an *outward* resemblance between certain acts of behavior of the Hebrew prophets of Israel and those of other religions. But there is a real danger in mistaking, as critical scholarship so often does, *a superficial and outward resemblance as indicative of the same prophetic psychology*. On the basis of the symbolic acts of some of the prophets, the behavior of the prophets of Baal, and the exceptional cases of the heathen soothsayer Balaam and the rebellious King Saul, in which there appears to be a complete suspension of personality (the normal consciousness being suspended by the divine overpowering of the Spirit), all true prophets are said to have experienced, to some

---

[14]Theophile James Meek, *Hebrew Origins*, p. 156.
[15]H. H. Rowley, *Prophecy and Religion in Ancient China and Israel*, p. 15.
[16]Yehezkel Kaufmann, *The Religion of Israel*, p. 100.
[17]Rowley (ed.), *The Old Testament and Modern Study*, p. 137.
[18]J. Lindblom, *Prophecy in Ancient Israel*, p. 106.

degree, such abnormal or ecstatic behavior. However, with regard to Balaam, a heathen prophet who purposed to curse Israel, and Saul who sought to slay David, there was of necessity a complete subjection of their personalities and suppression of their rebellious wills in order for God to communicate His message. In neither case were the recipients in sympathy, nor their minds in harmony, with the divine revelation given them, hence the necessity of a divinely imposed passivity and the suppression of their self-will and personality. Thus nothing can be proven from these exceptional instances with respect to the characteristic behavior of the prophets of Israel.

The view that erratic, abnormal behavior and the prophetic role are to be equated is also based upon a misinterpretation of certain passages in which the Old Testament critics contend that the prophets are said to have been popularly called madmen (II Kings 9:11; Hosea 9:7; Jer. 29:26) or fools (Hosea 9:7). Thus, it is contended that to "act the prophet" is to behave in a mad or extremely abnormal manner (I Sam. 18:10). However, this was not the proper view of the prophets at all, and such interpretation is merely an attempt to force these passages to conform to a preconceived notion that the Hebrew prophets were raving ecstatics in the same sense as their heathen counterparts. These passages do not prove, as the critics assert, that the popular conception of the prophet was that of a madman or fool, for in Jeremiah 29:26 and Hosea 9:7 the term refers to false prophets, and in II Kings 9:11 it is used scoffingly of the prophet sent by Elisha to Jehu. At times the behavior of the prophet was unusual or abnormal, but a careful consideration of each of these instances will reveal some divine purpose or spiritual significance.

In the first place, the very fact that the prophetic call, as well as the messages and revelations themselves, often came in the form of a supernatural vision, dream, theophany, or by audible voice, was abnormal, and most certainly not the normal experience of the ordinary Israelite (cf. Exodus 3; Nahum 1:1; Ezek. 1-3; Jer. 1; Zech. 1; Isa. 6, etc.). When the divine Presence and holy word are unveiled to the eyes of man, certainly we should not expect his response to the spiritual dimension to be on a plane comparable to that in the natural sphere.

Again, the symbolic acts of some of the prophets were not ordinary or normal behavior. Jeremiah walked the streets of Jerusalem with a yoke about his neck, acting out his message that Babylon was soon to place a "yoke" upon the nations including Israel (Jer.

27-28). Isaiah walked naked[19] and barefoot three years as a sign of the fate awaiting Egypt and Ethiopia (Isa. 20).

With Ezekiel the symbolic acts multiplied. He remained "dumb" for seven days after his call (3:15); he enacted the flight of the Israelites from Jerusalem by knocking a hole in the wall of his house and carrying forth his goods (12:1-7); he portrayed Jerusalem on a clay tile and then symbolically enacted the siege of the city (4:1-2); he lay alternately upon his right and left sides for a long period to illustrate Jerusalem's tribulation (4:4-8); by eating coarse food cooked with dung he prophesied of the approaching famine (4:9-17); by the symbolic cutting of his hair he portrayed the desolation of Jerusalem. These strange actions, together with his allegories, exhibit abnormal behavior.

The Prophet Hosea's marriage to a harlot was hardly the normal, customary behavior of most Israelites. Nevertheless, this rather unusual conduct on the part of the prophets does not indicate ecstatic aberrations, nor pathological behavior, as, for example, some have erroneously understood Ezekiel's behavior.[20] On the contrary, the prophets themselves admit to divine motivation and purpose in their behavior. These symbolic acts were *acted parables* to a perverted hardheaded people who seemed incapable of understanding ordinary speech.

> And he said unto me, Son of man, go, get thee unto the house of Israel, and speak with my words unto them. For thou art not sent to a people of a strange speech and of a hard language, but to the house of Israel; not to many peoples of a strange speech and of a hard language, whose words thou canst not understand. Surely, if I sent thee to them, they would hearken unto thee. But the house of Israel will not hearken unto thee; for they will not hearken unto me: for all the house of Israel are of a hard forehead and of a stiff heart (Ezek. 3:4-7).

Furthermore, inasmuch as inspiration and revelation imply not a *static* but a *dynamic* state of mind, the prophet may at times experience a spiritually heightened and rapturous, or trancelike state of

[19]Possibly stripped of his outer garments, wearing only the short tunic underneath.

[20]It has been charged by some critics that Ezekiel suffered from pathological abnormalities—temporary dumbness (aphasia) and partial paralysis (hemiplegia). (Cf. 3:24-27; 24:25-27; 4:4 ff.; James Hastings [ed.], *Encyclopaedia of Religion and Ethics*, X, 391.)

mental exaltation in which he is the recipient of supernatural visions and revelations of a profound nature. On such occasions he would find himself "in the Spirit," under the influence and power of the divine Presence, whereby consciousness of the mundane and temporal might be suspended. This, of course, clearly has no relation to self-induced ecstasy, nor to the frenzied, irrational behavior of the heathen prophets, nor to the mediumistic trance, in which there is no remembrance later by the speaker of what was uttered.

This *revelatory, prophetic state* is seen frequently in Scripture. Consider, for example, Ezekiel's unusual experience at the time of his inaugural vision (Ezek. 3:14 f.) and his visions wherein he was transported "in spirit" to Jerusalem (8:11); Daniel's visions and their effect upon him (Dan. 8:15-18; 10:7-10); Abraham's "deep sleep" preparatory to God's revelations to him (Gen. 15:12 f.); Zechariah's night visions which are not to be regarded as mere dreams, but a visional state, for he was "awakened" in preparation for the revelation "as a man that is wakened out of his sleep" (Zech. 1-6; cf. 4:1); the visions and revelations of the Apostle Paul wherein he was caught up to paradise, the experience being of such an exalted nature he was unable to ascertain whether he was transported in the body or spirit (II Cor. 12:1 f.); his experiences of ecstasy mentioned in II Corinthians 5:13, as well as his "trance" and vision in the temple (Acts 22:17 f.); Peter's trance and vision (Acts 10:9 f.); and the rapturous experiences of John who was caught up "in the Spirit" and given visions and revelations of things to come. The word translated "trance" in the English is the Greek term for ecstasy (*èkstasis*, Acts 10:10; 11:5; 22:17).

Therefore, the Scriptures do not deny the reality of some form of an ecstatic experience to the Hebrew prophets, but describe it as a *divinely induced revelatory condition* of a more or less restrained nature which was not in a continuum with pagan prophetism. The heathen and false prophets, on the other hand, induced an aberrant, ecstatic state or trance themselves by artificial means through the use of drugs, mass excitation, flagellation, frenzied dancing and magical ritual. In the case of Israel's true prophets it was a divinely induced state of the mind preparatory to the reception of revelation, the proclamation of the divine word (either verbally or by symbolic act), or the exalted expression of praise or worship (cf. Exodus 15; Judges 5; I Sam. 2). In contrast, magic and sorcery were resorted to by the heathen in an attempt to produce a self-induced ecstatic trance conducive to divination, so that through contact with the spirit world some favor or revelation of hidden knowledge could be secured from the gods or spirits.

One passage often cited by liberal interpreters as evidence of extreme ecstatic behavior among Israel's prophets is found in I Samuel 10:1-13. In this passage Samuel, upon anointing Saul as king, advised him that upon his return home he would meet a band of prophets coming down from the hill of God playing upon the psaltery, timbrel, pipe and harp, prophesying as they went, and the Spirit of the Lord would come upon him and he too would prophesy and be turned into another man. H. Wheeler Robinson states that this account is an example of the ecstatic behavior of the early prophets, and that Saul "caught the contagion of their influence and displayed the same physical and psychical excitement."[21] This is said to be an example of the ecstatic dance induced by the musical instruments. A parallel passage cited to prove that music was used by the prophets to induce the ecstatic experience is II Kings 3:1-20. In this instance Elisha is asked to give God's counsel respecting Israel's campaign against Moab which had rebelled upon the death of Ahab. "Elisha said ... but now bring me a minstrel. And it came to pass, when the minstrel played, that the hand of Yahweh came upon him" (vv. 14-15).

In the former case, E. J. Young argues with conviction that the company of prophets may have been on a pilgrimage to Gibeah, since the fact that they were preceded by musicians seems to indicate a festal procession. The text does not state that the prophesying was brought on by the music, but the musical instruments were carried *before* the prophets and were probably employed merely as an accompaniment.[22] The Old Testament itself gives ample evidence in the records of Chronicles of the practice of prophesying in this early period to the accompaniment of musical instruments, including prophecy in the form of song and praise. I Chronicles 25:1-3 states:

> Moreover David . . . set apart for the service certain of the sons of Asaph, and of Heman, and of Jeduthun, who should prophesy with harps, with psalteries, and with cymbals: . . . [and they] prophesied in giving thanks and praising Yahweh.

In the case of Elisha we see that music is harmoniously related to the poetic element in prophecy;[23] and the prophet, by thus elevating his mind and freeing himself from the mundane, might prepare himself for the divine revelation.[24] Furthermore, dancing, which is singled out as a characteristic of the pagan prophets in I Kings 18:26, is not

---

[21]H. Wheeler Robinson, *The Religious Ideas of the Old Testament*, p. 111.
[22]Edward J. Young, *My Servants the Prophets*, pp. 85-86.
[23]Cf. Num. 24:2; II Sam. 23:2; Ps. 40:3; Exodus 15; Judges 5; Deut. 33.
[24]J. Barton Payne, *The Theology of the Older Testament*, p. 52.

mentioned as a part of the behavior of the prophets in I Samuel 10. In neither this account nor that of Elisha in II Kings 3 is there any indication of ecstatic frenzy or self-induced trance brought on by the music. On the contrary, there is every indication, as the account in II Kings 3 clearly shows, that the prophet, although under the influence of the Spirit of God, was in full possession of his rational faculties and proceeded to utter an intelligible and comprehensible message from the Lord which is so unlike the self-induced trance of the shaman or spiritist medium in which, upon awaking, there is no remembrance of what was spoken.

Another passage to be noted with regard to the question of ecstasy is I Kings 20:35. In this passage one of the sons of the prophets commanded his companion to smite him. Here, it is said, is an example of a self-inflicted wound, comparable to the behavior of the heathen prophets on Mount Carmel, in order to bring upon oneself the ecstatic rapture conducive to prophesying. But even a casual examination of this text will reveal the absurdity of this contention. For one thing, the prophet was wounded *after* he had already received the revelation, and therefore did not seek by this means to transport himself into an ecstatic trancelike state. Verse 35 states that he asked one of his companions to smite him "*by the word of Yahweh*," thus indicating that his action and consequent message to King Ahab were on the basis of revelation already in his possession. The entire critical argument breaks down here, because the basic purpose in the heathen rites of frenzied dancing and flagellation was to induce the ecstatic state in order to receive the revelation. Furthermore, this was not a case of a self-inflicted wounding, but the prophet insisted that God had revealed that another should smite him. This fact is emphasized in that when one of his companions refused to do the smiting, he sought out another for the task. Certainly if the prophets had been accustomed to inflicting themselves in such a manner, he would now have been justified in so doing. An unprejudiced reading of the passage will show the divine purpose in his behavior, unusual to be sure, but no more so than that of Jeremiah, Isaiah, Ezekiel and Hosea. God intended by means of this symbolic act to rebuke Ahab for his leniency in releasing Ben-hadad and to show him what would be his own fate.

A final passage cited as evidence of the excessive ecstatic behavior of the prophets is found in I Samuel 19:19-24. When word was brought to Saul that David, whose life he sought, was hiding in Naioth, he sent messengers on three different occasions to seize him. Each time they were met by a company of prophets who were prophesying, and the Spirit of the Lord came upon them and they also prophesied. Upon learning of these events, Saul himself determined to go, and upon his arrival in Naioth the Spirit of God came upon him and he too prophesied. Of Saul it is also related that he "stripped off his clothes, and he also prophesied before Samuel, and lay down naked all that day and all that night. Wherefore they say, Is Saul also among the prophets?" From this single instance of Saul stripping off his clothes, prophesying and falling down naked before Samuel, it has been concluded by some that this kind of behavior was also characteristic of the bands of the prophets and proof of their similar ecstatic condition when prophesying.

However, this conclusion misses entirely the intended meaning of this unusual occurrence in connection with King Saul. The point, overlooked by the critics, is that the people who saw Saul prophesying were surprised to see him among the company of prophets and *prophesying with them.* They understandably asked, "Is Saul also among the prophets?" not because he stripped off his clothes and fell down naked, but because he too was prophesying! This is without question the clear meaning of the text. This is proven by virtue of the fact that this was the identical question asked by the onlookers as recorded in I Samuel 10:10-12, when they saw Saul prophesying with the company of prophets. There is absolutely no evidence on that occasion of Saul exhibiting unusual behavior or stripping off his clothes in prophesying. On that occasion, as in chapter 19, the people were prompted to ask the question "Is Saul also among the prophets?" *because he was acting like a prophet by his prophesying*, not because he was exhibiting so-called prophetic or ecstatic behavior in stripping off his clothes and falling down naked.

The significance of his behavior is not to be found in the suggestion that his nakedness was characteristic of the bands of the prophets, since there is nowhere the slightest hint in Scripture that any other prophet ever stripped off his clothes and fell down naked in some sort of ecstatic trance while under the influence of God's Spirit.[25] Saul's behavior at Naioth is unique in Scripture and was no doubt intended by God to be the means of humbling this proud, rebellious king. Saul had repeatedly resisted the will of God and was determined to destroy David. He acted as did Balaam, who determined to curse Israel but was overcome and brought under the subjection of God's Spirit (Num. 22-24), and as King Nebuchadnezzar,

[25]Isaiah 20:1-6 notwithstanding, for that has to do with a rational, self-conscious, symbolic act which was "for a sign and wonder concerning Egypt and concerning Ethiopia" (v. 3).

who through pride sought to exalt himself above God and was subjected to humiliation before God and the people (Dan. 4). Self-willed, proud King Saul, on his murderous mission to slay David, God's anointed, was not only compelled to turn from his intention and act as a prophet by prophesying, but was brought down in humiliation before God and his own subjects. God had given young Saul a "new heart" to the end that he was enabled to become a different kind of man in that he could conduct himself in a royal manner and think and act as a king ought (I Sam. 10). Now God was to strip Saul of his unworthy dignity and compel him to exhibit unkingly behavior, in that he was subdued and compelled to strip off his royal garments and fall down naked all day and night.

From all this it seems safe to conclude that negative criticism has not proven its case with respect to the existence of ecstatic prophets in Israel comparable in behavior to those in Canaan and throughout the Near East. Occasional instances of abnormal behavior are not evidence of irrational utterances, self-induced trances, nor frenzied, orgiastic and ecstatic behavior on the part of the Hebrew prophets. As has been shown, the behavior of Israel's prophets is explicable when the dynamic nature of the revelatory state of mind is considered, when the divine purpose of the symbolic acts of the prophets is understood, and the legitimate use of music in some types of prophesying is acknowledged.

PROPHETIC INSPIRATION

Now that the essential distinction between the so-called ecstatic prophets of the heathen religions and the prophets of Israel has been shown, there remains the need of arriving at a proper biblical understanding of the prophetic consciousness with respect to inspiration. The psychological conviction of the prophets was that God had supernaturally revealed Himself and had spoken His word to them. This is reiterated again and again by such phrases as "Thus saith the Lord," "The Lord hath spoken," "I saw the Lord," "I heard the voice of the Lord," "The vision of Isaiah ...which he saw," "Hear the word of the Lord," "The Lord said unto me," "Daniel had a dream and vision," "The vision of Obadiah," "Behold, I have put my words in thy mouth," "God spoke unto me," "The word of the Lord came unto me." Frequently the personality of the prophet disappears, as it were, and God superimposes Himself as the speaker: "But thou, Israel, my servant, Jacob whom I have chosen, the seed of Abraham my friend..." (Isa. 41:8). Hence, the prophet of Israel spoke under the conviction that he was the personal recipient of divine revelation;

or to state it another way, the prophet of Israel believed himself to
be *divinely inspired*. It will be necessary, therefore, to examine at this
juncture the various theories which have attempted to explain this
phenomenon as it pertains to the Old Testament prophets. Several
theories have been proposed in an effort to define the nature of
Hebrew psychology with respect to inspiration. The most significant
are as follows.

DIFFUSED CONSCIOUSNESS THEORY

This is the view of H. Wheeler Robinson who held that according
to Israelite belief each physical organ of the body could function in
quasi independence of his will when some external influence, such as
the Spirit of God, acted upon it. This, Robinson believes, can explain
the psychical experience of the prophet whose personality came temporarily under the influence and control of the Spirit of God. He
explains this psychological phenomenon thus:

> . . . Hebrew psychology enables us to understand something of
> the manner of this "possession" by invasive energy. The concep-
> tion is facilitated by that of diffused consciousness or localized
> psychical function. The Hebrews knew nothing of the nervous sys-
> tem and the psycho-physical function of the brain, which to them
> was no more than "the marrow of the head." Neither did they
> know anything of the circulation of the blood from the heart as its
> central organ. In the absence of such unifying conceptions, they
> were left free, like other ancient peoples, to imagine that each
> part of the body was to some degree a self-contained enti-
> ty. . . . Each part of the body is conceived to have psychical and
> ethical as well as physiological functions of its own. This applies
> not only to the central organs, the heart, liver, bowels, kidneys,
> but also to the peripheral, the eyes, ears, mouth, hands, and
> indeed to the flesh and bones in general. It was therefore much
> simpler for the Hebrews than for ourselves to believe in "inspira-
> tion"; an invasive energy could take possession of any one of
> these organs, such as the mouth and tongue, and use it in
> quasi-independence of its owner. It is this kind of conception that
> explains the reference to Jeremiah's mouth in the account of his
> call; his objection that he is too young to be made a prophet is
> answered by the hand of Yahweh touching his mouth and so
> making it His own organ: "I have put my words in thy mouth"
> [Jer. 1:9]. . . . In vision their eyes were made to see, in audition
> their ears were made to hear, by Him to whom they had surren-
> dered themselves.[26]

[26]H. Wheeler Robinson, *Inspiration and Revelation in the Old Testament*, pp. 181-82.

Thus Robinson proposed the view that according to Hebrew psychology the prophet believed that an external influence could take possession of any of the organs of the body and use and control them. Diffused consciousness would explain the spiritual vision given their eyes, the supernatural audition of their ears, and the control of their mouths by the Spirit of God.

CORPORATE PERSONALITY THEORY

The concept of corporate personality as applied to Israel views the one as identified with the many, and the many as embodied in the one. It should be briefly noted here in order to evaluate properly the theory of A. R. Johnson which follows, because his theory is influenced by this concept.[27] The strong sense of solidarity that prevailed in ancient Israel has been called the concept of corporate personality. The individual was subordinated to the family, tribe and nation to such an extent that he had no independent rights or worth.[28] The individual found satisfaction in the belief that immortality consisted in the hope that he lived on in his descendants and the nation.

H. Wheeler Robinson applied this concept of corporate personality to the prophets in an effort to help further explain the Hebrew prophetic consciousness. He said that "the prophet was one able to identify himself with both man and God, being the eye of Israel turned to God [Isa. 29:10], and the mouth of Yahweh opened to Israel [Jer. 15:19]."[29] According to Robinson the prophet's personality was temporarily merged in that of God. He writes:

> The closeness of this double identification is explained only when we remember such things as the story of Achan and of the slain descendants of Saul, the doom of toil and suffering which came upon the race because of the sin of Adam . . . all of them examples of the group, instead of the individual, as the unit. It is difficult for us, with centuries of individualism behind us, to recall the sense of social solidarity in its ancient form. . . . To those who could conceive of the merging of the individual in the family and the clan and the nation it must have been much easier for man's personality to be conceived as temporarily merged in that of God.[30]

[27]See also B. D. Napier, "Prophet, Prophetism," *The Interpreter's Dictionary of the Bible,* III, 913.

[28]Albert C. Knudson, *The Religious Teachings of the Old Testament,* p. 383.

[29]Robinson, *Redemption and Revelation,* p. 149.

[30]*Ibid.,* pp. 149-50.

Thus possessed by the invasive Spirit of Yahweh the prophet was conscious of "uniting Israel to God and God to Israel."[31] The prophet's peculiar relation to his people, Robinson asserts, is expressed by the concept of "corporate personality." The prophet could feel not only that he represented the nation, but that he actually *was* Israel before God and the actual voice of God to Israel: "They felt the beating of God's heart as their own; their eyes became the eyes of God seeing things unseen by men; their ears rang with the cry of human rebellion as though they were His."[32]

EXTENSION OF PERSONALITY THEORY

A. R. Johnson refutes the "diffused consciousness theory" on the basis that what is involved in these instances where the physical organs are depicted as having a quasi independence of their own is the prophetic writers' use of synecdoche, in which a part comes to represent the whole.

Influenced by the concept of corporate personality, Johnson proposed the theory of the "extension of personality" in which the prophet regarded himself as an extension of the divine Personality for "the personality (on what we may call its human side) has been absorbed, as it were, in that of the Godhead; the prophet has become temporarily, at least, an important 'Extension' of Yahweh's Personality."[33] Johnson states that this idea is thought to appear also in the importance attached to the family name, in which the personality survived after death. Also the household servant could be thought of as an extension of his master's personality, acting as his agent and representative. Even Elisha's staff, sent in charge of his servant Gehazi as the means of restoring the Shunammite's son to life, is an expression of the extension of the prophet's personality. This same concept is said to be present with respect to God. His Spirit is seen as an extension of His personality, as are His Word, His name and the ark. Hence, the ministry of the prophet is seen to be an extension also of the divine Personality. Johnson writes that "the prophet, in functioning, was held to be more than Yahweh's 'representative'; for the time being he was an active 'Extension' of Yahweh's Personality and, as such, *was* Yahweh—'in Person.' "[34]

[31]Robinson, *The Old Testament: Its Making and Meaning*, p. 84.
[32]*Ibid.*
[33]Aubrey R. Johnson, *The One and the Many in the Israelite Conception of God*, p. 33.
[34]*Ibid.*

SYMPATHETIC-PATHOS THEORY

A relatively recent explanation of the prophets' understanding of God is that proposed by Abraham J. Heschel in his book *The Prophets*. Heschel regards the prophetic consciousness as the sympathetic communication by the prophet of the divine pathos to men. Pathos expresses God's perpetual, solicitous concern for man. He writes:

> To the prophet . . . God does not reveal Himself in an abstract absoluteness, but in a personal and intimate relation to the world. He does not simply command and expect obedience; He is also moved and affected by what happens in the world, and reacts accordingly. Events and human actions arouse in Him joy or sorrow, pleasure or wrath. He is not conceived as judging the world in detachment. He reacts in an intimate and subjective manner, and thus determines the value of events. Quite obviously in the biblical view, man's deeds may move Him, affect Him, grieve Him or, on the other hand, gladden and please Him. This notion that God can be intimately affected, that He possesses not merely intelligence and will, but also pathos, basically defines the prophetic consciousness of God.[35]

Prophecy, according to Heschel, consisted in the inspired communication of this divine attitude to the prophet's consciousness. This understanding of God is echoed in almost every prophetic utterance.

This view is criticized by others. H. Wheeler Robinson contends that the emotional element in human and divine personality is not the most fundamental aspect in the religion of Israel. "It is the prophet's will, rather than his emotions, which reproduces the divine."[36] However, Heschel insists that God's pathos is not mere passion, or "an unreasoned emotion, but an act formed with intention . . . signifying God as involved in history, as intimately affected by events in history, as living care."[37]

It cannot be denied that this concept of divine pathos is a valid element in prophetic thought, indicating a sympathetic concern and involvement on the part of God in the world He created. However, pathos denotes more the prophets' communication of the divine "attitude" or "concern," called forth in response to man's moral and ethical conduct, rather than expressing the essential meaning and basis of the prophetic consciousness of God. Pathos is but one element, even if an important one, in the prophetic consciousness itself—

---

[35]Abraham J. Heschel, *The Prophets,* pp. 223-24.
[36]Robinson, *Inspiration and Revelation* . . . , pp. 184-85.
[37]Heschel, p. 231.

it is not the ground of the prophets' unique consciousness of their calling and ministry.

The Biblical Concept of the Prophetic Consciousness—Divine Inspiration by God's Spirit

The primary criticism of most of these theories is that although there are elements of truth in some of them, they are, nevertheless, generally inadequate expressions of the prophetic consciousness. The weakness of the "diffused consciousness" theory has already been observed by A. R. Johnson, for here we have the use of synecdoche by the prophets. The entire concept of "corporate personality" as it related to Old Testament studies is distorted and considerably overemphasized. The strength and weaknesses of the view propounded by Heschel of "sympathetic-pathos," in which the prophet could enter sympathetically into the divine pathos, has already been noted. The "extension of personality" theory of Johnson in which the prophet, in functioning, was not merely a representative, but was, for the time being, an extension of God's personality, is to a certain degree not lacking in scriptural support. Certainly this is implied in God's charge to Moses:

> And thou shalt speak unto him [Aaron], and put the words in his mouth: and I will be with thy mouth: and with his mouth, and will teach you what ye shall do . . . and *thou shalt be to him as God* (Exodus 4:15-16).[38]

And again in Exodus 7:1 Moses was told: "See, I have made thee *as God to Pharaoh.*" Nehemiah revealed the close identification of the prophet's word with God Himself when he said: "Thou . . . testifiedst against them by thy Spirit through thy prophets" (Neh. 9:30), as did Zechariah who declared that God's words were "sent by his Spirit by the former prophets" (Zech. 7:12).

Over and over again the personality of the prophet recedes and the Lord speaks in the first person: "I will heal their backsliding, I will love them freely"; "Hear, O Jacob my servant: and Israel whom I have chosen." On the other hand, of course, the prophet was ever conscious of the divine transcendence, and any suggestion of a kind of mystical absorption was foreign to Hebrew thought (cf. Isa. 6; Jer. 1:6; Exodus 4:10-14; Jonah 1, etc.). However, the concept of the prophet being, as it were, an extension of God's personality

---

[38]All italics used in Scripture references are the author's.

during the time when under the power of God's Spirit he spoke the very words which God gave him or inspired him to speak, does help to elucidate an important aspect of the prophetic consciousness.

The supernatural influence which clothed certain Old Testament figures and enabled them to see and hear things which were otherwise hidden (even to them), and by which they were compelled to speak forth in the name of the God of Israel, is described by various terms in the Old Testament, but all of them connote the idea of _divine inspiration by the Spirit of God_. Consider, for example, the following statements of the Scriptures: "The Spirit of God came upon him" (Num. 24:2); "The hand of the Lord Yahweh fell ... upon me" (Ezek. 8:1); "The Spirit of Yahweh fell upon me" (Ezek. 11:5); "The hand of Yahweh came upon him" (II Kings 3:15); "The Spirit came upon Amasai" (I Chron. 12:18); "The Spirit of God came upon Zechariah" (II Chron. 24:20); "The Spirit rested upon them ... and they prophesied" (Num. 11:26); "Thou ... testifiedst against them by thy Spirit through thy prophets" (Neh. 9:30); "The Spirit of the Lord Yahweh is upon me; because Yahweh hath anointed me to preach good tidings" (Isa. 61:1); "The words which Yahweh of hosts had sent by his Spirit by the former prophets" (Zech. 7:12); "And it shall come to pass afterward, that I will pour out my Spirit upon all flesh; and your sons and your daughters shall prophesy" (Joel 2:28); "The Spirit of Yahweh spake by me" (II Sam. 23:2). Such statements in the Old Testament which could be multiplied over and over, declare with one accord that the divine power which came upon certain Old Testament figures was the *Spirit of God*. And that divine power came upon them for the express purpose of opening their spiritual eyes and speaking into their inner ear revelations of truth that were otherwise unknown.

Liberal theology, in its attempt to discredit biblical inspiration, contends that Old Testament prophecy had its analogy in human genius. Israel is represented as a people of unique religious disposition, the Old Testament religion being the result of their natural piety and spiritual endowment. Therefore, the prophets of Israel are depicted as men who have the intuitive gifts of moral and spiritual insight heightened to such a degree that they are able to discern the issues of good and evil more clearly than their contemporaries and, because of this spiritual sensitivity and moral awareness, are able to announce reasonably accurate predictions respecting the future. However, the Old Testament almost goes out of its way to emphasize that prophecy is not a native faculty. No prophet of Israel claimed any special genius for discerning the unknown. Moses was an inarticulate stammerer by nature (Exodus 4:10; 6:12, 30). Jeremiah complained that he was but a novice (Jer. 1:6). Balaam's ass was able to see more than Balaam until God opened his eyes (Num. 22-24). Samuel the prophet was unable to discern which of Jesse's sons had been chosen by God (I Sam. 16:6 ff.). Nathan did not accurately interpret the divine will to King David on one occasion (II Sam. 7:1-3). Old Testament prophecy cannot be regarded as a native talent. The prophetic Spirit does not belong to the prophet, but "comes upon" him at certain periods.[39]

Thus the prophet of Israel was not one by virture of any innate talent which he possessed, nor did he take up the office by his own will (Amos 7:14-15). The true prophet insists that his messages do not originate in his own heart nor result from his own personal reflections, but they are divinely revealed counsels through the Spirit of God. Micah declares: "But as for me, I am full of power by the Spirit of Yahweh ... to declare unto Jacob his transgression, and to Israel his sin" (Micah 3:8). The prophet, under a divine anointing by God's Spirit, declares the word of the Lord received from the Spirit by inspiration or revelation. Sometimes it may run counter to his own preference (Jonah 1-4). Often it is not fully comprehended by the speaker himself (Dan. 7:15; 12:8; cf. I Peter 1:10-11). Sometimes he is called upon to make tremendous sacrifices and endure excessive hardships (Hosea 1-3; Jer. 16). The message frequently brings deep grief and suffering to his soul (Isa. 6:11; Hab. 3:1-2; Lam.). The word of the prophet is often rejected (Ezek. 2:1-7), and the prophet persecuted (Jer. 11:18-19; 18:18; 26:8; Dan. 6). But so conscious is he that he is anointed by God's Spirit and not speaking out of his own heart that he cannot keep silent. "There is in my heart as it were a burning fire shut up in my bones, and I am weary with forbearing, and I cannot contain" (Jer. 20:9). The prophetic consciousness was the result of divine inspiration by the Spirit of God: *"Men spake from God, being moved by the Holy Spirit"* (II Peter 1:21). They wrote and spoke, conscious of, and by means of the influence and operation of the Holy Spirit.

Therefore, in view of the obvious and significant relationship of the question of inspiration with the subject of Old Testament prophetism, an examination of the scriptural view of revelation and inspiration follows.

[39]Kaufmann, p. 96.

Chapter 4

REVELATION AND
INSPIRATION

REVELATION

MAN'S QUEST FOR GOD

THE FIRST CHAPTER of Genesis declares that man was created in the image of God. When he fell into sin the image was marred but not completely destroyed, otherwise he would have become merely an irrational beast without moral and spiritual faculties. The image of God in man was primarily his divinely endowed moral, spiritual, rational and religious nature. Both the Bible and history testify to the fact that man is by nature religious. Because of this, he subscribes in various ways to some concept of spiritual reality, and seeks to postulate some fundamental principle which will transcend and explain the created order. This is to be seen in man's relentless search for the meaning of life, in his restless quest for truth, for reality, for knowledge and for the highest good; or we may, generally speaking, call his quest *a search for God*. Man, as a sinner, has sought to relate himself to absolute reality by three paths: philosophy, science and religion.

Philosophy. All philosophical systems are attempts to find absolute truth, that is, the answers to questions of ultimate reality. The questions never change, only the philosophical answers. Since Christianity alone can satisfactorily answer the questions concerned with ultimate reality, questing human reason must look to the revelation of God for the solution to its problems. The philosopher can formulate the questions, but only the Christian faith can supply the correct answers. The answers are supplied by God, not human reason. "Philosophy," said Plato, "begins with wonder." Man wonders about the meaning of life and the universe which surrounds him. He wonders and asks questions about the mystery of birth, life, death. He questions the meaning of pleasure, pain, happiness, the meaning of moral and natural evil. Man's quest for knowledge and reality is persistent; his questions are endless. What is man? What was his origin and

74

what are his destiny and purpose? What are justice, beauty, right and wrong? What are love, goodness, hate, sin? What is God? Is man immortal? What is the soul? Sinful man holds that by his unaided reason he can supply correct answers to these important questions by way of the philosophical quest. But this belief is based upon two fallacies which reveal the inadequacy of philosophical speculation to discover ultimate truth and reality. What are these fallacies?

1. Man's reason was unaffected by the fall. This statement is erroneous inasmuch as the Scriptures insist that man's reason, because he is a sinner, is darkened and perverted, and he cannot see things aright. Jeremiah establishes this fact by his universal charge "Every man is become brutish and is without knowledge" (10:14). It is confirmed by God's indictment through the psalmist:

> The fool hath said in his heart, There is no God . . . . Yahweh looked down from heaven upon the children of men, to see if there were any that did understand, that did seek after God. They are all gone aside; they are together become filthy; there is none that doeth good, no, not one. Have all the workers of iniquity no knowledge, who . . . call not upon Yahweh? (Ps. 14:1-4).

The Apostle Paul asserts that natural man perverts God's revelation of certain truths in creation concerning His power and divinity for the precise reason that men, as sinners, "became vain in their reasonings, and their senseless heart was darkened. Professing themselves to be wise, they became fools, and changed the glory of the incorruptible God for the likeness of an image of corruptible man, and of birds, and four-footed beasts, and creeping things. Wherefore God gave them up . . ." (Rom. 1:21-24). Thus the fall has so adversely affected man's reason that "the natural man receiveth not the things of the Spirit of God: for they are foolishness unto him; and he cannot know them, because they are spiritually judged" (I Cor. 2:14). The greatest proof of this is that the more man speculates and philosophizes about God and the universe the farther from true reality his quest carries him. Instead of seeing God, in his sinful imagination he postulates a god in his own image and a universe governed and controlled by the laws of his own theories and hypotheses.

There is a permanent antagonism between philosophy and Christianity because the ultimate questions of philosophy are the basic truths of Christianity. Philosophy at its best is little more than an intellectual introduction to the questions of truth and ultimate reality. It cannot supply the final answers to these questions. This does not mean that philosophy cannot arrive at any degree of truth. It does mean, however, that sinful reason cannot plumb the depths of spiritual truth—it cannot answer the questions which faith alone can comprehend and to which revelation can supply the answers. Philosophy cannot, for instance, by mere metaphysical speculation, cope adequately with the being and nature of God, the problem of sin, the ultimate standard or norm for right and wrong, and the nature of the soul. Philosophy cannot supply *ultimate* answers to any question, religious or not, since all truth must ultimately be grounded on an authentic, divine revelation which the philosopher bypasses in his quest for truth. Hence, the answers supplied by philosophy are, at best, relative answers distorted by sin. The first fallacy of the philosophical quest for ultimate reality is that it fails to take into consideration the fact that the fall seriously affected man's reason—it has become darkened and perverted and is quite unreliable, especially in the metaphysical sphere. All this only tends to emphasize the second fallacy of philosophy.

2. Man can know ultimate truth apart from divine revelation. The basic criticism of philosophy is that it tends to *absolutize the finite.* Reason is thought to be infallible and the reality of a divine revelation of truth is scorned. Philosophy is to be criticized because of its rationalistic basis in its contention that reason alone is sufficient to solve all the problems concerning ultimate reality. But as the Scriptures have shown, whatever man knows about ultimate truth apart from revelation is limited, earthly and perverted.

> For it is written, I will destroy the wisdom of the wise, and the discernment of the discerning will I bring to naught. Where is the wise? Where is the scribe? Where is the disputer of this world? Hath not God made foolish the wisdom of the world? (I Cor. 1:19-20).

Even Solomon, in all his wisdom, confessed that finite reason, even when combined with the most diligent study and speculation, could not comprehend the inscrutable designs of God's providence and works in the world. He humbly admits:

> Then I beheld all the work of God, that man cannot find out the work that is done under the sun: because however much a man labor to seek it out, yet he shall not find it; yea moreover, though a wise man think to know it, yet shall he not be able to find it (Eccles. 8:17).

Thus sinful reason and the philosophical speculations of human wisdom are inadequate to provide us with trustworthy answers to the vital questions concerning man's existence.

Science. The second road of quest for reality and final truth is that of the scientific laboratory. It has been aptly designated as "scientism." This is the contemporary belief held by most people, including a great portion of professing Christendom, that *scientific discovery*, not revelation, is the only valid means of knowing reality and final truth. Science has become, in a real sense, the god of this age, and is being worshiped as the savior and great benefactor of mankind. Scientific materialism is one of the greatest threats which confront the Christian church of the twentieth century, inasmuch as most people do not seem cognizant of the narrow limits of its "absolute" knowledge in any area of reality, nor the artificiality of many of its presuppositions. The average Christian, unfamiliar with the technical language of science, with little or no background in scientific studies, has too often fallen victim to an inherent human weakness, which is to accept without question the dogmatic assertions of scholars and scientists in their respective fields. This is especially true in the areas of medicine, science and philosophy. The untrained in these fields, which are highly technical, stand in awe, as it were, with heads bowed, almost reverently acquiescing to their declarations, whether factual or purely speculative.

This respect for truth is commendable, and where the scientist can demonstrate his conclusions factually there is no objection; but it is an all-too-patent fact that science does not limit itself to proven and demonstrable facts, for such terms as theory, hypothesis, supposition and speculation are household words in scientific laboratories. It is too often overlooked, but it is well to remember that science in order to discover knowledge and factual information must, as a part of its methodology, resort to speculation, theorizing and hypothesizing. The scientific method involves the steps of observation, hypothesis, experimentation and verification. Only at the last stage, verification, can it be said that the original assumption, contained in the working hypothesis, has become a demonstrable fact. Until verified it is but a theory.

This is highly significant when one becomes aware of just how much of the alleged scientific "facts" of today are pure speculation, incapable of demonstration. An obvious example is the *theory* of evolution, which is presented as a *fact* and widely accepted as such. However, it needs to be reiterated again and again that the theory of evolution is precisely that—*a theory still unsustained by scientific proof!* Where scientific speculations are in conflict with biblical revelation, as evolution unquestionably is, man has but one of two recourses: he may drift with the current of popular and changing scientific theories, or he can resort to faith in the integrity of the Scriptures in which there is no variableness, whereas the scientific "facts" of one decade become, all too frequently, obsolete conjectures merely to be discarded by the next.

Moreover, the subtle danger of twentieth century scientific materialism is to be seen from the fact that, unlike old mechanistic materialism, it is now frequently seen in a religious robe, no longer denying the existence of a Supreme Being, nor the validity of the moral and religious. More and more we are told of the "principle of faith" involved in all scientific inquiry. Many scientists, repudiating the grosser aspects of atheism and agnosticism, now assure us that it is illogical not to affirm the existence of some "higher power" or "Creator"; some would even venture to demonstrate rationally for us the logic of such a reality. Furthermore, moral and religious values are now admitted to be beneficial. Moral values arose, we are told, as man in the process of evolution adjusted himself to his environment and sought to control it. Morality had survival value for society. Religion meets an inner need inherent in man's higher nature and promotes respectability; hence, it too is worthwhile. The religious aura of modern science is perhaps its most deceptive aspect, for it enables science to propagate the popular notion that while the Scriptures may have something to say in the sphere of *religion* which men may heed, yet since the scientific method is infallible, the Scriptures are to be considered authoritative only insofar as they agree with the discoveries and postulates of science. However, science, like philosophy, not only commits the basic fallacy of believing that sinful, unaided reason is capable of discovering and comprehending ultimate reality apart from revelation; also it must be criticized for its erroneous presupposition that all truth is *mechanically measurable and perceptible by the physical senses.*

Religion. The worship or religion of man is itself, outside the Judeo-Christian faith, a quest by which man attempts to discover metaphysical truth and relate himself to divine Reality by his own efforts and on his own terms. However, the Scriptures clearly indicate the futility of all such attempts by fallen creatures to span the impassable gulf between God and man, whether they be in the form of the crude rites of heathenism, self-justification through ritual and the sacraments, or the religio-social efforts of Liberalism. Without exception, all the religions of mankind are based on *discovery;* the religion of the Scriptures alone is that of *disclosure* or *revelation.* Every religion outside the Bible is a *quest* for ultimate reality instead

of a *response* to divine revelation. The religions of men are presump-
tuous attempts on the part of fallen creatures to devise and contrive
means by which they might uncover God's hiddenness and relate
themselves to Him for their own ends and purposes.)

GOD'S SELF-DISCLOSURE: REVELATION

Revelation, not speculation and discovery, is the source and content of metaphysical truth. As has been noted, the unique distinction
between the Judeo-Christian religion and the religions of the world is
that all other religions are a quest, whereas the faith of Israel and
the church is grounded in a revelation. The religion of the Scriptures
is not a quest for, but a response to, truth; it is not a discovery of
God; it is being discovered by Him. This fact is evident throughout
Scripture. In Genesis after the fall, we find that it is God who takes
the initiative and comes seeking man, whereas Adam in his guilt of
conscience hides from His presence! "And the Lord God called unto
the man, and said unto him, Where art thou?" (Gen. 3:9). Again, in
Genesis 12, we find that it is God who, in His sovereign grace, reveals
Himself and His will and purpose to Abraham. This self-disclosure of
Himself and His will, according to His purpose in history, occurs
again in Exodus 3 in His appearance to Moses. Over and over the
fact that the religion of Israel is the result of supernatural revelation, not speculation, is constantly reiterated. Zophar, the friend of
Job, established this fact when he asked, "Canst thou by searching
find out God?" (11:7). The testimony of the New Testament is the
same: "No man knoweth the Son, save the Father; neither doth any
know the Father, save the Son, and he to whomsoever the Son
willeth *to reveal* him" (Matt. 11:27; cf. Luke 19:10).

In theology the doctrine of revelation is customarily treated under the divisions of Special and General Revelation, the former
referring primarily to the revelation of God through His Word and
supremely in Jesus Christ (John 1:1-18), and the latter dealing with
the general disclosure of God's power and wisdom in creation and
nature (Ps. 8; 19). Special Revelation, as it is expressed in the Old
Testament, is considered first.

Special Revelation. There are three distinctive elements which
characterize Special Revelation. The first is that it is *redemptive.*
The development of the special or redemptive revelation of God had
its beginning in Eden (Gen. 3:15) when the intimate relationship
between God and man was interrupted by the fall.[1] At this time,
according to His eternal purpose, there began a series of divine

---

[1]Gen. 1-2 would constitute "preredemptive" revelation.

interventions in human history whereby God was to reveal Himself redemptively. With the call of Abraham (Gen. 12) the Old Testament traces the formal beginning of God's gracious revelation for the expressed purpose of the ultimate blessing of the whole world. Israel was chosen to be the particular recipient of the knowledge of God and His Word. To Israel alone God communicated His redemptive Word and made known His statutes and precepts. The psalmist emphasizes this when he declares:

> He showeth his word unto Jacob, His statutes and his ordinances unto Israel. He hath not dealt so with any nation: And as for his ordinances, they have not known them (Ps. 147:19-20).

The Old Testament insists that the religion of Israel is a supernaturally revealed religion for the purpose of redemption and thus sets itself over against all other religions which are the products of unregenerate men (cf. Deut. 4:7 ff.; 7:6; Exodus 3 ff.; Rom. 3:1-2).

The second distinctive element of special revelation is that it is *supernatural.* The biblical view of revelation discloses the inadequacy of the presuppositions of negative critical theology and the evolutionary theories of religion. Liberal scholarship, which treats the Old Testament revelation as merely the evolution of religion, sees within the framework of the Old Testament simply an expression of man's quest for religious knowledge as he progressively speculated upon matters concerning his past in an attempt to develop an acceptable form of religion and worship. Revelation, at best, in this view is little more than a divine influence acting upon and working with human reason, which is left in the final analysis to develop its own course. Religion, along with philosophy, the arts and sciences, culture and civilization, is directed by the evolutionary laws of inevitable progress which will carry it through various stages of development to higher moral and ethical forms. Hence, all religions are said to show a progressive development upward from animism and fetishism; the polytheistic religions become more pure and gradually more monotheistic in the course of their development. Hence, the Scriptures, according to the Wellhausen school, are not to be regarded as a trustworthy, infallible revelation, either in their historical references or in their religious concepts, but simply as the product of growth and development in the religious history of Israel.

A study of Israel's environment and historical development will reveal, we are told, the significant conditioning factors which precipitated and directed the evolution of her religious ideas. Prophecy is seen merely as one stage in religious evolution. However, this hypothesis has never been capable of effectively demonstrating why Israel's religion did not undergo the same religious evolution as that of the heathen nations. The polytheistic religions of Israel's neighbors quite obviously did not develop more pure and more monotheistic concepts in the course of their evolution but, on the contrary, became increasingly more idolatrous, superstitious and corrupt. Israel, on the other hand, emphasized an exclusive monotheism from the beginning, and this, together with the Old Testament view of God's holiness, distinguished Israel's religion from that of her contemporaries. Moreover, there were many such distinctives in Israel's religion, and whatever it might have had in common with other religions in some external form was purely nonessential.

Religious evolution is based upon the fallacy that there are inexorable laws of progress in religion and morality which must work themselves out in every civilization and culture. W. Robertson Smith, a critical scholar of the last century, was constrained to reject the extreme position of Wellhausen that all religions have evolved as a result of religious reflection, and are merely products of their environment. "To say," he writes, "that God speaks to all men alike, and gives the same communication directly to all without the use of a revealing agency, reduces religion to mysticism."[2] Nevertheless, the basic assumption of criticism is still that the Bible is not a supernatural revelation from God, but an unreliable account concerning man's reflections about God.

An understanding of the meaning of the term "revelation" will help to illustrate its supernatural character. The Old Testament shows that revelation means that something hidden has been made known. Revelation means literally "an uncovering or unveiling" (Hebrew, *gālâh*; Greek, *apokalupsis*); hence, it is the antithesis of "discovery," for revelation is a *disclosure* of knowledge otherwise unknown. Isaiah 48:6-7 confirms this fact: *God's self disclosure to man*

> I have showed thee new things from this time, even hidden things, which thou hast not known. They are created now, and not from of old; and before this day thou heardest them not; lest thou shouldest say, Behold, I knew them.

Revelation is essentially a means of acquiring knowledge completely opposite to the usual human method by means of observation, speculation, research and the thought processes. Revelation, in the biblical sense, means the disclosure of knowledge given in a supernatural way which man by his own rational powers could neither know nor discern. This does not deny a certain knowledge of

[2]W. Robertson Smith, *The Prophets of Israel,* p. 11.

God which is disclosed in nature, but even here it is a revelation and disclosure (Ps. 19:1). It is apparent that this concept is diametrically opposed to the rationalistic view that the religion of Israel was the result of growth, development and discovery. Revelation issues from a sphere beyond man's rational and natural faculties, and the essence of all that man can discover is limited and confined to the material cosmos. The Bible testifies to the fact that there is no true knowledge of God except in the revelation of Himself to His creatures (Matt. 11:27). Furthermore, we may identify this revelation, in a real sense, with the total content of the Scriptures.

According to neoorthodox thought, however, "what is revealed to us is not a body of information concerning various things of which we might otherwise be ignorant."[3] Revelation does not include, we are told, such historical facts as the dates of accession of the kings of Israel and Judah, the genealogy of Joseph, the husband of Mary, and dogma in the form of propositional truths, but what God reveals to us is Himself. Brunner contends that revelation is always personal— it is God communicating Himself in personal encounter to man. Thus faith is not the acceptance of some particular doctrine or proposition about God, but a personal relationship with God.[4]

However, it is not an insignificant question to ask, Why is the idea always presented by the liberal writers in such a way that one must choose between believing certain propositions or doctrinal truths about God, and faith in the form of a personal encounter with God? Quite obviously salvation is not the result of mere formal assent to certain theological truths. Nevertheless, saving faith in Christ, through personal encounter, is inseparably bound up with the historical biblical witness about Him. That is to say, such facts as the virgin birth, incarnation, deity of Christ, substitutionary atonement, resurrection and personal bodily return of Christ are not merely some propositions which one can affirm or deny as he pleases, as if all that is necessary is a mystical encounter with Christ. But faith in these doctrinal truths, to which the Scriptures witness, is not something different from personal faith in the One about whom they witness. These propositions and truths about Christ are as much the revelation as God's personal encounter with the seeker. In a word, one could not know God savingly apart from the fact that He had revealed Himself historically to the prophets and apostles and had given them His Word. This does not overlook the necessity, however, as Calvin observed, that "the same Spirit . . . who spoke by the mouth of the prophets, must penetrate our hearts, in order to convince us

[3]John Baillie, *The Idea of Revelation in Recent Thought,* pp. 28-29.
[4]Emil Brunner, *Revelation and Reason,* pp. 36-40.

that they faithfully delivered the message with which they were divinely intrusted."[5]

For Barth, however, nothing is a vehicle of revelation unless one hears God speaking to him through it, simply because all parts of the Bible are not equally inspired. John Baillie writes: "There are indeed many things in the Bible that seem to have no revelatory quality at all."[6] It is necessary, he continues, "to distinguish also between its essential message and its numerous imperfections—historical inaccuracies, inaccurate or conflicting reports, misquotations or misapplied quotations from the Old Testament in the New."[7] But unless we identify the total content of the Holy Scriptures with revelation, how can we be sure that we have received the true knowledge of God and redemption? This brings into focus the third distinctive element of biblical revelation.

Biblical revelation is primarily a revelation of *facts through history in the form of the spoken or revealed Word*. This truth is opposed to the neoorthodox theory that the Bible is not an inerrant body of revelation, consisting of historical facts and theological propositions or truths, but contains merely the inferences and interpretations, first by Israel and later the church, of what they believed God had done in history. Unless the truth of a historical revelation of the factual Word is presupposed, it is futile and unavailing to attempt to arrive at a saving knowledge of God or speak of the uniqueness of the Christian religion. The only alternative is to follow the course of negative criticism and study comparative religions, since, in this view, the great fundamental principles of all religions are the same. But it is a patent fact that the Old Testament, especially the message of the prophets, testifies to the supposition that all history is the story of something that God is doing (cf. Isa. 46:9-10). The Scriptures are fundamentally a revelation *through* historical events—God *speaking* His Word to man through history. The interpreters of these historical events and recipients of this Word were primarily the divinely inspired prophets of whom Moses was the first. The result was a concurrence of the historical event and the interpretive Word—the Holy Scriptures. The Old and New Testaments view revelation as the divine communication of truth through inspired men of God called to interpret for us the spiritual or metaphysical significance of these historical events. Thus, biblical revelation is a revelation of facts. These facts deal with God, creation, man, sin and

[5]John Calvin, *Institutes of the Christian Religion*, trans. Henry Beveridge, I, 72.
[6]Baillie, pp. 117-19.
[7]*Ibid.*, p. 120.

redemption. Moreover, they include the formation of a nation of priests; the exodus of a people from Egypt; the institution of a system of worship; conquests; establishment of a theocratic kingdom; social, cultural and political developments; wars and oppressions; the exile and restoration of the Hebrew nation; and many other historical events concerning the relation of God to the world in general and Israel in particular.

The facts of history stand on the one side as it were and the recorded testimony and interpretation of these facts, the divine Word, on the other. That is, on the one side is God's act in history, and on the other is the prophetic consciousness illuminated by the Word from God; the result—divine revelation. The waters of the Red Sea were parted by a great wind, and to the uninformed observer this is all that the historical event signified. But the presence of Moses, God's prophet, to interpret the event as an act of God, reveals this particular fact of history to be a supernatural event; and the subsequent recorded testimony to the supernatural character of this event, the written revelation, we call *Holy Scripture*. Again, the destruction of Sennacherib's army (II Kings 19:35-36) would ordinarily have been viewed simply as a mysterious catastrophe of fate. But there was an Isaiah to interpret this event by means of divine illumination as the judgment of God. The exile of Israel would not have been seen as the divinely appointed judgment of God upon the nation because of her sins apart from revelation through the inspired preaching and writings of the prophets, especially Jeremiah, Daniel and Ezekiel. The fact of the exodus may have had no particular significance in history simply as an event without divine interpretation, inasmuch as the migration of peoples was not an uncommon occurrence in history. But the historical fact taken together with the divine revelation of the meaning of this event to the inspired writer gives the event spiritual and supernatural significance.[8] Now a mutual correspondence exists between the two—the historical event and the divine testimony to it; the result is *infallible revelation*. The Prophet Amos points to the close correspondence that exists between the facts or events of history and the prophetic word of revelation: "Surely the Lord Yahweh will do nothing, except he reveal his secret unto his servants the prophets" (Amos 3:7).

[8]J. Barton Payne concurs in this when he states: "The Flood offers a case in point. God granted a revelation through an act in nature, namely, the rainbow; but God's action would have been meaningless without His special explanation first (Gen. 9:12-17)" (*The Theology of the Older Testament,* p. 45).

There is, of course, a fundamental distinction between this understanding of revelation as the supernatural communication of the *Word* of truth through historical events as revealed to the divinely inspired writers and the viewpoint of those who, as G. Ernest Wright in his book *God Who Acts*, contend that revelation has been almost exclusively communicated in deeds or acts rather than in words. Revelation, according to Wright, is for redemptive purposes, and the manner in which God has revealed Himself to man is through the performance of His mighty saving acts in history. Thus revelation is the recital of God's redemptive acts in history, namely, the exodus from Egypt, the covenant instituted at Sinai and the incarnation and death of Christ. The central religious festivals were intended to be recitals in which the historical saving acts of God were rehearsed.[9] History is the arena of God's activity. "Biblical theology," Wright contends, "is first and foremost a theology of recital, in which Biblical man confesses his faith by reciting the formative events of his history as the redemptive handiwork of God."[10] In his view Israel's religion is not the result of an inspired *verbal* revelation, but was derived by virtue of her attempt to explain the historical events through which God had revealed Himself. "The knowledge of God was an *inference* from what actually had happened in human history."[11] "Israel inferred from the Exodus event that God had chosen her. . . ."[12] Inasmuch as revelation is primarily the product of inference and the interpretation of history, the Old Testament, alleges Wright, contains many epithets and images borrowed from Canaanite religion,[13] later editorial interpretations by the priestly cultus,[14] numerous traditions[15] and sagas.[16]

On the contrary, the biblical concept of revelation is that it is the disclosure of factual truth through historical events in the form of the divinely spoken and revealed *Word*. The creation account, as well as the record of man's sin, the flood, the call of Abraham, the election of Israel, the miraculous plagues upon Egypt and Israel's subsequent deliverance in the exodus are all equally factual and reliable historical accounts for the precise reason that God revealed Himself to Moses the prophet and communicated His Word to him (cf. Exodus

[9]G. Ernest Wright, *God Who Acts,* p. 28.
[10]*Ibid.,* p. 38.
[11]*Ibid.,* p. 44 (italics added).
[12]*Ibid.,* p. 54.
[13]*Ibid.,* pp. 46-47.
[14]*Ibid.,* p. 55.
[15]*Ibid.,* p. 28.
[16]*Ibid.,* p. 51.

3:1 ff.). That this is also true with respect to the other prophets, beginning with Samuel, that is, that God spoke His word of revelation to them, is the claim of the entire Old Testament. Revelation is, therefore, something which is *given*. To limit the meaning of revelation to inferences and interpretations drawn from history—these having different degrees of reliability—is to obscure and prostitute the biblical meaning of the term. God did not merely leave numerous redemptive acts to explain themselves, but the interpretative word always accompanied the acts.[17]

General Revelation. This brings us to the second division of the doctrine of revelation. General or natural revelation means that God has revealed something of Himself to man through creation, providence, physical nature, and in the conscience. General Revelation refers to that knowledge of God which comes to man outside the Scriptures and the other special modes mentioned in Scripture, that is, revelation through the Urim and Thummim, theophanies, visions, dreams and miracles. Natural or general revelation is often sharply differentiated from supernatural or Special Revelation, although this distinction must not obscure the fact that all revelation, even when mediated through only natural means, has a supernatural basis in that supernatural knowledge is revealed.[18] The Scriptures testify, as Warfield correctly observes, that there is a revelation which God continuously makes to all men, and through it His power, wisdom, glory and divinity are made known. This form of revelation is communicated through the media of natural phenomena and is addressed generally to all rational creatures.[19]

Some religions have personified and deified the sun, moon and stars, as well as other objects and powers of nature, ranging from the tree to the wind; but the religion of the Old Testament, which admits of a revelation in and through nature, is decidedly not nature worship. On the contrary, the God of Israel stands behind nature as its Author and Master and uses it for His own providential purposes, and through nature reveals something of His almighty power and unsurpassed glory. In contrast to the heathen religions round about Israel,

---

[17]E. J. Young also challenges Dr. Wright's circumscribed view of revelation. He reminds us that "historical events are of no significance to man unless they are interpreted in words. And when God performed mighty acts of deliverance He accompanied those acts with words of explanation" (*Thy Word Is Truth*, p. 224). The authoritative Word is itself a "redemptive act," concludes J. I. Packer, *Fundamentalism and the Word of God*, pp. 91-94.

[18]James Orr, *Revelation and Inspiration*, pp. 60 f.

[19]Orr (ed.), *The International Standard Bible Encyclopaedia*, IV, 2574-75.

nature worship and deification of the objects of creation is severely condemned in the Old Testament (cf. Deut. 4:15-19).[20]

Although the created order was not to become an object of worship, the Old Testament just as emphatically asserts that the universe is, in a real sense, a source of knowledge about God. "The heavens declare the glory of God; and the firmament showeth his handiwork," confesses the Psalmist David (19:1). The first speech of God to Job sets forth the wonders of His power and wisdom as revealed in and through nature (Job 38; cf. Ps. 104). Contemplation of God's handiwork in the heavens caused David to exclaim: "O Yahweh, our Lord, how excellent is thy name in all the earth, who hast set thy glory upon the heavens!" (Ps. 8:1; cf. vv. 3-4.) Other passages which attest to the fact of natural revelation are: Psalm 29:1-5; 104; 119:89-91; Isaiah 40:12-14; Acts 14:15-17; Romans 1:19-20; 2:14-15.

One of the most significant passages in the Scriptures which speaks of the reality of natural revelation is the Apostle Paul's "cosmological argument" for the existence of God in Romans 1:18-23.

Creation itself, the apostle declares, is a source of knowledge of God wherein His attributes and perfections, especially His everlasting power and divinity, are made manifest to all men. God so designed the universe and the nature of man at creation that they should bear witness to Himself: "He left not himself without witness" (Acts 14:17; 17:26-27). In Romans 2 the apostle particularizes this revelation of God in that he posits it in men themselves, who by virtue of their moral nature "show the work of the law written in their hearts, their conscience bearing witness" (Rom. 2:15). Man, according to Calvin, was created to be a spectator of this world, and eyes were given him that he might, by looking upon God's glorious handiwork, see the Author Himself.[21] But the tragedy that the apostle would have us realize is that this elementary knowledge of the divine perfections, rather than eliciting from man a response of adoration and thankfulness, resulted in a gross perversion of the revelation. Instead of seeing God behind His creation, man fixed his eyes upon *the creation itself and turned it into idols!* This raises the question of the *purpose* of natural revelation. The apostle's cosmological argument for the existence of God reveals that atheism and agnosticism cannot be justified even among the heathen, yet at the same time history and experience emphatically confirm the fact of

[20]Cf. also 17:3 ff.; II Kings 17:16; 21:3; 23:5; Jer. 8:2; Ezek. 8:16, etc.
[21]A. N. Arnold, *Commentary on the Epistle to the Romans,* Vol. IV of *An American Commentary on the New Testament,* ed. Alvah Hovey, p. 47.

the insufficiency of natural or general revelation to give men a saving knowledge of God and of their need of special revelation.

While the universe is a source of "natural theology"[22] and knowledge about God's attributes, this revelation is limited and cannot, in spite of the claims of Pelagians and Deists, lead a sinner to salvation. "It does not even afford an adequate basis for religion in general, much less for true religion."[23] The universe is a revelation of God's power, wisdom and glory, but not of His redeeming grace and salvation. It is precisely at this place that man is in need of *special* revelation. "Nature does not give propositional truth. It gives data from which inferences are reasonably drawn."[24] Man by reason and apart from special revelation can, through the data of general revelation in nature, (1) assume the existence of God and (2) understand something of His nature and being. But it is only through the testimony of biblical revelation that the general truths in natural revelation can be fully understood and issue in salvation.

Generally speaking God has revealed Himself in two ways to men, objectively and subjectively. The revelation of Himself in nature and providence (objective) and the conscience (subjective) we call general or natural revelation; the revelation of Himself in His Word and the incarnation of Christ (objective) and through the Holy Spirit (subjective) we call special revelation. General revelation is inadequate to give a saving knowledge of God and the means of salvation. "The heavens declare the glory of God," but reveal nothing of His redeeming grace in Christ. God, the apostle reminds the idolatrous Gentiles at Lystra, administers common grace to all men in that He "left not himself without witness, in that he did good and gave you from heaven rains and fruitful seasons"; but the means of special grace is confined to the revelation of Himself in His Word.

[22]By "natural theology" the writer does not mean the classical Catholic view of Thomas Aquinas that man by his *unaided* reason is able, by inference from nature and creation, to deduce certain facts about God. That is, man can know that God exists, not because God is revealing Himself in nature, but because he can reason from what he sees in creation up to God. Quite the contrary, by natural theology it is meant that there is a rapport between knowing and being (cf. Augustine's ontological argument), and that man can know nothing that God does not reveal to him; by his unaided reason he could not even know himself or his world. We can know about God only insofar as He speaks to us in nature and in His Word (Acts 17:22-28; John 1:9; Rom. 1:19; Job 32:8).

[23]Louis Berkhof, *A Summary of Christian Doctrine*, p. 12.

[24]Merrill C. Tenney (ed.), *The Zondervan Pictorial Bible Dictionary*, p. 721.

Again, when Paul asserts that "the invisible things of him since the creation of the world are clearly seen," he speaks of a general knowledge of God's divine attributes, namely, "his everlasting power and divinity," not specifically of saving truth.[25] From this revelation of His power, wisdom and glory in creation, and on the basis of the inner witness in the conscience (Rom. 2:15), man may deduce certain truths about God. But there are certain facts which are basic for obtaining a saving knowledge of God that man cannot know apart from special revelation. This body of saving truth transcends the general truth revealed in nature and consists of such essential facts as the incarnation, virgin birth, the cross, the resurrection, the Son of God, salvation by faith—in a word, the gospel of redemption in Christ. Salvation comes solely from *knowing God as He is revealed in Jesus Christ*, not by knowing *about* God as He is revealed in nature (cf. John 17:2; Rom. 10:17).

What then is the divine purpose in natural revelation? Why does God give a general revelation of Himself if it cannot save? The Scriptures indicate that His purpose was threefold. First, its value stated positively is that general revelation is, in a sense, *preparatory to special revelation*. In Acts 17 the Apostle Paul confirms this in his address to the Athenians, where he builds his entire argument "that they should seek God, if haply they might feel after him and find him" (v. 27), on *theistic evidence* in *creation* (v. 24), *nature* and *providence* (vv. 25-26), and *man's rational and moral constitution* (vv. 28-29). The Prophet Jonah likewise informed the terror-stricken sailors during the storm at sea that it was "Yahweh, the God of heaven, who hath made the sea and the dry land" (Jonah 1:9), who was responsible for the great tempest they were experiencing. Through the phenomena of *nature* the prophet directed their attention to the covenant *God of Israel, Yahweh*, as the Creator and Controller of the universe. Little wonder, then, when the storm abruptly ceased upon the casting of Yahweh's disobedient prophet into the sea, that we read: "Then the men feared Yahweh exceedingly; and they offered a sacrifice unto Yahweh, and made vows" (Jonah 1:16).

General revelation forms the background, as it were, for special

---

[25]When the apostle in the next verse (Rom. 1:21) says "when they knew God, they glorified him not as God," he does not refer to saving knowledge, but as Haldane notes, this is "a reference to the knowledge of God which He communicated in the first promise after the fall, and again after the flood, but which, not liking to retain God in their knowledge . . . mankind had lost" (Robert Haldane, *Exposition of the Epistle to the Romans*, I, 60).

revelation. Special revelation, as Warfield suggests, does not supersede general revelation, but supplements it.

> Without general revelation, special revelation would lack that basis in the fundamental knowledge of God as the mighty and wise, righteous and good maker and ruler of all things, apart from which the further revelation of this great God's interventions in the world for the salvation of sinners could not be either intelligible, credible or operative.[26]

A second purpose in natural revelation is that which is frequently stated in Scripture, namely, for *God's glory.* "The heavens declare the glory of God; and the firmament showeth his handiwork" (Ps. 19:1). "O Yahweh, our Lord, how excellent is thy name in all the earth, who hast set thy glory upon the heavens!" (Ps. 8:1). "When I consider thy heavens, the work of thy fingers, the moon and the stars, which thou hast ordained; what is man, that thou art mindful of him?" (Ps. 8:3-4). "O Yahweh, how manifold are thy works! In wisdom hast thou made them all: the earth is full of thy riches" (Ps. 104:24). "Let the glory of Yahweh endure for ever; let Yahweh rejoice in his works" (Ps. 104:31). "For the invisible things of him since the creation of the world are clearly seen, being perceived through the things that are made, even his everlasting power and divinity" (Rom. 1:20). The entire universe was intended to be the theater for God's glory, whereby He might demonstrate His incomparable power and wisdom to the end that man might praise Him. But through sin's entrance into the world, God's handiwork in nature was obscured and its truth and purpose perverted, until man, the sinner, could no longer discern aright the original meaning and purpose of natural revelation. This fact leads to the third and final purpose in general revelation.

The value of general revelation stated negatively is that it is *judicial* in its purpose. While general revelation does not lead to a true knowledge of God due to man's sin, nevertheless, as the apostle affirms, it does render man *without excuse.* "For the invisible things of him since the creation of the world are clearly seen, being perceived through the things that are made, even his everlasting power and divinity; that they may be without excuse" (Rom. 1:20). The Scriptures do not say that God does not reveal Himself in nature. On the contrary, there is a divine revelation through nature, asserts the Apostle Paul, but man's sin blinds his eyes to any true knowledge of God. That knowledge of God which comes breaking through in gen-

---

[26]Orr, *The International Standard Bible Encyclopaedia, IV,* 2575.

eral revelation is perverted by man's sinful imagination; and instead of seeing the majesty, wisdom and power of God, he vainly imagines idols and turns the creature into the Creator (Rom. 1:21-23)! Nevertheless, the revelation is there. Man's perversion of what he sees does not destroy the revelation, nor totally obscure it—the revelation remains—hence, it renders man without excuse.

> The heavens declare his righteousness, and all the peoples have seen his glory. Let all them be put to shame that serve graven images, that boast themselves of idols (Ps. 97:6-7).

INSPIRATION

The doctrine of inspiration is inseparably related to the doctrine of revelation. Inspiration, however, has primarily to do with the writing of the Scriptures; hence, the subject under consideration is the inspiration of the Scriptures, although technically inspiration would also include the oral utterances or preaching of the prophets, apostles and others.

DEFINITIONS

The relationship between revelation and inspiration may be more clearly seen if these concepts are defined. *Revelation* means that God through the Scriptures, providence, creation, nature, the conscience, prophecy, miracles, visions and other supernatural means has *unveiled* all that mankind needs to know about Him, His purposes and His will. *Inspiration* is that divine influence of the Holy Spirit upon the writers of Scripture whereby their writings were made *verbally infallible*.

God has revealed Himself particularly in His Word, as well as through His mighty acts in the creation of the universe, in nature, the conscience, etc. This *unveiling* of Himself is revelation—God making Himself and His will known to men. The *record* of this revelation, made under the guidance of the Holy Spirit, is the result of inspiration. Revelation involves God's disclosure of truth to men; inspiration concerns man's accurate reception and recording of this truth. Perhaps a third concept, *illumination*, needs clarification in order to facilitate understanding of the terms revelation and inspiration. Illumination is the divine ministry of the Holy Spirit in the mind and heart of the believer, whereby he is enabled to *understand* the inspired record of revelation.

In summary, then, *revelation* is God unveiling truth; *inspiration* is God assuring the accurate reception, interpretation and recording of the revelation; and *illumination* is the believer's enlightenment by God to understand the inspired record of revelation.

Occurrence of the Term Inspiration
in Scripture

The term "inspiration" and the verb "inspire" do not occur in the original Hebrew and Greek, although the translations employ the terms in two passages, Job 32:8 and II Timothy 3:16 (AV): "But there is a spirit in man: and the inspiration of the Almighty giveth them understanding." "All scripture is given by inspiration of God, and is profitable for doctrine, for reproof, for correction, for instruction in righteousness."

In Job 32:8 the word translated "inspiration" in the King James Version is *neshāmâh* in the Hebrew, meaning "breath," and the verse should read ". . . and the breath of the Almighty giveth them understanding" (cf. ASV). Although it is not the intention of this verse to teach the inspiration of Scripture, it does, however, convey the fact that the phrase the "breath of God," which is certainly used here in the sense of inspiration, is the source of human understanding. Furthermore, the fact that the term "inspiration" does not occur in the Old Testament, but the Hebrew term used is "breath," does not weaken the concept of inspiration. On the contrary, when considered in connection with the term used in the New Testament text in II Timothy 3:16, it actually strengthens the idea.

In II Timothy 3:16 the word translated "inspired of God" is *theopneustos*, a compound word in Greek meaning literally "God-breathed." Hence, the verse would read, "All Scripture is God-breathed," indicating that God is the source and origin of the Scriptures. Thus the Greek term has more force with respect to the divine nature and origin of Scripture than the term "inspiration" itself suggests. That is to say, the English word "inspire" connotes the idea of the *in*breathing of some thought, emotion, idea or influence into something. One might say, "The general's courage inspired the troops to action," or "The book inspired him to speak." But as B. B. Warfield has so ably shown in his monumental work, *The Inspiration and Authority of the Bible*, the Greek term in no sense denotes the idea of *in*spiration, but rather conveys the sense of *spiration*, that is, *ex*piration, "breathing out":

> There is obviously some confusion here arising from . . . the Vulgate translation *"a Deo inspiratus"* . . . . There is . . . nothing in the word *theopneustos* to warrant the *in*- of the Vulgate rendering:

this word speaks not of an "*in*spiration" by God, but of a "spiration" by God.[27]

The English versions are influenced by the Vulgate which renders the Greek *theopneustos* as "God-*in*breathed" or "God-inspired." But the preposition "in" is lacking in the Greek term, which term does not intend to convey the idea of God breathing something *into the writers*, but that *God Himself breathed out* something by divine spiration, *namely, the Holy Scriptures.* This is the most significant term the apostle could have chosen, since the "breath of God" in Scripture is used to denote His personal creative power (cf. Gen. 2:7; Ps. 33:6). Thus II Timothy 3:16 has to do with the *divine origin* of the Scriptures. They are the product of the creative breath of God; their infallibility and inerrancy cannot, therefore, be denied.

This same emphasis is seen in II Peter 1:21 where the prophets are said to have been "borne along" by the Spirit of God, that is, they spoke what the Spirit conveyed to them. Likewise Hebrews 1:1 states that "*God* spake *in* the prophets," that is, God did not merely sanctify what men spoke or wrote, but He Himself *breathed out* His Word to them and carried them along by His Spirit as they spoke and wrote His Word which He had revealed to them. However, since the term "inspiration" has by popular usage become a vital part of our theological vocabulary, intending to convey the same idea as *theopneustos* of the infallibility and inerrancy of Scripture, it would seem best to continue its general use while strengthening the concept as noted.

NATURE AND EXTENT OF INSPIRATION

Influenced by rationalistic thinkers, it has become common practice for many theologians either to deny or in some manner limit the biblical doctrine of inspiration. Several theories of inspiration have been proposed which so greatly alter the biblical teaching that they are seen to be, upon examination, quite inadequate.

The nature of inspiration. A few of the most common theories of inspiration are reviewed and answered as preparatory to an examination of the biblical expression of the nature and extent of inspiration.

1. The Intuition Theory

a. Definition. Inspiration is said to be a higher development of the natural or inherent insight into the truth possessed by all men to some degree. In men like Isaiah and Paul, Plato and Shakespeare,

[27]Benjamin B. Warfield, *The Inspiration and Authority of the Bible,* p. 277.

this intuitive insight appears in an intensified degree. The Hebrews had a genius for religion, as the Greeks had a genius for philosophy and art, and the Romans for government and law.

b. Evaluation. In matters of religion and morals, man's natural insight into the truth is distorted by sin (I Cor. 2:14). Furthermore, Numbers 12:6-8, Genesis 12:1-3, and Exodus 3 show that the Hebrews had no genius for religion; on the contrary, Israel's religion was a revelation. That Israel had no natural inclination toward religious matters is made quite clear by Moses in Deuteronomy 9:4-7.

The theory that all men have an inherent insight into moral and religious truth contains a self-contradiction in that we have the anomalous situation in which one person is inspired to utter as *true* what another is inspired to pronounce as *false*. Such a conclusion would naturally follow from the all-too-obvious fact that there is no agreement, outside the Scriptures, among those who have claimed inspiration, even less among the various religions of the world. The alleged revelations of such individuals as Ellen G. White, Muhammad, Joseph Smith and others, who all contradict one another, as well as the Bible, *cannot be inspired to contradict each other!*[28]

2. The Illumination Theory

a. Definition. The Holy Spirit illuminates the believer's mind to perceive moral and spiritual truth. Among the Scripture writers, this illumination differs only in degree from the spiritual illumination of all believers, affecting only their mental powers, not their writings, except perhaps indirectly.

b. Evaluation. This is the liberal and neoorthodox viewpoint. The Bible, it is said, is not in its entirety the Word of God, although it contains, in a limited way, a somewhat reliable account. We answer, however, that the illumination of the believer's mind gives us no new truth in the form of revelation or Scripture, but only an enlightened understanding of the truth already revealed to the sacred writers. The difference between the divine *inspiration* of the prophets and apostles and the spiritual *illumination* of all believers is clearly seen in the following texts:

Inspiration, II Peter 1:21; II Samuel 23:2

Illumination, Titus 2:11-12; I Corinthians 12:3

3. The Mechanical or Dictation Theory

a. Definition. The literal mechanical view holds that the writers were passive agents to whom God dictated the Scriptures word for word as to a secretary.

28Augustus Hopkins Strong, *Systematic Theology,* pp. 203-4.

b. Evaluation. Although this view is also inadequate, it is not one proposed by rationalistic scholars; rather it is that view which rationalists contend characterizes conservative theology. It will be shown, however, that although this concept does have some scriptural basis, it is too restrictive, therefore an inadequate expression of the full biblical teaching on this subject.

First, we must certainly admit that the Scriptures themselves show that on repeated occasions God spoke and in effect dictated the message He wished to communicate, commanding that it be written or spoken. There are numerous examples of this. The Apostle John writes: "I was in the Spirit on the Lord's day, and I heard behind me a great voice, as of a trumpet saying, *What thou seest, write in a book*" (Rev. 1:10-11). When Moses protested that he was not an eloquent speaker, God rebuked him and said: "Now therefore go, and *I will be with thy mouth, and teach thee what thou shalt speak*" (Exodus 4:12; cf. 7:1-2; 34:27-28). The Prophet Balaam who desired to curse Israel for reward, lamented to King Balak that he was powerless to do so: "Have I now any power at all to speak anything? *The word that God putteth in my mouth, that shall I speak*" (Num. 22:38; cf. 23:20). Jeremiah too writes that he speaks the very words that God had given him: "Then Yahweh put forth his hand, and touched my mouth; and Yahweh said unto me, *Behold, I have put my words in thy mouth*" (Jer. 1:9).

Repeatedly the prophets recorded their messages which were received through dreams and visions by introducing them with the formula "Thus saith the Lord." Many times what is written is seen to be God Himself speaking in the first person (cf. Isa. 1:2 ff.). However, in every case there are evident peculiarities of style and content which distinguish and characterize the various writers. Compare for example the style of Amos the herdsman with Isaiah the prophet, or Peter the fisherman with Paul the theologian. Also the authors gathered their material, in part, from sources at hand. This, of course, does not imply that they were not directed by the Holy Spirit in the selection of this material. Note the following texts: I Kings 11:41; 14:29; I Chronicles 29:29; Luke 1:1-4. Compare also the following parallel accounts: Isaiah 2:2-4 with Micah 4:1-3; II Kings 25 with Jeremiah 52; II Chronicles 36:22-23 with Ezra 1:1-3*a*. Note that Psalms 14 and 53 are identical. Again, the minor variations in details and wording in parallel accounts in the Gospels emphasize the differences in style and content: Matthew 20:30 (two blind men); Luke 18:35 (one mentioned). This does not imply contradiction, however, but merely a difference in reporting details—they are verbally different. Hence, no purely mechanical theory is adequate because of the obvious differences in style and content and the presence of material gathered from sources available to them.

B. The Divine-Human Relationship View

This view we believe to be the biblical one inasmuch as it alone seems to give adequate consideration to the *divine-human relationship* in inspiration, and thus is able to account satisfactorily for the differences of style and content among the various authors of Scripture. This view is called the Dynamical Theory by A. H. Strong and the Organic Theory by Louis Berkhof. It will be well to recall the author's definition of inspiration at this time which is an expression of this view. Inspiration is that *divine influence of the Holy Spirit upon the writers of Scripture* whereby their writings were made verbally infallible. It should be evident that this definition is intended to express the divine-human relationship involved in the inspiration of Scripture.

What is meant by the divine-human relationship? It means that God used the personalities of the writers as well as their persons. This is why their individualism is as clearly seen as their inspiration. The Holy Spirit moved upon the hearts of the writers in a dynamic way that was in harmony with their own personalities, not completely suppressing their own peculiar temperament, style, education and culture. It is God who created man as it pleased Him, each with his own particular individualistic personality. He did not make men all alike, as He reminded Moses whom He had commanded to go speak His Word to Pharaoh.

> And Moses said unto Yahweh, Oh, Lord, I am not eloquent, neither heretofore, nor since thou hast spoken unto thy servant; for I am slow of speech, and of a slow tongue. And Yahweh said unto him, Who hath made man's mouth? Or who maketh a man dumb, or deaf, or seeing, or blind? Is it not I, Yahweh? Now therefore go, and I will be with *thy* mouth, and *teach thee* what *thou* shalt speak (Exodus 4:10-12).

Thus we see that God made the particular molds into which He poured His Spirit. It was through these different personalities which *He* had made that He chose to speak His Word; hence, He would use *their* lips, *their* culture, *their* characteristics, *their* temperament, *their* style—in a word, *their own individual personalities*—to speak *His* Word. This is not to imply, as we shall presently see, that God merely inspired their thoughts and left them free to choose the words, for biblical inspiration means God breathed out *His Word* by His Spirit through the prophets and writers of Scripture. Although He used their individual personalities, when the Spirit of God moved upon them their vocabulary became heightened, their style elevated and often poetic, and their very words inspired, being energized with divine life and power. Moreover, when God spoke through them in the first person, the personality of the writer or speaker would, at such times, recede into the background. One writer has aptly summarized this unique divine-human relationship in inspiration with these words:

> We may regard the *Incarnate* Word as a fitting parallel to the *Inspired* Word; for, as in the Person of our Lord the Divine and human elements of His Nature were inextricably blended, so in the pages of His Holy Word every passage is alike human and Divine.[29]

The extent of inspiration. Having ascertained something of the nature of the inspiration of Scripture, one final question remains to be answered: What was the extent of inspiration? Influenced by negative criticism, some theologians have come either to reject the inspiration of Scripture altogether, or attempt to refute the equal inspiration and validity of all its parts, rejecting as inspired, for example, the so-called "imprecatory" psalms, which allegedly are ethically beneath the New Testament teachings concerning love of one's enemies, and rejecting as being unworthy of canonicity such books as Ecclesiastes or the Song of Solomon.

Others, often conservative Christians, who contend for the total inspiration of Scripture, nevertheless in seeking to account for the differences of style and content among the various writers, have postulated the theory that the Holy Spirit merely inspired the *thoughts* of the writers, but left the actual choice of words to the individual. A. H. Strong proposes this view which actually is a denial of the plenary verbal view of inspiration. He writes:

> The theory of verbal inspiration is refuted by the two facts: 1. that the N.T. quotations from the O.T., in 99 cases, differ both from the Hebrew and from the LXX; 2. that Jesus' own words are reported with variations by the different evangelists.[30]

In this view only the "thoughts" are said to have been inspired, and that inspiration did not involve a direct communication of words. But the obvious and almost elementary question immediately sug-

[29]William C. Procter, *The Authenticity and Authority of the Old Testament,* p. 7.
[30]*Ibid.,* p. 216.

gested by this theory is: How can the communication of thoughts be separated from a communication of words? E. J. Young asks:

> In what manner . . . has God seen fit to reveal . . . thoughts to us? To ask the question is to answer it. He has revealed them through the media of words . . . . When we wish in adequate fashion to communicate our thoughts we are compelled to employ words.[31]

The *plenary verbal* view of the inspiration of the Scriptures is the only correct view for the precise reason that the Bible itself teaches it. While there is no teaching to be found in Scripture that the thoughts of the writers were inspired, the Scriptures everywhere do declare that the words of Scripture are *the words of God*: "the word of God" (Mark 7:13; cf. Rom. 10:17; Heb. 4:12; I Thess. 2:13); "the word of Yahweh that came to Jeremiah" (Jer. 14:1); "Hear this word that Yahweh hath spoken against you" (Amos 3:1); "It is written, Man shall not live by bread alone, but by every word that proceedeth out of the mouth of God" (Matt. 4:4); "I will be with thy mouth, and teach thee what thou shalt speak" (Exodus 4:12); "Heaven and earth shall pass away, but my words shall not pass away" (Matt. 24:35); "Then Yahweh put forth his hand, and touched my mouth; and Yahweh said unto me, Behold, I have put my words in thy mouth" (Jer. 1:9). Such passages completely refute the idea of the mere inspiration of the thoughts of the sacred writers, but declare conclusively that inspiration extends to the very words themselves. Such texts, explicitly teaching verbal inspiration, could be multiplied hundreds of times from the Old and New Testaments (note I Cor. 2:13). The classic warning expressed by B. B. Warfield is worth remembering here. He writes:

> If criticism has made such discoveries as to necessitate the abandonment of the doctrine of plenary inspiration, it is not enough to say that we are compelled to abandon only a "particular theory of inspiration". . . . We must go on to say that that "particular theory of inspiration" is the theory of the apostles and of the Lord, and that in abandoning *it* we are abandoning *them*. . . .[32]

Plenary verbal inspiration means that the Scriptures in their entirety are the very words of God and are, therefore, infallible and inerrant in the original autographs. In spite of the fact that the Scriptures themselves claim such inerrancy, the rationalistic critics, on the basis of human logic, seek to discredit this truth. Their

[31]Young, p. 49.
[32]Warfield, p. 180.

reasoning expressed in the form of a simple syllogism may be stated thus:

> All men are fallible.
> Men were authors of the Bible.
> Conclusion: The Bible is fallible.

We answer, however, that such an inference does not properly distinguish between the writer and his writings. That is, the *writers* were *sometimes* inspired, but their *writings always*. The writers were, as they would have humbly admitted, fallible men who could and did sometimes sin, but their writings they knew to be *God-breathed* and therefore inerrant, a fact which they, without exception, insisted to be true. Hence, inspiration was, with respect to the *inerrancy* of Scripture, *independent of the culture, conduct and character of the writers.*[33] This fact is nowhere more clearly seen than in the case of the rebellious King Saul (I Sam. 19:18-24), and that of Balaam the prophet who would have cursed Israel but was compelled, in spite of his wicked character, to speak the words of God: "Have I now any power at all to speak anything? The word that God putteth in my mouth, that shall I speak" (Num. 22:38). Hence, inspiration is independent of the character, culture and conduct of the speaker or writer. One must, therefore, with regard to the inerrancy of Scripture, distinguish between the writer and his writings.

This is evident also from the fact that the prophet did not always speak in an inspired state. That is to say, although the call came to the prophet or apostle for a lifetime, each prophetic message or revelation which he received came as the result of a special enlightenment for that particular situation. For instance, in II Samuel 7:3 Nathan the prophet, with sincere motive, gave David encouragement to proceed with the building of the temple, saying, "Go, do all that is in thy heart; for Yahweh is with thee." However, verses 4-7 clearly indicate that in this case the prophet had not spoken by inspiration God's will in the matter, and was, in fact, commanded by God the same night to correct his well-meaning, but nevertheless incorrect, advice. Again, Christ said David wrote of Him in the Psalms by inspiration of the Holy Spirit (Matt. 22:43 f.). David himself claims to speak by the inspiration of the Spirit in II Samuel 23:2. However, we find that in 11:14-15, where he writes instructions to Joab to have Uriah killed, he is obviously not inspired by the Spirit of God. Moses spoke the words of God to Israel according to Exodus 4:10-12, but

[33]Procter, p. 5.

- sinned with his lips when he angrily denounced the people at the time
he twice smote the rock in the wilderness (Num. 20:10-13; cf. Ps.
106:32-33). Peter spoke by the Holy Spirit on the day of Pentecost
(Acts 2; cf. 4:8; I Peter 1:12), but was later rebuked by the Apostle
Paul for his legalistic conduct at Antioch (Gal. 2:11 ff.). He spoke by
inspiration one moment (Matt. 16:16-17), but was rebuked by Christ
the next for speaking by Satan's influence (vv. 21-23).

Thus the writers were sometimes inspired, but their writings, with
respect to Scripture, always. This is precisely where the Bible itself
places the emphasis: "*All scripture* is given by inspiration of God"
(II Tim. 3:16, AV); therefore, the *Scriptures* claim to be infallible,
inerrant and God-breathed. However, the same Scriptures candidly
reveal the fallibility and sins of its writers as just noted. Thus it is
here we must attack the erroneous arguments of the rationalist with
respect to plenary verbal inspiration. Their logic may appear irrefu-
table, but their basic presuppositions are fallacious and deceptive.
This is to be seen in that they seek to disprove the inspiration of
Scripture on the basis of man's fallibility, whereas the biblical doctrine of plenary verbal inspiration, set forth in II Timothy 3:16, does
not speak of inspired *men* (although they were when speaking or
writing God's Word), but of inspired *Scripture:* "All scripture is . . .
[God-breathed]." The writers were inspired and inerrant only when
they "spake from God, being moved by the Holy Spirit" (II Peter
1:21); but *all* Scripture is God-breathed and is therefore verbally
infallible. The critics of verbal inspiration must contend with the
sacred Scriptures themselves which have been breathed out by God,
not with discursive questions as to whether or not fallible men can
record infallible revelation. Such an approach does not even deal
with the real nature of the question at all.

Chapter 5

TRUE AND FALSE
PROPHETS

THE SCRIPTURES recognize the existence of both false and genuine prophecy inasmuch as false and true prophets were to be found in Israel. Genuine prophets, such as Jeremiah and Ezekiel, denounced the mercenary prophets who, motivated by self-interest and a desire for acceptance and popularity, foretold peace and security for a corrupt and rebellious nation. Jesus also warned that false prophets would arise and deceive many (Matt. 24:11). The Apostle Paul (Acts 20:29-31) and the Apostle John (I John 4:1) also warned of this. Moreover, false prophetesses were not unknown in Israel (Ezek. 13:17; Neh. 6:14) nor to the church (Rev. 2:20).

Significantly, both false and true prophets claimed to be inspired and to speak on behalf of God! This problem is quite evident in the account in I Kings 22 of the conflict between the Prophet Micaiah and the four hundred prophets of Ahab. Micaiah charged that the prophets of Ahab were "lying prophets," upon which Zedekiah, one of the king's prophets, took issue with Micaiah and "came near, and smote Micaiah on the cheek, and said, Which way went the Spirit of Yahweh from me to speak unto thee?" (v. 24). Here the lying prophet in no unmistakable terms claims to speak by inspiration of God's Spirit. That this is no isolated incident in which a false prophet claimed to speak the word of God can be seen in other passages of Scripture, as for example, Jeremiah 28. Here the Prophet Hananiah uses the prophetic formula "Thus saith the Lord," seeking to authenticate his message which is in contradiction to that of Jeremiah (cf. vv. 2, 11). Jeremiah likewise, in this same passage, authenticates his message with this formula "Thus saith the Lord." How then could the people discern who was a genuine prophet of Israel? How could they distinguish him from the false prophet? Contrary to what Mowinckel held, the difference did not lie in the premise that the so-called ecstatic prophets who possessed the "Spirit" were set over against the canonical prophets who possessed the "Word." This view is disproved by the fact that both groups claimed to possess the Spirit and to speak Yahweh's word. Nor is true prophecy to be considered an outgrowth of the false in which some men, such as Isaiah and Jeremiah, by means of keen spiritual perception, rose above their contemporaries and emerged as the great prophets of Israel. The tests by which Israel might distinguish between true and false prophets were given by God Himself in His Word.

BIBLICAL TESTS OF A TRUE PROPHET

SPOKE ONLY IN THE NAME OF YAHWEH

This first test by which Israel could differentiate the genuine prophet from the impostor is set forth in Deuteronomy 13:1-5 and 18:20.

First of all, it appears from these passages that if a prophet spoke in the name of any god other than Yahweh, even though he substantiated his claims with the prediction of a sign which should come to pass or through the performance of some miracle, he was not to be believed but put to death as a false or lying prophet. The fact that he sought to persuade Israel to forsake Yahweh was a sufficient test to prove him an impostor. How could that prophet who sought to turn them from the worship of Yahweh be sent by Yahweh? It is significant to note that Deuteronomy 13 does not suggest that the sign or wonder which the false prophet gave was not authentic. On the contrary, the Scriptures show that Satan can perform signs and miracles (e.g., II Thess. 2:9; Rev. 13:13-15). Also, according to Ezekiel 14:9-11, God might even allow a false prophet to be self-deceived and in turn deceive the sinful and unfaithful nation as punishment.

Therefore, this single test was not in itself sufficient to prove unmistakably the genuineness of the prophet, for the false prophets also often spoke in the name of Yahweh:

> For thus saith Yahweh of hosts, the God of Israel: Let not your prophets that are in the midst of you, and your diviners, deceive you; neither hearken ye to your dreams which ye cause to be dreamed. For they prophesy falsely unto you *in my name:* I have not sent them, saith Yahweh (Jer. 29:8-9).

Illustrative of the fact that it was no easy matter to distinguish between the true and false prophet on the basis of a single test alone is the account of a prophet from Judah sent to prophesy against Jeroboam I at Bethel. Although he, as God's prophet, had been forewarned by God not to tarry nor eat at Bethel, he himself was deceived by the false words of the old prophet of that city who claimed to speak in the name of the Lord and thus persuaded him to tarry and eat with him (I Kings 13). Here is the case of an authentic prophet being deceived by the words of another who claimed to be speaking in the name of Yahweh. As is noted later, he could have avoided deception by subjecting the old prophet's message to another test which would have proven the falseness of his words.

SPOKE ONLY BY REVELATION OR INSPIRATION

Another test to differentiate between the true and false prophets concerns revelation and inspiration. If a prophet, claiming to speak on behalf of Yahweh, practiced divination, augury, sorcery and the like, he was to be rejected as false. Deuteronomy 18:9-14 sets forth the methods used by the heathen nations in seeking to uncover the secrets of the spiritual realm or to obtain knowledge of future events. These methods were condemned by God without reservation as attempts to acquire hidden knowledge from demonic sources. Thus the prophetic institution itself was to be established as the sole means by which Israel was to receive the true revelation. When God chose to speak His word to Israel, it would come *through His prophets unsolicited,* apart from divination and augury; moreover, they were to speak only when He spoke to them. This appears as one of the greatest distinctions between the religion of Israel and the heathen religions. The nations sought to discover truth by means of divination and sorcery, whereas Israel received it by revelation. The heathen practice of obtaining oracles by divination was not to be practiced by the true prophets. When it appears (Ezek. 12:24; 22:28; Jer. 14:14; and Micah 3:7, 11), the prophet is a deceiver who prophesies lies in the name of the Lord. He is not inspired, but speaks out of his own heart (Jer. 23:16, 26; Ezek. 13:2). The true prophet receives the revelation through the media of dreams and visions, according to Numbers 12:6: "And he said, Hear now my words: if there be a prophet among you, I Yahweh will make myself known unto him in a vision, I will speak with him in a dream" (cf. Amos 3:7).

However, there might be times when a false prophet would not resort to the heathen method of divination, but would prophesy in the name of the Lord and claim to speak a message from the Lord which he had received by dream or vision. Such could either be a false claim by the prophets as in Jeremiah 23:16, 32 where they are charged with speaking "a vision of their own heart" and prophesying "lying dreams," or an actual case of self-deception on the part of the prophet whereby God sought either to prove or punish Israel as in

Deuteronomy 13:1-5; I Kings 22:13-28; Ezekiel 14:9-11. How then would the people distinguish the false from the true prophet and know when he was speaking by divine revelation? It becomes clear that no single test could authenticate the claims of the prophet. Several other biblical tests were given which, when taken together, would assure the validity of the prophet's claims.

COULD BE IDENTIFIED BY THE TESTIMONY OF HIS OWN MORAL CHARACTER

False prophets were characterized by their low morality; hence, true and false prophets could be distinguished by a personal or intrinsic test. The false prophet was a mercenary who prophesied for hire (Micah 3:5, 11); he was a drunkard (Isa. 28:7); he was profane and wicked (Jer. 23:11); he conspired with others to deceive and defraud (Ezek. 22:25); he was light and treacherous (Zeph. 3:4); he committed adultery, walked in lies and supported the evildoers (Jer. 23:14); and he was generally immoral in life and conduct (Jer. 23:15).

The false prophet was, moreover, a religious opportunist, prophesying only what the degenerate people wished to hear (Isa. 30:10-11; Micah 2:11); he proclaimed an optimistic message of peace and prosperity (Ezek. 13:1-16; Jer. 14:13; 23:17; Micah 3:5); he often practiced divination (Ezek. 22:28; Jer. 14:14), and prophesied lies out of his own heart (Ezek. 13:2; Jer. 23:16). Thus, in a real sense, the moral character of the prophet himself would attest to his authority. He who professed a divine commission from the holy God of Israel must reflect conduct and character consistent with that claim (cf. Matt. 7:15-20).

WAS CONSCIOUS OF A DEFINITE CALL EXPERIENCE

The prophetic office was not one into which any individual could inject himself. Neither religious disposition nor spiritual training could make a man a prophet. Nor did one inherit the office. God alone equipped and called men to this office, as numerous instances in Scripture show. Moses, the greatest prophet of the Old Testament, experienced just such a call and was informed by God in this experience that He Himself prepares and equips men for this calling (Exodus 4:10-12). Jeremiah, at the time of his call, was advised that he had been ordained by God to be His prophet before he had been conceived in the womb (Jer. 1:4-10). Amos insists on his divine calling to the office in his reply to Amaziah's rebuke:

Then answered Amos, and said to Amaziah, I was no prophet, neither was I a prophet's son; but I was a herdsman, and a dresser of sycomore-trees: and Yahweh took me from following the flock, and Yahweh said unto me, Go, prophesy unto my people Israel (Amos 7:14-15).

The divine origin of the call experience of Samuel is clearly set forth in I Samuel 3. This is especially evident in verses 19-20: "And Samuel grew, and Yahweh was with him, and did let none of his words fall to the ground. And all Israel from Dan even to Beer-sheba knew that Samuel was established to be a prophet of Yahweh." The call of Ezekiel was preceded by a heavenly vision authenticating his divine commission and message. All the true prophets of Israel were conscious of a definite personal call experience of which the people themselves were quite aware, not only from the prophets' clear statements of this fact (cf. Jer. 1:6-9), but also because of its effect upon their messages. The prophet of God never sought the office on his own initiative, but was constrained to speak by a sense of divine compulsion; hence, his message carried its own divine seal of authority and conviction of this fact.

COMMISSION OFTEN WAS AUTHENTICATED WITH SIGNS OR MIRACLES

This test of a true prophet or spokesman of God was another means by which the prophet could authenticate himself. We are reminded here of the signs and miracles of Moses in Egypt given as evidence of his divine commission (Exodus 4:1-9, 21); the parting of the waters of the Jordan to authenticate Joshua as the successor to Moses (Joshua 3:7-13); Samuel's miracle of thunder and rain to validate his words to Israel (I Sam. 12:16 ff.); the miracles of Elijah and Elisha; and the signs of Isaiah (7:14), Micaiah (I Kings 22:28), Ezekiel (chaps. 4-5) and Amos (8:1-3). (See also I Kings 13:1-5.)

However, as with the other tests, we find that this too, when taken alone, is inconclusive and not an infallible confirmation; for the false prophets also were said to give signs and wonders in an effort to establish their authority as noted in Deuteronomy 13:1-5 (cf. Exodus 7:8-13, 20-22; 8:7; Matt. 24:24; Mark 13:22; II Thess. 2:9).

MESSAGE WAS IN HARMONY WITH PREVIOUS REVELATION

According to Deuteronomy 13:1-3, the prophet's word must not contradict nor disagree with the previous revelation of truth, but must confirm or build upon it. The prophet of Judah in the account in I Kings 13 who had been forewarned by God not to tarry nor eat at Bethel would not have been deceived by the old prophet's contradictory word had he heeded this basic principle. Jeremiah charged the lying prophets with speaking things which subverted and contradicted the previous revelations of God and thereby led the people astray (chap. 23). A classic illustration of this from Israel's history is found in Jeremiah 26 where Jeremiah predicted the destruction of Jerusalem, whereupon the incensed inhabitants, led by the priests and prophets, sought to slay him. Certain of the elders, however, recalled that the Prophet Micah had previously preached this same message during the reign of Hezekiah, and the king had not put him to death. The significance of this incident lies in the fact that Jeremiah's life was spared for the precise reason that his message was authenticated as a revelation from God because it was in exact harmony with the previous revelation made by God to the Prophet Micah years before! (cf. Isa. 8:20).

HISTORICAL CONFIRMATION AUTHENTICATED TRUE PROPHET

The actual fulfillment of a prophecy was to be evidence of its truth. The confirmation of the prophet's word by history would differentiate between true prophets and mere professional prophets who conformed their message to please their hearers. This test of the true prophet is found in Deuteronomy 18:21-22:

> And if thou say in thy heart, How shall we know the word which Yahweh hath not spoken? When a prophet speaketh in the name of Yahweh, if the thing follow not, nor come to pass, that is the thing which Yahweh hath not spoken: the prophet hath spoken it presumptuously, thou shalt not be afraid of him.

The prophet's message was to be verified by its fulfillment in history. An actual historical example of the validity of this test is found in Jeremiah 28. After the deportation of Jehoiachin and the temple treasures to Babylon, the Prophet Hananiah in the presence of the people predicts a speedy restoration within two years:

> Thus speaketh Yahweh of hosts, the God of Israel, saying, I have broken the yoke of the king of Babylon. Within two full years will I bring again into this place all the vessels of Yahweh's house, that Nebuchadnezzar king of Babylon took away from this place, and carried to Babylon: and I will bring again to this place Jeconiah the son of Jehoiakim, king of Judah, with all the captives of Judah that went to Babylon, saith Yahweh (vv. 2-4).

Hananiah makes this prediction in direct opposition to Jeremiah's earlier prophecy (25:11-12) of a seventy-year captivity (cf. 27:16-22). Because of Hananiah's false prophecy, God instructs Jeremiah to pronounce judgment upon him:

> Then said the prophet Jeremiah unto Hananiah the prophet, Hear now, Hananiah: Yahweh hath not sent thee; but thou makest this people to trust in a lie. Therefore thus saith Yahweh, Behold, I will send thee away from off the face of the earth: this year thou shalt die, because thou hast spoken rebellion against Yahweh. So Hananiah the prophet died the same year in the seventh month (28:15-17).

The prediction of Jeremiah, in respect to Hananiah's death, was confirmed within the year, whereas Hananiah's words were proved false when the events of history failed to confirm them at the end of two years. The long-range prophecy of Jeremiah was also verified with the exile of Israel in Babylon for seventy years.

Another historical example of the application of this test is found in I Kings 22 where Micaiah, in order to prove the divine origin of his message in contrast to that of the false prophets of Ahab's court, submitted his own predictions to this rigid test. In opposition to the favorable predictions of Ahab's prophets, he declared before all the people that Ahab would be slain in battle, and said, "If thou return at all in peace, Yahweh hath not spoken by me. And he said, Hear, ye peoples, all of you" (I Kings 22:28). The events of history confirmed his word. The validity of this test is likewise confirmed by Zechariah when he reminds the returned exiles that the events of history verified the predictions of the prophets of God concerning them:

> But my words and my statutes, which I commanded my servants the prophets, did they not overtake your fathers? And they turned and said, Like as Yahweh of hosts thought to do unto us, according to our ways, and according to our doings, so hath he dealt with us (Zech. 1:6).

Thus the predictions of the true prophets, in contrast to those who prophesied peace, found fulfillment in the exile and other events of history. Stated negatively, nonfulfillment was a test of false prophecy. However, it must not be forgotten that, according to Deuteronomy 13:1-5, if a prophet taught idolatry, even the fulfillment of some sign or a miracle would not authenticate his ministry. Amos grounded the authority of the words of a true prophet in the fact that "the Lord God will do nothing, except he reveal his secret unto his servants the prophets" (3:7). The prophets themselves required no historical

confirmation to assure them that the events predicted would surely
come to pass. Had not God revealed His word to them by visions and
dreams? (Num. 12:6; Amos 1:1: "The words of Amos ... which he
saw"). Nor do they feel it incumbent to try and prove to gainsayers
the authority of their words until the predictions were confirmed by
the events of history, inasmuch as there were other tests which
authenticated the words of a true prophet. Because of the important
relationship between prophecy and fulfillment, and in view of the fact
that some question whether or not all prophecy was intended to be
literally fulfilled, the question of *fulfillment* and *nonfulfillment* of
prophecy is taken up later in this chapter.

MORAL QUALITY OF THE MESSAGE DIFFERENTIATED
BETWEEN TRUE AND FALSE

Whatever value the other tests of true prophecy possess, none is
more significant than the test of the moral quality and spiritual
essence of the prophet's message itself. The messages of the false
prophets were motivated by two things: their overzealous sense of
nationalism and their desire for personal advantage. Thus, on the one
hand their preaching was calculated to appeal to the people's patriotism by encouraging Israel to become a military state, thereby trusting in her own strength rather than the Lord. The prophets to whom
Ezekiel, Micah and Jeremiah were opposed were those who cried
peace and security and who insisted upon the inviolability of
Jerusalem in spite of the glaring national sins and apostasy of the
people. Ezekiel announced God's word of condemnation upon the
false prophets who daubed over with "whitewash" (ASV margin) the
insecure walls the people built (13:10-16), that is, they superficially
covered over the sinful lives of the people with soothing words of
peace.

> Because, even because they have seduced my people, saying,
> Peace; and there is no peace; and when one buildeth up a wall,
> behold, they daub it with untempered mortar. Thus will I accom-
> plish my wrath upon the wall, and upon them that have daubed
> it with untempered mortar; and I will say unto you, The wall is
> no more, neither they that daubed it; to wit, the prophets of
> Israel that prophesy concerning Jerusalem, and that see visions of
> peace for her, and there is no peace, saith the Lord Yahweh
> (Ezek. 13:10, 15-16).

Micah likewise expresses the message of a true prophet when after
God rebukes "the prophets that make my people to err ... and cry,

Peace" (3:5), he declares: "But as for me, I am full of power by the Spirit of Yahweh, and of judgment, and of might, to declare unto Jacob his transgression, and to Israel his sin" (3:8).

On the other hand, their desire for popular acceptance caused the false prophets to approve the sins of the people and their moral wickedness:

> In the prophets of Jerusalem also I have seen a horrible thing: they commit adultery, and walk in lies; and they strengthen the hands of evil-doers, so that none doth return from his wickedness. They teach you vanity; they speak a vision of their own heart, and not out of the mouth of Yahweh. They say continually unto them that despise me, Yahweh hath said, Ye shall have peace; and unto every one that walketh in the stubbornness of his own heart they say, No evil shall come upon you. Behold, I am against them that prophesy lying dreams, saith Yahweh, and do tell them, and cause my people to err by their lies, and by their vain boasting (Jer. 23:14, 16-17, 32).

In addition to the fact that the false prophets prophesied lying dreams and visions, God also accused them of lacking in originality in many respects in their message due to plagiarism. When the prophecies of the true prophets of God suited their purposes, they would "steal" their words and proclaim them as their own in order to authenticate their own ministry. "Therefore, behold, I am against the prophets, saith Yahweh, that steal my words every one from his neighbor" (Jer. 23:30).

Furthermore, had they been true prophets they would have called the people to repentance and turned them from their wickedness. "But if they had stood in my council, then had they caused my people to hear my words, and had turned them from their evil way, and from the evil of their doings" (Jer. 23:22). Whereas the false prophet calculated, from the contemporary situation, which result would most probably occur and would be most in harmony with the religious convictions of the sinful people, the true prophet proclaimed things completely contradictory to outward appearances and contrary to the popular religious convictions of the people. Inspired by Yahweh, the true prophet had a holy disregard for the acceptability of his message and a personal unconcern for the consequences with respect to his own welfare.

In this regard Jeremiah proposed a test (28:5-9) to differentiate between the false and true prophets. Hananiah the prophet prophesied an optimistic message to Judah, thereby glossing over her wickedness and need of divine punishment. He stood with those who prophesied peace and security. In Jeremiah 28:1-4 Hananiah predicted the overthrow of the Babylonian oppression of Judah within two years in opposition to Jeremiah's prophecy of seventy years in exile (25:11-12). Jeremiah then proposed a test based upon the moral or ethical content of the prophetic message itself:

> Then the prophet Jeremiah said unto the prophet Hananiah in the presence of the priests, and in the presence of all the people that stood in the house of Yahweh, even the prophet Jeremiah said, Amen: Yahweh do so; Yahweh perform thy words which thou hast prophesied, to bring again the vessels of Yahweh's house, and all them of the captivity, from Babylon unto this place. Nevertheless hear thou now this word that I speak in thine ears, and in the ears of all the people: The prophets that have been before me and before thee of old prophesied against many countries, and against great kingdoms, of war, and of evil, and of pestilence. The prophet that prophesieth of peace, when the word of the prophet shall come to pass, then shall the prophet be known, that Yahweh hath truly sent him (28:5-9).

The moral quality and spiritual content of the prophet's message are the basis of this test. The prophet who predicts judgment for a sinful nation is following in the succession of the former prophets; hence, his message needs no further authentication, whereas the prophet who prophesies peace and safety to a degenerate and wicked people, let the *fulfillment* of such a prediction prove him true!

HEARER'S DISCERNMENT INDICATED TRUE AND FALSE

This test was enunciated by Moses in Deuteronomy 18:15-19 and confirmed by Christ in John 7:17. The principle set forth in these passages, while it applies specifically to Christ's prophetic ministry, nevertheless is a valid test respecting all true prophecy. There is an inner witness in the believer's heart by the same Spirit who inspired the prophetic Word that enables him to discern it as the truth and the Word of God. The witness in the believer's heart answers to the truth contained in the Word. In the final analysis the corroboration of the prophet's word rested with the hearers and thus was wholly subjective. The moral ability of the people to discriminate between true and false prophets in any age gives evidence of their spiritual condition. Israel's persistent rejection of the true prophets was indicative of her moral and spiritual declension. This fact is nowhere more evident than in Ezekiel 2:3-7.

The difference between the true and false prophet was spiritually discerned. The Word of God carries its own evidence and authority, and thus commends itself to the hearts and consciences of the children of God: "Is not my word like fire? saith Yahweh; and like a hammer that breaketh the rock in pieces?" (Jer. 23:29). "If any man willeth to do his will, he shall know of the teaching, whether it is of God, or whether I speak from myself" (John 7:17). "And ye have an anointing from the Holy One, and ye know all things" (I John 2:20). The subjective test presupposed a certain moral and spiritual discernment which the people did not always possess, consequently in times of moral declension the false prophets predicting smooth things for the nation, independent of the need of repentance and moral improvement, were honored above the true prophets who emphasized judgment and the need of inward righteousness. Is it not thus in every age?

In conclusion, no one single test was sufficient to authenticate the claims of a prophet. Both the true and the false prophets could prophesy in the name of Yahweh. Both could claim divine inspiration. Lying dreams and visions were presented as genuine revelations. Signs and wonders could accompany the message of a false prophet as well as the true. And since the false prophet sometimes copied the prophetic truths of genuine prophets, the basic evidences which must accompany and undergird these tests would be as follows: The prophet's message would be in harmony with the previous revelations. The character of the prophet would be consistent with the holy and righteous nature of God as He had revealed Himself to Moses. The high moral quality and spiritual content of the message itself would differentiate it from the compromising platitudes of the false prophets. Finally the truth in the believer's own heart would confirm the truth of the prophet's word.[1]

PROBLEM OF FULFILLMENT AND NONFULFILLMENT OF PROPHECY

In Old Testament prophecy, fulfillment constitutes an essential aspect of the prophet's message. In Deuteronomy 18:21-22, this constitutes one of the evidences of its genuineness. The verification of the prophet's word by the events of history was evidence of its truth and divine origin (cf. Jer. 28); nonfulfillment was an indication of false

[1]In the N.T. yet another test is given in addition to these. The spiritual discernment of other true prophets will judge the genuineness of a prophetic utterance (I Cor. 14:29; cf. Jer. 28; I Kings 22). The test proposed in I John 4 is in harmony with the first and sixth tests set forth in this study.

prophecy.[2] In Isaiah 41:21-23 the significance of the relationship between prophecy and fulfillment is seen when God disdainfully challenged the idol-gods, in which Israel vainly trusted, to predict events lying in the distant future; their fulfillment would be proof of the existence and authority of these gods. However, the idol-gods could announce no predictions, whereas God, knowing the end and the beginning of all events, again and again demonstrated the truth of the word of His prophets through the fulfillment of their forecasts and signs: "Therefore Yahweh himself will give you a sign" (Isa. 7:14); "I have showed thee new things from this time, even hidden things, which thou hast not known. They are created now, and not from of old; and before this day thou heardest them not; lest thou shouldest say, Behold, I knew them" (Isa. 48:6-7).

If fulfillment constitutes the evidence of the genuineness of the prophecy, what then of those predictions which are said not to have been *literally* fulfilled and of those instances of the nonfulfillment of the prophecy of a true prophet? Kirkpatrick, in his effort to solve this problem, rejects the idea that "prophecy and fulfillment [are]... related as the reflection in a mirror to the object reflected,"[3] or that "prophecy [is]. . .'inverted history.' "[4] Thus fulfillment, he holds, does not correspond exactly to the prediction, "but fulfillment is related to prophecy rather as the plant with all its beauty of leaf and flower and fruit is related to the seed from which it has sprung. . . . The inner idea, and not the form in which that idea is conveyed, is the essential part of prophecy."[5] Precisely what he means by concept is to be seen in the following statement: "The form in which the idea is embodied is largely human, determined by the conditions of the prophet's age and varying from time to time accordingly. The fulfillment, which is the evolution of the essential idea, is greater than the prophecy."[6] However, is this an adequate as well as biblical explanation of the problem of the nonfulfillment of prophecy? Some instances of alleged nonfulfillment of prophecy are the prediction of the Prophet Ezekiel with regard to the ruin of Tyre by Nebuchadnezzar

2This does not overlook the fact that Deut. 13:1 f. states that Satan can sometimes announce a sign or wonder through the false prophet which may come to pass. Israel is not to be deceived by signs and wonders if they are not in harmony with God's previous revelation (vv. 2-3). Fulfillment is just one of the evidences of the genuineness of prophecy. The question under consideration here has reference only to the problem of fulfillment or nonfulfillment of genuine prophecy.

3A. F. Kirkpatrick, *The Doctrine of the Prophets,* p. 15.

4*Ibid.*

5*Ibid.,* p. 16.

6*Ibid.,* pp. 16-17.

(Ezek. 26:7-14; 29:17-20); Jonah's prophecy of the destruction of Nineveh (3:4); the prophecy of Elijah against Ahab concerning the murder of Naboth (I Kings 21:17-29); Isaiah's prophecy of the destruction of Damascus (Isa. 17:1).

The critical school seeks to disparage the trustworthiness of true prophecy by parading a few alleged instances of predictions by genuine prophets that were unfulfilled, especially the prophecy of Ezekiel 26:7-14. However, in their eagerness to discredit biblical prophecy it becomes all too obvious that they willfully ignore the hundreds of fulfilled prophecies attested to by history, such as Jeremiah's prediction of the death of Hananiah within the same year, Micah's prediction of the birthplace of the Messiah, Isaiah's forecast of the overthrow of Sennacherib's army, Micaiah's predicted defeat and death of King Ahab, Zechariah's forecast of the betrayal of Christ for thirty pieces of silver, and so on. But what of the alleged nonfulfillment of such passages as those previously cited? Is there a satisfactory explanation from Scripture? We believe the reply is to be made in the affirmative, and that the problem can be resolved from the following threefold consideration.

The nonfulfillment of certain prophecies is to be explained from the threefold nature of predictive prophecy itself; that is, prophecy may either be *literally* fulfilled, *essentially* fulfilled, or *conditionally* fulfilled. Examples of literally fulfilled prophecies have already been cited. Prophecy may also be intended by God to accomplish only an essential fulfillment; the details, therefore, are not necessarily always to be pressed. An example of this is perhaps found in the prophecy of Elijah concerning Ahab and his murder of Naboth. In I Kings 21:19 Elijah says: "Thus saith Yahweh, Hast thou killed and also taken possession? . . . In the place where dogs licked the blood of Naboth shall dogs lick thy blood, even thine." Verse 13 indicates that Naboth was slain outside the city of Jezreel and presumably this is where the dogs licked his blood. In the fulfillment of this prophecy we read in 22:34-35 when King Ahab was slain in the battle of Ramoth-gilead that his blood ran out in his chariot, after which he was carried back to Samaria and buried. Whereupon "they washed the chariot by the pool of Samaria and the dogs licked up his blood . . . according unto the word of Yahweh which he spake" (v. 38). The prediction in 21:19 had said "*in the place* where the dogs licked the blood of Naboth shall dogs lick thy blood." Actually Naboth was slain outside the city of Jezreel and Ahab at Ramoth-gilead, and the king's blood which was washed out of his chariot was licked up at the pool of Samaria. However, the *essential* elements of the prophecy were fulfilled in that the dogs licked up his blood as they had the blood of

Naboth. Quite evidently the precise location of Naboth's body in relation to Ahab's is not the main thrust of this prophecy with respect to fulfillment, but this is rather to be found in God's just retribution *in kind* against Ahab for his murder of Naboth.

Another example of the essential fulfillment of prophecy is found in the oracle concerning Damascus in Isaiah 17:1: "Behold, Damascus is taken away from being a city, and it shall be a ruinous heap." However, the city of Damascus exists yet today. This prophecy is to be interpreted not as absolutely but essentially fulfilled. The prophet does not necessarily mean a literal permanent destruction of the city, but a severe judgment upon it, as occurred when King Ahaz made an alliance with Tiglath-Pileser to deliver Judah from the threat of Syria and Israel. The Assyrians destroyed Damascus and displaced the dominance of the city and the power of Syria for a long time (cf. II Kings 16:5-9).

The prophecy of Ezekiel 26:7-14, according to the critics, is said to promise Nebuchadnezzar the spoil of Tyre as his reward for acting as God's agent of judgment in the destruction of that city. However, according to Ezekiel's own later admission in 29:17-20, this prediction was unfulfilled. The primary verses in question are as follows: "For thus saith the Lord Yahweh: Behold, I will bring upon Tyre Nebuchadrezzar king of Babylon . . . with horses, and with chariots, and with horsemen, and a company, and much people. And they shall make a spoil of thy riches, and make a prey of thy merchandise" (26:7, 12). The alleged admission by Ezekiel of the nonfulfillment of the prediction in 29:17-20 reads thus:

> And it came to pass in the seven and twentieth year, in the first month, in the first day of the month, the word of Yahweh came unto me, saying, Son of man, Nebuchadrezzar king of Babylon caused his army to serve a great service against Tyre: every head was made bald, and every shoulder was worn; yet had he no wages, nor his army, from Tyre, for the service that he had served against it. Therefore thus saith the Lord Yahweh: Behold, I will give the land of Egypt unto Nebuchadrezzar king of Babylon; and he shall carry off her multitude, and take her spoil, and take her prey; and it shall be the wages for his army. I have given him the land of Egypt as his recompense for which he served, because they wrought for me, saith the Lord Yahweh.

On the basis of the statements in verses 18 and 20, Old Testament critics insist that this is an admission of the nonfulfillment of the earlier prophecy in chapter 26. That this is not the case at all is evident from certain considerations. First of all, such an admission

would be to charge God with the error because in both chapters 26
and 29 it is the Lord Himself speaking in the first person throughout!
The obvious serious implications involved should compel one to
weigh very carefully his conclusions concerning the proper interpretation of this prophecy. Furthermore, it is difficult to believe that the
Prophet Ezekiel could expect his audience to take his prophecies and
preaching seriously if he admitted that he had been in error previously in some of his predictions, especially in view of the fact that he
also claimed at that time to be speaking the word of the Lord!
However, in spite of the statements by the critics, the Prophet
Ezekiel does not think his earlier prophecy was unfulfilled. It would
be sufficient to say that it had been fulfilled in essence; however,
even this is not necessary from a simple unbiased reading of the two
passages. Ezekiel does not say in 26:12, as it is alleged, that Nebuchadnezzar will *profit* materially from the siege of Tyre. This is
not even the concern of this prophecy. What God is predicting
through His prophet is that Tyre will be besieged and overthrown,
many of the inhabitants slain, their riches and merchandise made a
spoil to the enemy, and the city made "a bare rock . . . a place for the
spreading of nets." The prophecy does not remotely concern Nebuchadnezzar's receiving a profitable reward for his destruction of
Tyre—there is not a single promise made to him in this regard. This
theory is but a figment of the imagination of the critics. Any conqueror takes as spoil what he can find of the possessions of the
defeated enemy. This is the precise limit of what is said respecting
Nebuchadnezzar. Chapter 29 simply states a historical fact, namely,
that the long siege of Tyre which lasted thirteen years was not
profitable to Nebuchadnezzar and his army and that God was to
recompense him for his services (i.e., as God's agent of judgment)
by giving him Egypt. Chapter 29 does not say Nebuchadnezzar did
not take spoil from Tyre, but expresses the fact of the costliness of the
long siege. The prophecy of chapter 26 was fulfilled; Tyre was overthrown and despoiled. Furthermore, chapter 29 is not a prophecy
concerning Tyre at all, but predicts the overthrow of Egypt. In this
connection, God would again use Babylon to execute His judgment;
and since Nebuchadnezzar had not realized a profit from his long
siege of Tyre, God would recompense him in the Egyptian campaign.
Nor is it necessary to insist that the statement "and he had no
wages, nor his army" (29:18) means that Nebuchadnezzar took no
spoil at all from Tyre, but simply that they had not received sufficient recompense for the immense expense of such a long campaign, as
if he were to say "we did not meet our expenses," or "we did not even

make our wages." An army might obtain huge sums in spoil and still not make their wages, especially in such a prolonged siege. It should not be forgotten that God does not say in 26:12 that they would. Thus this is not a case of an unfulfilled prophecy respecting Nebuchadnezzar's wages and profit from the siege of Tyre for the precise reason that Ezekiel made no such prediction in the first place! What he did predict, the overthrow and spoil of Tyre, was completely fulfilled. Nebuchadnezzar destroyed the mainland city of Tyre, and it was never rebuilt. Later, Alexander the Great did scrape the area as "a bare rock" in building his causeway out to the island city of Tyre, which he conquered and destroyed.

There are times when we find actual instances of the nonfulfillment of certain prophecies. This does not mean that the prophet made an erroneous prediction, but can be explained by the conditional nature of some types of prophecy. Such prophecies did not always have to be fulfilled like an edict of fate. Such prophecies are seen to be morally and ethically conditioned. God could, and sometimes did, revoke a threatened judgment upon repentance. A clear example of this was Jonah's prophecy of judgment concerning Nineveh: "Yet forty days, and Nineveh shall be overthrown" (3:4). However, in verse 10 we read: "And God saw their works, that they turned from their evil way; and God repented of the evil which he said he would do unto them; and he did it not."

The scriptural basis for the conditional element of some prophecies is found in Jeremiah 18:1-10. Just as the potter can shape the clay as it suits him, marring it if it displeases him, or reshaping it again into another vessel, so too God can determine the fate of a nation as He wishes. Hence, His threats and promises may be conditioned by the conduct and response of the people concerned. God in His sovereignty has the absolute freedom to deal with nations according to their moral conduct toward Him. This is to be seen in the case of Nineveh's repentance at the preaching of Jonah. When the city heard the announcement of the forthcoming judgment upon them, they turned from their evil and repented. God's suspension of the predicted destruction of the city was the result of the conditionality of some prophecies as set forth in Jeremiah 18. Another instance of this is found in the case of King Ahab who humbled himself before God when he heard the prophecy of Elijah against his house, and as a result God delayed the execution of the threatened judgment until after Ahab's death (I Kings 21:17-29). In the same way the prediction of blessing can be recalled if the people prove themselves undeserving (cf. Jer. 18:9-10; Deut. 28).

Hence, many of the prophecies of Scripture present alternatives and are therefore conditional. If Israel were obedient she would be blessed; if she disobeyed she would suffer divine punishment (Deut. 28). Jeremiah informed Zedekiah of this fact when he delivered a conditional prophecy concerning the fate of Jerusalem (Jer. 38:17-18; cf. 42:10-13). Ezekiel also confirms this principle of God's dealing with men (Ezek. 33:13-15).

Therefore, prophecy may be either conditional or unconditional, for as noted previously not all prophetic utterances are conditioned. There are some predictions and promises concerning which "Yahweh hath sworn, and will not repent" (Ps. 110:4). All those prophecies, for instance, which foretell the advent of the Messiah, His work and kingdom (cf. Isa. 7:14; Micah 5:2; Isa. 53; II Sam 7; Dan 2, 7, etc.); the prophecies concerning the restoration of Israel (cf. Amos 9:11-15; Ezek. 37, etc.); the judgment and overthrow of the nations (Joel 3; Matt. 25, etc.); and the second advent (Matt. 25; Acts 1:11, etc.), are unconditional, as was the promise in Genesis 8:22 that "while the earth remaineth, seedtime and harvest, and cold and heat, and summer and winter, and day and night shall not cease." Moreover, the promises God made to the patriarchs concerning Israel's future blessing shall yet be realized, declared the apostle, "for the gifts and the calling of God are not repented of" (Rom. 11:29).

Chapter 6

THE LANGUAGE OF
PROPHECY

THERE WERE BASICALLY three methods by which the prophets delivered their messages: (1) *orally*, that is, through the preaching or proclamation of God's word as seen, for example, in Micaiah's prophecy to Ahab (I Kings 22), or Nathan to David (II Sam. 12); (2) through the *written Word* (the Scriptures) such as the books of Isaiah, Jeremiah; (3) by means of the *symbolic act* as when Isaiah walked naked and barefoot as a sign to Egypt and Ethiopia of their pending judgment, or when Hosea was instructed to marry "a wife of whoredom," thereby depicting God's relationship to adulterous Israel.

In the language of prophecy, the form itself was not limited to one kind, but the word of God was expressed in various ways. Some prophecies were clearly stated without the use of symbolism, figures of speech, parables and the like, such as Jeremiah's prediction of Hananiah's death (Jer. 28), the actual naming of the future King Josiah by the prophet of Judah (I Kings 13:1-2) and the forewarnings of Israel's exile of seventy years' duration (Jer. 25:11-14). At other times, the prophets made use of various kinds of literary expression. The parable was frequently used, as seen in Nathan's parable of the poor man's ewe lamb (II Sam. 12:1-14) and Isaiah's parable of the vineyard (Isa. 5:1-7). They employed allegory as a medium of prophetic utterance, a form of expression for which the book of Ezekiel is noted (cf. allegory of the worthless vine, 15:1-8; allegory of the foundling child, 16:1-43). Metaphor was frequently employed, as in Isaiah's prophecy concerning Assyria: "Ho Assyrian, the rod of mine anger, the staff in whose hand is mine indignation" (10:5). The prophets make extensive use of every kind of figure of speech by employing simile, metonymy, synecdoche, hyperbole, personification and the like. The use of symbolism is especially abundant in the prophecies of Daniel, Ezekiel and Zechariah.

Typical Language

One of the most unique forms of Old Testament prophecy was the use of *typical* language in which persons, things and events depict some future fulfillment. The marked prophetic element of the Old Testament establishes the principle that the New Testament is latent in the Old and that the Old is patent in the New. Prophecy may be either verbally predictive or typically predictive.[1] Hence, a "type" is in reality a *species of prophecy* of which the Old Testament Passover, Levitical sacrifices, the temple and priesthood are examples.[2] The justification for the typological interpretation of many Old Testament passages is threefold according to Bernard Ramm: (1) the general relationship the Old Testament sustains to the New; (2) Christ's own use of the Old Testament and His invitation to us to find Him predicted and typified therein; and (3) the vocabulary of the New Testament with reference to the Old,[3] to be seen in such phrases as "Christ our Passover," "Lamb of God," "Son of Man," or in terms like "sacrifice," "Redeemer," "blood" and "Messiah." Old Testament types which were subjects of prophecy were: *persons,* such as David who typified Christ; *institutions,* like the Sabbath, pointing to salvation's rest, or the Passover, typifying redemption; *offices* of such nature as prophet, priest and king, as typical of Christ; *events,* such as the exodus depicting future spiritual deliverance; *actions,* like the lifting up of the brazen serpent in the wilderness typifying the crucifixion; and *things,* such as the curtain of the tabernacle expressing principles involving access to God.[4] The type foreshadows a future event which is the antitype. "It must serve in the divine economy," observes Terry, "as a shadow of things to come (Col. ii, 17; Heb. x, 1). Hence it is that sacred typology constitutes a specific form of prophetic revelation. The Old Testament dispensations were preparatory to the New, and contained many things in germ which could fully blossom only in the light of the Gospel of Jesus."[5] Therefore, that which is interpreted as typical in the Old Testament is not something foreign to or superimposed upon the text, but arises from the divinely intended unity between the two Testaments.

[1]Bernard Ramm, *Protestant Biblical Interpretation,* p. 139.

[2]Girdlestone has shown how the Old Testament expressed the future in terms of past events, e.g., Sodom and Gomorrah are types of God's future dealing with the wicked (II Peter 2:6; cf. Isa. 1:9-10; Jer. 23:14). See R. B. Girdlestone, *The Grammar of Prophecy,* pp. 66-73.

[3]Ramm, pp. 138-39.

[4]*Ibid.,* p. 147.

[5]Milton S. Terry, *Biblical Hermeneutics,* p. 248.

THE WORD OF THE LORD

Another significant concept concerning the language of Hebrew prophecy is the Old Testament phrase *d^ebhar Yahweh*, "*the word of Yahweh*" (or "the word of the Lord"). In Hebrew thought the *d^ebhar Yahweh* was itself dynamic and efficacious once it was uttered: "So shall my word be that goeth forth out of my mouth: it shall not return unto me void, but it shall accomplish that which I please, and it shall prosper in the thing whereto I sent it" (Isa. 55:11). To the Israelite, as it was commonly conceived in the Near East, a person's word was not merely the audible voice, but possessed a certain objectivity of its own, for example, *dābhār* means both "word" and "act," thus *dībhrê 'awōnōth* are "acts of iniquity" or *dībhārîm ṭôbhîm* are "good deeds."

At this point the significance of the Hebrew *curse* or *blessing* comes into view. When a curse or blessing was uttered it was thought in some sense to have a definite effect upon the other person. This conception is clearly to be seen in the case of the blessing of Isaac upon Jacob and Esau. Although Isaac had, by prophetic utterance, pronounced his blessing upon the head of Jacob whom he thought to be Esau, once the words had actually gone forth he could not recall them. When Isaac, then blind due to age, learned that he had been deceived, he cried out to Esau: "Who then is he that hath taken venison, and brought it me, and I have eaten of all before thou camest, and have blessed him? Yea, and *he shall be blessed*. And he said, Thy brother came with guile, and *hath taken away thy blessing*" (Gen. 27:33, 35). Once the prophetic word had been pronounced upon another, it began its work and could not be recalled.

The same concept is found in the account in Numbers 22-24 when Balak, king of Moab, sends for the Prophet Balaam to come and curse Israel for him:

> Come now therefore, I pray thee, curse me this people; for they are too mighty for me: peradventure I shall prevail, that we may smite them, and that I may drive them out of the land; for I know that he whom thou blessest is blessed, and he whom thou cursest is cursed (Num. 22:6).

Balak echoes the prevalent conception that the word of the prophet is always efficacious, a valid concept, of course, in the case of the utterances of the true prophets. God declares in Isaiah 44:26 that He "confirmeth the word of his servant, and performeth the counsel of his messengers" (cf. 55:11). Ezekiel is commanded by God to warn Judah of her approaching judgment: "Thus saith the Lord God: There shall none of my words be deferred any more, but the word which I shall speak shall be performed, saith the Lord God" (Ezek. 12:28). The word of the prophet of Judah spoken against the altar at Bethel was immediately effective, and the great altar was rent and the ashes poured out as announced (I Kings 13:1-6). Elisha's curse upon his mockers resulted in their immediate punishment (II Kings 2:23-25). By the word of Elijah, fire was called down from heaven to consume his would-be captors (II Kings 1); and again by his word the waters of the Jordan were parted (II Kings 2:8). The plagues upon Egypt were the direct result of the spoken word of the Prophet Moses; and the death of Ahab was the result of the prophetic word pronounced against the king by the Prophet Micaiah. So effective was the word of the prophets that when uttered over nations and kingdoms they had the power of destruction or restoration. God said to Jeremiah: "Behold, I have put my words in thy mouth: see, I have this day set thee over the nations and over the kingdoms, to pluck up and to break down and to destroy and to overthrow, to build and to plant" (Jer. 1:9-10). Zechariah emphasizes the truth that the prophet's word was always effective. God reminded the returned exiles of this fact:

> But my words and my statutes, which I commanded my servants the prophets, did they not overtake your fathers? And they turned and said, Like as Yahweh of hosts thought to do unto us, according to our ways, and according to our doings, so hath he dealt with us (Zech. 1:6).

There was nothing magical in the Hebrew conception of the *dᵉbhar Yahweh,* "the word of Yahweh," but a recognition of the *divine source* of the prophetic utterance. The prophets themselves are careful to distinguish between the word of the Lord and their own words. This is to be seen in the prophetic formula "Thus saith the Lord." Never in the course of his utterances did the prophet fail to distinguish the boundary line between the divine and human elements in prophecy. Thus Amos could reply to those who would challenge his authority and the divine source of his utterances: "I was no prophet, neither was I a prophet's son; but I was a herdsman, and a dresser of sycomore-trees: and Yahweh took me from following the flock, and Yahweh said unto me, Go, prophesy unto my people Israel. Now therefore *hear thou the word of Yahweh*" (7:14-16). And again, "The lion hath roared; who will not fear? The Lord God hath spoken; who can but prophesy?" (3:8). This emphasis upon the divine source of the prophetic message helps explain the stress placed upon the objectivity of the spoken word by the Hebrews. This concept was further strengthened by the belief that the divine word was creative. With its utterance the desired result was invariably achieved. Thus in Psalm 33:6 we are told how God created the universe through His spoken word: "By the word of Yahweh were the heavens made, and all the host of them by the breath of his mouth." God has but to speak His word and the result is effected: "And God said, Let there be light: and there was light" (Gen. 1:3). "For he commanded, and they were created" (Ps. 148:5; cf. Heb. 11:3: "By faith we understand that the worlds have been framed by the word of God").

The divine efficacious word is said to be put into the mouth of the prophet; hence, the prophet's word is likewise unfailing in its effectiveness. This was seen in the commission of Moses: "Now therefore go, and I will be with thy mouth, and teach thee what thou shalt speak" (Exodus 4:12). In the call of Jeremiah we read: "Then Yahweh put forth his hand, and touched my mouth; and Yahweh said unto me, Behold, I have put my words in thy mouth" (1:9). Ezekiel was commanded to eat the roll of the book containing God's prophetic word of judgment against the rebellious nation, and then was instructed to go speak those words to Israel (Ezek. 2-3; note also Deut. 18:18; Isa. 6:6 ff.; I Kings 22:14). Thus, when the Old Testament prophet spoke he was to be heeded, because his word was the *d*e*bhar Yahweh* and, being of divine origin, unfailingly initiated and effected what it predicted: "For I am Yahweh; I will speak [through the prophets]; and the word that I shall speak shall be performed" (Ezek. 12:25).

THE PROPHETIC PERFECT

A third aspect concerning the language of prophecy that requires consideration is the Hebrew verbal form known as the *prophetic perfect*. In classical Hebrew there are no tenses indicating time. The time of a verb is determined from the context. Instead of tenses there are two states, designated as "perfect" and "imperfect," indicating completed or incompleted action respectively. However, since the Hebrew perfect state indicates completed action, usually it is used to describe action or events in the past. The imperfect, expressing incompleted action, is normally used to express future events which obviously are incomplete, not yet having occurred. Nevertheless, the perfect, which indicates completed action, could also be used in future time when the speaker or writer wished to express confidence in the certainty of an event which was yet to take place. This is usually called a "perfect of confidence"[6] or "perfect of certainty," as

---

[6]J. Wash Watts, *A Survey of Syntax in the Hebrew Old Testament*, p. 17.

in Genesis 30:13: "And Leah said [upon the birth of a second son to Jacob], Happy am I! For the daughters *will call* me happy" (cf. Num. 17:12; Gen. 23:11). The verb in this verse translated in the future tense as "will call" is actually a perfect indicating the event, which has not yet occurred, as completed. The confidence of the speaker that the daughters would call her blessed was such that she spoke of it as having already taken place. This use of the perfect state occurs most frequently in prophetic language and is called the prophetic perfect. That is, when the Scripture passage indicates that the word which the prophet speaks is a word from God predicting some future event, then the perfect state of a verb (i.e., a verb indicating completed action) is used. This is because from the standpoint of the unfailing divine purposes, the fulfillment of these events was regarded as so certain it could be spoken of by the prophet as perfected or completed as surely as if it had already occurred. The perfect of prophecy is a perfect state (completed action) in future time that describes the future event as if it had already taken place, based upon the authority of the divine word revealed to the prophet. In Isaiah 9:6, for example, the prophet, speaking of the future birth of the Messiah centuries later, declares (literally): "a child *has been born*," the prophet using here the perfect state of the verb indicating completed action and the certainty of the fulfillment of the event in the mind of God. It is of course to be translated as the versions render it, as a future event: "A child *shall be* born." Again in 11:9 the prophet speaking of the future millennial conditions predicts: "For the earth shall be full of the knowledge of Yahweh," literally, "The earth *is full* of the knowledge of Yahweh," since the prophet again uses a perfect verb to speak of a future event as certain. Again in Numbers 24:17 we read: "There shall come forth a star out of Jacob," which is an event so certain that the speaker actually said: "There *has come* forth a star out of Jacob." (See also Isa. 5:13; 8:8; 10:28; 28:2; 53:12; Hosea 4:6; Amos 5:2; Ps. 67:7; 110:5.) In Numbers 24 the prophetic perfect occurs repeatedly. Long before the captivity, Isaiah, using this unusual verbal construction, could cry: "Therefore my people *have gone* into captivity" (Isa. 5:13). From these examples, it can be seen how the language of predictive prophecy in the Old Testament is a unique phenomenon which describes future events as already completed on the basis of divine certainty.

SYMBOLIC ACTS

Finally, the *symbolic acts* of the prophets were a significant form of the prophetic method for expressing the word of the Lord. The symbolic acts of the prophets were not expressions of "symbolic magic" as some critics have contended, but rather a symbolic method of proclaiming the divine revelation. H. Wheeler Robinson expresses the critical interpretation of these acts thus:

> These acts . . . initiated the divine action in miniature, and thus helped towards the fulfillment of what was foretold. Genetically, they spring from the widespread practice of symbolic magic, but the prophets have transformed them into religion by assimilating them to the will of God.[7]

In heathenism the use of symbolic magic is common, whereby the priest seeks to control events, initiate an action, or make efficacious a pronounced curse upon an enemy, by symbolically enacting in miniature what he desires to see accomplished in actuality. However, this is not the case in the Old Testament, for what we have in the symbolic act of the prophet is a *prophetic act* which was itself as much a method of divine revelation as the spoken word of the prophet.

The symbolic acts of the prophets were quite numerous and each was intended by God as a *vehicle* for divine revelation. Jeremiah wore a yoke around his neck through the streets to depict the impending Babylonian bondage (Jer. 27-28). Hosea was commanded to marry a wife of whoredom, thus symbolizing by her adulterous conduct the unfaithfulness of Israel (Hosea 1-3). Isaiah walked naked and barefoot as a sign to Egypt and Ethiopia of their similar fate at the hands of Assyria (Isa. 20:1-6). Ezekiel's symbolic acts are the most numerous. He was commanded to lay mock siege to Jerusalem by portraying it upon a tile (4:1-3); to lie for a stated period upon his side to depict the period appointed to Israel as punishment for her iniquity (4:4-8); to eat unclean food by measure as a sign of Israel's physical privations in exile (4:9-17); to burn a portion of his hair, thus foretelling the coming destruction of Jerusalem and its inhabitants (5:1-4). On other occasions he was commanded to prophesy to the mountains, dig through the wall and carry out his personal belongings, join two sticks, one marked with the name of Judah and the other Ephraim, to prophesy to the dry bones, set a caldron on the fire, and in many ways depict by symbolism the future course of God's dealings with Israel. The Prophet Ahijah, upon meeting Jeroboam, rent his garment in twelve pieces, thus symbolizing the division of the kingdom (I Kings 11:30 ff.). Jeremiah symbolically gave signs to Israel by the "marred girdle" (13:1 ff.), the

[7]H. Wheeler Robinson, *Inspiration and Revelation in the Old Testament*, p. 227.

potter and the clay (18:1 ff.), a broken bottle (19:1 ff.), and the "cup of the wine of wrath" (25:15 ff.).

Furthermore, the prophets were sometimes commanded to give symbolic names to their children, thus prophetically symbolizing God's intentions toward Israel, as when Isaiah called one of his sons Shear-jashub, meaning prophetically "a remnant shall return" (7:3), and calling another Maher-shalal-hash-baz, "the spoil speedeth, the prey hasteth" (8:1), signifying judgment. Hosea was instructed by God to give all his children symbolic names. Jezreel, the name of his first son, was a prophetic symbol of God's intention to "avenge the blood of Jezreel upon the house of Jehu" (1:4). And by the names Lo-ruhamah, "no mercy" (1:6), and Lo-ammi, "not my people" (1:9), God indicated His rejection of Israel.

Thus, the symbolic act, like the prophetic Word, was by divine intention to be a vehicle for the proclamation of God's revelation through His prophets. The symbolic act was a graphic, prophetic method of arresting the attention of the recipient, thereby dramatically impressing upon Israel's consciousness the divine word itself.

Chapter 7

MESSIANIC PROPHECY

MESSIANIC PROPHECY, in a real sense, may be regarded as the New Testament in the Old. Messianic prophecy is that which *predicts the fulfillment of redemption and the establishment of the kingdom of God through the Messiah.* Such prophecy is not confined in the Old Testament to the prophets, nor is it limited to any particular form of literature. It is to be found in the early historical narratives, in the poetical books and the writings, as well as in the prophetic books themselves.

TWO STREAMS OF MESSIANIC PROPHECY IN THE OLD TESTAMENT

Messianic prophecy in the Old Testament proceeded along two lines of development, both grounded in the twofold promise God made to Abraham. One aspect had to do with the future *nation* or *kingdom*; the other spoke of *salvation* and *blessing*. These two aspects of God's prophetic promise are to be found in His call to Abraham recorded in Genesis 12:1-3: "Now Yahweh said unto Abram, Get thee out of thy country, and from thy kindred, and from thy father's house, unto the land that I will show thee: and I will make of thee *a great nation* . . . and *in thee shall all the families of the earth be blessed.*" Out of this twofold promise two streams of Messianic prophecy were to develop. One stream would emphasize the glorious future of the nation or kingdom of Israel, ruled over by a Davidic monarch, the Messianic King. The other stream would speak of the work of the Messiah, portraying Him, not as a reigning king, but as a suffering servant who would be slain on behalf of His people. Prophecies foretelling the future glory of the kingdom of Israel ruled over by the *Davidic* Messiah are quite numerous (see II Sam. 7:5-17; I Kings 11:36; 15:4; II Kings 8:19; Isa. 9:6-7; Jer. 23:5-6; 33:14-17; Zech. 14:9, 16). To this stream of prophecy concerning the Davidic Messiah are to be added all those prophecies which foretell the glorious future of Israel and the restoration and glorification of Zion, the holy city (see Deut. 30:1-10; Isa. 2:2-5; 10:20-23; 11:10-16; Hosea 1:10-11; 2:14-23; 3:4-5; Amos 9:11-15; Zeph. 3:8-20; Zech. 1:12-17; 2:4-13, etc.).

It was this promise made to Abraham which created the Jewish expectancy of the kingdom of God, to be realized through Israel as a nation of priests upon earth. With the establishment of the theocracy under Moses and the anointing of Saul as king by Samuel this nationalistic conception of Israel as the kingdom of God was advanced. The subsequent successful reign of David heightened this expectancy even more. Furthermore, in the divine promise made to David of an everlasting kingdom, the Hebrew expectation of an eternal glorious kingdom ruled over by a Davidic monarch was all but realized: "And thy house and thy kingdom shall be made sure for ever before thee: thy throne shall be established for ever" (II Sam. 7:16). However, the ensuing disappointments which resulted from the wickedness and apostasy of the kings who followed David (none of whom obviously could fulfill Messianic expectations), together with the division of the kingdom itself into two opposing realms, and the resultant tragic experience of the destruction of the sacred city and the exile, caused the hope of a Messianic king to be coupled with that of a Messianic deliverer and restoration, upon which the ancient promises of the glorious Davidic kingdom would be realized. Nevertheless, with their restoration to Palestine by Cyrus, the glorious future was still not to be an actuality, and Zerubbabel was not their expected Messiah. Furthermore, one of the principal promises, that of blessing and freedom from foreign domination, as set forth, for example, in Joel 2-3 and Amos 9:11-15, had not yet been fulfilled, which fact Nehemiah 9:32-38, Haggai 2:3 and Ezra 3:11-13 clearly indicate. Hence, the kingdom of God was yet somewhere in the remote future. Therefore, during the intertestamental period there was a development of the eschatological nature of the kingdom in Jewish thought.

The other stream of prophecy, based upon the redemptive implications in the promise made to Abraham in Genesis 12:1-3, as stated before, portrayed the future Messiah, not as a reigning king, but as a suffering servant, afflicted and slain on behalf of the people whose sins He bears. This other side of Messianic prophecy is graphically portrayed in several passages, such as Zechariah 13:7; Psalm 22; and Isaiah 53. The ancient rabbis were puzzled by the two apparently conflicting streams of prophecy in reference to the Messiah's person and mission. One series of prophecies depicted Him as a babe to be born in Bethlehem, and as a man of sorrows, acquainted with grief and smitten unto death for the transgressions of His people, thereby making vicarious atonement. The other prophecies portrayed Him as the Son of Man coming in the clouds of heaven with great power and glory, sitting upon the throne of David. Because of this the rabbis formulated the doctrine of *two* Messiahs: a Messiah ben Joseph who would suffer and die for Israel; the other, the Messiah ben David who would conquer and rule. But what they saw as two Messiahs, we now know had reference to *two advents*—the first and second comings of the Lord. That is, the prophecies concerning His sufferings and death were to be fulfilled in His first advent (Luke 24:25-27, 44-46; cf. Isa. 53); the prophecies concerning His glory and reign will be realized in His second advent (Matt. 24:29-31; cf. Zech. 14).

MEANING AND USAGE OF THE TERM "MESSIAH"

The Hebrew term Messiah has a twofold meaning, namely, "to smear" (as smearing cakes with oil, Exodus 29:2), or "to anoint." The noun Messiah is *māshîaḥ* from the verb *māshaḥ*, "to smear or anoint." It is in the sense of "anoint" that the term is used with reference to the Son of God. There is a close connection in the Old Testament between anointing and consecration, that is, the setting apart of anyone or anything for service to the Lord. In this regard the term "anoint" is used both literally and metaphorically. In literal usage men were actually anointed with oil, signifying their divine selection and consecration to an office. Metaphorically, the term is used to designate those who are called and set apart for God's purposes as, for example, Cyrus, king of Persia, and the nation of Israel. Thus in the former employment of the term both persons and inanimate objects were consecrated by anointing with oil: the Aaronic priests (Exodus 28:41); the tabernacle (Num. 7:1); its vessels (Num. 7:1); King Saul (I Sam. 10:1); David (I Sam. 16:13); the Prophet Elisha (I Kings 19:16); and the heathen king of Syria, Hazael (I Kings 19:15). Metaphorically, the term anointed is used of the Jewish patriarchs who are called "my anointed ones" (Ps. 105:15), and of the nation of Israel (Hab. 3:13). Cyrus, king of Persia, whom God called His "anointed" (Isa. 45:1), was commissioned by the Lord to be the deliverer of God's people from the Babylonian exile. Finally, the term Messiah or anointed One had special reference to the Davidic King, who as God's Son was to inherit David's everlasting kingdom (Ps. 2:2; 18:50; 89:38, 51; 132:10, 17; I Sam. 2:10, 35; Dan. 9:25-26).

Hence, we see that in the Old Testament the term "anointed," or "the Lord's anointed," does not always refer to the Messiah (i.e., Christ), but may refer to the nation of Israel, a king, the Jewish patriarchs, or even the Persian ruler Cyrus. The term simply means "anointed"; the context, therefore, must determine whether or not it is being used as a technical designation of the Messiah (e.g., Dan.

9:25-26). The origin of the concept of a Davidic Messiah is found in II Samuel 7. Although the term "anointed" is not used in this passage, the divine establishment of the everlasting kingdom of David, upon whose throne the Son of God would sit, is clearly predicted. The first association of the term Messiah with the idea of a king who would rule in Zion (thus signifying a Davidic king of Judah) is found in Psalm 2 (cf. vv. 2, 6-7), which doubtless was written by David (Acts 4:25-26). In this psalm the King is called Messiah (anointed One) and God's Son; and since He is to reign in Zion, He obviously is the same Davidic King who is set forth as God's Son in II Samuel 7. This association is confirmed in other psalms where the term appears. Daniel 9:25-26 identifies the Messiah with "the prince," and the term *māshîaḥ* appears here without question as a title. In other Old Testament passages where the term was used with reference to the future eschatological King, it was probably not regarded so much as a technical name or title, but rather was descriptive of the Davidic King—He was "the Lord's anointed." Such usage, however, caused the term to assume the signification of a title, as it certainly appears in Daniel and in the New Testament (cf. Matt. 2:4; 16:16; John 1:41; Acts 19:4).

Chapter 8

CESSATION OF OLD TESTAMENT PROPHECY, AND PROPHECY IN THE NEW TESTAMENT

MALACHI WAS REGARDED by the Hebrews as the last genuine prophet in Israel. According to I Maccabees 4:46; 9:27; 14:41, there were no canonical prophets in the Hebrew nation during the intertestamental period. During this period, apocalyptic and religious literature flourished; however, none of it emerged as canonical in Judaism. The attitude of the Palestinian Jews toward the Apocrypha was without question negative; they excluded these writings from the Old Testament canon for several reasons. It was believed that Ezra brought together the Old Testament canon and that after his work, prophecy ceased and no sacred Scripture was written. Hence, no book later than Ezra could be included in the canon of Scriptures. Another criterion used by the Jewish scholars of Jamnia around A.D. 90 to affirm the genuineness of a book was whether or not it was extant in the original Hebrew. The Apocryphal books were either written or survived only in the Greek and thus were rejected as noncanonical. Furthermore, these books contain historical inaccuracies and some enunciate doctrines contrary to the inspired Scriptures.

On the other hand, it was firmly believed among the Hebrews during the period between the Testaments that prophecy would be revived in the Messianic age on the basis of such forecasts as contained in Joel 2:28-29: "And it shall come to pass afterward, that I will pour out my Spirit upon all flesh; and your sons and your daughters shall prophesy, your old men shall dream dreams, your young men shall see visions," and in Malachi 4:5-6: "Behold, I will send you Elijah the prophet before the great and terrible day of Yahweh come. And he shall turn the heart of the fathers to the children, and the heart of the children to their fathers." In addition Moses had foretold a Prophet like unto himself whom the Lord would send and to whom all must hearken or fall under God's judgment (Deut. 18:15-19). The way was thus prepared by such prophecies for the ministry of John the Baptist as the forerunner of Christ as well as for Christ Himself. John is designated by Christ as the greatest of the prophets inasmuch as he forms the connecting link between the Old Testament prophets who foretold the Messiah and the appearance of the Messiah Himself (Luke 7:28). But it was Jesus Christ of whom Moses spoke (Deut. 18) as the Prophet that God would raise up and put His words in His mouth (cf. Acts 3:22-23; 7:37). Jesus is acclaimed as a prophet in the New Testament (Matt. 21:11, 46; Luke 7:16; John 4:19; 9:17); and He refers thus to Himself (Matt. 13:57; Luke 13:33).

In the church the office of prophet continues (I Cor. 12:28; Eph. 4:8-11), differing from the proclamation of the gospel by the apostles, evangelists and teachers.[1] New Testament prophecy is to be found, for example, in the prediction of a famine by the Prophet Agabus (Acts 11:27 ff.); in the prophecy of Paul's afflictions (Acts 21:10 ff.); and in the call of Paul and Barnabas through the prophets at Antioch to undertake their missionary work (Acts 13:1 ff.). Judas and Silas are mentioned as prophets in the early church (Acts 15:32), and Timothy was the recipient of spiritual gifts through prophecy (I Tim. 4:14; 1:18). The Apocalypse of John classes him as a significant prophet as well as an apostle. The prominent place of the prophet in the church is seen from the fact that God has "set" this office in the church and it is frequently mentioned in close connection with the apostles (I Cor. 12:28-29; Eph. 2:20; 3:5; 4:11). The purpose of the gift in the church is for (1) "edification, and exhortation, and consolation" (I Cor. 14:3-4); (2) learning (I Cor. 14:19, 31); (3) conviction of the unbelievers and convincing the unlearned (I Cor. 14:23-25); (4) special communication of revelation from God (Acts 13:1; I Cor. 14:29-30); (5) the occasional prediction of future events (Acts 21:10-11; I Tim. 4:1).

Warnings against false prophets occur frequently in the New Testament as well as in the Old. Jesus warned of their coming (Matt. 7:15; 24:11, 24); and the Apostle Paul predicted that false prophets would arise within the church at Ephesus after his departure (Acts 20:27-31); while John spoke of them as already present

---

[1]The offices and functions of prophet and preacher (as well as teacher) are never equated or confused in the New Testament, but are carefully distinguished (cf. I Cor. 12:28-29; 14:6; Eph. 4:11; Rom. 12:6-7; Acts 13:1). Moreover, the Greek terms differ for prophesying and preaching.

(I John 4:1-2). Finally, the Scriptures forewarn that the false prophet will play a significant role in the end-time events (Rev. 16:13; 19:20; 20:10).

PART II

THE BOOKS OF THE PROPHETS

INTRODUCTION

THE OLD TESTAMENT CANON is divided in the Hebrew Bible into three sections: the Law, the Prophets and the Writings. The second division consists of the Former Prophets: Joshua, Judges, Samuel and Kings; and the Latter Prophets, also called the Literary or Writing Prophets: Isaiah, Jeremiah, Ezekiel and the twelve Minor Prophets, which were regarded by the Hebrews as forming a single book called "The Twelve." They were first designated the Minor Prophets by the Latin church in the time of Augustine and Jerome on account of their brevity as compared to the so-called Major Prophets. The Twelve were grouped together by the Hebrews because they were small and as separate rolls might have become lost. Daniel, usually included among the Major Prophets in the English arrangement, appears in the third division of the Hebrew canon, the Writings. In the Alexandrian Canon of the Old Testament it appears among the Prophets, however. This classification of the book in the Hebrew text seems to be because of its historical emphasis, and because Daniel, while he had the prophetic gift and was a prophet, nevertheless appears in the capacity of a Hebrew statesman at the Babylonian court. Because of the prophetic nature of the book it belongs, therefore, as it is found in the LXX and English arrangement among the Prophets.

The chronological ministry of the prophets ranges from the ninth century B.C. (Obadiah and Joel) to the fifth (Malachi), and thus provides on the one hand a continuous witness concerning the contemporary moral, spiritual and political situation of Israel and Judah, as well as a prophetic testimony concerning the future of God's people, the Gentile nations, and the Messianic kingdom. Hosea stands first in the book of the Minor Prophets. In the arrangement of The Twelve in the Hebrew Bible the chronological principle which seems to have determined the over-all order was as follows: (1) the prophets of the Assyrian period were placed first (Hosea to Nahum); (2) then followed those of the Babylonian period (Habakkuk and Zephaniah); (3) the series closed with the three prophets of the Persian period after the exile (Haggai, Zechariah and Malachi). Hosea was probably placed first because it is the longest of

135

those books in the first series (whereas Obadiah would come first chronologically), and because he exercised his ministry much longer than all the other prophets. The Major Prophets were arranged chronologically: Isaiah, Jeremiah, Ezekiel.

The Hebrew prophets may be classified in several ways:

1. According to the recipient of the message:
   a. to Israel: Hosea, Amos
   b. to Judah: Joel, Isaiah, Micah, Zephaniah, Jeremiah, Habakkuk, Haggai, Zechariah, Malachi
   c. to Nineveh: Jonah, Nahum
   d. to Babylon: Daniel
   e. to the exiles: Ezekiel
   f. to Edom: Obadiah

2. According to the Hebrew text:
   a. Major Prophets: Isaiah, Jeremiah, Ezekiel
   b. Minor Prophets: The Twelve, in the following order: Hosea, Joel, Amos, Obadiah, Jonah, Micah, Nahum, Habakkuk, Zephaniah, Haggai, Zechariah, Malachi (Lamentations and Daniel are put in the Hagiographa, or Writings)

3. According to the Septuagint:
   a. Major Prophets: Isaiah, Jeremiah (Lamentations), Ezekiel, Daniel
   b. Minor Prophets: Hosea, Joel, Amos, Obadiah, Jonah, Micah, Nahum, Habakkuk, Zephaniah, Haggai, Zechariah, Malachi (this arrangement is followed by the English translations)

4. According to chronological periods:
   a. preexilic: Obadiah, Joel, Jonah, Hosea, Amos, Isaiah, Micah, Nahum, Zephaniah, Jeremiah, Habakkuk
   b. exilic: Daniel, Ezekiel
   c. postexilic: Haggai, Zechariah, Malachi

5. According to the periods of Gentile world power:
   a. Assyrian period: Obadiah, Joel, Jonah, Hosea, Amos, Isaiah, Micah, Nahum
   b. Babylonian period: Zephaniah, Jeremiah, Habakkuk, Daniel, Ezekiel
   c. Persian period: Haggai, Zechariah, Malachi

6. According to the dates of the prophets themselves (suggested date of the *approximate* beginning of the prophet's ministry[1]):
   a. Obadiah   845 B.C.

[1]The amount of confusion that prevails concerning the dates of the prophets is astounding, no two commentators being in precise agreement. The author feels that the above suggested dates are sufficiently substantiated by the evidence which follows as set forth in the introduction to each book.

b.	Joel	835
c.	Jonah	782
d.	Hosea	760
e.	Amos	760
f.	Isaiah	739
g.	Micah	735
h.	Nahum	650
i.	Zephaniah	640
j.	Jeremiah	627
k.	Habakkuk	609
l.	Daniel	605
m.	Ezekiel	593
n.	Haggai	520
o.	Zechariah	520
p.	Malachi	433

Chapter 9

OBADIAH

Servant of Yahweh

I. THE NATURE OF THE BOOK

OBADIAH, the shortest prophecy in the Old Testament (27 vv.), is concerned primarily with the punishment and destruction of Edom for her sins against Israel. The book follows Amos in the Hebrew canon, due perhaps to the reference to the dispossession of Edom near the close of that prophecy (Amos 9:12). Chronologically, however, the book stands as the earliest of the canonical prophets, dating from the ninth century B.C.

The occasion for the prophecy is to be found in verses 10-14 of the book. After denouncing the pride of Edom (vv. 1-4), the prophet predicts that nation's utter ruin (vv. 5-9), concluding with the warning "For the violence done to thy brother Jacob, shame shall cover thee, and thou shalt be cut off for ever" (v. 10). He then proceeds to rebuke Edom's unbrotherly conduct toward Jacob "in the day of his disaster" (v. 12), "in the day of ... calamity" (v. 13), and "in the day of distress" (v. 14), when Edom not only rejoiced in the calamity which had befallen Jerusalem, but also actually assisted the enemy in their affliction of Jacob.

The prophet's denunciation of Edom suggests that sin's chief element is pride (vv. 1-4). The fruits of sinful pride are self-exaltation and arrogant self-confidence. The rugged inaccessibility of their mountain fortress encouraged a false sense of security on the part of the Edomites and they considered themselves impregnable. From their habitation on high they threw down the challenge "Who shall bring me down to the ground?" (v. 3). God reminds them that the sinful pride of their hearts has deceived them, for in their arrogant confidence that they were impregnable from their enemies below, they were deluded into thinking themselves secure from every standpoint; but they had overlooked the God of heaven to whom they were quite vulnerably exposed. "Though thou mount on high as the eagle, and though thy nest be set among the stars, I will bring thee down from thence, saith Yahweh" (v. 4).

139

As Edom had treacherously dealt with Judah, her brother, so Edom would be betrayed by her friends and allies (v. 7). Edom's vaunted wisdom and might would fail her in the day when God would cut her off, for as Edom had aided in the plunder of Jerusalem, participated in the violence done against her, and rejoiced in her distress, Edom would reap the consequences of such treachery under the divine principle of retributive justice: "As thou hast done, it shall be done unto thee; thy dealing shall return upon thine own head" (v. 15; cf. Rom. 2:5-6).

The prophecy consists of a denunciation of Edom (vv. 1-16) and a promise of the future deliverance of God's people (vv. 17-21). Obadiah regards (1) the judgment upon Edom as a figure of the ultimate retribution upon all nations ("for the day of Yahweh is near upon all nations," (vv. 15-16) and (2) the restoration of Israel in Zion as predictive of the establishment of the kingdom of God ("and the kingdom shall be Yahweh's," v. 21). Eschatologically, Edom appears as representative of the heathen world regarded as hostile to God's kingdom. Retributive judgment is to fall upon her in the "day of the Lord."

II. THE DATE

Questions concerning the date and authorship of the prophets are usually considered together. However, for the sake of clarity they are discussed separately in this introduction. Problems of authorship, where they occur, are considered in the discussion of the problems of each book.

In order to ascertain a date for Obadiah an occasion must be found for the invasion and plunder of Jerusalem which, according to verses 11-14, occurred sometime previously. There are known to have been four such events in Old Testament history: (1) The earliest was an invasion by Shishak, king of Egypt, in 926 B.C. during the reign of Rehoboam of Judah (I Kings 14:25-26; II Chron. 12). This occasion is unlikely for two reasons: (a) Edom remained subject to the Hebrews at this time, and (b) there is no record in the Egyptian campaign of any such wholesale plunder and distress as is pictured in Obadiah. (2) During the reign of Jehoram of Judah (848-841) the Philistines and Arabians made a devastating attack upon Judah (II Chron. 21:16-17). This appears to be the most likely date for reasons which will follow. (3) Provoked by King Amaziah of Judah, Jehoash of Israel invaded Judah about 790 (II Kings 14; II Chron. 25). But this must be rejected since Obabiah 11 calls the invaders "strangers." (4) The destruction of Jerusalem by Nebuchadnezzar in 586. The final overthrow of Jerusalem in 586 is generally held by Old Testament critics to be the date and occasion for the prophecy.

In favor of a date around 845 for the invasion and plunder of Jerusalem during the reign of Jehoram rather than 586 are the following considerations: (1) Edom had revolted during the reign of Jehoram and was a bitter antagonist of Judah at this time (II Kings 8:20-22; II Chron. 21:8-20). (2) There is no mention in Obadiah of the deportation of the whole population as occurred in 586. (3) The captives were not taken to Babylon as in 586, but to Phoenicia and the West (Obad. 20). (4) All the later prophets who speak of the fall of Jerusalem and the captivity mention the Chaldeans, often including the name of Nebuchadnezzar himself, whereas Obadiah leaves the enemy unidentified. If Obadiah speaks of the destruction of Jerusalem in 586, such silence is inexplicable. (5) No reference is made to the total destruction of the city and temple which took place in 586.[1] (6) Amos (760) and Jeremiah (627) show an acquaintance with Obadiah, thus suggesting a preexilic origin for the prophecy. Compare Obadiah 14 with Amos 1:6; Obadiah 4 with Amos 9:2; Obadiah 19 with Amos 9:12. Jeremiah evidently quotes from Obadiah 1-6 in his book (49:7 ff.). Furthermore, Joel 3:3-6 (835) seems to allude to the same occasion described by Obadiah.

III. THE PROPHET

Nothing is known of the author of this brief prophecy except the name which in Hebrew means "servant of Yahweh." The name is not infrequent in the Old Testament. Obadiah was (1) an officer over the house of Ahab (I Kings 18:3); (2) one of the princes whom Jehoshaphat commissioned to teach the law in Judah (II Chron. 17:7); (3) one of the overseers who participated in the repairing of the temple under Josiah (II Chron. 34:12); (4) a priest in the time of Nehemiah (Neh. 10:5). Therefore, there is no ground for contending as some do that Obadiah is simply a symbolic name or pseudonym meaning "the servant [or prophet] of Yahweh." The contents of the prophecy indicate that he belonged to the kingdom of Judah (cf. vv. 10, 11-12, 17, 21).

IV. THE HISTORICAL BACKGROUND

The nation of Edom was descended from Esau (Gen. 25:30; 36:1 ff.). The Edomites lived in the rocky fortress of Mount Seir south of

---

[1]Obadiah 13 (ASV) points to a future calamity to befall the city, such words being inappropriate if the present disaster was that of 586 B.C.

Palestine, the capital of which was Sela (Petra), displacing the
original inhabitants, the Horites. The rugged inaccessibility of the
Edomites in their fortified mountain settlement caused them to feel
proud and secure, as Obadiah 1-9 indicates, scorning all threats to
their safety.

The enmity that existed between the Edomites and the Hebrews,
so graphically depicted in Obadiah's book, had its origin in Jacob's
triumph over his brother Esau in the matter of the birthright (Gen.
27), although their striving with one another is to be seen even at
their birth. While Jacob and Esau had become reconciled, it is
evident from Old Testament history that their descendants had not.
This is seen quite clearly in Edom's refusal of passage to Moses and
the children of Israel during the exodus march to Canaan. King Saul
later fought against Edom (I Sam. 14:47); and David, during his
reign, brought her into subjection (II Sam. 8:13-14). The Edomites
unsuccessfully tried to rebel under King Solomon (I Kings
11:14-22), but were unable to achieve freedom until their revolt
during the reign of Jehoram of Judah about 845 B.C. (II Kings
8:20-22). Outbreaks of conflict between the two nations continued
until the destruction of Jerusalem in 586 B.C. when the Edomites
encouraged its downfall (Ps. 137:7). The impending judgment of
God because of their cruelty toward and lack of compassion for their
brother Jacob is set forth in many Old Testament passages in addition
to Obadiah (Ezek. 25:12-14; Amos 1:11-12; Isa. 34:5 ff.; Jer. 49:7
ff.; Lam. 4:21-22).

By 312 B.C. the Nabataeans, an Arab people, had displaced the
Edomites from Petra as predicted by Obadiah. The Edomites then
occupied southern Judea which the Greeks called Idumaea. During
the Maccabean period John Hyrcanus subdued them, imposing upon
the Edomites (Idumaeans) Jewish law and circumcision. Julius Caesar appointed Antipater, an Idumaean, procurator of Judea in 47 B.C.;
and Herod, his son, became king of Judea in 37 B.C. The Idumaeans joined in the rebellion against Roman domination in A.D. 70 and
suffered the fate of the Jews in the destruction of Jerusalem by
Titus. From this time the Edomites disappear from history, thus
fulfilling the prophecy of Obadiah: "For the violence done to thy
brother Jacob, shame shall cover thee, and thou shalt be cut off for
ever" (v. 10; cf. v. 18).

V. Problems

Various views have been propounded concerning the authorship
of Obadiah. According to some critics the book is not a unity, but

simply a collection of oracles against Edom, and the authors are unknown. Eichhorn was the first to question the unity of the book, dating it after 586 B.C., regarding verses 17-21 an appendix from the time of Alexander Jannaeus.[2] Pfeiffer holds that the original oracle against Edom is contained in two places in the Old Testament: in Obadiah 1-9; and in Jeremiah 49:7-22. Both recensions are derived from a lost original. He dates verses 1-14, 15*b* about 460 B.C., and verses 16-21 as even later additions.[3] According to Ewald, the book is the work of an exilic prophet who used the older prophecy contained in verses 1-10 as his basis.[4] Wellhausen dated verses 2-9 as from the fifth century B.C.[5] About the only agreement among the negative critics is that verses 1-9 were written by some unknown prophet and became the basis for the later additions, verses 11-21. But there are no sound historical, literary or exegetical reasons for rejecting the book as a unity, the work of the Prophet Obadiah in the ninth century B.C.

A second problem might be designated as an ethical one. The book's critics call it "an indignant oration" and "intensely nationalistic," expressing not a prophetic revelation of God, but the ancient enmity and hate of the Israelites for the Edomites. However, there is nothing in the prophecy inconsistent with Old Testament ethics, for, on the basis of Genesis 12:3, judgment is quite often pronounced in the Old Testament upon the persecutors of God's people, and is graphically pictured as an absolute destruction. Compare for example the stern prophecies against Egypt, Babylonia, Assyria and others. Moreover, the offense of Edom was aggravated because of her blood kinship to the Hebrews (v. 10).

OUTLINE OF OBADIAH

I. THE DESTRUCTION OF EDOM PREDICTED	Verses 1-9
A. The Nations Called to Destroy Edom	1-2
B. The Inevitable Destruction of Entrenched Evil	3-4
C. Edom's Treasures to Be Taken Away	5-6
D. Edom's Destruction to Result from the Treachery of Her Allies	7
E. Edom's Wise and Mighty Men to Be Slaughtered	8-9
II. THE CAUSES FOR EDOM'S DESTRUCTION	Verses 10-14
A. Violence Done to Jacob	10

[2]Julias A. Bewer, "Introduction to Obadiah," *The International Critical Commentary,* ed. S. R. Driver *et al.,* p. 5.

[3]Robert H. Pfeiffer, *Introduction to the Old Testament,* pp. 585-86.

[4]Bewer, *ibid.*

[5]Aage Bentzen, *Introduction to the Old Testament,* p. 143.

Chapter 10

God is Love
Man is worth saving
Man is free to choose
Israel Chooses sin
God Punishes

JOEL Yahweh is God

I. The Nature of the Book

The occasion for the prophecy of Joel was a devastating locust plague and drought (chap. 1). On the basis of this natural calamity, the people are called to repentance in view of the imminent coming of the day of the Lord of which the present calamity is the forerunner. On the condition of their repentance, the nation is promised present security and blessing and a future outpouring of the Spirit of prophecy which will be showered upon all the faithful, after which shall ensue an era of righteousness and peace.

The prophecy may be divided into two parts: (1) the national call to repentance on the basis of God's judgments and the promise of deliverance and blessing in the day of the Lord (chaps. 1-2) and (2) judgment upon the enemies of Israel (chap. 3). In the first division the unprecedented plagues of locusts and drought are described, and all are called to lament their effect, especially the priests because of the necessity to suspend the daily sacrifices (chap. 1). This calamity is a token of the great day of the Lord which is to come. The army of locusts is a graphic picture of the future hosts of the Lord sent in judgment; but the threatened judgment may be averted by humble repentance (2:1-17). Then follow the promises of God to the repentant. God will deliver His people from present dangers and bestow upon them material blessings and prosperity (2:18-27). For the future, even greater blessings are promised. The coming day of the Lord will be a day of salvation for Israel and a day of terror and destruction for her foes (2:28—3:21).

In the Hebrew Bible, 2:28-32 of the English text forms 3:1-5; chapter 3 in the English text corresponds to chapter 4 of the Hebrew. With respect to the unity of the book, even the negative critics for the most part freely admit that it is the product of one author.

The central theme of the book is the emphasis upon the *day of the Lord*. This unique eschatological phrase "the day of Yahweh," which was first noted in Obadiah (v. 15), is reiterated again and again by the Prophet Joel (1:15; 2:1-2, 11, 31; 3:14, 18). Its spiritual significance is to be found in the nature and purpose of this day; it is to be a day of wrath and judgment upon the wicked and a day of salvation to the righteous.

The day of Yahweh will be heralded by divine portents: "And I will show wonders in the heavens and in the earth: blood, and fire, and pillars of smoke. The sun shall be turned into darkness, and the moon into blood, before the great and terrible day of Yahweh cometh" (Joel 2:30-31). Quite evidently such apocalyptic phenomena did not find fulfillment at Pentecost, but point to the latter days and the second advent, as our Lord Himself confirms in Matthew 24:29-30, where He uses the same apocalyptic imagery in connection with His second coming.

Such heavenly phenomena are frequently specified in the Old Testament as portents of the approaching day of judgment (Joel 2:2, 10-11; 3:15-16; Jer. 4:23; Amos 5:18; Zeph. 1:14-16; Ezek. 32:7; cf. Rev. 6:12). The prophetic usage of these apocalyptic figures always refers to a future day when God's wrath and judgment will fall upon the earth. It is to be a day of darkness and gloominess (Joel 2:2), wrath (Zeph. 1:15, 18), destruction (Joel 1:15) and punishment (Isa. 24:20-21). Hence, the wonders in heaven, and upon earth—blood, fire and smoke, as well as the darkening of the sun, moon and stars—are to be understood as literal precursors of the calamities and destruction announcing Christ's return in judgment in the day of the Lord.

There are two key time concepts in prophetic thought. One looks back to the exodus and God's judgment upon Egypt and the deliverance of Israel; the other is eschatological and has a future reference, and is designated in Scripture as the day of the Lord. It too is to be a day of judgment and a day of deliverance. It is the time of Yahweh's final intervention in history when He will judge the wicked, deliver the righteous, and establish His kingdom. On the basis of her election and subsequent deliverance from Egypt, Israel, although disobedient, was presumptuously considering only one aspect of the day of the Lord as applicable to her—that of salvation and deliverance: the day was to be a time of judgment when Yahweh would punish her enemies and destroy the nations. However, Amos corrects this misconception and warns sinful Israel that in contrast to the popular conception it is to be a day of darkness and not light—a day of punishment for the rebellious and disobedient in Israel as well (Amos 5:18-20). The Prophet Zephaniah also depicts the day as a time of wrath, a day of distress and anguish, a time of devastation and judgment upon all the wicked (Zeph. 1:14-18). This day of judgment will be universal and will fall upon all nations (cf. Zeph.

2-3; Amos 1:3—2:3; Joel 3; Zech. 12-14; Isa. 13:6, 9; 14:28-32; 17:1 ff.; 20:1-6; 31:1-5; Jer. 46:10; Ezek. 30:3 ff.). Joel 3 locates this event in the "valley of Jehoshaphat," a term which means in Hebrew "Yahweh judges." Here all nations will be gathered when God will execute judgment at the second advent in the day of the Lord.

However, the day of the Lord is not just a day of wrath upon the disobedient, declares Joel, but it is also to be a day in which God will preserve and deliver a remnant. In the great and terrible day of Yahweh "it shall come to pass, that whosoever shall call on the name of Yahweh shall be delivered; for in mount Zion and in Jerusalem there shall be those that escape, as Yahweh hath said, and among the remnant those whom Yahweh doth call" (Joel 2:32; cf. Zech. 14; Zeph. 3:8-20; Isa. 2, 11; 65-66; Amos 9:11-15; Ezek. 20:33-44, etc.). Thus the day of the Lord is that day when Christ returns to reveal His power, majesty and glory both in judgment and salvation—it is to be a day of wrath and a day of grace.

II. THE DATE

The book is undated in the superscription, which has led scholars to suggest dates ranging from early preexilic times to the late postexilic date of 350 B.C. as maintained by R. H. Pfeiffer. Critical scholars favor a postexilic date based upon the following arguments:

1. Judah and Jerusalem alone are the subject of the prophecy. The prophet does not once mention northern Israel, which would be inexplicable if the northern kingdom were still in existence. "Israel," where the term occurs (2:27; 3:2, 16), is used generically for the kingdom of Judah.

2. Joel makes no mention of a king or royal princes; he mentions only priests and elders as officials, and the priests and priestly offerings are prominent. This is to be expected if the book is postexilic, when such conditions prevailed, when the nation was without a king and priestly leadership was prominent.

3. There is no mention of idolatrous worship, which the preexilic prophets constantly rebuke. This implies a time when the nation is united religiously.

4. The enemies of Judah are the nations collectively who are assembled outside Jerusalem destined for defeat by Yahweh. This is a prominent feature in the later prophets (e.g., Ezek. 38-39; Zech. 14). The earlier prophets speak of specific nations as enemies of Judah, such as Assyria and Babylon.

5. Joel 3:2 is said to refer to the Babylonian captivity which is past.

6. The mention of the Grecians (Javan) in 3:6 to whom Jewish

slaves were sold is said to suit the late date for Joel, since it is unlikely that the Hebrews would have known of the Greeks before the exile.

7. The apocalyptic portion of Joel (1:15; 2:1-11, 20, 28-32; 3:1-20) depicting judgment upon the nations, deliverance of Jerusalem and establishment of the millennial kingdom, which has close affinities with Zechariah 9-14 (dated after 200 B.C. by the critics), indicates a date not earlier than 200 B.C. for this material when apocalyptic literature flourished in Palestine during the last two centuries B.C. Thus some critics, as Oesterley and Robinson and Bewer, view Joel as a book of composite authorship, the original postexilic prophecy of Joel being added to by an "apocalyptic editor" somewhat later. Most critics, however, while arguing for a postexilic date for the book, nevertheless insist upon its unity of authorship.[1]

These arguments for a late date for Joel are inconclusive, however, and a preexilic date for the book during the reign of Joash of Judah (*c.* 835) is highly probable for the following reasons:

1. The argument that the northern kingdom of Israel is not mentioned, which is said to prove that it has already been destroyed (722), is at best an argument from silence. Moreover, the writer is concerned with only the chosen nation of Judah and not the apostate kingdom in the north.

2. The absence of the mention of a king by Joel is not unusual, since neither do Obadiah, Jonah, Nahum and Habakkuk, all of whom were preexilic prophets, mention a king. Moreover, the prominence of the priests with no mention of a king is quite easily explained from the political situation which prevailed from 841 to 835 when Athaliah usurped the throne of Judah upon the death of her husband, King Ahaziah. During this period of political upheaval, Joash, the legitimate heir to the throne, was in seclusion and was a minor under the guardianship of Jehoiada, the high priest. Later when Joash ascended to the throne in 835 he ruled under the regency of the high priest, which explains the absence of his name in the superscription (Joel 1:1) and the prominence of the priests (see discussion under Historical Background).

3. Lack of any mention of idolatry carries little weight for dating the book. Joel does not rebuke moral and social sins either. Furthermore, idolatry would not be as great a problem in Judah during the ninth century B.C. as it was in Israel as a result of the earlier influence under Jeroboam and Ahab.

4. The prophecy in chapter 3 of the future universal judgment

---

[1]E.g., Robert H. Pfeiffer, *Introduction to the Old Testament,* pp. 574-75.

upon all nations, rather than the mention of some specific enemies of Judah, does not prove a postexilic date, but is in complete harmony with the eschatological nature of chapters 2-3. However, the Prophet Joel does in fact make specific reference to certain enemies who will be the object of God's judgment: the Phoenicians, Philistines, Egyptians and Edomites. Moreover, the very naming of these particular nations is strong evidence for a preexilic date for the book, inasmuch as they were the early preexilic enemies of Judah, not the later nations of Assyria, Babylonia and Persia.

5. Joel 3:2 is not an allusion to the Babylonian exile, since the whole context in chapters 2-3 is quite clearly eschatological, the verse in question being a prophetic reference to the present-day Diasopora of Israel which began with the destruction of Jerusalem in A.D. 70.

6. The mention of the Grecians (Javan) this early is not impossible, since they are mentioned in archaeological records dating from the eighth century B.C.

7. Finally, the position of the book in the Hebrew canon between Hosea and Amos suggests a preexilic date.

III. THE PROPHET

The Prophet Joel's name means "Yahweh is God." There is no information concerning the prophet outside the book itself, and his birthplace and conditions of life are unknown. He was the son of Pethuel, who is otherwise unknown. He was doubtless from Judah and possibly a native of Jerusalem (1:9; 2:15-17, 23, 32; 3:1). Some have thought him to be of the priestly line because of his knowledge of and references to the temple, the sacrifices and the priesthood. However, there is no necessity for this presupposition, since he does not include himself among the priests in 1:13-14; 2:17. His style is clear, fluent and of high lyrical quality. At the same time his descriptions are graphic, terse and quite picturesque. As a servant of God he emphasizes the need of prayer, fasting and repentance to avert divine judgment. He has sometimes been called the Prophet of Pentecost because of his prediction of the outpouring of the Holy Spirit (Acts 2).

IV. THE HISTORICAL BACKGROUND

Sometime toward the middle of the ninth century B.C. a locust swarm invaded Judah, more ominous and catastrophic than any that had ever been experienced before, which sounded the alarm for a call to repentance in view of a greater judgment to come. The prophet's call to the priests and ministers of the altar (1:13), while there is no mention of a king in the superscription, indicates that he exercised his prophetic office in Judah quite probably in the time of the boy king, Joash, about 835 B.C., when Jehoiada, his uncle who was the high priest, acted as regent (II Kings 11). Upon learning of the death of Ahaziah, Athaliah the queen mother, daughter of Ahab and Jezebel, put to death all her grandchildren except the youngest, Joash, who was taken by his aunt Jehosheba and the high priest Jehoiada and secreted for six years in the temple precincts. At the end of this time, Jehoiada enlisted the aid of the captains of the royal guard and on a predetermined day brought the young king forth and crowned him ruler over Judah at the age of seven. The ensuing celebration attracted the attention of Athaliah, who was quickly disposed of by the guards when she made an appearance at the temple.

It was apparently during some part of the young king's seclusion or early reign that Judah was stricken by the locust plague and drought; hence, Joel made his appeal to the people and priests, with no reference to the royal house.

V. PROBLEMS

One of the problems of the book is concerned with chapter 2. After a devastating locust plague and a drought are described in chapter 1, another invasion of locusts is predicted in chapter 2. The problem of chapter 2 may be stated as follows: Is the locust plague of chapter 2 to be interpreted literally, allegorically, or apocalyptically and symbolically? That is, does Joel in chapter 2 describe God's judgment in the form of another *actual* locust plague? Or does he describe under the *figure* of locusts a future invasion by an army from the north? Three interpretations of the book have been suggested.

The *allegorical* interpretation was advocated by the church Fathers, the Jewish rabbis and later interpreters such as Hengstenberg and Pusey. Pusey suggests that the prophet means something more than a literal locust plague in the form of a great scourge of God upon the nation. Under the figure of the locusts he speaks of great future judgments. The four kinds of locusts in chapter 1 are to be identified with the four invasions of Israel by her enemies: Assyria, Babylonia, Greece and Rome. Chapters 2 and 3 delineate in greater detail these judgments upon Israel and the church which culminate in the affliction through Antichrist in the end of the age.[2] The locusts of chapter 1 are typical and prophetic of the events of history during the "times of the Gentiles" from the kingdom of Babylon to the overthrow of the final Gentile world power (Dan. 2). Chapters 2 and

2E. B. Pusey, *The Minor Prophets,* I, 159-221.

3 describe the events of Daniel's "seventieth week" (Dan. 9) and the establishment of the millennial kingdom.

However, it would appear that the locusts in chapter 1 are to be understood literally, since there is nothing in the description of the events of this chapter to suggest otherwise. On the other hand, such is not the case in chapters 2-3, where apocalyptic imagery abounds, and where the locusts of chapter 2, as is shown later, are symbolic of a greater judgment to come.

The arguments for a *literal* locust plague in chapter 2 are as follows:

1. Locusts are one of the instruments of divine judgment for Israel's sins as predicted in Deuteronomy 28:38-39, 42; I Kings 8:37.

2. Joel's description agrees in detail with an actual locust plague which is common to that part of the world.

3. They devour the vines, strip the bark from the trees, and consume the vegetation of the land. There is no reference to death, plunder, the destruction of cities and the taking of captives, as would be the case if Joel were describing an invasion of Palestine by a literal army. And when restoration is promised it has reference only to the damage to the land and crops, not to the rebuilding of cities and the healing of the ravages of warfare.

4. The locusts are described under the figure of horses and horsemen (2:4 ff.), not vice versa. Hence, since the locusts themselves are compared to an army they cannot also be symbolical of a literal army. That is, if Joel describes the locusts as being *like* horses, they cannot also be symbolic of horses, which in effect would have him say "horses are like horses." Thus the prophet uses a simile to compare a literal locust with a horse, or a plague of locusts to an invasion by horsemen. The prophet would not have compared a real army with itself (cf. 2:4-7).

5. The invaders are called an army in 2:11, it is true, but they are identified with the locusts of chapter 1 in 2:25.

Therefore, the predicted calamity of 2:1-11 was to be a judgment of the same nature, although to a greater degree, as that which they had already experienced (chap. 1). The day of the Lord is imminent and will be ushered in by a locust plague more terrible and devastating than that which, according to chapter 1, Judah had recently experienced.

Some who advocate the literal view *idealize* the locusts of chapter 2. The actual locust plague of chapter 1 suggested to Joel the imagery by which he described the day of the Lord in chapter 2. In chapter 2 the locusts are idealized; "they are creatures of the imagination, invested with appalling size and power, the prototype of the 'apocalyptic' locusts of Rev. 9:3-10."[3]

The *apocalyptic* interpretation likewise views the locust plague of chapter 1 literally, an actual historical occurrence which was the occasion for Joel's prophecy. However, chapter 2 is held to be symbolic of a literal, future invasion by the enemies of Judah. On the basis of this natural calamity, the nation, in chapter 2, is called to repentance in view of the imminency of the day of the Lord which this present devastation foreshadows. A more terrible judgment than that of the present calamity is described in chapter 2 *under the imagery drawn from the locust plague of chapter 1*. With the recent plague as the background, the prophet uses this calamity as the *symbol* for his apocalyptic imagery in chapter 2.

In favor of the apocalyptic and symbolic interpretation are several significant considerations.

1.   The imagery of chapter 2 far exceeds the description of a locust plague. A literal plague of locusts is not accompanied by the cataclysmic phenomena as described in Joel, such as an earthquake, the shaking of the heavens and the darkening of the sun, moon and stars (2:10; cf. vv. 30-31; Matt. 24:29). It is true that locusts are one of the instruments of divine judgment upon Israel according to Deuteronomy 28:38-39. This is precisely what we have recorded in Joel 1! (cf. Amos 4:9). However, the language of chapter 2 is far too ominous to be limited to a literal plague of locusts.

2.   The absence of any mention of personal injury to the inhabitants is in harmony with the imagery of locusts, since it would be inconsistent with the figure to attribute destruction to other than vegetation. However, it should be noted that the assault is said to be upon the city, its inhabitants and their houses (6-9).

3.   It has been objected that since the locust plague is compared to an invasion by an army it cannot signify a literal army itself. This would have the effect of comparing an army with itself. However, this objection is faulty in that it overlooks the remarkable way in which the prophet uses symbolism. In chapter 2 the locusts under the appearance of a hostile army can be intended by the prophet to suggest that locusts are the *symbols* and *forerunners* of a greater devastation by Judah's enemies in the latter days. It cannot be insisted upon that such usage would be a violation of the use of simile, since the prophet, with the recent plague of chapter 1 as the background, uses *that* calamity as the basis of his imagery for the apocalyptic symbolism of chapter 2. In nonbiblical Near Eastern

[3]S. R. Driver, *An Introduction to the Literature of the Old Testament,* p. 308.

literature, armies are often compared to locusts or vice versa in both number and destructiveness. This can be seen in the Ugaritic legend of King Keret, and in the Egyptian texts of the inscriptions of Ramses II and of Merneptah. Many passages in Assyrian royal annals compare invading armies to locusts.[4]

4. The invaders of chapter 2 are actually called: "people" (2:2, 17); an "army" (2:11); the "nations" (2:17); "the northern one" (2:20).

5. In 2:17 the "nations" are depicted as seeking to rule over Judah. (The marginal reading of the ASV does not sufficiently fit the context, nor is such usage for this passage supported by the Brown-Driver-Briggs Hebrew lexicon.) The term "nations" could hardly refer to mere locusts in such a context, but is to be equated with the nations of chapter 3, whom all interpreters take to be actual nations and enemies of Judah.

6. The army of 2:11 cannot be identified with the "army" of 2:25 except in a typical way, but is to be equated with the "northern [army]" of 2:20. The "army" in 2:25 could just as easily refer to the plague in chapter 1:4 where the same terms occur. Joel 2:21-27 does not necessarily have to be limited to the future millennial blessings, but could also encompass a present promise to the repentant, in view of the plague of chapter 1. Such a twofold application is by no means uncommon in prophetic literature (cf. Zech. 1:7-17).

7. The invasion is from the north (v. 20), whereas locusts do not enter Palestine from that direction.

8. It can hardly be said of locusts that they had "done great things" (v. 20) in contrast with Yahweh who "hath done great things" (v. 21).

9. The term "northern one" would be an unsuitable designation for locusts (v. 20). The term in Hebrew is an adjective meaning "northern," but with the definite article prefixed, as it occurs here, it is a noun meaning "the northerner," or "the northern one." Even critical interpreters admit that the term is unsuitable to designate literal locusts (e.g., Driver, Bewer, Pfeiffer).

The "north" is a technical term in the Old Testament which often appears in passages of an apocalyptic nature and in such contexts is always symbolic of the enemies of Israel. In this connection it is also used to indicate the direction from which calamity and misfortune came upon Palestine. Assyria and Babylon came out of the north against the Hebrew nation and appear in Scripture not only as

[4]See John A. Thompson, *Journal of Near Eastern Studies,* XIV, No. 1 (January, 1955), 52-55, "Joel's Locusts in the Light of Near Eastern Parallels," although the author concludes that these facts strengthen the literal view!

contemporary enemies of Israel, but also as typical of her end-time foe who was to come out of the north, that is, the eschatological "northerner." (Cf. Zech. 6:8; Jer. 1:14-15; 6:1, 22; Ezek. 38:6, 15; 39:2; Isa. 14:31; Zeph. 2:13.)

A second problem is concerned with the *fulfillment* of Joel 2:28-32. The question to be answered is: Was Joel 2:28-32 completely fulfilled or only partly fulfilled on the day of Pentecost as recorded in Acts 2? Five views have been proposed in solution to this problem.

The first theory may be designated as the *termination at Pentecost* view. Grotius, for example, held that the fulfillment of Joel's prophecy (2:28-32) is to be sought for in certain events of Joel's own time, as well as on Pentecost at which time the prophecy terminated. Several Jewish interpreters, according to Keil, saw in the prophecy a reference to some event in Joel's own time, with its fulfillment terminating at the advent of the Messiah.[5]

Others, however, contend that the prophecy of Joel found *fulfillment at Pentecost*. Advocates of this interpretation, of whom E. J. Young is representative, hold that this is

> a prophecy of the Messianic age, when the Spirit of God is poured out upon all flesh, and the Gospel will be offered to all . . . . The fulfillment of this prophecy of grace is found in Acts 2:17 when the Holy Spirit was outpoured at Pentecost.[6]

In his exposition of the Prophet Joel, A. C. Gaebelein proposes a third interpretation which may be designated as the *nonfulfillment* or *eschatological* view:

> When the Holy Spirit came on the day of Pentecost it was not in fulfillment of Joel's prophecy. This prophecy has never been fulfilled nor will it be fulfilled during this present age, in which the church is being formed . . . . After this is accomplished the Lord will begin His relationship with His earthly people [Israel]; when He appears in His day then they will experience the fulfillment of this great prediction.[7]

A fourth interpretation, the *typical fulfillment* view, which sees the prophecy of Joel as being fulfilled "in earnest" at Pentecost, but not fully realized until the millennium, is set forth in the Jamieson, Fausset and Brown commentary on the Old Testament. Commenting on the term "afterward" in 2:28, Fausset writes:

> . . . "in the last days" (Isaiah 2:2) under Messiah, *after* the invasion and deliverance of Israel from the *Northern army.* Having heretofore stated the outward blessings, he now raised their

[5]C. F. Keil and F. Delitzsch, *The Twelve Minor Prophets, Biblical Commentary on the Old Testament,* trans. James Martin, I, 216.

[6]Edward J. Young, *An Introduction to the Old Testament,* pp. 247-48.

[7]A. C. Gaebelein, *The Prophet Joel,* p. 136.

minds to the expectation of extraordinary spiritual blessings, which constitute the true restoration of God's people (Isaiah 44:3). Fulfilled in the earnest (Acts 2:17) on Pentecost; among the Jews and . . . Gentiles: hereafter more fully at the restoration of Israel (Isaiah 54:13; Jeremiah 31:9, 34; Ezekiel 39:29; Zechariah 12:10). . . . That the promise is not *restricted* to the first Pentecost appears from Peter's own words: "The promise is (not only) unto you and your children (but also) to *all that are afar off* (both in space and time), even as many as the Lord our God shall call" (Acts 2:39).[8]

    5 A fifth view might be called the *continuous fulfillment* view. The prophecy of Joel will have continuous fulfillment from Pentecost to eschatological times. R. A. Torrey advocates this view. Referring to the promise of Christ in Acts 1:4-5, 8 which the disciples experienced at Pentecost, he writes:

The baptism with the Holy Spirit is an operation of the Holy Spirit distinct from and subsequent and additional to His regenerating work . . . an impartation of power, and the one who receives it is fitted for service. . . . [It is] not merely for the apostles, nor merely for those of the apostolic age, but for "all that are afar off, even as many as the Lord our God shall call," as well: i.e., it is for every believer in every age of the Church's history.[9]

This we take to be the correct interpretation, although most expositors ignore a future application of the prophecy, confining the fulfillment of Joel's prophecy (2:28-32) to the day of Pentecost and perhaps continuing in some merely mystical or symbolic sense throughout the church age. Such an interpretation requires not only a spiritualization of much of the prophecy of Joel, especially the references to the wonders in heaven and on earth, blood, fire and smoke, a darkened sun and blood-red moon, but also an application of the day of the Lord (v. 31) to the destruction of Jerusalem in A.D. 70 with the subsequent scattering of the Jews.

It is interesting that many expositors use the word "fulfillment" in connection with this prophecy, even saying that Peter on the day of Pentecost said that the outpouring of the Holy Spirit that day was a fulfillment of Joel's prophecy. Actually the term "fulfillment" was not used at all by Peter, whereas in many passages of the New Testament where the writer intends to convey the idea of fulfillment it is clearly stated "that it might be fulfilled." What Peter said was "This is that which was spoken by the prophet Joel" (Acts 2:16). By the phrase "this is that" he refers to their utterances as that which

[8]R. Jamieson, A. R. Fausset and David Brown, *A Commentary, Critical and Explanatory, on the Old and New Testaments,* I, 695-96.
[9]R. A. Torrey, *What the Bible Teaches,* pp. 271-78.

was predicted by Joel, but cautiously omits the use of the term "fulfillment." The outpouring of the Holy Spirit was taking place as Joel had predicted, declared Peter to the scoffing Jews who had charged that the disciples were drunken. However, he did not say that the event was the full and final completion of Joel's prediction; on the contrary, he insisted that their experience was but the *beginning* of a continuous fulfillment, that the "gift of the Holy Spirit" is for all who ask (Luke 11:13). "For to you is the promise, and to your children, *and to all that are afar off, even as many as the Lord our God shall call unto him*" (Acts 2:39; cf. 8:14-17; 9:17; 10:44-47; 11:15-17; 19:1-7; Gal. 3:14).

OUTLINE OF JOEL

EIGHTH CENTURY
PROPHETS

THE LONG MINISTRY of Elisha had ended at the beginning of the eighth century B.C. Contemporary with him in the ninth century had been the first two literary or writing prophets, Obadiah (845) and Joel (835). The prophets of the eighth century B.C. were: Jonah (782), Hosea (760), Amos (760), Isaiah (739) and Micah (735). On the contemporary scene a new era of Assyrian conquest began with the rise of Tiglath-pileser III, which was to have an unprecedented effect upon the life of Israel, as well as upon the other nations of the Near Eastern world of that period. The significant influence of the nation of Assyria upon the course of Israel's history during the eighth century B.C. is quite evident from the extensive references to Assyria by prophets of this period.

THE SIGNIFICANCE OF THE EIGHTH CENTURY B.C. IN ISRAEL

There are several reasons why the eighth century B.C. requires special consideration. First of all, this period is an unusually significant era in the history of the Hebrew people due to the fact that a considerable number of prominent Hebrew kings reigned during this time in Judah, among whom were Joash, Uzziah, Ahaz and Hezekiah. On the other hand, during the eighth century B.C. the last nine rulers of the northern kingdom of Israel reigned prior to its downfall to Assyria in 722. The most notable of these rulers was Jeroboam II. In no other century did so many important monarchs rule over Judah, nor so many comparatively insignificant ones over the northern kingdom of Israel.

Israel was, in the second place, unusually successful during the first part of the eighth century B.C. The independence as well as the territory of both kingdoms was still intact at the beginning and during the first half of the eighth century. Under Jeroboam II Israel had restored to her sovereignty most of the dominion formerly subject to Solomon (II Kings 14:25, 28). Judah was equally prosperous under the reign of Uzziah (II Chron. 26:1-15) and attained a considerable degree of wealth, influence and culture. Before the eighth century was to close, all these achievements would be lost, the northern kingdom would fall to the Assyrians, and Judah herself would begin to decline.

Furthermore, during this period three great crises confronted the Hebrew nation, each of which involved the nation of Assyria:

1.   The Syro-Ephraimitic Crisis, 734 B.C.

In 734, Rezin, king of Syria, and Pekah, king of Israel, formed a military alliance to oppose Tiglath-pileser III, king of Assyria. Judah, under Ahaz, apparently refused to join this resistance against Assyrian aggression, whereupon Syria and Israel moved against Judah. Ahaz, in alarm, appealed to Assyria for aid in spite of Isaiah's warning to trust in God for deliverance. Ahaz' refusal brought forth the great Immanuel prophecy of Isaiah 7 (cf. II Kings 16). Tiglath-pileser captured Damascus, the Syrian capital, slew Rezin, its king, and carried its population captive to Kir (II Kings 15:29). He invaded Israel and, after ravaging its northern and eastern districts, carrying off many captives (the Galilee captivity), made Pekah a vassal of Assyria.

2.   The Fall of Samaria, 722 B.C.

Pekah, after a reign of twenty years, was assassinated in 732 by Hoshea, who then became Israel's last king. Upon the death of Tiglath-pileser in 727, Hoshea, weary of paying heavy tribute to Assyria, turned to Egypt for help and withheld his annual tribute. The new Assyrian king, Shalmaneser V, invaded Israel and laid siege to Samaria. During the three-year siege Shalmaneser died and Sargon II, his successor, continued the siege, Samaria falling to him in 722. The fall of Samaria resulted in the utter collapse of the northern kingdom of Israel, and its territory became a part of the Assyrian Empire.

3.   The Sennacherib Crisis, 701 B.C.

Sennacherib succeeded his father Sargon in 705. As often happened upon a change of sovereigns, the subject nations under Assyria, including Palestine, revolted. When Sennacherib had suppressed the rebellions in the East, he turned to the West once more, subjugating the peoples. Hezekiah, king of Judah, sent messengers to Lachish to pay tribute to Assyria (II Kings 18). But the Assyrian monarch decided to lay siege to the city and plunder its resources, whereupon Isaiah was sent by God to assure the king of Judah that the city would stand. As the Assyrian army lay encamped about Jerusalem the angel of the Lord went forth and smote 185,000 in the Assyrian army, and the humiliated Sennacherib was compelled to return to Assyria (II Kings 19; Isa. 36-37).

Finally, this is an important century because its first half was the period in which Jonah, a prophet of Israel, was sent to the chief city of Assyria, Nineveh, with his stern message of judgment. Perhaps through the ministry of this prophet God proposed to turn the Assyrian nation temporarily from her unparalleled wickedness and bloodthirstiness, thus delaying her actual conquest of Israel until the time intended by Him later in the century (722). Including Elisha, whose ministry extends into this period, God raised up six prophets during the eighth century B.C. to proclaim His word to the nation.

Chapter 11

JONAH

I. The Nature of the Book

THE BOOK OF JONAH contains two events of supernatural significance: the account of the prophet being swallowed by a fish, and the
gourd which miraculously grew overnight. To these might be added
an event of even greater import—the repentance of the pagan city of
Nineveh as a consequence of the preaching of an unknown Hebrew
prophet. Because of these events the book's historicity has been
called into question and the prophecy variously viewed as mythological, symbolical, fictional, allegorical, and as a poetic parable much
like Isaiah's parable of the vineyard (Isa. 5) or the parable of the
good Samaritan.

The *mythological* view, which regards the fish episode as parallel
to such tales known the world over in which a person upon being
swallowed by a sea monster and remaining in it for a period of time
is later delivered from it unharmed, may be dismissed as unworthy of
serious consideration. H. Schmidt in his book *Jona* cites alleged
parallels from the mythical stories of the Greeks, such as Hercules'
deliverance of Hesione from the sea monster, and the rescue of An-
dromeda by Perseus from the same fate, and suggests that such tales
of miraculous deliverances were common along the coast of Palestine. The author of Jonah took this impressive motif and used it to
illustrate his own religious tale concerning Israel.[1]

Oesterley and Robinson view the book as purely *symbolic.* The
three-day sojourn of Jonah in the great fish is symbolical of Nineveh, the "great city of three days' journey"; his being vomited
out symbolizes the prophet going out of the repentant city as he was
out of place there. The name Jonah, which means "dove," was chosen
by the author because Nineveh was the chief sanctuary of the goddess
Ishtar whose sacred bird was the dove. The author was a propagan-
dist whose purpose was to teach the "universal Fatherhood of God,"

[1]Hans Schmidt, *Jona, eine untersuchung zur Vergleichenden Religion-
ageschichte* (Gottingen: 1907) follows L. Frobenius on this concept.

and as a consequence sought to overcome the proud, narrow nationalism of the Jewish nation.

Robert H. Pfeiffer dismisses the book as being neither an actual history nor an allegory, but contends that it is a *fiction—a religious short story with a moral.* The author, drawing upon ancient myths and folktales, making use of the legendary stories of Elijah and Elisha, and borrowing from the books of Joel and Judith, builds his plot around Jonah, the main character, in order to teach a moral lesson, that God's love and compassion are not restricted to the Jews but are extended to the Gentile nations as well. (Cf. 4:3 with I Kings 19:4*b*; 4:5 with I Kings 19:4*a*, 5*a*; 3:5 with Joel 1:13 f.; 3:9 with Joel 2:14; 4:2 with Joel 2:13; 3:7-8 with Judith 4:10.)

Basically, however, there are two prevailing views of the book: the allegorical, or parabolic, and the literal, or historical. One school of opinion (Cheyne, G. A. Smith *et al.*) claims that the book of Jonah is an *allegory* concerning Israel, and is no more to be taken literally than the allegories of Ezekiel or the parables of Jesus. In this view, proposed by negative criticism, Jonah symbolizes Israel. Israel was called to make God known to the world both in message and by conduct. But Israel failed in her responsibility and was "swallowed up" in the Babylonian exile (cf. Jer. 51:34, 44). As Jonah was delivered from the fish, so too Israel in her affliction turned and prayed and was liberated in order that she might accomplish her divinely ordained mission to the world. After liberation, however, she too was dissatisfied with Yahweh's long-suffering with the Gentile nations and impatiently awaited their overthrow and destruction. Bewer also follows this view of the book, contending that it is a *parable:*

> Surely this is not the record of actual historical events nor was it ever intended as such. It is a sin against the author to treat as literal prose what he intended as poetry. . . . His story is thus a story with a moral, a parable, a prose poem like the story of the Good Samaritan.[2]

But there is no valid reason for regarding the book as a parable or an allegory as the following considerations indicate:

1. It should be noted, in contradiction to the parabolic interpretation, that the book presents itself as an authentic *historical narrative,* not a parable (which is a simple comparison), for a parable would be easily discernible as such. An allegory, on the other hand, is a symbolical narrative in which every detail has a figurative meaning.

[2]Julius A. Bewer, "Jonah," *The International Critical Commentary,* ed. S. R. Driver *et al.,* p. 4.

Moreover, in the allegories of the Bible the interpretation is either given or clearly implied (cf. Ezek. 15). These features are noticeably absent in the book of Jonah. Chapter 4 in which God teaches Jonah a lesson from the gourd is not in contradiction to this. The account is not an allegory, but was an actual experience, as the entire book purports to be, by which God taught the prophet (and Israel) a spiritual lesson. As with the parable, an allegory is easily discernible as such and a writer intends his readers to recognize this literary form when so employed. (However, such a literary form must be superimposed on the book of Jonah which stresses its historical nature.)

2.   Ancient Jews regarded the book as historical (cf. Tobit 14:4 ff.; Josephus, Ant. IX, 12:2), as have the Christians.

3.   Jonah himself, on the basis of Scripture testimony, was an actual historical person whose prophetic ministry is recorded in II Kings 14:25.

4.   Christ believed in the historicity of the book, testifying both to the miracle of Jonah's three days' imprisonment in the fish, as well as to the prophet's successful mission to the Ninevites (Matt. 12:38-41; 16:4; Luke 11:29-32).

It is pure conjecture to maintain, as critical interpreters do, that Christ's words connecting Jonah's experience with His own resurrection, and His reference to Nineveh's repentance, do not imply His belief in the actual historicity of these events. The critics maintain that He merely accommodated Himself to the inaccurate views of His contemporaries. On the contrary, His references to Jonah do imply such a belief; and to suggest that His ethics were such as to comingle truth with error by the device of accommodation, or, as others have suggested, to deny the accuracy of Jesus' knowledge of past events, is markedly out of harmony with the biblical view of Christ.

Conservative Christians have always held to the *literal historicity* of the book, viewing it as an actual account of the experiences of the Prophet Jonah in the eighth century B.C. Those who hold the book to be historical also view the prophecy as having *symbolic* and *typical* reference to Israel and Christ. Hengstenberg, Lange and Keil, for instance, admit a symbolico-typical character to the book. Lange, however, places such an emphasis upon the symbolical aspect as it pertains to Israel that he practically interprets the prophecy allegorically, although he applies it typically to Christ. Jonah, he believes, symbolizes Israel; and Nineveh represents the heathen world to whom Israel has the mission of proclaiming God's truth and law. The experiences of Jonah are precisely those of Israel. Hence, the story is recorded primarily to show God's concern for all nations and to impress upon Israel her missionary obligations to the world.

However, while it is true that the book has symbolic and typical application, it should be emphasized that the fundamental purpose of Israel's calling was not to be a missionary nation to the world of her day in the literal sense of making converts to the religion of Israel. But the Old Testament shows that Israel was primarily called (1) to be the recipient and custodian of the true revelation of God (Exodus 3; Ps. 147:19-20; Rom. 3:1-2); (2) to exhibit to the world true religion and morality through her *separation* from other nations and by her obedience, righteousness and holiness (Deut. 7:6; Lev. 20:24-26); (3) to prepare the way for the Messiah (Gen. 12:1-3; II Sam. 7; Rom. 1:3; Gal. 3:16). Such Old Testament prophecies as Isaiah 2; 45:22; 66:18; Micah 4; Zechariah 8, 14, concerning the salvation of the Gentile nations, clearly have regard, not to the Old Testament dispensation, but to the future Messianic era as the context of these passages indicates. True missionary work could only come after the cross (John 12:20-24; Acts 1:4-8). Israel infrequently made proselytes, but there is no command to do so as a missionary effort in all the Old Testament.[3]

Therefore, the mission of Jonah, as Keil correctly observes, had symbolical and typical significance which was intended to enlighten Israel in regard to the *future* adoption of the repentant heathen nations into the fellowship of the blessings of salvation prepared in Israel for all nations (cf. Gen. 12:1-3). The object of Jonah's mission to Nineveh was to combat a delusion on the part of Israel whereby, as the result of her election and separation from the heathen, she had developed a false view concerning her responsibilities to the Gentiles. The attitude of Israel toward God's design to show mercy to the Gentiles is depicted by Jonah's response to God's commission to go preach to Nineveh (chap. 1) and his reaction to God's removal of their judgment upon their repentance (4:1-4). The manner in which God reproved the prophet for his anger because Nineveh had been

[3]This, of course, does not overlook the fact that there were always "strangers" (non-Israelites) dwelling in Palestine who through circumcision and observance of the Mosaic law entered into the blessings and privileges of the covenant (Exodus 12:48-49; Deut. 23:3-8), but the initiative was always theirs, being attracted to Judaism for various reasons, sometimes merely out of expediency. Not until the period of the Pharisees were positive efforts made to proselytize Gentiles, and these efforts were rebuked by Christ because of their improper motivation and character (Matt. 23:15).

spared (4:9-11) was intended to show Israel the magnitude of divine compassion which embraces all mankind.[4]

This symbolical meaning, however, does not exhaust the deeper significance of the history of Jonah that culminates in the typical character of Jonah's three days' imprisonment in the belly of the fish which Christ applied to His own death and entombment: "For as Jonah was three days and three nights in the belly of the whale; so shall the Son of man be three days and three nights in the heart of the earth" (Matt. 12:40). The book is not to be considered mere history, concludes Unger, for then it would have no place among the twelve Minor Prophets in the Hebrew canon, but it is to be viewed as predictive or typical history.[5]

But there was also another typical and prophetic lesson providentially designed and recorded in this book with which Christ rebuked His impenitent contemporaries. The repentance of Nineveh at the preaching of Jonah was used by Christ to accentuate the obduracy and impenitence of the Jewish nation which had been granted a unique privilege—the presence and preaching of the Son of God Himself. He contrasts the repentance of the Gentiles in Nineveh, who possessed so little spiritual light and understanding, with the unbelieving Jews who were the recipients of the revelation which testified of the One whom they now reject. Hence, the repentance of the unenlightened Gentiles was to serve as a rebuke to the privileged Jews of Jesus' day, and it will be the cause of their severer judgment at the second advent: "The men of Nineveh shall stand up in the judgment with this generation, and shall condemn it: for they repented at the preaching of Jonah; and behold, a greater than Jonah is here" (Matt. 12:41; cf. 11:20-24).

With respect to the miraculous elements of the book, while they might present some problems to modern scientific rationalists, yet they are not in any sense impossible in view of the biblical revelation of the omnipotence of the God of Israel. The miracles concerning the providential storm at sea, the lot falling upon the guilty prophet, the story of the fish and Jonah's miraculous preservation, the marvel of the gourd and the repentance of Nineveh are not more incredible than those miracles to which the whole body of Scripture testifies, for example, the exodus, the plagues of Egypt, the flood, the pillar of cloud and fire, the manna from heaven, the fall of Jericho and the New Testament testimony concerning Christ and His resurrection.

[4]C. F. Keil and F. Delitzsch, *The Twelve Minor Prophets, Biblical Commentary on the Old Testament,* trans. James Martin, I, 383-86.
[5]Merrill F. Unger, *Introductory Guide to the Old Testament,* p. 345.

The structure of the book is simple, consisting of four chapters logically divided according to their contents. Chapter 2 consists of a poetic prayer of thanksgiving; the remaining chapters are plain historical narrative devoted to an account of the experiences of the Prophet Jonah.

II. The Date

Those who reject the historical character of the book date it in the postexilic period between 400 and 200 B.C. and hold that it was written by an unknown author to whose work additions have been made, the most notable of which is the "thanksgiving psalm" (2:2-9). The reasons generally given for the late date are: (1) The book does not claim to have been written by Jonah. (2) The prophet is referred to in the third person throughout. (3) The presence of Aramaisms indicates a postexilic date. (4) The author's denunciation of the narrow Jewish exclusivism is an advanced universalistic conception not found in preexilic Israel. (5) The expression in 3:3 that "Nineveh *was* an exceeding great city" indicates that the author is writing after the destruction of Nineveh in 612 B.C.

Conservative scholars, on the other hand, date the book during the reign of Jeroboam II who ruled 782-753. In reply to the critical view several factors should be noted:

1. The fact that the book does not state that Jonah wrote the prophecy which bears his name is an argument from silence, and moreover proves nothing with respect to its date. The use of an amanuensis is not unknown in Scripture (cf. Baruch who wrote for Jeremiah). This could also explain the use of the third person in the book, although such usage was an acceptable Old Testament literary style (cf. Moses in Exodus 11:3; Num. 12:1-8; Exodus 6:27; 7:1, 20; and Samuel in I Sam. 12:11, etc.).

2. The presence of Aramaisms in the book can prove nothing in determining the date, since Aramaisms occur in early as well as late Old Testament books and are found in Ras Shamra (Ugaritic) texts which date from about 1500-1400 B.C.

3. The universalistic emphasis of the book is not evidence of its "late" date, for universalistic ideas appear throughout the Old Testament (cf. Gen. 9:27; 12:3; Joel 2:28-32; Lev. 19:33-34; I Sam. 2:10; Isa. 2:2, etc.).

4. Furthermore, the expression in 3:3 that "Nineveh *was* a great city" does not describe Nineveh as a city of the past, but simply indicates its size and importance in Jonah's day (cf. Luke 24:13 for a similar usage of "was"). As Aalders notes, "We can view the perfect

tense as synchronistic; it says no more than that when Jonah went to Nineveh it was a great city."[6]

Therefore, under the view that the book of Jonah is a historical narrative (predictive or typical history), there is no reason to deny that the book is the work of the Prophet Jonah himself in the eighth century B.C. at the time of Jeroboam II of Israel and King Uzziah of Judah. The date 782, which was the first year of Jeroboam's reign, is suggested for the beginning of Jonah's ministry (II Kings 14:25), the exact time of his preaching to Nineveh being uncertain (see Historical Background for further details).

III. The Prophet

Jonah, whose name in Hebrew means "dove," was known as Jonah ben Amittai from two Old Testament sources: II Kings 14:25 and Jonah 1:1. He is described as a prophet of Gath-hepher in Zebulon, a town of lower Galilee. As a member of the northern tribes he would therefore be considered a prophet of Israel. The historicity of the prophet is confirmed in a remarkable way through the reference to his ministry in II Kings 14:25. It is said there that he prophesied under Jeroboam II (c. 782-753), and that Israel regained its ancient boundaries from Hamath on the north to the Sea of the Arabah on the south, according to his word. While the Old Testament bears ample testimony to the historicity of the prophet, nevertheless, some critics have designated Jonah as a symbolic name for the prophetic order, and thus Jonah was to be a warning example to others. But the naming of the prophet and his father in II Kings 14:25, his mention by Christ in the New Testament, and the narrative of the book itself, indicate a historical figure who was an early contemporary of Amos, Hosea, Isaiah and Micah.

IV. The Historical Background

The Israelite Prophet Jonah, the son of Amittai, received a divine commission to pronounce judgment against the great city of Nineveh because of its extreme wickedness. However, the prophet attempted to evade the command by flight and embarked on a ship headed for Tarshish. He had refused to go, according to 4:2, because he wanted to avoid the futility of predicting Nineveh's overthrow and then having his proclamation appear inaccurate when God spared the city. Mingled with this apprehension doubtless was the Hebrew national abhorrence for the ruthless and idolatrous Assyrians. During a

[6]G. C. Aalders, *The Problem of the Book of Jonah,* pp. 12-13.

severe storm at sea the sailors, aware of divine wrath, discovered its cause in Jonah. Cast overboard, he was swallowed by a fish especially prepared by God. He was thus miraculously preserved; he repented, and subsequently was cast upon the land. He then faithfully obeyed his commission, preaching a terse message of judgment, "Yet forty days, and Nineveh shall be overthrown," to which the Ninevites responded generally, from the greatest to the least. The narrative indicates history and not an allegory or parable.

Assyria was a powerful empire, and Nineveh was at this time a great city surrounded by a complex of lesser cities or villages. If a few years after the death of Jeroboam II, Menahem became tributary to the Assyrian King Pul (II Kings 15:19), it is no rash assumption that even in the time of Jeroboam and Jonah the Assyrians were no strangers to Israel. Assyria had frequent contacts with Palestine. Tiglath-pileser I (1114-1076) had extended the conquests of Assyria westward to the Mediterranean Sea. In 853 B.C. Shalmaneser II, at Karkar, fought a confederation of kings including Ahab of Israel; and later Jehu (841-814) was compelled to pay tribute to Assyria. Nineveh was the last capital of the Assyrian Empire located on the east bank of the Tigris River, and was destroyed in 612 B.C. through a military alliance of Medes, Babylonians and Scythians. Nimrod had been its founder (Gen. 10:9-11), and the city is mentioned in early Babylonian cuneiform records. By "Nineveh the great city" the Hebrews designated both the city itself and its neighboring communities (Gen. 10:11 ff.). It had been one of the royal residences from 1100 B.C. The description of the size and importance of the city in the book of Jonah harmonizes with secular and archaeological records. Its deep moral corruption and wickedness are attested by the Prophet Nahum.

It was either in the reign of Adad-nirari III (810-783), Shalmaneser IV (782-773), Ashur-dan III (772-755), Ashur-nirari V (754-745), or Tiglath-pileser III (744-727) that Jonah appeared in Nineveh. If his appearance is put within the reign of Ashur-dan III (772-755 B.C.), then the plagues recorded in Assyrian history in 765 and 759, and the total eclipse of 763, possibly could have been regarded as portents of divine wrath which prepared the city for Jonah's message.

V. PROBLEMS

The problems concerning the historicity and date of the book have already been considered. However, several related questions require analysis. First of all the miraculous element of the book of

Jonah is dismissed by the rationalists upon the grounds of incredibility. That Jonah could have remained in a fish for three days and three nights, while he prayed a psalm of thanksgiving, exceeds the limits of credibility, charge the negative critics.

Besides this there are said to be other problems, for example, in what language did Jonah, a Hebrew, preach to the Ninevites? Since he did not know the Assyrian language, how could they have understood him? Also there is no record in contemporary history of Nineveh's repentance. If the story were true, then Jonah accomplished something that the greatest prophets in Israel were unable to do for their own nation. And what of the unprecedented growth of the plant? Hence, the book is not the record of actual historical events, but the author's aim is didactic. As such it is a sin against the author's intention, contend the critics, to treat the story as literal prose; it is a prose poem, not history. However, these objections are not as cogent as negative criticism presumes.

The problem with respect to the fish can be resolved by the observation that according to the text it is said that "Yahweh *prepared* a great fish to swallow up Jonah" (1:17). The whole argument must turn upon these words, and the question becomes simply: Is God able to prepare providentially a fish that could accommodate a man and keep him alive for as long as seventy-two hours? The answer is obvious. Moreover, the miracle is no more incredible than God's preservation and deliverance of Shadrach, Meshach and Abednego from the fiery furnace (Dan. 3). Those who need objective evidence of the scientific possibility of such a miracle may refer to such books as *The Harmony of Science and Scripture* by Dr. Harry Rimmer, where similar experiences are cited (chap. 5) in which men have been swallowed by fish and survived the ordeal.[7] However, one should take caution that his faith in the miracles of the Scriptures is not grounded in the possibility of finding some analogy elsewhere or rational explanation for the occurrence, lest if perchance the alleged analogy or rational proof be disproved one's faith then collapse with it. The miraculous in Scripture is not subject to rational proof—it is to be received by faith (I Cor. 2:1-5). The matter of the gourd's phenomenal growth is likewise no problem to enlightened faith.

The complaint that there is no record of Nineveh's repentance in secular history is not only a valueless argument from silence, but ignores the fact that the event *is* recorded in biblical history in the book of Jonah. *Remember the Hittites!*[8] In addition there are nu-

---

[7]See also A. J. Wilson, "The Sign of the Prophet Jonah," *Princeton Theological Review*, XXV (January, 1927), 630-42; G. Macloskie, "How to Test the Story of Jonah," *Bibliotheca Sacra*, LXXII, No. 286 (April, 1915), 334-38.

merous events of just as great importance contained in the biblical accounts that are not recorded in secular history, such as the exodus, the crossing of the Red Sea, the giving of the law at Sinai, the fall of Jericho, the slaying of Sennacherib's army and the "conversion" of the city of Gibeon without a word being preached to its inhabitants (Joshua 9)! Neither is it a valid objection, as to the truth of Nineveh's repentance, to argue that since it produced no permanent effect, it must never have occurred. Ahab repented at the announcement of judgment by Elijah (I Kings 21), but three years later stood in bold opposition to the word of God as proclaimed by the Prophet Micaiah (I Kings 22).

As to the Ninevites being unable to understand the message of Jonah, a Hebrew, it would be a sufficient reply to say that the prophet's message consisted (as far as the Hebrew text shows) of exactly six words: "Yet forty days, and Nineveh [shall be] destroyed!" Even the critics could have memorized that much of the Assyrian tongue! However, even apart from divine enabling (as seen, for example, at Pentecost), Israel's contacts with Assyria could well account for a sufficient knowledge of their language so that the prophet could have made himself understood, since the Assyro-Babylonian and Hebrew tongues were subdivisions of the northern Mesopotamian Semitic languages. Besides all this, Aramaic was the lingua franca of the Near East, having been spread by merchants everywhere. Could not this common tongue have been used by the prophet? Jonah's knowledge of this trade language of western Asia could also help explain the Aramaisms in the book. Isaiah 36:11 is conclusive evidence that Aramaic was familiar to some of the Hebrews during this period.

Two or three other problems need mentioning. It is objected that the phrase "Now Nineveh was an exceeding great city, of three days' journey" (3:3) is an inaccuracy, in that Nineveh was never so large a city as to require three days' journey to travel through it. But the phrase may be intended simply as a designation of the city's circumference. The appellation Nineveh is not always restricted to the city proper but may at times comprise the cities which lay close together and whose remains are now known as Kuyunjik, Nimrud and Karamles. Or the writer may simply mean Jonah took three days to visit

---

[8]An ancient people mentioned in more than a dozen O.T. books. Of the Hittites no trace could be found, leading some critics to view these O.T. references with suspicion. Archaeological discoveries in the early part of the twentieth century, however, not only confirmed the biblical references as accurate, but also revealed the Hittites to be an important people with an extended empire during the fourteenth and thirteenth centuries B.C.

the various quarters of this large metropolis. George L. Robinson cites a personal experience which illustrates this. On a trip to Palestine he asked a native of Nazareth concerning a proposed visit to see the principal points of interest, "Which city, Nazareth or Beirut, is the better?" The reply was, "Oh, Beirut is a city of three days!" referring to its superior size, and inferring that three days would be required to visit all the points of interest.[9] Nor does the phrase "Jonah began to enter into the city a day's journey" (v. 4) mean that he walked as far as possible into the city in one day, but that he went about preaching throughout one day.

Another question is raised by critical scholarship with respect to the designation of the king as "the king of Nineveh" rather than "the king of Assyria." The king, it is contended, was ruler over the nation of Assyria, not merely the city of Nineveh, such an error giving further evidence that the author of the book lived after the Assyrian period, since one living in the eighth century B.C. would have known better. The writer, however, simply intends to refer to the ruler residing in Nineveh, since the prophet's concern was with the city of Nineveh itself. Moreover, similar analogies are quite frequent in the Old Testament. Although Ahab was called king of Israel he was also referred to as "King of Samaria" (I Kings 21:1). Also see "the king of Damascus" (II Chron. 24:23), "the king of Salem" (Gen. 14:18) and the king of Zion (Jer. 8:19).

The final problem concerns the unity of the book. The psalm in chapter 2 is alleged to be from a different source than the rest of the book. The following arguments are given in support of this theory:

1. The psalm of thanksgiving for deliverance is said to occur before the deliverance takes place in verse 10.

2. Wellhausen argues that the mention of weeds in verse 5 excludes the idea that Jonah was in the fish's belly.

3. It has been maintained that the text reads smoothly without this psalm, if 2:10 is placed immediately after 2:1. Others contend that the psalm, borrowed from another source, was incorrectly inserted after 2:1 and should have come after 2:10. E. J. Young is quite correct in his observation that the prayer of thanksgiving is not for deliverance from the whale's belly, but thanksgiving for deliverance from drowning in the sea. Yahweh prepared the great fish to rescue Jonah from the sea. This also explains the reference to the seaweeds which obviously do not grow in a whale's belly. Finally, the argument that the text reads smoothly by an omission of the psalm is hardly

[9]George L. Robinson, *The Twelve Minor Prophets*, p. 80.

admissible, since such reasoning could be applied to many portions of the biblical text.

OUTLINE OF JONAH

Chapter 12

HOSEA Salvation

I. THE NATURE OF THE BOOK

THE BOOK OF HOSEA consists of two sections: chapters 1-3 which are symbolic narrative, and chapters 4-14 which consist of addresses by the prophet. In the first three chapters the prophet's wife and her three children, together with the tragedy of the prophet's married life, are all symbolic of the relationship that existed between God and Israel. In the second section there is a collection of addresses consisting of appeals, denunciations, warnings, exhortations and promises. There is no strict chronological order to be discovered in this section, since chapters 4-14 probably do not contain a collection of the complete separate addresses delivered to Israel.

The book begins with a symbolical action. To show the unfaithfulness of Israel and the long-suffering love of God, the prophet was commanded to perform a public act which would forcefully and effectively demonstrate these two truths. Hosea was commanded to take a wife of "whoredoms" to illustrate Israel's state of spiritual adultery; and by the names of the three children born of this marriage, he was to signify the fate of the people. Their names indicate the fruits of idolatry, that is, the rejection and exile of Israel to Assyria. The first son was called Jezreel, which means "sown or scattered by God," perhaps referring to the coming exile. In addition, the historical importance of the place called Jezreel may be here referred to. Jezreel was the place of Jehu's bloody brutality (II Kings 10:14); and on this plain, the scene of many bloody conflicts, the kingdom of Israel was going to be destroyed. Lo-ruhamah was the name of the second child meaning "uncompassionated" or "without compassion," indicating Israel was to find no mercy when judgment fell. The third child called Lo-ammi meaning "not my people" signified the climax of Israel's fate, implying her rejection and renunciation by God. After a time Gomer deserted her husband and proved unfaithful to him. But her paramours soon tired of her; and Hosea, seeking her by God's direction, found her deserted, despised and apparently sold as a slave. In his love he purchased her freedom and restored her; not, however, to her former status to enjoy the privileges and blessings of a wife which she had cast away, but he placed her in a position of restraint, separated from her paramours, until her discipline should be complete.

On the ground of the bond and covenant relation existing between God and Israel, represented often under the figure of marriage (cf. Exodus 34:15; Isa. 62:5; Hosea 2:19; Jer. 3:14), the idolatry of Israel is exhibited as whoredom and adultery. Thus the prophet's marriage to adulterous Gomer was to illustrate this apostasy, and the names of her children, the exile and judgment (chap. 1). Next the Lord announced that He was to put an end to Israel's whoredoms, and after the discipline of exile and punishment would betroth Himself to her again forever (chap. 2). The prophet was commanded to restore his unfaithful wife, symbolically signifying God's unceasing love for Israel (chap. 3). He was, however, to keep her in such a position that it would be impossible for her to commit whoredom any longer. By this the present state of Israel is described in which she is separated from her ancient rites of worship, yet free from her idolatries, until her restoration when her long period of discipline is completed:

> For the children of Israel shall abide many days without king, and without prince, and without sacrifice, and without pillar, and without ephod or teraphim: afterward shall the children of Israel return, and seek Yahweh their God, and David their king, and shall come with fear unto Yahweh and to his goodness in the latter days (3:4-5).

In the second division of the book, consisting of the prophet's discourses throughout, there is an absence of symbolic acts. However, the theme is essentially the same as in the first section. Punishment and judgment are announced upon the northern kingdom of Israel because of its apostasy, but at the same time it is predicted that Israel shall one day be restored and become once more the object of God's love and divine favor.

Hosea stands first in the book of the Minor Prophets. The prophecy is not arranged according to chronological order, however, since Hosea is preceded in history by Obadiah, Joel and Jonah, and was a contemporary of Amos, Micah and Isaiah. The influence Hosea exerted can be measured in the book's use by other biblical writers, as more than thirty direct and indirect quotations from the prophet are contained in the Gospels and Epistles (cf. Hosea 11:1 with Matt. 2:15; 6:6 with Matt. 9:13 and 12:7; 10:8 with Luke 23:30; 2:23 with

Rom. 9:25; 13:14 with I Cor. 15:55). The entire book is the work of
the prophet himself, although some critical scholars deny to Hosea
the passages of hope and restoration such as 2:14 ff.; 3:5; 11:8-11;
14:2-9.

The references to Judah and the southern kingdom are said to be
later interpolations. However, Hosea's references to the southern
kingdom are no more numerous than those which Isaiah, a prophet of
Judah, makes concerning the northern kingdom.

God's love for Israel is expressed as *ḥesed* in the Old Testament.
This Hebrew term more clearly expresses the unique nature of God's
love for Israel than any other. The root meaning suggests "steadfast-
ness," then "mercy" and "loving-kindness." The usage of the term in
the Old Testament indicates that it is always operative within the
covenant, and never means simply "kindness" in general to all without distinction. Thus, originally *ḥesed* was used to denote the attitude of loyalty and faithfulness, or the moral obligation which both
parties of a covenant were to observe toward one another. *Ḥesed*
became the binding relationship in the covenant—it was *steadfast
faithfulness*. *Ḥesed* with respect to God's relationship to Israel might
be translated as "covenant-love."[1]

As Hosea is known as the prophet of love in the Old Testament,
he has also rightly been called "the prophet of *ḥesed*." It was *ḥesed*
(viz., mercy or kindness expressed as steadfast faithfulness as a result
of her convenant with Yahweh) that the Lord wanted from Israel,
rather than mere outward conformity to religious ritual (6:6). Israel's unfaithfulness is described as a violation of the covenant relationship (6:7). Hosea shows that sin, with respect to God's people, is
essentially spiritual infidelity. Their *ḥesed* was as transient as the
morning cloud and as dew (6:4); *ḥesed* is lacking altogether in the
land (4:1-2); hence, the prophet exhorts the people to keep *ḥesed*
(10:12; 12:6). Hosea's own experience with Gomer was illustrative of
God's steadfast love for Israel. Israel may be faithless and forget
ḥesed, but God's love for her is eternal and steadfast. Israel may not
be faithful to her covenant vows, but God, on His part, will be
faithful; hence, His unchanging love, His *ḥesed*, will not fail on her
behalf for He will "heal their backsliding" and "love them freely."
Because of His *ḥesed* He would one day espouse her to Himself again
in such a way that she too would practice *ḥesed*:

> I will betroth thee unto me for ever; yea, I will betroth thee unto
> me in righteousness, and in justice, and in lovingkindness

[1]Norman H. Snaith, *The Distinctive Ideas of the Old Testament,* pp.
94-130.

[*hesed*] and in mercies. I will even betroth thee unto me in faithfulness (2:19-20).

II. THE DATE

*also kings in
Isaiah's time*

The scope of Hosea's ministry is indicated in the superscription: "in the days of Uzziah, Jotham, Ahaz, and Hezekiah, kings of Judah, and in the days of Jeroboam, the son of Joash, king of Israel." The limits of Hosea's ministry would thus be from the reign of Uzziah (790-739 B.C.) to that of Hezekiah (715-686). Although only Jeroboam II is mentioned of the kings of Israel, the inclusion of Hezekiah indicates that Hosea's ministry extended well beyond Jeroboam's death and included the reigns of all the final kings of Israel: Zechariah, Shallum, Menahem, Pekahiah, Pekah, and Hoshea whose reign ended with the fall of Samaria in 722.

The contents of the book indicate that Hosea's ministry may have extended over a period in excess of forty years, from the latter years of Jeroboam II into the reign of Hezekiah. Keil suggests that Hosea held his prophetic office for about sixty or sixty-five years.[2] The first portion of the book (chaps. 1-3) has obvious reference to the reign of Jeroboam II, and the superscription would place the *beginning* of the prophet's ministry at some time during the latter years of his reign, after the beginning of the reign of Uzziah in Judah (767).[3] In 1:4 the overthrow of the house of Jehu (to which Jeroboam belonged) is depicted as yet future, although near at hand. The kingdom of Israel is pictured as yet prosperous (2:8) with no allusions to the state of anarchy and confusion that prevailed after the death of Jeroboam (753). Hence, the suggested beginning of the prophet's ministry might be placed at about 760.

Several factors indicate a lengthy ministry for the prophet:

1. The mention of Hezekiah (715-686) unquestionably extends the prophet's ministry until after 715.

2. Many scholars believe that the term "Shalman" in 10:14 refers to Shalmaneser and his expedition into Galilee which occurred, according to II Kings 17:3, at the beginning of Hoshea's reign (732-722). The event according to Hosea has already taken place, while a fresh invasion of the Assyrians is threatened. This could only refer to Shalmaneser's final expedition against Hoshea (who had rebelled against him) which ended in the fall of Samaria in 722 in the sixth year of Hezekiah (II Kings 18:10).

[2]C. F. Keil and F. Delitzsch, *The Twelve Minor Prophets, Biblical Commentary on the Old Testament*, I, 15.

[3]Uzziah reigned as coregent with Amaziah from 790-767.

3.   It has also been urged that Jareb (5:13; 10:6) is the natal name of Sargon II.

4.   The predictions of an Assyrian invasion in 10:5-6; 13:15-16 seem to refer to the near future.

5.   The statement in 8:10 may refer to the tribute paid to Pul by Menahem (752-742).

6.   The allusions to the Egyptian relations (7:11; 11:11) are satisfied by the events of Hoshea's reign (732-722).

7.   As Keil correctly maintains, it cannot be proven (as some contend) from 6:8 and 12:11 that the active ministry of Hosea did not extend beyond the reign of Jotham (739-736) on the ground that, according to these passages, Gilead (depopulated by Tiglath-pileser in 734; II Kings 15:29) was still in possession of Israel. These words could well have been uttered after the Assyrians had conquered Gilead. And by virtue of the nature of Hosea's book, a compendium of the sum and substance of all that he prophesied during a long period, the book would of necessity contain historical allusions to events already past when it was compiled. Consequently there are no grounds for denying the genuineness of the superscription and shortening the period of Hosea's ministry. A prophetic career of such length is not without parallel; Elisha prophesied for over fifty years,[4] and Isaiah for probably at least forty years. The suggested length of Hosea's prophetic ministry is from about 760[5] until sometime into the reign of Hezekiah (715-686).

III. The Prophet

The name Hosea means "salvation" and is found in the Scriptures in various forms. It is the equivalent to Joshua, the successor to Moses; to Hoshea, the last king of Israel; and in its Greek form to Jesus. Hosea was probably a citizen of the northern kingdom and exercised his prophetic office in Israel. His familiarity with the circumstances and topography of the northern kingdom (cf. 5:1; 6:8-9; 12:12; 14:6 ff.) and the fact that he speaks of Israel's king as "our king" (7:5) are further confirmation of this fact. His frequent references to Judah do not necessarily invalidate his northern origin, since the book indicates his ministry as exclusively occupied with the religious, moral and political events which transpired there. All that

---

[4]Keil and Delitzsch, I, 16.

[5]As Schultz notes, a minimum of three to ten years should be allowed for Hosea's marriage and the birth of his three children, although it is not indicated how much of this period was contemporary with Jeroboam's reign which terminated in 753 B.C. (Samuel J. Schultz, *The Old Testament Speaks*, p. 387, n.).

is to be learned about the prophet himself must be ascertained from his book, which simply states that he was the son of Beeri. Hosea has been called the Jeremiah of Israel. As Jeremiah saw the rapid decline of Judah and the final destruction of Jerusalem and the captivity of the people which he commemorated in Lamentations, so too Hosea first predicted and then no doubt witnessed the downfall and exile of his people Israel.

IV. THE HISTORICAL BACKGROUND

From the historical record in II Kings 14-17 it would appear that Hosea exercised his prophetic ministry in a chaotic period, filled with disorder, bloodshed and strife. Under Jeroboam II Israel had been prosperous and successful, but the sin of idolatry remained. Impiety, oppression, carnal luxury and moral and spiritual degeneracy were found everywhere, and when Jeroboam died a scene of anarchy and confusion ensued (cf. 4:1-2; 7:1, 7; 8:3-4; 9:15).

Jeroboam's son Zechariah was assassinated by Shallum after a brief reign of six months. Shallum then usurped the throne but was himself murdered after one month by Menahem, one of his generals. This apostate and wicked tyrant ruled for ten years, during which the Assyrians under Tiglath-pileser invaded Israel and made the northern kingdom a tributary. Menahem's son, Pekahiah, after a reign of two years, was murdered by Pekah, one of his officers, who seized the throne and in an alliance with Rezin of Damascus turned against the southern kingdom of Judah. Ahaz, the king of Judah, appealed to the Assyrians, who devastated Damascus and took Samaria.

Pekah was assassinated by Hoshea who usurped the throne and at first paid tribute to the Assyrians. Later, however, Hoshea made an alliance with Egypt and discontinued the yearly tribute. This resulted in an invasion by Shalmaneser V, successor to Tiglath-pileser. Hoshea was taken captive, and after a siege of three years Samaria fell into the hands of Sargon in 722 B.C. Vast numbers of the remaining tribes of Israel were deported to Mesopotamia. Their places were repopulated by foreigners brought in by the Assyrians from Babylon, Cuthah, Avva, Hamath and Sepharvaim (II Kings 17:1-24).

Such was the tumultuous period in which Hosea prophesied. The moral condition of Israel, as evidenced by the Historical Books, as well as the prophecy itself, was exceedingly corrupt. The priests, instead of leading the people into righteous living, encouraged them in their sins (cf. 4:6-9; 5:1; 6:9). The kings set an example of drunkenness and debauchery (7:3-5). The people confounded the worship of Yahweh with Baal, while calf worship was prevalent on every hand. The nation rejected God and trusted in foreign alliances (8:9-10). Moral and spiritual declension, political chaos, idolatrous worship, and apostasy from Yahweh characterized the nation when the Lord moved Hosea to pronounce His warnings, rebukes and prophecies to Israel.[6]

V. PROBLEMS

Inasmuch as there is no record in the book of Hosea of the actual fall of Samaria in 722, critical scholars view the reference to King Hezekiah as well as the other Judean kings (Uzziah, Jotham and Ahaz) as a later gloss, and assign the *terminus a quo* of Hosea's prophecies to shortly before 753 B.C. and the *terminus ad quem* to around 735. Why, they contend, should Jeroboam alone be mentioned of the kings of Israel, when, if Hosea's ministry extended into the reign of Hezekiah (715-686), the prophet must have worked also during the reigns of all the Israelite kings after Jeroboam II, namely, Zechariah, Shallum, Menahem, Pekahiah, Pekah and Hoshea? Moreover, if Hosea was a northern prophet, why then is his work dated in the superscription by southern kings? Some have suggested as a solution that the use of the names of rulers of both kingdoms perhaps indicates birth in one and work in another, that is, that Hosea, like Amos, went up from Judah to preach to Israel. Since there is no incontrovertible proof to the contrary (except perhaps the reference to "our king" in 7:5), and since Hosea's birthplace is not known, this has been cited as one possible solution to the problem, inasmuch as frequent references are made to Judah (1:7, 11; 4:15; 5:5, 10-14; 6:4, 11; 8:14; 11:12; 12:2).

In connection with the idea that Hosea might have been a prophet of Judah, it may be also that the superscription dates the total ministry of the prophet in terms of the kings of Judah, whereas the name of Jeroboam was given to indicate only that period of his prophetic activity in Israel which was during the reign of Jeroboam II. This would also help solve the problem of the absence of any mention of the actual fall of Samaria.

Two other solutions have been suggested. Keil, with others, believes that the names of the southern kings were added because of the inward relation Hosea assumed toward that kingdom in common with all true prophets, since the Judean kings alone were recognized

[6]W. J. Deane, "Introduction to the Book of Hosea," *The Pulpit Commentary,* eds. H. D. M. Spence and J. S. Exell, XIII, i-iii.

by the prophets as legitimate representatives of the theocracy; and he thus fixes the date of his prophecy by the reigns of these kings. Therefore, he gives a complete list of the kings of Judah, whom he places first, whereas he mentions the name of only one king of Israel, Jeroboam, because he is the king in whose reign he began his prophetic ministry, and because of the importance of Jeroboam as contrasted to the kings of Israel who succeeded him.[7] Others suggest that the names of the remaining kings of Israel were omitted because they were all (except in the case of Zechariah who reigned only briefly for six months) usurpers of the throne and were not regarded as the true kings in Israel. Hence, Hosea in the superscription simply passes over this period of anarchy in which, over the short span of thirty years, six kings occupied the throne of Israel. The absence of any mention of the fall of Samaria is explained from the fact that the prophecies of Hosea are doubtless only a compendium of his addresses. The prophet does, however, foretell the destruction of Samaria and the captivity of Israel (10:5-8; 13:16); and the absence of any recorded word as to the actual occurrence of the event in the book of Hosea does not necessarily prove the cessation of his ministry before this time.

A second difficulty concerns the interpretation of the marriage of Hosea in chapter 1 where the prophet is commanded by God to take "a wife of whoredoms." The various interpretations may be classified under two heads: those that object to a literal interpretation and those who hold that an actual marriage took place. Basically there are two views proposed by those who object to the literal interpretation: (1) The story is said to be based upon a *vision* or *dream*, and the transaction never actually was carried out in real life. (2) The story is a *parable* or *allegory* to illustrate the relation of Israel to Yahweh.

In defense of these two views as against a literal interpretation, four points are argued:

1. To take the story literally, whereby the prophet was actually commanded to marry a harlot, is to propose a moral difficulty, which not only reflects upon the holiness of God, but also requires conduct on the part of Hosea that is inconsistent with the character of a prophet. Hence, the account is of a vision, dream or an allegory.

2. There is an emphasis upon symbolism in the names given the three children.

3. Too much time would be required by the events in chapters 1 and 3 for Hosea to use them in teaching a moral and spiritual object

[7]Keil and Delitzsch, I, 11-12.

lesson to Israel. For instance, at least a year would elapse between the births of each of the three children, to say nothing of the time required for Gomer to desert her husband and, after a period, be restored.

4.   The woman in 3:1 is not the same as the wife of chapter 1, and it is improbable that Hosea would have made two such marriages.[8]

However, in reply to these arguments and in favor of a literal interpretation several things are apparent:

1.   Indication is nowhere given by the prophet that this is a vision, parable or allegory (cf. Jer. 25:15 ff.; Zech 1:8; 4:1; Ezek. 1, 8; note especially Ezek. 20:49). Moreover, the style is that of narrative and not of an allegory or parable. Furthermore, that which is morally objectionable in actual practice becomes no more palatable, nor defensible, simply because it is presented as a vision or allegory.

2.   Prophets were accustomed to give symbolical names to their real children (cf. Isa. 7:3; 8:3). Moreover, the name Gomer has no known symbolical significance, and too, no symbolical meaning can be found in the fact that the second child is a girl rather than a boy.

3.   The length of time required by this symbolic marriage to teach Israel a spiritual lesson is not unreasonable due to the nature of the sin God was to rebuke. On the contrary, it would heighten the analogy between Hosea's experience with Gomer and that of God with Israel. Also, the symbolic acts of some of the other prophets were over extended periods. Compare Isaiah 20 where the prophet is commanded to walk naked and barefoot for three years as a sign to Egypt, and Ezekiel 4 where, as a sign to Israel and Judah, the prophet is instructed to lie on his side for an exceedingly long period.

4.   The woman of 3:1 is Gomer, since Hosea is commanded to love a sinful woman as Yahweh has loved His people, although they have turned to other gods. The parallel would best fit Gomer, who had deserted Hosea for her paramours.

Those who hold that a *literal* marriage took place suggest several interpretations in explanation. It is held by some that Gomer was a *public harlot* whom Hosea was commanded to marry, who either (a)

---

[8]Many and varied are the critical attempts at solution to the problem of chapter 3. One writer suggests that Hosea does not remarry Gomer, but purchases a cult prostitute connected with a shrine of the type seen in the Hammurabi and Assyrian codes. He thus is in a position to control her actions and isolates her from all men as a symbol of Israel's period of quarantine (A. Douglas Tushingham, "A Reconstruction of Hosea, Chapters 1-3," *Journal of Near Eastern Studies,* XII [July, 1953], 150-59).

already had children as a result of her whoredoms, or (b) bore them after marriage to Hosea (1:3, "bare him a son"), or (c) they were the result of her adulteries while married to the prophet. The marriage thereby becomes an intentionally obvious sermon against Israel to direct their attention to their sins against Yahweh.

But there are two principal objections against the view that Gomer was a public harlot: (a) The text (1:2) does not speak of a harlot (singular), but of a "wife of harlotries." This would seem to characterize her *nature* which only manifested itself after marriage, whereas the singular would probably have been used had a literal, professional harlot been meant here. (b) Such a view would be inconsistent with the symbolical representation that Israel had been faithful and chaste at the time of her marriage to Yahweh in the exodus, later becoming unfaithful and following after other lovers (gods).

Another interpretation by the literalists is the view that *spiritual adultery* is meant here, Gomer being a worshiper of other gods, like most of the Israelites of Hosea's day. But if Gomer were simply an idolatress who had forsaken God for idols and so was a spiritual adulteress, Hosea's use of his wife for purposes of illustration would probably have had little effect upon a people who were idolaters like her and saw no evil in their conduct. Also, this does not adequately explain why the children were called "children of whoredom" (v. 2).

Other interpreters have suggested that Hosea took Gomer, not as a real wife in marriage, but only as a *concubine*. However, this view not only has no basis whatever to support it from the text, but it fails to escape the very moral problem which such an interpretation endeavors to solve. Luther suggested a *symbolical* interpretation of the marriage in an effort to escape the problem of Hosea marrying an actual harlot. Gomer and the children were virtuous, but Hosea simply called them adulterous for symbolical purposes. This view would seem to create more problems than it solves, not the least of which would be the stigma or disgrace which would fall upon his wife and children as a consequence.

Finally, there is the *unfaithful wife* interpretation which holds that the marriage actually took place between Hosea and Gomer, who was a chaste woman at the time of her marriage, but who had a disposition toward unfaithfulness which did not manifest itself until after the marriage. The obvious advantages of this view are as follows:

1. It accepts the narrative as historic fact as it is intended, rather than as an allegory or vision.

2. It eliminates all the moral difficulties involved in the other views.

3. It gives proper recognition to Hosea's evident love for his wife as a genuine affection, not something artificial or symbolical, as would have perhaps been the case if the marriage were contracted merely for the purpose of symbolizing a spiritual lesson to Israel.

4. It better explains the close relationship between Hosea's experiences and the lesson it is intended to teach of Israel's unfaithfulness after her marriage to Yahweh.

5. This view is supported by chapter 3 which describes Hosea as taking back his wife, who had been rejected because of adultery (chaps. 1-2). This rejection would not seem justifiable if Hosea had married a common harlot with full knowledge of her nature.

6. This view also aids in the solution to the problem of the children being called "children of whoredom." The phrase may mean simply that since Gomer is a "wife of whoredom," the children of such a wife are called "children of whoredom," rather than signifying that these were children already born as the result of Gomer's harlotries before her marriage to Hosea. Or as some suggest, it may mean that the term is descriptive of the children born through adultery after the marriage, begotten by another than the prophet. Although the first child called Jezreel is said to be born to him, this is not said of the other two. Moreover, the contention by some that Hosea would not have kept Gomer as a wife when he discovered her infidelity after the birth of the first child, Jezreel, forgets the analogy of the prophet's marriage to Gomer and that of Yahweh to Israel in which God is depicted as long-suffering toward Israel, although she repeatedly manifests her unfaithfulness to Him, and it is only after numerous pleas and warnings that God finally rejects her.

OUTLINE OF HOSEA

Chapter 13

Jeroboam II

Uzziah - Judah

AMOS
load or Burden

I. The Nature of the Book

THE BOOK OF AMOS is a prophetic writing of nine chapters, containing chiefly the announcements of judgment upon the northern kingdom of Israel because of her social injustices, moral degeneracy and apostasy. The prophet foretells not only the coming dissolution of Israel but also the expectation of judgment upon the surrounding nations. He sees justice and ethical conduct between men as the foundation of society, and maintains that worship by a people whose lives are characterized by selfishness, greed, immorality and oppression is an abomination to God.

The book of Amos consists of three groups of oracles under one title: "The words of Amos . . . which he saw concerning Israel in the days of Uzziah king of Judah, and in the days of Jeroboam . . . king of Israel, two years before the earthquake" (1:1). Chapters 1 and 2 consist of eight "burdens" against the surrounding nations, including Judah and Israel. The oracles are directed against the crimes of these nations and culminate in a detailed denunciation of the social and moral evils of Israel. The second section, chapters 3-6, consists of three sermons against Israel for her sins. The sermons of judgment are easily perceptible since each begins with the prophetic formula "Hear this word" which stands at the head of chapters 3, 4 and 5. Each of the three denunciations is concluded with an emphatic "therefore" (3:11; 4:12; 5:16; 6:7) which announces the nature of the judgment to follow. Hence, in the first part of each sermon is set forth the cause of judgment, and in the latter, the nature of the judgment. The third oracle, chapters 7-9, consists of five visions: (1) locusts (7:1); (2) fire (7:4); (3) plumbline (7:7); (4) summer fruit (8:1) and (5) the altar (9:1). In 7:10-17 there is a parenthetical narrative containing the high priest Amaziah's rebuke to Amos because of his preaching, which makes judgment inevitable since the nation indicates by this action that it has chosen a final course of rebellion against the word of the Lord. The prophecy is concluded (9:11-15) with a promise of restoration and glory for Israel.

The principle which Amos insists upon is that the external prac-

184

tice of religion divorced from right ethical conduct is unacceptable to God. The people are deceived in believing that perfunctory religious observances, while their lives are filled with selfishness, greed and gross immorality, will provide them security from the consequences of divine judgment. With a touch of irony the prophet invites the sinful people who have been accustomed to make a great display of their religious enthusiasm:

> Come to Beth-el, and transgress; to Gilgal, and multiply transgression; and bring your sacrifices every morning, and your tithes every three days; and offer a sacrifice of thanksgiving . . . and proclaim freewill-offerings and publish them: for this pleaseth you, O ye children of Israel, saith the Lord Yahweh (4:4-5).

The prophet insists that religion and morality are inseparable; there can be no absolute separation between worship and conduct, between religion and life:

> I hate, I despise your feasts, and I will take no delight in your solemn assemblies. Yea, though ye offer me your burnt-offerings and meal-offerings, I will not accept them; neither will I regard the peace-offerings of your fat beasts. Take thou away from me the noise of thy songs; for I will not hear the melody of thy viols. But let justice roll down as waters, and righteousness as a mighty stream (5:21-24).

God declares here that He considers worship, divorced from right conduct, an abomination.

The nation's unprecedented prosperity and luxury, together with their sinful indulgences, ease and idleness were indicative of national decay and moral depravity. Israel, as well as Judah, is denounced in chapter 6 as living in sinful self-security, satisfied in their present state of wantonness and revelry, oblivious to the approaching judgment. "Woe unto them that are at ease in Zion, and to them that are secure in the mountain of Samaria" (6:1). Their condition is characterized here as one of carnal security. The city of Samaria believed itself impregnable; thus in their pride they "put far away the evil day" (6:3). While both Israel and Judah ignored the inevitable judgment and lived at ease in their false self-security, sin multiplied and abounded in their capitals.

Israel's moral corruption is described by the prophet as: carnal security (6:1); scorn of judgment for sin (v. 3a); violence and oppression (v. 3b); indolence (v. 4a); wanton luxury and gluttony (vv. 4b, 6b); idle pleasures (v. 5); drunkenness (v. 6a; cf. 4:1); lack of compassion (v. 6b). By ignoring the approaching calamity, the nation blindly pursued such a course of sinful wantonness as to hasten its arrival. In order to demonstrate the magnitude of the people's depravity the Lord threatened their certain judgment by swearing a solemn oath that their wickedness would not go unpunished (vv. 8 ff.).

God's relation to Israel was a special one based upon her divine election. Because of His sovereign choice of Israel from among the nations, she became the recipient of special favors and privileges. However, the lesson she failed to learn was that the greater the privileges the greater the responsibilities that accompany them (cf. Luke 12:48). Israel prided herself in her election but rejected her moral and ethical responsibilities. Therefore God forewarned her that she could expect full punishment for her sins: "You only have I known of all the families of the earth: therefore I will visit upon you all your iniquities" (Amos 3:2).

While the election of Israel gave her special privileges, it did not give her the right to sin with impunity; thus Amos declared: "Therefore... prepare to meet thy God, O Israel" (4:12). Election is never to be looked upon as arbitrary and meaningless; election is for a purpose. Amos, as well as the other prophets, insisted that Israel's election did not give her a monopoly on divine favor, but called her to special moral responsibility; she was called to be "a holy people unto Yahweh...Yahweh thy God hath chosen thee to be a people for his own possession, above all peoples that are upon the face of the earth" (Deut. 7:6). They had been given revelations that had never been granted to other nations (Ps. 147:19-20), but this only increased their responsibility and made judgment upon their failures more certain (3:2).

Israel was called to service and moral responsibility; she was chosen to become a kingdom of priests and a holy nation (Exodus 19:6) who was to receive and cherish the special revelations granted to her, and through her own response of loyalty, faithfulness and obedience, exhibit to the world the nature of true religion and morality. God's revelation of Himself to Israel in her election was to be reflected in holiness and obedience; her election meant election to responsibility. However, in her pride and carnal self-complacency she failed in her moral and spiritual obligations, viewing her election as providing her with special advantages in the day of the Lord. But the Prophet Amos rebuked this mistaken conception (5:18-20, 27).

II. THE DATE

There is little difficulty in dating the prophecy due to the chronological data of the superscription (1:1), which place the book in the period of King Jeroboam II of Israel (782-753 B.C.) and of King Uzziah of Judah (767-739). Since the reigns coincide between 767-753 this might well define the limits of the prophecy.

The title of the book states that Amos began to prophesy during the reigns of Uzziah and Jeroboam two years before the earthquake. The date of the earthquake cannot be determined with exactness, although it is mentioned again in Zechariah 14:5-7 after the exile. However, a comparison of 6:2, 13 with II Kings 14:25 seems to intimate that Amos' ministry took place after Jeroboam had regained Israel's territory as predicted by the Prophet Jonah, but before the death of Jeroboam in 753 (7:11*a*) or the fall of Samaria in 722 (7:11*b*).

In view of all this it would appear that the beginning of Amos' ministry took place about 760 B.C. Amos' silence concerning the death of Jeroboam and the state of anarchy and confusion which followed would doubtless confine his prophetic ministry to the period 760-753.

III. The Prophet

Amos, whose name means "load or burden," is not to be confused with Isaiah's father Amoz. Considerable information concerning the prophet is given in the book itself. He lived in Tekoa, a town about five miles southeast of Bethlehem. His occupation was that of a herdsman of sheep (1:1) and "a dresser of sycomore-trees" (7:14). He was not of the priestly nor prophetic line but was called to be a prophet of Israel while engaged in his humble occupation. He himself describes his unique call: "I was no prophet, neither was I a prophet's son; but I was a herdsman, and a dresser of sycomore-trees: and Yahweh took me from following the flock, and Yahweh said unto me, Go, prophesy unto my people Israel" (7:14-15).[1]

Amos has been called the prophet of righteousness because of his bold preaching against the moral decay of Israel and Judah. His fearless preaching against Israel in Bethel aroused Amaziah, the apostate high priest, who denounced him to King Jeroboam. He was a prophet from Judah to Israel, and while his ministry was concerned primarily with the northern kingdom (7:15), yet he prophesied also

---

[1]Inasmuch as the verb "to be" does not occur in 7:14, some critical interpreters translate it: "I *am* not a prophet, and *am* not a son of a prophet," Amos thereby allegedly repudiating the prophetic institution. However, this is an erroneous assumption, as Amos merely denies here the implications of Amaziah's statements. Moreover, the verb "was" should be supplied here, it would seem, on the basis of his previous statements concerning himself in 1:1; 3:3-8.

with respect to Judah (2:4-5) as well as the surrounding nations of Damascus (Syria), Gaza (Philistia), Tyre (Phoenicia), Edom, Ammon and Moab. His ministry was exercised at the main religious sanctuary of Israel, Bethel (7:10), although he may have denounced sin also at Samaria (3:9-12; 4:1-3) and at Gilgal (4:4; 5:4-5; cf. 7:10).

IV. THE HISTORICAL BACKGROUND

At the time Amos prophesied, Israel was secure from outward enemies and inwardly prosperous. She was far removed from any expectation of judgment and ruin which was to befall her about forty years thence. Jeroboam II was politically and militarily the most successful of the kings of northern Israel. The details of his reign, although brief in the book of Kings, nevertheless indicate unusual military successes. "He restored the border of Israel from the entrance of Hamath unto the sea of the Arabah" (II Kings 14:25). According to verse 28 he also recovered Damascus and Hamath which had formerly been subject to Judah in the days of David and Solomon. The book of Amos portrays the nation enjoying its prosperity and reposing in carnal ease and self-security as the result of peace and freedom from outward threats (6:13).

Prosperity had produced its inevitable fruits—pride, luxury, selfishness, greed, oppression and moral decay. These sins were accentuated in Israel by the idolatrous calf worship which centered at Bethel. It was to Bethel that Amos was commissioned to go and preach a message of rebuke against transgression and iniquity and to forewarn of the approach of divine judgment. Israel, however, at the height of its power and material prosperity, was so sunken in the depths of corruption, and was so complacent in its newly won security, that the words of the simple shepherd from Tekoa were fruitless. Although no one gave thought to the Assyrians at this time, the prophet, as did his contemporary Isaiah, saw that kingdom as the instrument of God's wrath upon Israel's apostasy (cf. Isa. 10 with Amos 7:11, 16-17 and especially 5:27).

V. PROBLEMS

The problems connected with the book of Amos are fewer in number than those of any of the other prophets, and have to do with alleged literary additions. Critics maintain certain annotations and additions were made by later editors. This secondary material is said to consist of: 1:1-2, 9-10, 11-12; 2:4-5, 12; 4:7*b*, 8*a*, 13; 5:8-9, 18*b*,

22*b*; 6:2, 9-11*a*; 7:1*d*, 8*a*; 8:2*a*, 6, 11*a*; 9:8*c*-15. These alleged insertions comprise later historical events foretold by Amos, as well as the passages of hope, the chief of which is the Messianic prophecy of 9:9-15.

Negative criticism, rejecting any possibility of predictive prophecy or the admixture of passages of hope with those of judgment, postulates the hypothesis that such passages where these are found are later glosses. Amos himself, alleges Harper, did not leave a book, but certain addresses compiled later by his disciples, to which numerous insertions were added in the succeeding centuries. The last of these was in the period of Zechariah and Zerubbabel, when the hope of the restoration of the throne of David was high, at which time there was added the Messianic promise of 9:8*c*-15.[2] The obvious weaknesses of these conjectures by the critics are all too apparent. There is no evidence to controvert the belief that Amos was the author of the entire book. It is cited in the New Testament by Stephen who quotes from Amos 5:25-27 (Acts 7:42-43). And James cites Amos 9:11 at the Jerusalem conference (Acts 15:16).

OUTLINE OF AMOS

---

[2]W. R. Harper, "Amos and Hosea," *The International Critical Commentary,* ed. S. R. Driver *et al.,* pp. cxxxiii-xxxiv.

Principles of Biblical Sociology
1. *Universal Sovernity of God*
2. *Sin of inhumanity*
3. *Moral responsibility of all mankind*

Chapter 14

ISAIAH

I. The Nature of the Book

Isaiah's ministry was concerned primarily with Judah and Jerusalem (1:1) at a very crucial period of the nation's history (c. 739-700 B.C.) which formed the background for his prophecies. Several of his most significant messages are directly related to the critical circumstances encountered by Judah in the second half of the eighth century B.C., such as the Syro-Ephraimitic war (734) and the Sennacherib crisis (701). His prophecies are by no means limited to Judah, however, as he pronounces judgment upon Babylon, Assyria and Egypt, as well as upon the surrounding nations, and occasionally upon Israel.

The importance of the prophecy is indicated by the frequent quotations from it by the New Testament writers and by the Lord Himself. Besides numerous allusions and quotations where the prophet's name is not given, there are twenty-one quotations by name. Christ inaugurated His public ministry with a quotation from the Prophet Isaiah (Luke 4:17 ff.), and later referred to him in explaining the parable of the sower (Matt. 13:14 f.). Isaiah has always been considered the greatest of the Hebrew prophets and is known as the evangelist of the Old Testament. There are two principal themes in the book: *judgment* (chaps. 1-39) and *redemption* (chaps. 40-66). As chapter 1 introduces the first theme whereby the prophet denounces the corruption of Jerusalem and its impending judgment, chapter 40 announces the second with a message of comfort and the promise of redemption. As a sign of the latter, Isaiah predicts the birth of a Deliverer (7:14) as well as His spiritual work of deliverance (chap. 53).

The book of Isaiah abounds with Messianic prophecies concerning the Messiah's person, work, and kingdom, especially in its millennial aspect. Isaiah predicts His virgin birth (7:14); His deity and eternal kingdom (9:1-7); His humanity (a branch of the root of Jesse, 11:1) and righteous reign (11:2-5); and His vicarious sufferings and death (52:13—53:12). Among the prophecies concerning

191

the millennium and related events are chapters 2; 11-12; 24-27; 59-66.

While the principal theme of the first section of the book is judgment and that of the latter, redemption and deliverance, prophecies concerning both judgment and redemption occur throughout the two divisions of the single prophecy. These two major divisions consist of eight subdivisions: chapters 1-12; 13-23; 24-27; 28-35; 36-39; 40-48; 49-55; 56-66. A brief analysis of these will illustrate the principal themes of the book.

Chapters 1-12: prophecies concerning the corruption of Judah (and Jerusalem) and her inevitable punishment, closing with the millennial promise of restoration and blessing. Chapters 13-23: prophecies of judgment, chiefly against the foreign nations whose activities affected Israel and Judah. Chapters 24-27: the *apocalypse* of Isaiah. A prophecy depicting the tribulation and judgment upon the nations, issuing in the millennium. Chapters 28-35: prophecies concerning Samaria and Judah in relation to Assyria, warning of the fall of Israel and condemning alliances with Egypt. Chapters 36-39: historical section concerning Sennacherib's invasion, Hezekiah's sickness and recovery, and Isaiah's prophecy of the Babylonian captivity in judgment upon Judah for her sins. Chapters 40-48: comforting promises of salvation and restoration to the exiles. Chapters 49-55: salvation and deliverance to be accomplished through God's Servant, the Messiah. Chapters 56-66: admonitions to obedience, and promises concerning Israel's future glory. The first thirty-five chapters are didactic, admonitory and predictive, being concerned primarily with judgment. These are followed by a historical narrative of four chapters, and the work is concluded with twenty-seven chapters, chiefly consolatory and Messianic.

The opening chapter of the book graphically illustrates the moral and spiritual condition of the degenerate nation at the time Isaiah began his ministry. The nation, he warns, can avoid her inevitable judgment only if she, by genuine repentance, turns from her present course back to the Lord, who in vain invites the sinful people, "Come now and let us reason together, . . .though your sins be as scarlet, they shall be as white as snow; though they be red like crimson, they shall be as wool. If ye be willing and obedient, ye shall eat the good of the land" (1:18-19).

Divine pardon, according to Isaiah, is conditioned on sincere repentance which manifests itself in the forsaking of sins and in righteous conduct. Hence, the prophet admonishes the sinful people: "Wash you, make you clean; put away the evil of your doings from before mine eyes; cease to do evil; learn to do well; seek justice, relieve the oppressed, judge the fatherless, plead for the widow" (1:16-17). The prophet condemns mere religious formalism divorced from right moral and ethical conduct (vv. 1-15). In this Isaiah and his contemporary Amos are in accord, namely, that genuine religion and morality are inseparable. The nation had come to believe that her punctilious attention to ritual and mere ceremonialism could atone for her sins however great. Isaiah denounces her as "rebellious," "a sinful nation," "a people laden with iniquity," "a seed of evil-doers," "children that deal corruptly," whose "whole head is sick, and the whole heart faint," but who, nevertheless, continues in a perfunctory observance of religion, presumptuously assuming that this makes her acceptable before God. It is from this outward formalism as well as sinful disobedience that the prophet seeks to call the nation.

II. The Date

According to the superscription (1:1), Isaiah's ministry was "in the days of Uzziah, Jotham, Ahaz, and Hezekiah, kings of Judah." It has been generally held that Isaiah began his ministry in the last years of Uzziah's reign (790-739 B.C.), continuing at least until shortly after the invasion by Sennacherib in 701 B.C. (36:1). This would place the scope of his active ministry from about 739 to 700 B.C., a period of perhaps forty years. However, Isaiah records the death of Sennacherib in 37:38, which occurred in 681, indicating that he survived the death of Hezekiah in 686. This is confirmed by II Chronicles 32:32 where it is stated that Isaiah wrote the history of Hezekiah (Isa. 36-39, from which the author of II Kings 18:13— 20:19 acquired his information), thus extending his ministry into the reign of Manasseh, the successor to Hezekiah. According to Hebrew tradition, Isaiah suffered martyrdom by being sawn asunder during the reign of the wicked king Manasseh (cf. Heb. 11:37). The reign of Manasseh is not mentioned in the superscription; hence, Isaiah's visions were no doubt limited to the period of the kings listed therein, ending with Hezekiah, although his writings would extend to 681 B.C. (37:38).[1]

The general arrangement of the book appears to be largely chronological as all the dates mentioned occur in historical sequence: 6:1, "in the year that king Uzziah died" (739 B.C.); 7:1, "in the days of Ahaz" (735 ff.); 14:28, "in the year that king Ahaz died"

---

[1]It may be, as Keil suggests concerning the superscription in the book of Jeremiah, that the period given in 1:1 includes only the time of Isaiah's principal labors, while no reference is made to his later work under Manasseh which was, in a sense, of subordinate importance.

(715); 20:1, "in the year that Tartan came unto Ashdod, when Sargon the king of Assyria sent him" (711); 36:1, "in the fourteenth year of king Hezekiah" (701); 37:38, the year of the death of Sennacherib who was slain when "his sons smote him with the sword" (681).

It is not an easy matter to date the various prophecies precisely; but since the dates which are given are in historical sequence, it seems logical to conclude that the prophet followed a general chronological arrangement throughout. Hence, *chapters 1-6* doubtless belong to the closing period of Uzziah's reign and that of Jotham his successor (*c.* 739-735 B.C.). It probably cannot be maintained, as some interpreters suggest, that chapter 6 represents the initial call of Isaiah to the prophetic office, and is out of its chronological order, belonging instead before the events of chapter 1. The contents of the chapter suggest a call for a special mission. Furthermore, the original call of a prophet, where recorded, occupies the beginning section of his book. Thus Isaiah's initial call is unrecorded, as is the case with most of the prophets.[2] Isaiah's early prophecies (chaps. 1-5) were probably written in the closing period of Uzziah's reign when Jotham his son was regent. Then "in the year that king Uzziah died" (6:1), Isaiah received his vision and special recommission as recorded in chapter 6. *Chapters 7-12* belong to the reign of Ahaz (735-715 B.C.) and the period of the Syro-Ephraimitic war (734) which called forth the great Immanuel prophecy (7:14). *Chapters 13-39* are assigned by George L. Robinson to the reign of Hezekiah before 700 B.C., with the single exception of 14:28-32 which is assigned to the year Ahaz died (715).[3] If, however, Ahaz died after Hezekiah began to reign, then 14:28-32 would not be out of chronological order. The oracles against foreign nations (chaps. 13-23) belong to various dates preceding Sennacherib's invasion in 701 B.C. and the death of Hezekiah in 686, and are grouped together here because of their similar theme. *Chapters 40-66* belong to the reign of Hezekiah after 701 according to Robinson,[4] and perhaps include, as J. Barton Payne suggests, a part of the reign of Manasseh, the prophet rebuking the national sins under the rising apostasy of this wicked monarch.[5]

[2]Schultz suggests, however, that perhaps his call is recorded in chap. 6 instead of chap. 1 because he wished to portray the extreme wickedness of his generation, thus providing the reader with a better understanding of Isaiah's reluctance in accepting the responsibility of this prophetic ministry (Samuel J. Schultz, *The Old Testament Speaks,* p. 304).

[3]George L. Robinson, *The Book of Isaiah,* pp. 48-53.

[4]*Ibid.,* pp. 53-56.

[5]J. Barton Payne, *An Outline of Hebrew History,* pp. 143-44.

III. The Prophet

The name borne by Isaiah, considered by many the greatest of the literary prophets, was symbolic of his message since it signifies "Yahweh is salvation" or "Yahweh saves." The name was not an uncommon one as may be seen from I Chronicles 25:3, 15; 26:25; Ezra 8:7; Nehemiah 11:7, where the form Jeshaiah is used. Isaiah was the son of Amoz, not to be confused with Amos, his contemporary. Amoz, Isaiah's father, according to Jewish tradition, was a brother of King Amaziah, which would make Isaiah a cousin to King Uzziah.

Isaiah was married, and his wife was called a "prophetess" (8:3). He had two sons, Shear-jashub (7:3) and Maher-shalal-hash-baz (8:1-4). The scene of his labors appears to have been chiefly in Judah and Jerusalem (1:1). He had intimate access to the royal court of both Ahaz and Hezekiah as is apparent from several passages (cf. 7:3 ff.; 37:21 ff.; 38:1 ff.; 39:3-8). He was also the historian of the reigns of Uzziah and Hezekiah, according to II Chronicles 26:21-22; 32:32. The questions of Isaiah's call and length of ministry are sufficiently discussed under the date of the book (II) and require no further mention here.

IV. The Historical Background

According to the superscription of his book, Isaiah labored during the reigns of Uzziah, Jotham, Ahaz and Hezekiah. During the early part of this period both Judah and Israel were politically and economically prosperous. Under Uzziah, Judah had attained an unusually high degree of prosperity (II Chron. 26). Israel, under the reign of Jeroboam II which had just ended, had recovered most of the territory formerly subject to Solomon (II Kings 14:25, 28). The material prosperity of the two kingdoms produced the usual social and moral evils, as well as religious declension, which inevitably results under such circumstances. The wealth and luxury which resulted from their economic prosperity, together with the spirit of optimism created by their military successes, produced an attitude of carnal self-confidence and careless security in the two capitals, which was also rebuked by Isaiah's contemporary, Amos (760-753).

Such was the situation, therefore, when Isaiah appeared upon the scene. Isaiah's mission was principally concerned with the rebuke of Judah for her iniquities, oppressions, injustices, foreign alliances and religious hypocrisy. He boldly denounced the sins of the people (chap. 1) and rulers alike (7:13), and predicted the overthrow of both kingdoms at the hands of Assyria and Babylon.

Three grave crises arose during Isaiah's ministry, namely, the Syro-Ephraimitic war in 734 B.C.; the fall of Samaria in 722; and the invasion of Judah by Sennacherib in 701 (see discussion under "Eighth Century Prophets"). The historical background for the period of Isaiah is set forth in II Kings 15-21 and II Chronicles 26-33.

V. PROBLEMS

Without question the problem of the unity of the book of Isaiah has been the subject of more discussion, by both critics and defenders of its integrity, than any other question concerning the prophetic books of the Old Testament. The critical school with one voice denies the unity of Isaiah, rejecting the Isaianic authorship of chapters 40-66 by assigning them to an unknown author or authors living near the close of the Babylonian exile. Criticism designates chapters 40-66 as Second Isaiah or Deutero-Isaiah.

Since J. C. Doederlein published his commentary on Isaiah in 1775, in which he denied chapters 40-66 as the work of the Prophet Isaiah, critical scholars have generally considered the book as two separate works. Duhm in 1892 went so far as to question the unity of chapters 40-66. He limited "Second Isaiah" to chapters 40-55, written in Babylon (*c.* 549-538 B.C.), and designated 56-66 as "Trito-Isaiah," written by another unknown author in Palestine (*c.* 460-445 B.C.). In addition, negative critics generally deny to Isaiah chapters 11:10-16; 12; 13:1—14:23; 15:1—16:12; 21:1-10; 24-27; 34-35; 36-39; 40-66, or about two-thirds of the book.

According to Driver, three independent lines of argument show that chapters 40-66 are not the work of the Prophet Isaiah, but were written near the close of the Babylonian captivity:

1. The *historical background* of chapters 40-66 presupposes the exile. Internal evidence indicates that the prophecy (40-66) was written from the standpoint of the exile, as the theme is the exile and the return.(*a*) Jerusalem is depicted as ruined and deserted (44:26*b*; 58:12; 61:4; 63:18; 64:10 f.). (*b*) The people are experiencing affliction at the hands of the Chaldeans (42:22, 25; 47:6; 52:5). (*c*) The prospect of return is imminent (40:2; 46:13; 48:20). (*d*) Those whom the prophet addresses are his contemporaries in Babylon whom he addresses in person, not those of Isaiah's day in Jerusalem (40:21, 26, 28; 43:10; 48:8; 50:10 f.; 51:6, 12 f.; 58:3 f.). Driver argues that on the analogy of prophecy wherein the prophet always speaks to his own contemporaries, the message being related to the circumstances of his own time, chapters 40-66 presuppose the exile. The prophets never abandon their historical position and throw themselves forward

to an ideal standpoint, describing future events as though they were past.[6]

2. The *literary style* of chapters 40-66 is said to be markedly different from Isaiah's writings in 1-39. (*a*) Many words and expressions used in 40-66 are not found in the earlier portions of the book. (*b*) Isaiah's style is stately, terse and grave, whereas the prophet of 40-66 is more flowing, lyrical, warm, and impassioned. (*c*) Personification is common in 40-66. (*d*) Chapters 40-66 are characterized by dramatic representation.[7]

3. The *theological ideas* of chapters 40-66 differ from those of Isaiah in 1-39. (*a*) Driver contends that Isaiah depicts the majesty of Yahweh, whereas in 40-66 the prophet emphasizes His infinitude. (*b*) Again the doctrine of a remnant is characteristic of Isaiah (6:13; 37:31 ff.). In 40-66 it is present only by implication (59:20; 65:8 ff.), and not expressed in Isaiah's terminology. (*c*) Chapters 1-39 speak of the Messianic King (9:6-7; 11:1 ff.); chapters 40-66 describe Yahweh's Servant (42:1 ff.; 49:1 ff.; 50:4-9; 52:13—53:12; 61:1-3).[8]

In addition to these arguments critics also contend that (1) the name of Isaiah does not occur in chapters 40-66; (2) Cyrus is mentioned by name one hundred fifty years before his time if these chapters are assigned to Isaiah (cf. 44:28; 45:1); (3) Zechariah 9-14 presents a similar case to Isaiah 40-66, where differences in style indicate a later date for this section by an unknown author.

That these arguments by the critics against the unity of Isaiah are inconclusive and based upon erroneous presuppositions is evident for several reasons:

1. First of all it is claimed that the historical background of chapters 40-66 presupposes the period of the exile. The writer speaks from the standpoint of the exile, not of events in the remote future. Conservative scholars have approached this question from two viewpoints. In the first place there are those evangelical expositors such as Alexander, followed by E. J. Young, J. Barton Payne and others, who contend that the standpoint of chapters 40-66 is *not* the Babylonian exile but the eighth century B.C. Alexander writes, "Let it be observed how seldom, after all, the book mentions Babylon, the Exile, or the restoration,"[9] for "the Prophet speaks of Babylon less

---

[6]S. R. Driver, *An Introduction to the Literature of the Old Testament*, p. 237.

[7]*Ibid.*, p. 242.

[8]*Ibid.*, pp. 238-42.

[9]Joseph Addison Alexander, *Commentary on the Prophecies of Isaiah*, p. 57.

frequently than Egypt."[10] Alexander concludes that "the downfall of Babylon is repeatedly mentioned, like the exodus from Egypt, as a great event in the history of Israel; but . . . the subject of the prophecy is neither the Egyptian nor the Babylonian bondage, nor deliverance from either, but the whole condition, character, and destiny of Israel."[11]

J. Barton Payne suggests that "much of 40-66, moreover, simply cannot refer to Babylon; 52:3-6 seems to make direct reference to deliverance from *Assyrian* captivity."[12] "Chapter 40 . . . constitutes an authentic prophecy of Isaiah, datable to 701 B.C., and directed to that chastened remnant of Judah which survived Sennacherib's devastations and deportations, seemingly more massive even than those of Nebuchadrezzar, exaggerated as the Assyrian claims of over 200,-000 captives may be."[13] Hence, the background for 40-66 is not the Babylonian captivity but the historical conditions of the eighth century B.C.

On the other hand, many interpreters of the conservative school hold the position that it is to be admitted that the standpoint of chapters 40-66 is the exile, since this is precisely the writer's intention. As Hengstenberg has shown, the prophet purposely assumes as his standpoint the time when Jerusalem was to be conquered by the Chaldeans; it is an ideal, not a real standpoint. In this future period he thinks and speaks; it has become for him the present. Hence, the question is merely whether one believes in the biblical view of prophecy whereby God through the inspiration of the Holy Spirit can reveal the future to His prophets.

Driver himself admits that the prophets did sometimes "throw themselves forward to an ideal standpoint, and describe from it events future to themselves, as though they were past (e.g., 5:13-15; 9:1-16; 23:1, 14)."[14] But he ignores this testimony as not being really parallel, since in these and other instances such transference to the future is only "transient," whereas in Isaiah 40-60 the standpoint of the exile is sustained throughout.[15] Skinner likewise concedes that no argument can be raised as to the "possibility" of such a projection of the prophetic standpoint into the remote future, since it does

[10]*Ibid.*, p. 59.

[11]*Ibid.*

[12]Payne, "The Unity of Isaiah: Evidence from Chapters 36-39," *Bulletin of the Evangelical Theological Society,* ed. Samuel J. Schultz, VI, No. 2 (May, 1963), 53-54.

[13]*Ibid.*, p. 53.

[14]Driver, p. 237.

[15]*Ibid.*, pp. 237-38.

occur in the Old Testament, but that no example can be produced where a prophet so immerses himself in the future throughout twenty-seven chapters.[16] It would be sufficient to point out that no "parallel" examples need to be produced to authenticate its occurrence here. Moreover, the critics' objection loses its force by their own admission that such instances do occur but to a lesser degree!

However, it is not true that parallel examples are absent in the Scriptures whereby the prophet, in a lengthy discourse, speaks from an ideal, future standpoint as if it were the present or past. Practically the entire book of Revelation in the New Testament presents just such an example where the writer is completely immersed in future events as if they were actually present before him. Again, Ezekiel throughout chapters 40-48 of his prophecy does not distinguish between the idealistic future standpoint of the millennium and the actual present. Nahum, in chapters 2-3, describes the destruction of Nineveh as if the prophet were actually present witnessing its devastation and imminent downfall. Psalm 22 cannot be limited to events in David's past experiences; in the Spirit he speaks prophetically of Christ's crucifixion and death. And so it is with Psalm 2 (cf. Acts 4:25 ff.; 13:33 ff.) and many similar instances throughout the Scriptures.

Not every prophecy needs to be traced to a definite contemporary historical situation, nor directly applicable to the generation to whom it is spoken. It cannot be maintained, as Driver contends, that "the prophet speaks always, in the first instance to his own contemporaries: the message which he brings is intimately related with the circumstances of his time: his promises and predictions . . . correspond to the needs which are then felt."[17] Obvious contradictions to this concept of prophecy are Zechariah 9-14; Daniel 11-12 (see especially 12:4, 8-9); Isaiah 24-27, in addition to those already mentioned. This is not to overlook, of course, a general relationship of prophecy to the historical situation which called forth the prophetic utterance.

It seems evident then that 40-55 are indeed written from the standpoint of the exile. Israel is projected there in prophecy, from which captivity she is promised deliverance. But more than this is foretold. Isaiah prophesies of the time when his people will be scattered among all the nations during her present dispersion and predicts her restoration and the glorious millennial kingdom. The prophet

---

[16]J. Skinner, "Introduction to the Book of the Prophet Isaiah," Vol. II of *The Cambridge Bible for Schools and Colleges,* ed. A. F. Kirkpatrick, pp. xvii-xviii.

[17]Driver, p. 237.

doubtless saw as one event what in reality were to be *two* restorations, the first from Babylon, the second in the latter days at the second advent (cf. Isa. 2; 11; 24-27; 34-35; 54-55; 60-66).

Furthermore, the numerous strictures against idolatry to be found in the supposedly postexilic chapters are, as Archer has observed, a most decisive objection to a postexilic date for the composition of chapters 40-66. Note for example 41:21-24; 44:9-20; 57:4-5, 7; 65:2-4; 66:17. The hilly terrain referred to excludes the possibility of this idolatrous worship being carried on in Babylonia which is a flat, alluvial plain. The forms of worship alluded to are those which characterized the reign of Manasseh. Scholars agree that the returning exiles brought back no idolatry to Judah, having been delivered of this iniquitous practice during their captivity. Not until the time of Antiochus Epiphanes in the second century B.C. was there any serious attempt to introduce it again in Israel. This is confirmed by the writings of the postexilic authors Haggai, Zechariah, Malachi, Ezra and Nehemiah who, although they denounce a variety of sins and shortcomings among the returned Jews, never lift their voices against the practice of idolatry.[18]

2. The differences in style between chapters 40-66 and 1-39 are not sufficient to indicate differences in authorship. As in the case of Zechariah 9-14, the change of subject matter can well account for this. Such literary arguments are wholly subjective and always precarious. An author's style can only be determined from the book which bears his name. "To derive our knowledge of his style from a part of that book on the presumption that he wrote it and then to deny his authorship for the remainder of the book, is reasoning in a circle."[19]

Moreover, the critics do not sufficiently take into consideration the *similarities* between the two sections of the prophecy in their effort to magnify alleged differences. The resemblances in style and language are not insignificant. The phrase "the Holy One of Israel" occurs a dozen or more times in each section, but is rarely used elsewhere in the prophets. God is "the Mighty One of Israel" in both 1:24 and 49:26; 60:16. The phrase "the mouth of Yahweh hath spoken it" in 1:20 is repeated in 40:5; 58:14. The promise of restoration to Zion in 35:10 is repeated verbatim in 51:11. "They shall not hurt nor destroy in all my holy mountain" in 11:9 is repeated in

[18]Gleason L. Archer, Jr., *A Survey of Old Testament Introduction,* pp. 329-31.

[19]John H. Raven, *Old Testament Introduction,* p. 189.

65:25. In fact, passages in which there is actual verbal agreement, or similarity in phraseology, metaphor, thought and figure between the two sections, are so numerous as to remove any doubt of the unity of the book to the unprejudiced mind. Literally hundreds are cited by Rawlinson in his introduction to Isaiah.[20] The similarities are so numerous and striking that some critics, rather than give up their theory of two books, were compelled to conjecture that "second Isaiah" was either a disciple of Isaiah, someone in the exile filled with the spirit of Isaiah, or one who wrote in conscious imitation of the prophet! But whatever differences in style may occur can readily be explained because Isaiah in 40-66 was writing upon another subject and from another viewpoint.[21]

3. The alleged theological differences between chapters 1-39 and chapters 40-66 are nonexistent. The more elevated ideas of God said to characterize "second Isaiah" may be accounted for in the same way as the alleged differences in style, on the basis of change of subject and viewpoint (cf. Zech. 9-14). Furthermore, there is no absence in 40-66, as Driver claims, of the deliverance of a faithful remnant (mentioned in 6:13; 37:31 ff.), for the precise reason that the entire section (40-66) concerns the salvation and deliverance of a remnant both in Israel and from among the Gentiles! George L. Robinson is correct when he states that 2:2-4, with chapter 6, is the key to Isaiah's horizon in 40-66.[22]

4. Isaiah appears as the author of the book bearing his name by virtue of the heading (1:1), which is clearly intended to apply to the entire prophecy of 66 chapters, not merely chapters 1-39. Critics who argue that since Isaiah's name does not occur in 40-66 it must not be by his hand, overlook the fact that most prophets did not head each new division of their prophecies by repeating the original superscription (cf. Zech. 9-14; Joel 2; Hosea 4, etc.). Furthermore, since it is customary for the negative critics to consider the superscriptions of books as suspect, rejecting them as often as not as later editorial glosses (cf. Hosea 1:1), had Isaiah's name occurred in 40-66, it would be rejected no doubt as a later editorial addition.

5. Moreover, there is no manuscript evidence to show that the entire prophecy is not a unified whole and written by the Prophet

---

[20]George Rawlinson, "Introduction to the Book of the Prophet Isaiah," Vol. X of *The Pulpit Commentary*, eds. H. D. M. Spence and J. S. Exell, pp. xii-xvii.

[21]Raven, p. 190.

[22]Robinson, p. 63.

Isaiah. This fact was further strengthened by the discovery of the
Dead Sea Scrolls in 1947. It is noteworthy that in the Isaiah Scroll,
dating from the second century B.C., chapter 40 begins on the last line
of the column which contains 38:8—40:2. This is a second century
B.C. witness to the unity of Isaiah. The LXX (*c.* 250-200 B.C.) ascribes
the entire contents of the book to Isaiah, the son of Amoz. The
Apocryphal book of Ecclesiasticus (*c.* 180 B.C.) regards the prophecy as a unity. Referring to Isaiah 40:1 we read: "He comforted them
that mourned in Sion" (Ecclus. 48:24). Concerning the future scope
of 40-55, the author writes: "He saw by an excellent spirit what
should come to pass at the last. . .[and secret things] or ever they
came" (Ecclus. 48:24-25). Quite evidently Ben Sirach, the author of
Ecclesiasticus, considered chapters 40-66 a prophecy by Isaiah of
future events concerning Israel, not the description of events by some
unknown writer at the close of the Babylonian exile. Furthermore,
allusions to Isaiah 40-66 by the preexilic prophets sustain the unity
of the book. (Cf. Zeph. 2:15 with Isa. 47:8, 10; Nahum 1:15 with Isa.
52:7; Jer. 31:35 with Isa. 51:15; and Jer. 10:1-16 with Isa. 41:7 and
44:12-15.)[23]

6. The author of the so-called "second Isaiah" was a Palestinian. "The writer of chapters 40-66," Raven notes, "does not show the
familiarity with the land or religion of Babylon which we would
expect from a man living among the captives."[24] On the other hand,
mention is made of Jerusalem and of things pertaining to Palestine,
or from the viewpoint of the promised land (cf. 52:11).

7. The witness of the New Testament to the unity of Isaiah is
without question the strongest defense of Isaianic authorship.
Alexander, in his commentary on Isaiah, notes that Isaiah is quoted
by name twenty-one times in the New Testament from both sections
of the book, and of the sixty-six chapters, forty-seven are directly
quoted or alluded to several times.[25] John 12:38-40 contains two
quotations from the book of Isaiah, one from 53:1, the other from 6:9
f.; and John adds, "These things said Isaiah" (v. 41), thus indicating that the quotations from both parts of the book have a single
author. Luke 4:17 states that "the book of the prophet Isaiah" was
delivered to Jesus who read from Isaiah 61:1, the alleged anonymous
portion. In Acts 8:30 the Ethiopian eunuch was reading from "Isaiah
the prophet" and the passage he refers to is Isaiah 53. Over and over
the New Testament states in its quotations from Isaiah that they are

[23]Merrill F. Unger, *Introductory Guide to the Old Testament,* p. 320.
[24]Raven, p. 195.
[25]Alexander, p. 13.

from "Isaiah the prophet" (cf. Matt. 3:3; 4:14; 8:17; John 1:23; Rom. 9:27, 29, etc.).

8. It is also claimed that the mention of Cyrus by name a century and a half before his time argues against Isaianic authorship of 40-66.[26] But this fact should present no problem to those who believe in predictive prophecy. Moreover, such a prediction is not without precedent. Josiah's reign was foretold about three centuries in advance and his name was given (I Kings 13:1-2). The virgin birth of Christ was predicted, as was His crucifixion, in the eighth century B.C. (Isa. 7; 53). The exact place of His birth was predicted by Micah, Isaiah's contemporary (Micah 5:2). Jeremiah foretold the captivity, indicating the precise number of years as seventy (25:11-12). Daniel's predictions, in minute detail, of the events of history, centuries in advance, are so precise that critics have been forced to assign the book to the second century B.C. after the events had occurred.

9. Finally, Isaiah 40-66 is admitted, even by the critics, to be an incomparable literary production and its author the greatest of Old Testament prophets. Why then, we may ask, is his identity unknown, and how did his work become attached as a mere appendix to the book of Isaiah?

A second problem of the book concerns the *Immanuel prophecy* of Isaiah 7:14. To understand the context in which this great prophecy was uttered a review of the background will be necessary. Rezin of Damascus and Pekah of Israel were endeavoring to force Ahaz, king of Judah, into an alliance with Syria and Israel against Assyria. His refusal resulted in an invasion of Judah in 734 B.C. by Syria and Israel upon which Ahaz sent an appeal to Assyria for aid. Isaiah the prophet warned him to trust in the Lord for deliverance and, to confirm his message, the prophet offered to work any sign Ahaz would desire. "Ask thee a sign of Yahweh thy God; ask it either in the depth, or in the height above" (7:11). The king scoffed at the offer, upon which the prophet gave a sign anyway—Isaiah 7:14, the Immanuel prophecy.

Various interpretations have been offered in an effort to deny the Messianic implications of the passage. The problem is twofold: (1) Who is the virgin of whom Isaiah speaks? (2) Is the term "virgin" a correct translation of the Hebrew word *'almâh* in this verse? First of

---

[26]For an excellent defense of the Isaianic authorship of the prophecies concerning Cyrus, see Oswald T. Allis, *The Unity of Isaiah,* chaps. 4-5; E. J. Young, *Who Wrote Isaiah?*

all then, who is the virgin of Isaiah 7:14? Five different solutions
have been proposed:

1. *The virgin was Ahaz' wife; the son, Hezekiah.* The mother
was Abi, the wife of Ahaz (II Kings 18:2), and the son, Hezekiah,
who delivered Judah from the Assyrians. But according to II Kings
16:2; 18:2, Hezekiah was nine years old in the first year of Ahaz, and
the prophecy predicts a future birth.

2. *The virgin was Isaiah's wife; the son, Maher-shalal-hash-baz.*
The mother was Isaiah's wife, the prophetess of 8:3, and the son was
Maher-shalal-hash-baz. Several arguments are usually cited in support of this view. (*a*) This fits the context of 8:1-4. (*b*) Immanuel is
simply a *symbolic* designation that "God is with us" of which the son
is the sign. (*c*) The Hebrew terms "shall conceive" and "shall bear"
used in this verse are not finite verbs but are participles, without
regard to tense or time, therefore do not have to refer to the future.
The literal translation should read: "Behold, the *'almâh* [is] pregnant and bearing a son."[27] The English versions translate these
participles incorrectly as future tenses. Hence, the woman has already conceived and is bearing a son to Isaiah. (*d*) Verse 16 proves
the sign would be fulfilled in Ahaz' time. The prophecy would have no
meaning to Ahaz if it referred to the birth of Christ in the future.
Moreover, the term *'almâh* has the definite article prefixed ("the
virgin") and must therefore have been a woman known to Ahaz and
Israel. (*e*) Furthermore, the Hebrew word *'almâh* does not mean
"virgin," but simply "a maiden" or "a girl of marriageable age." The
unequivocal term for virgin in the Old Testament is *bᵉthûlâh*. (*f*)
The miracle is in Isaiah's prediction of a *son* to be born (rather than
a daughter).

3. The theory that the "virgin" in Isaiah 7:14 is *a personification of the house of David* (Hofmann) has no valid basis whatever,
as Delitzsch has shown in his commentary on Isaiah, for we should
expect the prophet in this case to have used some phrase such as
"daughter of Zion," since the term "virgin" is unknown in a personification of this kind.[28]

4. *A double fulfillment.* A fourth view which has been proposed
suggests that the prophecy has a double reference and fulfillment. A
young woman of Ahaz' day (identity unknown) who was *then* a

---

[27]A similar formula, according to Old Testament critics, is said to be
found in the Ras Shamra texts. For an excellent evaluation of this question and
refutation of the assumptions of negative criticism, see Young, *Studies in
Isaiah.*

[28]C. F. Keil and F. Delitzsch, *The Prophecies of Isaiah, Biblical Commentary on the Old Testament,* I, 218.

virgin, but had married, would conceive and bear a son, calling his name Immanuel (this would not be a "virgin birth" however). The prophecy would then find fulfillment in Ahaz' day as the context suggests. But the immediate fulfillment did not exhaust the prophecy, which had a deeper meaning. The prophecy is so worded that its ultimate fulfillment was by the virgin Mary and the birth of Christ. All the expressions of the prophecy do not have to suit both fulfillments. Compare Matthew 2:15 with Hosea 11:1, for example.

5. *The exclusive Messianic view.* This view, which the author proposes as the correct one, understands Isaiah 7:14 as referring exclusively to the virgin birth of Christ, and that the prophet saw in one *prospectiveless* picture the birth of Immanuel together with more immediate events, a phenomenon common in Old Testament prophecy (cf. II Sam. 7:11-16; Zech. 6:9-15, etc.). There are several reasons which support this interpretation:

a. The prophecy cannot refer to a mere human, as the proponents of the first and second views suggest, since the child to be born is called Immanuel ("God [is] with us").

b. Chapter 8:8 removes all doubt as to whether or not the designation "Immanuel" could refer to Ahaz' or Isaiah's son. The phrase "thy land, O Immanuel" obviously could not mean that the land of Palestine belonged to either Ahaz' or Isaiah's son.

c. Isaiah 9:6-7 and 11:1-5 without question refer to the same child as that in 7:14, and the description in these passages is that of a divine Person.

d. It is incorrect to say that participles cannot be translated in future time, since it is always the context in Hebrew which determines the "time" of a participle. Compare, for example, Genesis 17:19 where the participle *yōledeth* ("shall bear") is identical with that of Isaiah 7:14 and is used to describe the birth of Sarah's son Isaac which, as the context shows, could only refer to the future. Moreover, the first term in question ("shall conceive") is not a participle, but a feminine adjective meaning "pregnant" ("woman with child"), and the adjective, just as the participle, is always in the same "time" as the context in which it is used. Nevertheless, the verse can be properly translated with the force of the present tense, namely, "the virgin is pregnant." In prophetic vision the Prophet Isaiah sees before him the virgin pregnant with the child who is to be called Immanuel. The emphasis in the vision is not upon time, but is concerned primarily with the fact that a virgin is with child. This is what constituted it as a sign.

e. If Isaiah were referring to his wife he probably would have used the common term for wife (*'ishshâh*). The use of the term *'almâh* must have signified some person other than his wife. The fact that the definite article is prefixed to *'almâh* ("the virgin") does not necessarily imply that it was someone whom Ahaz knew, but suggests that some special significance is to be attached to this particular virgin. Moreover, Isaiah's wife already had borne a son, Shear-jashub, and thus was not a virgin at the time of this prophecy. In addition, there is no mention of a father, as is also the case in Micah 5:2, Isaiah 9, and the gospel accounts.

Finally, the critics object to the claim that this is a prediction by Isaiah of an event in the distant future, since the prophet always speaks, first of all, to his contemporaries and never abandons his own historical position. This is seen in verse 16 where the prophet predicts that Judah will soon be delivered from Israel and Syria. In what sense could the purely Messianic view be a sign of the fulfillment of this event? What meaning, they ask, could the sign of the birth of Immanuel have for King Ahaz and the house of David in the eighth century B.C., if it refers to an event many centuries yet future to them? The answer is that the sign had no meaning to them necessarily. Ahaz, in disbelief, had refused God's offer to fulfill any sign that he might choose which would have had contemporary significance; hence, God would give a sign of His own choosing. Moreover, full or immediate comprehension is not always essential to a prophecy, nor is it necessarily the purpose in a sign. Jonah's experience in the eighth century B.C. was a sign of the death and resurrection of Christ centuries before the events occurred and before anyone knew the inward spiritual significance of Jonah's three days' confinement in the belly of the fish! Nevertheless, Christ speaks of it as a divinely intended *sign* of His own burial three days and three nights in the heart of the earth (Matt. 12:38-40). Again, in Zechariah 3:8 God gives Israel a sign concerning the Messiah who would come, which, at that time, could have no real meaningful significance to the prophet's contemporaries: "Hear now, O Joshua the high priest, thou and thy fellows that sit before thee; for they are men that are a sign: for, behold, I will bring forth my servant the Branch." It cannot be maintained, therefore, that the essential purpose in every sign is for it to have immediate significance to that particular generation in which it was given.

Therefore, these were *prophetic signs* just as in the case of Isaiah's sign to Judah. God had graciously condescended to fulfill any sign that Ahaz cared to ask in order to confirm for him Isaiah's predictions concerning the overthrow of Israel and Syria who had attacked Judah, but he, in disbelief, had scornfully refused. Where-upon, Isaiah rebuked his hardness of heart and carnal disbelief and declared that God Himself would give a sign. The sign was the utterance of a great Messianic prophecy—Isaiah 7:14: "Therefore the Lord himself will give you a sign: behold, a virgin shall conceive, and bear a son, and shall call his name Immanuel." All the events spoken of in the context (e.g., v. 16) would surely be fulfilled before the child grew to the age of discernment. As a matter of fact those events concerning Ahaz were fulfilled within a few years; the virgin birth, however, was not to find fulfillment until centuries later. Isaiah does not make any statement as to the time element involved. This is a frequent characteristic in Messianic prophecy (cf. II Sam. 7:12-16). The Messianic prophecy given to Judah was *itself* the sign![29] The *'almâh* of this prophecy, as Delitzsch has shown, was to remain an enigma throughout the Old Testament, stimulating inquiry (I Peter 1:10-12) and waiting for the historical solution, as was also the case with the suffering Servant in Isaiah 53. The sign in question was "a mystery smiling with rich consolation upon the prophet and all believers, and couched in the enigmatical terms, in order that those who hardened themselves [as Ahaz] might not understand it, and that believers might increasingly long to compre-hend its meaning."[30]

The second problem in connection with Isaiah 7:14 concerns the term *'almâh*. Is the designation "virgin" a correct translation of this Hebrew term? Old Testament critics insist that *'almâh* means a "young woman" sexually mature or of marriageable age, never a virgin, and can even designate a married woman.[31] Furthermore, had Isaiah intended to convey the idea of a virgin, he had such a term available, *bᵉthulâh* which means "virgin." But these claims are in-

[29]The declaration of Isaiah in vv. 15-17, which depicts Immanuel eating "butter [curds] and honey," food reflecting the poverty and desolation of Judah (v. 22), until He comes to the years of discretion, is a prediction, symbolically expressed, that Judah's desolation caused by the invasion of Rezin and Pekah would be of short duration. Young notes in his commentary on Isaiah that the infancy of the Messiah was symbolically made the measure of the time that Judah would be in danger from her two enemies (E. J. Young, *The Book of Isaiah,* I, 291-98). Likewise, in 8:4 the infancy of Maher-shalal-hash-baz is made the measure of time elapsing before Assyria would devastate Damascus and Syria. What was prophesied in 7:15-16 is confirmed in 8:4.

[30]Keil and Delitzsch, I, 220.

[31]Francis Brown, S. R. Driver and Charles A. Briggs, *A Hebrew and English Lexicon of the Old Testament,* p. 261.

conclusive and by no means convey the true nature of the situation when all the facts are considered.

It is significant that the meaning "virgin" fits the context of the passages where *'almâh* occurs and can be denied in none of them (Gen. 24:43; Exodus 2:8; Ps. 68:25; Prov. 30:19; Song of Sol. 1:3; 6:8). For example, in Genesis 24 both *bᵉthulâh* (v. 16) and *'almâh* (v. 43) occur. Rebekah is called a *bᵉthulâh* ("virgin") in verse 16 and an *'almâh* in verse 43. This can mean but one thing—both terms can, in certain instances at least, mean virgin. That is, inasmuch as Rebekah is called in verse 16 a *bᵉthulâh* ("virgin"), verse 43 indicates that *'almâh* can properly be applied to a girl who has already been designated as a virgin.

Why then did Isaiah use the Hebrew term *'almâh* instead of *bᵉthulâh* if he intended to convey the idea of a virgin birth? *Bᵉthulâh* often needs some qualification to clarify whether or not a virgin is meant. For example, in Genesis 24:16 Rebekah is described as "a virgin [*bᵉthulâh*], *neither had any man known her*" (cf. Judges 21:12). Also the word can be used to designate a married woman (Joel 1:8; Deut. 22:24). Quite often, then, unless some qualifying phrase is used one cannot tell from *bᵉthulâh* whether or not the woman in question is a virgin, whereas *'almâh* is never so qualified.

Furthermore, it is not true that *'almâh* can sometimes designate a married woman. In not one single instance either in the Scriptures or in extrabiblical literature is there any support to the critical claim that *'almâh* is used of a married woman. On the contrary, the presumption was that every *'almâh* was, by implication, a virgin and unmarried.[32] Thus, the prophet selected the term *'almâh* as more fitting than *bethulâh*, since the latter term would have needed qualification, whereas the term *'almâh* would sufficiently encompass the ultimate intended meaning of the prophecy. Hence, *'almâh* should be rendered "unmarried damsel" or "virgin."

The child described in 7:14 was to be *Immanuel*. In chapter 9:6-7 this child to be born is declared to be the "Mighty God," "Everlasting Father," "Prince of Peace." These are Old Testament prophecies of the incarnation of Deity; therefore, His birth would, of necessity, be unusual and miraculous. Unless *'almâh* be translated with the implication of "virgin" there is no announcement worthy of being constituted as a sign of the birth of Immanuel, who was to be called "Mighty God."

It is significant that the Septuagint translators, writing in the

[32]See Edward J. Young's scholarly study of Isaiah 7:14 in his *Studies in Isaiah.*

third century before Christ, rendered 'almâh by the Greek *parthenos*, "a virgin." Moreover, the Holy Spirit rendered Isaiah's term 'almâh as "virgin" (*parthenos*) in Matthew 1:23 (cf. vv. 18-22). This, of course, will settle the matter for the Christian. All the scholarly debate on the subject as to the precise meaning of 'almâh cannot change the fact that the concept which the Holy Spirit had in mind when He inspired Isaiah to use the term 'almâh in his prophecy was that of a *virgin!*

A third problem concerns the identity of the "servant" mentioned in the servant poems in Isaiah 42:1-9; 49:1-9; 50:4-9; 52:13—53:12.[33]

Few Old Testament problems have occupied the scholars more than the attempts to identify the servant in these passages.[34]

The various theories fall into two general groups: those which consider the servant of the Lord as descriptive of Israel or a pious remnant within the nation, and those which view the servant as an individual.[35]

1. *The servant is Israel.* The Jews abandoned the traditional Messianic interpretation of the servant due to the Christian testimony of the identification of the servant with Jesus of Nazareth, and applied the prophecies to certain ones of the prophets, or to the nation of Israel itself. Beginning with the nineteenth century, critical scholars have adopted one or another of the Jewish interpretations either categorically or with certain modifications. As H. H. Rowley notes in his work *The Servant of the Lord and Other Essays*, with the advent of the critical view, which contended that chapters 40-66 were not the work of Isaiah, there came a growing tendency to accept the common Jewish view that the suffering servant was the nation Israel.[36]

Those who view the servant as the nation Israel, or the pious

---

[33]The term "servant" occurs twenty times in Isa. 40-53. Only the four above mentioned passages are designated as "servant poems," although some would, with good reason, include 61:1-3 despite the fact that the word "servant" does not occur.

[34]See C. R. North, *The Suffering Servant in Deutero-Isaiah,* for a recent survey of the vast amount of literature on the subject.

[35]Grossmann, Gunkel, A. Jeremias and others were exponents of the mythological view of Isaiah 53, contending that this servant poem was based upon a hymn in honor of Tammuz-Adonis. A ritual song from the cultic myth of the dying and resurrected god allegedly influenced the writer of Deutero-Isaiah!

[36]H. H. Rowley, *The Servant of the Lord and Other Essays on the Old Testament,* p. 4.

remnant within the nation, contend that the two are repeatedly equated (cf. 41:8; 43:8-13; 44:1-2, 21; 45:4; 49:3). It is contended further that Isaiah 52:13—53:12 depicts the vicarious sufferings of the nation, especially in the Babylonian exile. It was representative suffering—God's means of redeeming the world. Israel paid double for her sins (40:2), but this was in Yahweh's purpose. Israel, redeemed and purified, became the servant of God to the nations. The sight of her sufferings moves the nations to repentance when it is interpreted in light of God's redemptive purpose in Israel's punishment and suffering. Thus the concept of vicarious and redemptive suffering is born.[37]

In marked contrast to this view of Israel's sufferings is the clear testimony of Scripture to the contrary. The Jewish exiles could hardly be said to be suffering vicariously on behalf of others, for it was in punishment for her own sins that Israel was sent into captivity (Jer. 25:1-10), whereas the servant of chapter 53 suffers *solely* for the sins of others. In fact, there could not be found a righteous person in Israel on whose behalf God would spare others (Jer. 5:1). Moreover, Israel was so wicked and obdurate that vicarious intercession or suffering in her behalf was impossible even if offered by such as Moses, Samuel and others whose intercession for Israel God had previously accepted in lieu of the nation's deserved punishment (Jer. 15:1; Ezek. 14:14, 20). How utterly impossible it was then that sinful Israel could suffer vicariously for the sins of others. The basic principle of redemptive and vicarious suffering depicted in Old Testament sacrifice, in which the substitute was always to be innocent and without blemish, was all too clearly absent in the case of Israel. Israel, as sinful, could not have constituted an acceptable substitute to God on behalf of other wicked nations.

Israel paying double for her sins (Isa. 40:2) had no redemptive significance, for the Scriptures clearly teach that Israel, because of her privileged position and election, must therefore undergo a severer judgment than the unenlightened heathen nations: "You only have I known of all the families of the earth: therefore I will visit upon you all your iniquities" (Amos 3:2; see also Jer. 16:17-18; Dan. 9:11-12).

Other interpreters have, equally without success, sought to identify the servant with some pious and suffering group or class within Israel, such as the body of prophets, the Davidic dynasty, the priesthood, the Hasidim, or Isaiah's own disciples.

[37]Otto J. Baab, *The Theology of the Old Testament*, pp. 235-36.

2. *The servant is an individual.* The suggestions as to the identification of the servant with a historical character of past, present or future history are so numerous they can only be mentioned briefly. The servant has been identified with the suffering Prophet Jeremiah, Zerubbabel, Jehoiachin, Moses, Josiah, Hezekiah, Uzziah, and with the so-called "Deutero-Isaiah" himself. In addition, others would equate him with an anonymous contemporary of the Prophet Isaiah, variously depicting the servant as a teacher of the Torah afflicted with leprosy, an exilic martyr or some other pious sufferer.[38]

3. *The servant is the Messiah.* The portrait of the servant depicted in Isaiah 52:13—53:12 is so clearly individualistic that it cannot justifiably be reduced to a mere personification of Israel. Likewise the conjectures that it refers to some historical character other than Christ Himself must also be rejected on the grounds that (*a*) the objective statements in 42:1 show that Isaiah cannot refer to himself; (*b*) the future references in 52:13, 15 and 53:11 exclude Moses, Uzziah or other past figures; (*c*) his sinless character (53:9), his resurrection (53:10) and the nature and magnitude of his work (42:4; 49:5; 53:4-6, 11) go infinitely beyond mere man's capabilities;[39] thus (*d*) the statement can refer to none save Jesus Christ to whom the term is applied by the Holy Spirit in Matthew 8:17; Mark 15:28; Luke 22:37; John 12:37-38; Acts 8:32-33; Romans 10:16; I Peter 2:24-25.

How then may one reconcile the individualistic interpretation with the fact that the servant is called "Israel" in several passages (e.g., 41:8; 43:8-13; 49:3)?

Some critical scholars suggest the idea of *corporate personality* in which there is a transition from the whole group to a single representative of it. Thus writes H. W. Robinson: "Israel is meant, but Israel as represented by its men of prophetic spirit, who have learnt to make an offering to God of their own and the nation's suffering."[40]

On the other hand, Alexander, Delitzsch, Young, Payne, Allis and others correctly identify the figure of the servant with *both* the nation and its head, the Messiah. The servant is "Israel" in its various aspects. The term is fluid, moving in these passages from the sinful nation as a whole (42:19 f.) to the righteous remnant within Israel

---

[38]Robert H. Pfeiffer, *Introduction to the Old Testament,* pp. 460-61.
[39]See J. Barton Payne, *Theology of the Older Testament,* p. 255, n.
[40]H. Wheeler Robinson, *The Old Testament: Its Making and Meaning,* pp. 110-11.

(49:3), and ultimately to an individual, or representative head, the Messiah (49:5; 53:11).

OUTLINE OF ISAIAH

Chapters 1-39

PROPHECIES OF JUDGMENT

I. PROPHECIES CONCERNING JUDAH AND JERUSALEM	Chapters 1-12
A. Introductory Prophecy: Condemnation of Israel's Corruption and Religious Formalism	1:1-31
B. Prophecy of the Universal Millennial Rule After Judgment	2:1—5:30
1. The Glory of the Millennial Kingdom	2:1-4
2. Judgments Preliminary to the Establishment of the Millennial Kingdom: The Day of the Lord	2:5—4:6
3. Grounds for Judgment: Parable of the Vineyard and Woes upon the Wicked	5:1-30
C. Isaiah's Vision of the Lord	6:1-13
D. Prophecies Concerning the Messiah, His Kingdom and the Nation's Punishment	7:1—12:6
1. The Immanuel Prophecy	7:1-25
2. The Sign of Maher-shalal-hash-baz	8:1-22
3. Prophecy of the Birth and Rule of the Messiah	9:1-7
4. Prophecy Against the Kingdom of Israel	9:8—10:4
5. Prophecy Concerning the Providential Use and Punishment of Assyria	10:5-34
6. Prophecy of the Reign of the Messiah and His Millennial Kingdom	11:1-16
7. Responsive Praise to Yahweh: A Song of Thanksgiving	12:1-6
II. PROPHECIES OF JUDGMENT AGAINST THE NATIONS	Chapters 13-23
A. Against Babylon	13:1—14:23
B. Against Assyria	14:24-27
C. Against Philistia	28-32
D. Against Moab	15:1—16:14
E. Against Damascus	17:1-14
F. Against Ethiopia	18:1-7
G. Against Egypt	19:1-25
H. Against Egypt and Ethiopia	20:1-6
I. Against Babylon, Edom and Arabia	21:1-17
1. The Burden of the "Wilderness of the Sea" (Babylon)	1-10
2. The Burden of "Dumah" (Edom)	11-12
3. The Burden of Arabia	13-17
J. Against Jerusalem: The Burden of the Valley of Vision	22:1-25

Chapter 15

MICAH

I. THE NATURE OF THE BOOK

THE BOOK CONSISTS OF three prophetic addresses clearly distinguished from one another by the introductory word "hear" (1:2; 3:1; 6:1). According to Keil, however, these three addresses (chaps. 1-2; 3-5; 6-7) are not three prophecies of Micah delivered to the people at three different times, but rather a condensation of the essential contents of his oral addresses committed to writing. Threatening and promise, judgment and mercy, alternate in these three addresses. There is much in common with Isaiah, and at times the words of both are identical. Being contemporaries, and confronted with the same circumstances, the two prophets would often be dealing with the same subjects.

The three prophetical addresses are differentiated from each other by their contents, tone and point of view, yet demonstrate a certain inward connection. Each division contains a description of the present corruption, an announcement of imminent judgment, and promises of a glorious future. Chapters 1-2 announce a general judgment upon Israel and Judah because of their sins, The second address, after pronouncing divine judgment upon the leaders of the nation, the wicked princes and false prophets (chap. 3), announces the future hope of the Messianic kingdom (chaps. 4-5). The third address consists of an admonition to repentance and hope of future deliverance and salvation (chaps. 6-7).

The essential requirements of true religion and acceptable worship are "to do justly, and to love kindness [mercy], and to walk humbly with thy God" (6:8). Micah sums up in this verse the cardinal principle of genuine religion in contrast to popular religion. From the time Israel escaped from bondage in Egypt until her exile in Babylon over eight centuries later, God, through His prophets, sought to teach her the nature of acceptable religion and worship. True religion was not mere outward conformity to a prescribed ritual, nor the mere bringing of sacrifices or the payment of tithes, but a life lived in accord with the divine principles of righteousness.

Wherewith shall I come before Yahweh, and bow myself before the high God? Shall I come before him with burnt-offerings, with calves a year old? Will Yahweh be pleased with thousands of rams, or with ten thousands of rivers of oil? Shall I give my first-born for my transgression, the fruit of my body for the sin of my soul? He hath showed thee, O man, what is good; and what doth Yahweh require of thee, but to do justly, and to love kindness [mercy], and to walk humbly with thy God? (Micah 6:6-8).

Micah, as did his contemporaries, Hosea, Amos and Isaiah, labored to impress Israel with the truth that certain principles of righteous conduct were required of men, not the mere exercise of external ritual. The inculcation of certain definite moral virtues is his aim in 6:8. The first two have regard to one's moral and ethical responsibilities toward his neighbor; the third stresses humble obedience in fellowship with God. Three inward principles are given: (1) "to do justly," to be motivated by the principle of equity in word and deed in every relationship with one's fellowman, which was the precise opposite to their present conduct (2:1-2, 8;9); (2) "to love kindness [mercy]." One may practice strict justice, as a judge who presides over a court of law, but the justice of the children of God is to be tempered with mercy, or loving-kindness (*hesed*). Justice requires honest and equitable treatment of one's neighbor, whereas mercy is an expression of love and compassion. The injunction here is not simply to *do* mercy, but to *love* mercy, to be merciful out of a spirit of love. "Be ye merciful, even as your Father is merciful," Christ taught His disciples (Luke 6:36; cf. the parable of the unmerciful servant, Matt. 18:23 ff.); (3) "to walk humbly with thy God." To walk in fellowship with God requires humility (having a proper evaluation of oneself in relation to God) and obedience. When the Scriptures speak of one's "walk," they intend to convey the idea of life and conduct. The patriarchs are said to have "walked with God"; the Christian is exhorted to "walk worthily of the calling wherewith ye were called, with all lowliness and meekness, with longsuffering, forbearing one another in love" (Eph. 4:1-2). Humility is constantly enjoined in Scripture upon those who would walk with God (II Chron. 7:14; James 4:6). These three cardinal moral and religious principles are summed up by Christ in Matthew 23:23 as justice, mercy and faith:

Woe unto you, scribes and Pharisees, hypocrites! For ye tithe mint and anise and cummin, and have left undone the weightier matters of the law, justice, and mercy, and faith: but these ye ought to have done, and not to have left the other undone.

No prophet of the Old Testament exceeds Micah in the propor-
tion of predictions respecting Israel's future and the advent of the
Messiah and His kingdom. Among his predictions are: the fall of
Samaria in 722 B.C. (1:6-7); the invasion of Judah by Sennacherib
(1:9-16); the fall of Jerusalem and the destruction of the temple in
586 B.C. (3:12; 7:13); the exile in Babylon (4:10); the return from
captivity and the future peace and supremacy of Israel (4:1-8, 13;
7:11, 14-17); the birth of the Messianic King in Bethlehem (5:2).

To Isaiah and Micah belong the two most unmistakable prophecies of the Messiah. The Prophet Isaiah foretold His birth of a
virgin; Micah described the location of His birthplace so clearly
that when the wise men came inquiring where the King of the Jews
was born, the answer was immediately given to Herod by the Jewish
scribes and priests (Matt. 2:5). Furthermore, Micah predicted that
the time of the Messiah's reign would be one of profound peace
(4:1-7), using the same words as Isaiah 2:2; and in 5:4, 8, as well as
elsewhere, he described His kingdom.[1]

Micah exhibits an acquaintance with the Pentateuch as well as
other books of the Old Testament. His allusions to early history and
the actual expressions he sometimes uses, indicate a knowledge of the
books of Moses. Other books referred to are II Samuel 1:20 (cf.
1:10) and I Kings 22:28 (cf. 1:2). Words are used from the Psalms
(cf. 2:1; 3:2 with Ps. 36:4; 53:4; 14:4; 27:2) and Proverbs (5:9, 11).
Images and language from Amos are adopted (2:3, 6, 11; 3:6).[2]
Micah 4:1-5 and Isaiah 2:2-5 are parallel passages.

Micah is quoted three times: (1) by the elders of Judah (Jer.
26:18 quoting Micah 3:12); (2) by the chief priests and scribes
informing Herod where Jesus was to be born (Matt. 2:5-6 quoting
Micah 5:2); (3) by Jesus when sending out the twelve (Matt.
10:35-36 quoting Micah 7:6).

In Micah 1:10-15 the vividness of the prophet's style is seen in
his unique employment of paronomasia (a play on words) in a
lamentation over Judah (cf. vv. 8-9). Here the forthcoming judgment upon Judah is exemplified by the fate of certain cities in the
surrounding region. The names of these towns become symbolic and
prophetic of their punishment. The meaning, and sometimes the
sound, of the names in Hebrew becomes the basis of a satirical play
on words which is lost in the English translation. For example, it is as
if the prophet had said, "Hightown will be laid low," "There will be
no peace in Concord," or "Cannon Falls will fall by the cannon."

---

[1]W. J. Deane, "Introduction to the Book of Micah," *The Pulpit Commentary,* XIV, iii.
[2]*Ibid.,* p. vii.

The play upon the names of these various towns in this lament is evident in the original. For example, in the first phrase *"tell it not in Gath"* (1:10), the Hebrew word for "tell" somewhat resembles the word "Gath" in sound; some authorities also relate the meaning of the two words etymologically.[3]

"Weep not at all" (1:10) in Hebrew is a play on sound which is literally "weeping, weep not," according to Pusey and Keil; or as Lange and others maintain, the apparent infinitive (weeping) is really a contraction for "in Acco," a city of Palestine, and is to be rendered "in Acco weep not." The play on sound is the same in either case in Hebrew.

"At Beth-le-aphrah have I rolled myself in the dust" (1:10). The name of the town in Hebrew means "house of dust," and the play on words (and sound) is obvious, the prophet referring to their forthcoming affliction and humiliation.

"Pass away, O inhabitant of Shaphir, in nakedness and shame" (1:11). The name of the city of Shaphir means "beauty" or "fairness," the prophet thus contrasting its meaning with their approaching dishonor, nakedness and shame.

"The inhabitant of Zaanan is not come forth" (1:11). Zaanan, probably meaning "going forth" or "departure," represents both a play on sense and sound.

"The wailing of Beth-ezel shall take from you the stay thereof" (1:11). Beth-ezel means "house at one's side," that is, "neighbor-town." The lamentation of Zaanan's neighbor-town, because of its distress, indicates that it will be able to offer no help or refuge to them; hence, Zaanan cannot go forth.

"For the inhabitant of Maroth waiteth anxiously for good, because evil is come down from Yahweh" (1:12). Maroth signifies bitterness. She waited anxiously for good, or relief from her bitterness (distress); but instead, there was simply more of the same, only bitterness from the Lord in punishment for her sins.

"Bind the chariot to the swift steed, O inhabitant of Lachish" (1:13). The paronomasia here lies in the sound, the Hebrew word for chariot, *rekesh*, rhyming with the name of the city, Lachish. The prophet warns them to flee from the enemy: "O inhabitant of Lachish, harness the *rekesh*."

"Therefore shalt thou give a parting gift to Moresheth-gath" (1:14). The prophet addresses Judah who is to give up, with a parting gift, one of her possessions, Moresheth-gath. The paronomasia

---

[3]John Peter Lange, *Minor Prophets, Lange's Commentary on the Holy Scriptures,* trans. Philip Schaff, XIV, 10, 13.

may be understood in one of two ways. A play upon meaning is intended since Moresheth may signify possession, and Judah is thus called upon "to give up possession of her possession." Keil, on the other hand, suggests a play upon sound between Moresheth and *mᵉ'-ōrāśâh* meaning "betrothed" (Deut. 22:23). The meaning would then be that as a father gives a parting gift at the departure of a daughter upon marriage, so Judah must give a farewell gift to Moresheth-gath, the prophet signifying in this manner that she must relinquish all claim to Moresheth, giving it up to the enemy.

"*The houses of Achzib shall be a deceitful thing unto the kings of Israel*" (1:14). The play is upon both sound and meaning in this clause. The translation here, "a deceitful thing," is '*akzāb*, an adjective in Hebrew meaning "deceptive," "lying," or "disappointing." The prophet announces that "the houses of '*Akzîb*[4] ["deception"] shall become '*akzāb* ["deceptive or disappointing"] to the kings of Israel." In Jeremiah 15:18 (cf. Job 6:15) a stream which dries up in summer and disappoints the thirsty traveler is spoken of as a deceptive or disappointing stream ('*akzāb*). The city of '*Akzîb* will surrender to the enemy and prove a disappointment ('*akzāb*). She will prove of no help in time of need.

"*I will yet bring unto thee, O inhabitant of Mareshah, him that shall possess thee*" (1:15). The paronomasia is seen in the play upon the name Mareshah meaning "possession"; hence, Mareshah ("possession") shall not escape the hand of the conqueror, the dispossessor (Assyria) into whose hands the city will pass, becoming the enemy's possession.

The final paronomasia is seen in the prophet's words that "*the glory of Israel shall come even unto Adullam*" (1:15). Adullam is from an Arabic root meaning "to turn aside," the noun *adullam* signifying retreat or refuge.[5] David fled to Adullam from Saul, taking refuge there in a cave (I Sam. 22:1). Thus the glory of Israel (the nobility) will retreat to the place of retreat (Adullam). The prophet concludes his lament over Judah's forthcoming judgment by calling upon Zion to mourn her punishment and captivity (1:16).

II. THE DATE

The superscription to the book indicates that Micah, a younger contemporary of Isaiah, was active under the reigns of Jotham (739-735), Ahaz (735-715) and Hezekiah (715-686). Critical schol-

---

[4]'Akzîb is a more accurate transliteration of the Hebrew than Achzib.

[5]Francis Brown, S. R. Driver and Charles A. Briggs, *A Hebrew and English Lexicon of the Old Testament*, p. 726.

ars have denied the accuracy of this title, but internal evidence confirms its genuineness nevertheless. That Micah prophesied in the days of Hezekiah is affirmed first of all by the clear statement of this fact in Jeremiah 26:18-19, where Micah 3:12 is quoted. This does not imply that all his prophecies were restricted to Hezekiah's reign. Perhaps the various oral prophecies delivered on different occasions were committed to writing during Hezekiah's reign.

Internal evidence indicates that the prophecies were delivered under the reigns of Jotham and Ahaz, as well as that of Hezekiah. The reference to the high places still existing, and the corruption and moral declension of the nation (1:5; 2:1-13), points clearly to the reigns of Jotham and Ahaz as the period when the first section of the book was delivered (cf. II Kings 15:35; 16:4; II Chron. 28:4, 25). The prophecy of the fall of Samaria (1:6) belongs to the years preceding the fall in 722 B.C. Hence, 1:5-6 gives ample evidence that Micah prophesied before both the reformation of Hezekiah (correcting Ahaz' abuses) and the fall of Samaria.

Other allusions are indicative of the scope of Micah's ministry and indicate it was not limited to the reign of Hezekiah. In 5:10 Micah denounces the horses and chariots of Judah, doubtless acquired during the prosperous reign of Uzziah, and on which his successor Jotham prided himself (II Chron. 26:11-15; 27:4-6; Isa. 2:7). When Micah denounces "the statutes of Omri" and "the works of the house of Ahab" (6:16), he obviously has reference to King Ahaz who, it is expressly stated, walked in the ways of the kings of Israel (II Kings 16:3). The allusion to human sacrifice (6:7) befits the time of Ahaz, who sacrificed his sons to Molech (II Kings 16:3; II Chron. 28:3). The syncretism of worship, when the people in the midst of idolatry and sin nevertheless paid lip service to Yahweh, suits the character of Ahaz (II Kings 16:10-16).[6]

Micah's denunciations of idolatry and great wickedness would not have been delivered after the reformation under Hezekiah. It is certain that Micah preached both before and after the downfall of Samaria in 722; hence, a date of 735-700 is suggested.

III. THE PROPHET

His name is a rather common one in the Old Testament, appearing numerous times in one form or another. Micah is a shortened form of Micaiah, meaning "Who [is] like Yahweh?" For other uses of the name see Judges 17:1; II Chronicles 13:2; 17:7; Jeremiah 36:11; I Kings 22:8-9. The prophet of I Kings 22 in the days of Ahab was

------

[6]Deane, p. v.

named Micaiah the son of Imlah; it is probably to distinguish the two that the minor prophet is called "Micah the Morashtite," that is, a native of Moresheth-gath (1:14), the name signifying a possession of Gath. Although the site of the city is not precisely known, it was in the Shephelah and is mentioned elsewhere (Joshua 15:44; II Chron. 11:8).

Although his father's name is not given, Micah's name indicates pious and faithful parents. He was from Judah and prophesied in Jerusalem. This is seen in that not only is his ministry confined to the reigns of the Judean kings, Jotham, Ahaz and Hezekiah, but his addresses condemn chiefly the corruptions of Jerusalem and Zion. He was direct and plain-spoken, possessed of strong convictions, courage and an uncompromising faith in God. He demanded justice among men and sympathized with the poor and oppressed as did his contemporary Amos. The source of his dynamic preaching is found in 3:8:

> But as for me, I am full of power by the Spirit of Yahweh, and of judgment, and of might, to declare unto Jacob his transgression, and to Israel his sin.

IV. THE HISTORICAL BACKGROUND

Micah, like his contemporary Isaiah, also belongs to the critical period of Israel's history in the latter half of the eighth century B.C. At this time Assyria was strong under Tiglath-pileser III, Shalmaneser V, Sargon II and Sennacherib. Uzziah, king of Judah, was succeeded to the throne by his son Jotham, who had been coregent with his father, reigning independently only a few years (739-735). Toward the close of his reign Judah was threatened with an invasion by the allied forces of Damascus and Israel, the real crisis not coming, however, until the reign of his son Ahaz. In fear Ahaz, against the protest of Isaiah, appealed to Tiglath-pileser III of Assyria. Damascus and Israel were overcome and Judah delivered, but at the cost of her national independence, for Judah became a vassal of the Assyrian king.

During the early years of Hezekiah, Judah continued to enjoy peace by paying yearly tribute to Assyria. The Assyrian might was seen in the conquest of Samaria and the captivity of Israel at the hands of Sargon after Hoshea of Israel sought to throw off the Assyrian yoke by an alliance with Egypt. Sennacherib, the successor to Sargon, upon the death of his predecessor was confronted with revolts in which Judah participated. In 702-701 he marched westward. Tyre, Sidon and other states fell before him, Judah was overrun, and Hezekiah was shut up in Jerusalem "like a caged bird," but through divine intervention was delivered by a supernatural occurrence (II Kings 18-19).

The moral and spiritual situation in Judah during these times was low. Religion was a matter of form; the observance of ceremonial ritual was believed adequate to insure divine favor and acceptance (6:6-7; 3:11). Idolatry was widespread, foreign elements were introduced into the worship, human sacrifice was practiced, and the priests and prophets taught and divined for hire. Nobles fleeced the poor, judges accepted bribes, and the rich took advantage of poor widows and orphans. The hopelessness of the social and moral situation is to be seen in the prophet's words: "Trust ye not in a neighbor; put ye not confidence in a friend . . . for the son dishonoreth the father, the daughter riseth up against her mother, the daughter-in-law against her mother-in-law; a man's enemies are the men of his own house" (7:5-6).

V. PROBLEMS

Problems connected with the prophecy are twofold, one dealing with the question of the unity of the book, the other with the parallel passages of Micah 4:1-3 and Isaiah 2:2-4.

As to the unity of the book, there is very little question among critical scholars concerning the genuineness of chapters 1-3 as the work of Micah (except 2:12-13 which was allegedly added after the exile). Chapters 4-5, according to Pfeiffer, were added during the exile since 4:1, 4:10 and 5:3 are said to show the people are already exiled. Chapters 6:1—7:6 are viewed as a later anonymous prophecy from the period of Manasseh. Wellhausen assigned 7:7-20 to the exile. The critics deny a unity of thought throughout the book, and thus reject its unity of authorship. They conclude that no part of chapters 4-7 should be ascribed to the Prophet Micah. The quotation of the last verse of chapter 3 in Jeremiah 26:18 is said to indicate that this was the conclusion of the book of Micah in Jeremiah's day![7] The remainder was added later.

However, in reply we may note with Raven that the expression "hear" in 1:2; 3:1; 6:1 indicates unity of the book. The similarity of chapters 6-7 and Isaiah 40-66 argues against an exilic date for these chapters since Isaiah and Micah were contemporaries. Nor is Micah required to present one continuous argument throughout the book in order for the prophecy to be a unity, since he deals with more than a single subject in his book. Furthermore, the peculiarities of Micah's

[7]Rolland E. Wolfe, "Introduction to the Book of Micah," Vol. VI of *The Interpreter's Bible*, ed. Nolan B. Harmon, p. 899.

style indicate unity of the book. He uses dramatic interruptions and answers: 2:5, 12; 3:1; 6:6-8; 7:14-15. He uses many historical references: 1:13, 15; 5:5; 6:4-5, 16; 7:20. He makes frequent use of the image of the shepherd: 2:12; 3:2-3; 4:6; 5:3-5; 7:14. The fact that such peculiarities appear in all parts of the book is strong corroborative evidence in favor of its being the work of one author.

In an attempt to solve the second problem, five solutions have been suggested in explanation of the parallel passages of Micah 4:1-3 and Isaiah 2:2-4; (1) Micah was the author and Isaiah borrowed from him. (2) Isaiah's passage is the original and Micah's the copy. (3) Both borrowed from an earlier anonymous prophecy. (4) The oracle was original in Micah and inserted by a later editor in Isaiah. (5) The passage was inserted late in both Micah and Isaiah. Inasmuch as the passage in Micah occurs in close connection and contrast with what immediately precedes, while in Isaiah the connection is not so obvious, E. J. Young suggests that the words may have originally belonged to Micah. Or it may be that both prophets drew from a current prophecy adapting it to their own purposes. On the other hand, this concept of a future era of universal peace and restoration was itself current in the eighth century B.C. among the prophets contemporary with Micah, as were other spiritual teachings (cf. Amos 9:11-15; Hosea 3; 14:4-8). Since Micah 4:1-3 and Isaiah 2:2-4 are not precisely identical, but have slight variations (cf. especially Micah 4:5 with Isa. 2:5), it is not impossible that both prophets received similar but, nevertheless, separate revelations of this great truth.

OUTLINE OF MICAH

Pride Oppression
Idolatry Ruthlessness Rebuked

Supreme aspects of Divine Holiness

MERCY   WRATH

Goodness   Severity
Compassionate   relentless in wrath

Chapter 16

NAHUM

Consolation or comfort

I. The Nature of the Book

THE PROPHECY OF NAHUM, like that of Jonah, is concerned with one
subject—the judgment of Nineveh. In the Septuagint it is placed
immediately after Jonah as being the complement to that book.
They form one moral history, the remission of God's judgment upon
repentance being illustrated in the one, the execution of God's judgment in the other (cf. Nahum 3:1 with Jonah 3:8; Nahum 1:2 with
Jonah 4:2). Jonah's preaching in the eighth century had produced
repentance; but now over a century later the nation, more wicked and
ruthless than ever, falls under the sentence of divine judgment pronounced by the Prophet Nahum. Their pride, oppression, idolatry and
ruthlessness are severely rebuked, and their inevitable and final destruction is pronounced.

The two supreme aspects of divine holiness are mercy (1:7, 15)
and wrath (1:2). In this both the goodness and severity of the Lord
are revealed. God is compassionate toward the penitent (Jonah
3:10), but uncompromising and relentless in His wrath toward en-
trenched wickedness (Nahum 3:1-7). These striking features of the
divine character, which reveal the inflexible justice of God, appear
throughout the prophecy. Against the wicked He is jealous of His
honor (1:2); an avenger (1:2); full of wrath (1:2); unwilling to
acquit the wicked (1:3); indignant (1:6); fierce in anger (1:6); full
of power (1:3-6). Toward the penitent and trusting He is slow to
anger (1:3); good (1:7); a stronghold in the day of trouble (1:7);
cognizant of those who trust Him (1:7); a Deliverer from the wicked
one (1:15).

Nahum's prophecy falls into three divisions: chapter 1 is an
introductory psalm of triumph over the impending fall of Nineveh;
chapter 2 depicts the siege and destruction of Nineveh; and chapter 3
sets forth the causes for her downfall. Although the prophecy does
not close with a Messianic hope, nor does it make reference to the
prospect of the establishment of that eschatological kingdom of the

Messiah, yet, as Keil has surmised, the prophecy stands in such close relation to Judah that it may be called a prophecy of consolation to that kingdom.[1] The predicted fall of the defiant capital of the mighty Assyrian Empire, the representative of all the godless nations which have sought to destroy God's kingdom of Israel, suggests that the kingdom of evil will be destroyed and the sovereign kingdom of righteousness exalted (cf. 1:2-3; 2:2; Micah 4:6-8; 5:5 ff.). Nineveh (Assyria), being Israel's most powerful foe at that time, is representative and symbolic, as in Micah 5:5-9, of all the enemies of God and His people in all ages who shall receive their final overthrow at the Messiah's second advent. The declaration of Nahum in 1:2-3 is the pledge of the inevitable divine judgment upon all enemies of God's people (e.g., Nineveh's destruction). "Yahweh is a jealous God and avengeth; Yahweh avengeth and is full of wrath; Yahweh taketh vengeance on his adversaries, and he reserveth wrath for his enemies" (v. 2). The prophecy is poetic in form and of excellent classical quality, being admitted by all scholars as comparable to Isaiah, and one of the finest in the Old Testament. His descriptions are vivid and graphic; the language is powerful, moving and forceful.

II. THE DATE

The date of Nahum's prophecy, although it lacks the usual mention of Hebrew kings in the superscription, can be determined in a general way on the basis of internal evidence. From the statement in 3:8-10 it is apparent that Nahum prophesied between the capture and destruction of No-Amon (Thebes) in Egypt in 663 B.C. by Ashurbanipal, an event spoken of as past, and the destruction of Nineveh itself in 612, an event still regarded as future. From the tone of the prophecy it may be inferred that the destruction of Thebes was a comparatively recent event still fresh in the minds of both Israel and Assyria.

The fact that no king is mentioned in the superscription points to the reign of the wicked Manasseh (686-642), whose name may have been suppressed in the title owing to that king's evil reputation, a thing unlikely if Josiah (640-609) had been on the throne. Also 1:12-13; 2:12-13; and 3:1-4 suggest that Assyria, whose power began rapidly to decline after the death of Ashurbanipal in 633, was still dominant in the West. Hence, Nahum's prophetic ministry may be dated about 650.

[1] C. F. Keil and F. Delitzch, *The Twelve Minor Prophets, Biblical Commentary on the Old Testament*, II, 4.

III. THE PROPHET

Of the Prophet Nahum nothing definite is known outside the prophecy itself. His name in Hebrew, which occurs nowhere else in the Old Testament (cf. Luke 3:25), is from a root meaning "comfort" or "consolation." The name probably has reference to the prophet's message of comfort to Judah from the threats of Assyrian oppression; but this does not indicate, as some critics allege, that the name is to be taken simply as an appellative, or as others assert, an abbreviation of Nehemiah, who lived long after the fall of Assyria (444 B.C.).

The prophet is called "the Elkoshite" (1:1), which means that he was a native of Elkosh. Its location has not been determined; and since it is mentioned nowhere else in the Old Testament, there is considerable difference of opinion as to its probable location. Four sites have been suggested.

The first suggestion, according to Ewald and Lange, identifies Elkosh with the modern village Alkush on the left bank of the Tigris River north of Mosul, where his tomb is allegedly located. This view regards the prophet as a descendant of one of the families of the northern kingdom of Israel carried into exile by Sargon in 722 B.C. In support of this view attention is called to the prophet's accurate knowledge of Nineveh and the Assyrians. He uses Assyrian words (2:7; 3:17); he is well acquainted with Nineveh, its walls (2:5), the river gates (2:6), its temples and images (1:14) and its immense wealth (2:9). But the evidence is not conclusive, because the knowledge is not so technical that the writer could not have obtained it while living in Palestine, since Assyria was well known in the seventh century B.C. from her contacts with Palestine. The prophet's knowledge of Thebes is no less precise, but few would insist the prophet had personal acquaintance with that city. Furthermore, this tradition dates back no farther than the sixteenth century A.D.

Another tradition locates Elkosh in Galilee, identifying it with the modern El Kauze (Elkesi). This was the view of Jerome, which if correct would make the prophet a descendant of one of the families left behind in 722 B.C. (cf. II Chron. 30:1, 5, 10, 18; 34:6). But the fact that the prophet refers to Judah and his silence respecting the northern kingdom seems against this view. Others seek to identify Elkosh with the city of Capernaum which means "city of Nahum." The original name of the city, it is supposed, was Elkosh, but was later changed to Capernaum in honor of its renowned citizen, Nahum. In support of this view it is pointed out that the prophet shows special interest in the northern portion of Palestine in his mention of Carmel, Lebanon and Bashan (1:4). Others, however, place Elkosh in the south of Judah in the territory of Simeon. About six miles east of Beit-jibrin is an old well called Bir el-kaus which might be Elkosh. A location in Judah is undoubtedly more in harmony with the prophet's interest in the triumph of the southern kingdom (1:15).

IV. THE HISTORICAL BACKGROUND

When Nahum prophesied, Assyria was at the height of its power. Having subdued its neighbors, the nation had extended its power into Palestine and distant Egypt. Ashurbanipal's wars were numerous and characterized by ruthlessness and cruelty. He boasted of his violence and shameful atrocities, which included among other things the tearing off of the limbs of his victims, putting out their eyes, impaling them, boiling them in tar, skinning them alive. Assyria prided itself on its cruel and violent atrocities, the number of its corpses and the pyramids of human heads left behind as monuments to its destruction.

The people of Judah had witnessed for many years an almost endless succession of the cruel Assyrian invaders into Palestine: Shalmanezer III (858-824) who made repeated campaigns against Syria and Palestine, Tiglath-pileser III (744-727), Shalmaneser V (726-722), Sargon II (722-705), Sennacherib (704-681), Esarhaddon (680-669), and now the barbarous Ashurbanipal. It was upon such a cruel oppressor, Assyria, that Nahum was called to pronounce the impending doom.

Nineveh was proud in her seeming invulnerability; but the prophet, rebuking Nineveh's pride, oppression, cruelty and idolatry, proclaims her inevitable destruction forever. In just a few short years her end came. A coalition of enemies under God's providential direction overthrew this mighty empire. Following Ashurbanipal were three undistinguished rulers who occupied the throne, and then the end came with sudden swiftness eradicating the Assyrian civilization. Egypt revolted as did Babylon; later Nabopolassar of Babylon joined with Cyaxares the Mede and the king of the Scythians in an allied attack upon Nineveh, which fell under their combined power in 612 B.C., and the city was destroyed.

Ashur-uballit II (612-606) reigned for a few years in Haran as king of Assyria, but this last capital was soon taken by the Scythians. Great Nineveh and Assyria had fallen never to rise again! The destruction predicted by Zephaniah (2:13-15) and Nahum had taken place.[2]

---

[2]Jack Finegan, *Light from the Ancient Past,* pp. 180-84.

I will make thy grave; for thou art vile. Woe to the bloody city! It is all full of lies and rapine; the prey departeth not. And it shall come to pass that all they that look upon thee shall flee from thee, and say, Nineveh is laid waste: who will bemoan her? Whence shall I seek comforters for thee? (1:14; 3: 1, 7).

V. PROBLEMS

The only problem concerning the book, apart from those already considered, is that of its unity. Until the nineteenth century no doubts were expressed as to the unity of Nahum. This change of opinion rests upon an alleged discovery by Gunkel of the remnants of an old alphabetic poem in chapter 1.

While some admit traces of an acrostic arrangement, yet this is not carried out consistently; and in order to restore the acrostic, it becomes necessary, especially from verse 7 onward, to take much liberty with the text. Frequently words must be inserted or omitted, words and clauses transposed, and sometimes passages almost entirely rewritten. In the presence of such violence to the text, the critical assumption is obviously groundless. Pfeiffer nevertheless would limit the work of Nahum to 2:3—3:19 to which a redactor about 300 B.C. prefaced the alphabetic psalm. However, Oswald T. Allis, in an article in *The Evangelical Quarterly*, demonstrates the futility of the critical attempts to reconstruct an acrostic poem in chapter 1.[3]

There is no objective evidence against the genuineness of chapter 1; and its unity with chapters 2 and 3 is apparent from the following internal considerations, in spite of the critical allegation that the psalm (chap. 1) has no vital connection with Nahum's prophecy of the fall of Nineveh (chaps. 2-3):

1. In 1:1 the superscription states that it is "the burden of Nineveh." There are no valid reasons for rejecting the superscription as genuine and by the hand of Nahum.

2. In 1:8 the prophet declares: "But with an over-running flood he will make a full end of her place," which may refer poetically to the fact that Nineveh was weakened by an unusually heavy and long-continued flood of the Tigris, which carried away a great section of the huge rampart that surrounded the city and permitted the enemy to force their way through this gap within the walls and capture the city (cf. 2:6).

3. In 1:9 it is said that God "will make a full end; affliction shall not rise up the second time," which was certainly fulfilled in

[3]Oswald T. Allis, "Nahum, Nineveh, Elkosh," *The Evangelical Quarterly*, XXVII, No. 2 (April, 1955), 67-80.

Assyria's utter destruction and her inability to afflict Israel a second time.

4. There is an account from secular history concerning the destruction of Nineveh which relates that after the Assyrians had repulsed the enemy they then gave themselves to drunkenness and feasting (e.g., Belshazzar, Dan. 5:1), and as a consequence were surprised by the Medes and the city was taken. If true, the words in 1:10 may have reference to this occurrence: "For entangled like thorns, and drunken as with their drink, they are consumed utterly as dry stubble."

5. In 1:11 it is said: "There is one gone forth out of thee, that deviseth evil against Yahweh, that counselleth wickedness." The obvious reference seems to be to Sennacherib and his impious threats when he had gone forth from Nineveh in 701 B.C. against Judah and Jerusalem (cf. II Kings 18-19).

6. In verse 12 the annihilation of Sennacherib's army may well be referred to and the assassination of Sennacherib (II Kings 19:35-37): "Thus saith Yahweh: Though [they were in] full strength, and likewise many, even so they have been cut down, and he has passed" (lit. trans.).[4]

7. In 1:13 it is predicted: "And now will I break his yoke from off thee, and will burst thy bonds in sunder," which apparently is a reference to the vassalage of Judah to Assyria (II Kings 18:14; II Chron. 33:11).

8. It is predicted in 1:14 that Nineveh's name would be blotted out, and that God would dig her grave, a prophecy which Ezekiel confirms in 32:22-23 of his book: "Asshur is there [in Sheol] and all her company: her graves are round about her; all of them slain, fallen by the sword: whose graves are set in the uttermost parts of the pit, and her company is round about her grave; all of them slain, fallen by the sword, who caused terror in the land of the living."

The destruction of Nineveh at the hands of the Medes, Babylonians and Scythians occurred unexpectedly. So deep and effectively did God dig her grave that every trace of the wicked city's existence disappeared for ages and even its site was unknown. Xenophon, the Athenian historian and general, thought the mounds were ruins of some Parthian city, when he and his army marched by about two hundred years after its destruction. When Alexander the Great fought nearby he did not know that a great world empire lay buried at his feet. So completely had all traces of the great Assyrian Empire

---

[4]Hebrew verbs are in the state of perfected action, whereas the ASV suggests future tense.

disappeared that many critical scholars held the biblical references to Nineveh in disrepute. It was not until 1845 when Layard definitely identified the site known as Kuyunjik to be the ancient city of Nineveh that the grave of this once magnificent capital was uncovered.

OUTLINE OF NAHUM

Supreme aspects of divine Holiness

Day of Lord
1. *Imminent*
2. *Day of Terror*
3. *Judgment because of Sin*
4. *Universal*
5. *Severe*

Chapter 17

ZEPHANIAH

Yahweh Hides

I. The Nature of the Book

THE THOUGHT OF THE BOOK is centered upon one central theme—the coming of the day of the Lord. The prophecy is almost wholly occupied with the subject of judgment. It begins with the announcement of a universal judgment: upon Judah in particular and the world in general. The day of the Lord will be an overwhelming terror in which the wrath of God will consume the whole earth. But since Zephaniah's interest is in his own people primarily, the first part of his message is directed to them. From them he turns to the surrounding nations, the Philistines, Moabites, Ammonites, Ethiopians or Egyptians, and Assyrians.

But this judgment, as the revelation of the wrath of God because of the general corruption of the world, is not the entire subject of the message of the prophet. The Lord will manifest Himself terribly to the nations by pouring out His wrath upon all idolaters and the wicked for the purpose of purifying a people from all nations who will call upon His name. The prophet concludes with the promise of Israel's restoration. The redeemed remnant will return to Zion, cleansed, humbled, trusting and faithful. Zion will then be the object of praise among all the peoples of the earth. Therefore, judgment is not regarded by Zephaniah as an end in itself; it will be the means of purifying a remnant and ushering in His kingdom.

Earlier prophets had spoken of this day (Obad. 15; Joel 1:15; Amos 5:18-20), but the entire teaching of Zephaniah centers around this theme. The nature of the day is described as: (1) imminent (1:14); (2) filled with wrath, trouble, distress, desolation, gloominess, and with clouds and thick darkness; hence, a day of terror (1:15); (3) occupied with judgment because of sin (1:17); (4) universal, falling upon all creation, man and beast, Jew and Gentile (1:2-3; 2:4-15; 3:8); (5) severe, as only a remnant will survive (2:3; 3:9-13). It is to be the day when God will fulfill His purposes, as predicted, of judgment upon sin and redemption of His people.

Some critics have spoken disparagingly of Zephaniah's style as

232

being prosaic and unoriginal. However, like other prophets he shows affinity with his predecessors, sometimes employing their language, not out of poverty of idea indicating a "decline" in prophecy during this period; the fundamental doctrines of judgment and salvation common to all prophets are brought to focus in Zephaniah.[1] The doctrines of purifying judgment upon Israel and retributive judgment upon the nations of the world seen in Obadiah, Joel, Isaiah, Micah and Nahum become the central theme in Zephaniah. He uses isolated expressions and striking words from his predecessors and applies them to his own purpose under the inspiration of the Holy Spirit.

The prophecy ranks as an "apocalypse" concerning universal judgment and salvation of a remnant. Along with the uniting of his predecessors' teachings of judgment, Zephaniah reiterates the prophetic doctrine of a remnant which had been enunciated by Obadiah (17); Joel (3); Amos (5:15; 9:11 f.); Isaiah (17:3; 37:32); and Micah (5:6 f.). Also the conversion of the heathen promised in Zephaniah 3:9-12 should be compared with Isaiah 2.

II. THE DATE

Dating of the book is quite easily determined from the superscription; it was during the reign of Josiah (640-609 B.C.).[2] A question arises as to the length of his ministry, whether it extended over the full time of Josiah's reign or was confined to a more limited period. Internal evidence suggests that most of Zephaniah's preaching was done prior to 621 B.C. Josiah's reign falls into two parts separated by the reform of 621. (1) From 2:13 it is evident that the destruction of Nineveh in 612 is yet future. (2) The idolatrous practices condemned by Zephaniah (1:3-6) are precisely those abolished in 621; and while traces may have remained, this would not warrant the wholesale condemnation seen in these verses (cf. 1:3-6 with II Kings 23:4 ff.). (3) The religious and moral conditions described in 1:3-6, 8-9, 12;

[1]W. J. Deane, "Introduction to the Book of Zephaniah," *The Pulpit Commentary,* XIV, iv-v.

[2]This assumes, of course, that one accepts the superscription as genuine. Some critics, as is to be expected, advance the theory of a later gloss. Hyatt suggests that the superscription in 1:1, which dates the prophecy in the reign of Josiah, is a later and inaccurate editorial addition, and that the book should be dated in the reign of Jehoiakim (609-598) since he thinks it reflects the social and religious conditions of this period rather than the reign of Josiah (J. Philip Hyatt, "The Date and Background of Zephaniah," *Journal of Near Eastern Studies,* VII, No. 1 [January, 1948], 25-29). However, there is no basis for this conjecture.

3:1-7 are explicable before 621, but not during the period of religious reformation.

III. THE PROPHET

The name Zephaniah means "Yahweh hides" (i.e., "protects"). His ancestry is traced back four generations in 1:1: "Zephaniah the son of Cushi, the son of Gedaliah, the son of Amariah, the son of Hezekiah." As it is usual to name only a prophet's father (cf. Isa. 1:1; Jer. 1:1; Hosea 1:1),[3] there must have been a reason for the more extensive genealogy here. Thus it is inferred that the Hezekiah mentioned is King Hezekiah of Judah, the contemporary of Isaiah and Micah. Zephaniah would be, therefore, a descendant of royal blood and a distant relative of Josiah. No satisfactory objection to this inference has been proposed, and the objection that if this were Hezekiah the king he would have been designated as such is an argument from silence. Moreover, Zechariah 1:1 mentions his ancestor Iddo only by name and not by his office of priest (cf. Neh. 12:4).

The prophet lived in the southern kingdom, probably in Jerusalem (cf. 1:4, 10-11). His prophetic activity may have been instrumental in stirring Josiah to his reforms (cf. II Chron. 34:1-7). He was a contemporary of Nahum and Jeremiah.

IV. THE HISTORICAL BACKGROUND

Manasseh, upon his death, was succeeded by his son Amon who reigned only two years. Amon continued in all the sins of his father and was finally assassinated by his servants. Josiah, his son, was just eight years old when he came to the throne of Judah, which was in a ruinous condition spiritually due to the corrupt influence of Manasseh and Amon. As early as his sixteenth year his heart was turned to the Lord (II Chron. 34:3) and he undertook a program of moral and spiritual reforms. In 612 B.C. a coalition of Babylonians and Scythians brought about the downfall of Nineveh. According to the Babylonian chronicle, when Ashur-uballit withdrew to Harran to establish the Assyrian court there, Pharaoh Necho came to his support, marching through Palestine to capture Carchemish before proceeding to Haran. This brought him in conflict with King Josiah of Judah whose challenge of Necho at Megiddo resulted in his untimely death in 609 B.C. (II Chron. 35:20-25).[4]

Zephaniah leaves no doubt as to the religious and moral condi-

[3]Zech. 1:1 excepted.
[4]D. Winton Thomas (ed.), *Documents from Old Testament Times*, p. 77.

tions of the early period of Josiah's reign. For confirmation of his denunciations, Jeremiah 1-12 and the historical account in II Kings 21-23 may be compared. Social injustice, idolatry and moral corruption were widespread (3:1-7). The religious situation was equally corrupt. Manasseh and Amon had turned the people to idolatry and the rejection of the worship of Yahweh. These were the conditions which called forth Zephaniah's denunciation of the rulers and religious leaders and the announcement of certain judgment. In the course of repairing the temple, Hilkiah found a copy of the book of the law. Josiah, upon hearing its teachings together with its warnings and rebukes, was moved to institute immediate reforms long overdue. Heathen pollutions of the temple were removed, high places destroyed, idolatrous priests slain and the purity of worship restored (II Kings 22:3 ff.).

V. PROBLEMS

Critical appraisal of the contents of the book has resulted in the division of certain portions of the text as belonging neither to Zephaniah nor to his times, but to a later period. The oracle against Moab and Ammon (2:8-11) is held to be late since its phraseology presupposes the conditions of the exile. The account of the fall of Nineveh in 2:15 is said to have been appended by a pious reader after the event had taken place. Following the critical presupposition that passages of judgment and hope cannot be comingled, critics consider the hope-filled passages as later additions (viz., 2:3, 11; 3:5, 12-13, 14-20). However, as with most literary criticism by the negative school, these arguments are based on subjective inferences.

OUTLINE OF ZEPHANIAH

Chapter 18

JEREMIAH

Yahweh appoints or establishes

I. The Nature of the Book

THE OPENING WORDS of Jeremiah are the key to understanding his prophecy for they reveal the background and tragic circumstances in which he was called to labor (1:1-3). These were times of misfortune and approaching catastrophe for the nation of Judah. The kingdom of Israel had come to ruin and utter destruction a century earlier because of its apostasy; but the graphic warning in Israel's judgment was lost upon Judah, who rushed headlong in her iniquity toward a similar fate. Jeremiah stood practically alone in an effort to stem the tide of apostasy and turn Judah from her iniquities, which he warned would lead to inevitable destruction at the hands of the Babylonians. In the face of the optimistic promises of the false prophets who cried "Peace, peace" to the sinful nation, his words of warning fell upon deaf ears. Hence, the consequences of the people's persistent rebellion against the word of the Lord were inevitable; the prophet was constrained to pronounce a solemn irrevocable message of judgment: "This whole land shall be a desolation, and an astonishment; and these nations shall serve the king of Babylon seventy years" (25:11).

The prophet begins his first oracle (2:1-8) with the joyful reminiscence of the happy relations which first existed between God and His people in the springtime of their spiritual betrothal to Him at the exodus. Then Israel had portrayed the characteristics of a chaste bride—pure love and fidelity. "I remember . . . the kindness of thy youth, the love of thine espousals; how thou wentest after me in the wilderness" (2:2). God was her first love when He appeared to her in Egypt. She was joyful then at the prospect of forsaking her former state with its afflictions, and following Him out of Egypt into a new home and a new life with Him. There was much delight in her early love and fidelity.

God is depicted here manifesting the characteristics of the husband who looks upon the wife of his youth as a kind of firstfruits devoted in a special way to him as he overshadows her with his

237

protective care. "Israel was holiness unto Yahweh, the firstfruits of his increase: all that devour him shall be held guilty; evil shall come upon them, saith Yahweh" (2:3). Thus the prophet pictures the idyllic days of the soul's first love for God, and its devotion and fidelity to Him, to which God responded with loving care and concern. As Israel's husband He jealously guards her against her enemies and oppressors, since he who touched Israel was guilty of trespassing against the holy, consecrated possession of the Lord (cf. Zech. 2:8).

Rebuking the ingratitude of the people, God appeals both to His character and past dealings with Israel to disprove that there is any reason in Him to account for the people's sin and infidelity. The first love has been forgotten, the remembrance of the past has become bitter. The cause for the change in the relationship does not lie in God—He has remained faithful and righteous in His dealings with His people, but they have become unfaithful toward Him. They have violated the solemn vows and pledges of fidelity made unto Him. The yielding up of the soul to God is likened to an espousal to God; to be unfaithful is to violate these sacred vows of marriage. These departures were self-instituted without any provocation from God and thus were an exhibition of their shameful ingratitude (cf. James 1:13-15). It is inexcusable desertion and infidelity and must be punished.

The shameful apostasy of Israel is unparalleled among the heathen nations of the world, God charges (2:9-13). Search through every pagan nation, inquire in every idol temple, investigate the religious life of the idolaters of the world, and there will be found a fidelity to these false gods that will put Israel's unfaithfulness to her God to shame. Israel's conduct was unheard of even among the heathen. The idolatrous nations remained true to their gods, in spite of the fact that they did not actually exist and could not help them in any way. God, as it were, marvels at Israel's unbelief (cf. Mark 6:5-6).

Israel is charged with two unprecedented evils. First, she is charged with forsaking the "fountain of living waters" (2:13a). The Lord is described in the Scriptures as a fountain of living waters. Jesus declared in John 7:37: "If any man thirst, let him come unto me and drink." Isaiah cried: "Ho, every one that thirsteth, come ye to the waters. . ." (Isa. 55:1; cf. John 4; Rev. 22:17). God, in depicting Himself as living waters, signifies that He is the source of life which flows forth freely to those who are thirsty. Thus, He here condemns an inconceivable act of spiritual folly—that they who are being nourished by fresh living waters would forsake them and invite death. But more, their folly becomes completely inexplicable when it

2 evils ① *forsaking the fountain of living waters*
② *Hewing out Broken cisterns.*

is seen that not only have they forsaken the fountain of living waters
but they have "hewed them out cisterns, broken cisterns, that can *II*
hold no water" (2:13b).

This, then, is the second evil with which Israel is charged: the
people have hewed out for themselves broken cisterns. Israel's forsaking of God is as irrational as if she had abandoned the clear, cool
waters of a fresh running fountain for the stagnant muddy mixture of
some cistern. But her folly is magnified when it is seen that the
exchange was not only for the foul waters of a cistern, but for
cisterns that were cracked, broken and unable to hold water at all.
Only the blindness occasioned by her apostasy could account for such
folly. This, then, was the burden of the prophet's message. Not only
had Israel forsaken the true God, whom she alone had been privileged to know (Amos 3:2), but she also magnified her sin and shame
by exchanging the only true and living God for worthless idols—
broken cisterns. Such apostasy could no longer remain unpunished;
Judah would be exiled and Jerusalem destroyed.

From chapter 36 it is evident that Jeremiah's prophecies were
first committed to writing in the fourth year of Jehoiakim (605 B.C.).
At this time the prophet dictated to his secretary Baruch the
messages which covered all his prophecies from the beginning of his
ministry (627 B.C.) until the fourth year of Jehoiakim. In the
following year the prophecies were read in the presence of
Jehoiakim, whereupon the king, indignant at their contents, seized
the roll, cut it with a knife and destroyed it in the fire. In consequence God directed the prophet to dictate another roll "and write in
it all the former words that were in the first roll, which Jehoiakim the
king of Judah hath burned" (36:28). Since this portion covered only
about half of Jeremiah's prophetic ministry, the remainder of the
book, including the foreign prophecies, was added later.

Jeremiah's prophecies are not arranged in chronological order.
For example, his prophecies under Josiah (1-20) are followed by a
prophecy in the period of Zedekiah (21), the last king of Judah,
whereas there were actually three kings whose reigns intervened between Josiah and Zedekiah. Again, chapters 35-36 precede in time
chapters 27-34. Some expositors (Keil among them) have suggested
that Jeremiah arranged his book topically according to subject matter; others (including Driver) believe that certain portions circulated
independently in small separate collections, being gathered together
later; still others explain the composite character of the book by the
nature of its composition. The earlier prophecies were destroyed and
redictated with additions (36:32). Later prophecies were collected

and edited by Baruch. The fact that the book was written in stages suggests why it is not arranged in strict chronological order, according to Unger.

The precise principle of arrangement is not easy to ascertain; however, the general arrangement of the prophecies is discernible since they are divided in accordance with their contents, those concerning Judah and the future Messianic kingdom coming first (chaps. 1-45), followed by the prophecies concerning foreign nations (chaps. 46-51), to which a historical appendix is added (chap. 52).

Furthermore, this general arrangement may be more specifically classified according to the reigns of the rulers under whom Jeremiah prophesied as follows:

Jeremiah's call (chap. 1).

Prophecies delivered under Josiah and Jehoiakim (chaps. 2-20). This section consists of six discourses which contain the substance of Jeremiah's oral preaching primarily during the reign of Josiah.

Prophecies delivered under Jehoiakim (chaps. 25-27; 35-36; 45; 46:1—49:33). Chapter 27 is dated in verse 1 in Jehoiakim's reign, whereas the contents of the chapter seem to indicate the period of Zedekiah (cf. vv. 3, 12, 20). Young suggests a "scribal error," Jehoiakim being written for Zedekiah. Keil cites another solution by Haevernick who suggests that the prophecy was delivered to Jeremiah during Jehoiakim's reign and was to be conveyed to the kings concerned at the proper intervals.[1] Chapter 45 is a promise addressed to Baruch and is dated in verse 1 in the fourth year of Jehoiakim. Keil suggests that due to its position in the book it may signify that it was not written down by Baruch until later in Egypt when he collected the prophecies of Jeremiah. This message of comfort to Baruch was then added as an appendix to the prophecies of Jeremiah since it was a fitting conclusion to what preceded.[2] The foreign prophecies (46-51) are difficult to date exactly. According to 36:1-2, God commanded Jeremiah in the fourth year of Jehoiakim to write all the prophecies which he had given up to that time concerning not only Israel and Judah but *all the nations*. The superscription in 46:1-2 contains the title for the collection of foreign prophecies which follow (viz., 46:1—49:33) and dates them in the fourth year of Jehoiakim (605 B.C.). There is a new heading given in 49:34 in the prophecy concerning Elam, dating it in the beginning

---

[1] C. F. Keil and F. Delitzsch, *The Prophecies of Jeremiah, Biblical Commentary on the Old Testament,* I, 396.
[2] *Ibid.,* II, 171-72.

of the reign of Zedekiah, in whose reign the prophecies against Babylon (50-51) were also uttered (51:59-64).

Prophecies delivered under Zedekiah (chaps. 21-24; 28-34; 37-39; 49:34—51:64).

Prophecies and events under Gedaliah (chaps. 40-42).

Jeremiah's ministry in Egypt (chaps. 43-44).

Historical appendix (chap. 52). The actual prophecies of Jeremiah end with chapter 51 on the basis of the statement in 51:64: "Thus far are the words of Jeremiah." Chapter 52 was added, no doubt by Baruch on the authority of Jeremiah, from II Kings 24-25.[3]

II. THE DATE

The Prophet Jeremiah received his call and commission in the thirteenth year of the reign of Josiah (627 B.C.) according to 1:2 and 25:3. The length of his ministry was rather extensive, the first phase covering a period of forty-one years (627-586). According to information given in 1:1-3, his first prophecy was in the thirteenth year of Josiah (640-609); he continued prophesying through the reigns of Jehoiakim and Zedekiah, the destruction of Jerusalem coming in the eleventh year of the latter's reign (586). The prophet's ministry also covered the brief reigns of Jehoahaz and Jehoiachin, although because of their brevity they are not mentioned except summarily (13:18-19, Jehoiachin; 22:11-12, Jehoahaz [Shallum]).

The second phase of the prophet's ministry commenced after the fall of the city and the deportation of its inhabitants to Babylon. Nebuchadnezzar permitted Jeremiah to remain in Palestine during the governorship of Gedaliah. Upon the treacherous murder of Gedaliah by Ishmael the remnant of the Jews made plans to flee into Egypt in fear of the reaction of Babylon to the murder of Gedaliah whom Nebuchadnezzar had appointed governor. The word of the Lord came again unto Jeremiah at this time, warning the remnant of Judah not to flee into Egypt (chap. 42). Nevertheless, they refused to heed his warnings and carried the prophet with them into Egypt where he continued his ministry until his death (chaps. 43-44). Thus, his ministry perhaps extended altogether for over half a century.

Keil states that Jeremiah's "later labours at Mizpah and in Egypt were but a continuation of secondary importance, which might consequently be passed over in the heading of the book,"[4] as were

---

[3]This chronological arrangement of the prophecies is generally accepted by conservative scholars. For more detailed analysis see E. J. Young, *Introduction to the Old Testament*, pp. 225-29.

[4]Keil and Delitzsch, I, 28.

the brief reigns of Jehoahaz and Jehoiachin. The superscription in 1:1-3 does not include chapters 40-44 (events after the fall of Jerusalem and in Egypt), but covers only his prophecies from the thirteenth year of Josiah[5] "unto the carrying away of Jerusalem captive in the fifth month." The period mentioned covers only Jeremiah's principal work, with no reference to those after the captivity of Judah.

III. THE PROPHET

Jeremiah, whose name perhaps means "Yahweh appoints or establishes," was the son of Hilkiah, a priest who lived in the priest city of Anathoth, a town of Benjamin a few miles northeast of Jerusalem. He was of the line of Ithamar and called to the prophetic ministry while still a youth (1:6), preaching in Jerusalem during the last forty-one years of the kingdom of Judah from the thirteenth year of Josiah until the fall of Jerusalem in 586 B.C. There is considerable information concerning the life and times of Jeremiah given in his book, far more in fact than about any of the other prophets in their writings. The history of his lengthy ministry can be traced from his call in the reign of Josiah to its close in Egypt sometime after the destruction of Jerusalem in the period of the Babylonian exile.

Jeremiah had been predestinated to his office before his birth and ordained to be a prophet of God (1:5). He was born of a priestly heritage into an age of religious and moral declension at the time of the decline of Judah. He was a man of strong character, sensitive to the sins of his people which he steadfastly rebuked.

Fearlessly predicting the inevitable judgment to fall upon Judah, Jeremiah was rejected and persecuted by the popular prophets, nobles, rulers and common people. He relentlessly waged a battle against the false prophets, announcing judgment in the face of their optimistic promises of peace and security. At the time of his call (1:10-19) he was introduced to the theme of judgment which was to

[5]Some critical scholars (viz., Hyatt, May) contend that Jeremiah did not begin to prophesy until near the close of Josiah's reign since there is no evidence the prophet participated in the Josian religious reforms, for it was the Prophetess Huldah (II Kings 22:14) and not Jeremiah who was consulted when the book of the law was found in the temple in 621. Moreover, the allusion to the Babylonians in 1:13 ff. indicates his call took place, not in 627 B.C., but after Babylon began to present a threat, i.e., about 612. Others, such as John Bright, "Jeremiah," *The Anchor Bible,* pp. lxxxiii-lxxxv, reject such conjecture as inconclusive. The fact that it is stated in two places (1:2; 25:3) that Jeremiah began his ministry in the thirteenth year of Josiah should settle the matter for us.

characterize his ministry, and which runs throughout his book. His insistence that Judah would inevitably fall because of her iniquities, and that she should submit to Babylon to prevent unnecessary bloodshed, made his ministry extremely unpopular and precarious. He was beaten and imprisoned, rejected by family and friends, considered a traitor to the nation, despised by the leaders and people, his prophecies were destroyed and his life threatened. His was to be a ministry of opposition against all classes of the people in rebuke of their apostasy, for when God first called the prophet He forewarned him of this fact. At the time of his call he was told that God was sending him "against the princes thereof, against the priests thereof, and against the people of the land. And they shall fight against thee" (1:18-19).

The unique character of Jeremiah's call is to be seen in the twofold nature of his ministry:

1.   It was to be destructive in its immediate purpose. "I have this day set thee over the nations and over the kingdoms, to pluck up and to break down and to destroy and to overthrow" (1:10a). The prophet is here appointed to speak the words of the Lord which will effect the destruction of the wicked. The divine power of the prophetic word is evidenced in its fulfillment as Zechariah declares after the exile which Jeremiah foretold, "But my words and my statutes, which I commanded my servants the prophets, did they not overtake your fathers? And they turned and said, Like as Yahweh of hosts thought to do unto us, according to our ways, and according to our doings, so hath he dealt with us" (Zech. 1:6). The prophet's words were God's words which were the unfailing instrument of His sovereign purposes: "So shall my word be that goeth forth out of my mouth: it shall not return unto me void, but it shall accomplish that which I please, and it shall prosper in the thing whereto I sent it" (Isa. 55:11; cf. Gen. 1:3; Ps. 33:6, 9). The divine word is described as a consuming fire and a hammer that crushes rocks in pieces (Jer. 23:29). Thus, the prophet is commissioned first of all to announce the forthcoming uprooting, overthrow and complete destruction of Judah, as well as the punishment of the nations for their wickedness.

2.   It was to be a constructive ministry in its ultimate aim. Not only was Jeremiah commissioned to announce the overthrow and destruction of the nations, but he was also called "to build and to plant" (1:10b). Two figures are employed to describe this twofold work: (a) the agricultural terms "to pluck up" and "to plant," and (b) the architectural terms "to break down" and "to build." His word was to be directed to Judah and the nations to announce their

destruction; but in the case of Judah and Israel, he was to promise the restoration of a remnant according to God's sovereign purposes and grace. After they had been "plucked up" and "broken down" in judgment, the nation would be built again and once more planted in its own land. "And it shall come to pass that, like as I have watched over them to pluck up and to break down and to overthrow and to destroy and to afflict, so will I watch over them to build and to plant, saith Yahweh" (Jer. 31:28).

The prophet's message of judgment is confirmed by two visions:

1. The vision of the almond tree. "Moreover the word of Yahweh came unto me, saying, Jeremiah, what seest thou? And I said, I see a rod of an almond-tree. Then said Yahweh unto me, Thou hast well seen: for I watch over my word to perform it" (1:11-12). In this vision there is a play on words to be seen in God's message to Jeremiah. The almond tree in Hebrew is literally "the wakeful tree" or "the watchful tree," so called because of its early waking out of winter's sleep before the other trees. The early budding of the almond tree is symbolical of the wakeful attitude of God and the early execution of His purpose with respect to judgment upon the nations, verse 12 literally reading: "I will be wakeful as to my word to perform it," or, as the American Standard Version renders it: "I will watch over my word to perform it."

The fact that Jeremiah was sent to prophesy concerning the judgment and overthrow of Jerusalem in the midst of an era of peace and prosperity would cause his word to be looked upon with disbelief and contempt by the people who saw no sign of the impending calamities, especially in view of the fact that the false prophets were promising peace and security. Therefore, Jeremiah is given the assurance at the time of his call that God will watch over His word and perform it on schedule at the predetermined and proper time.

The words of the spokesmen of God may for a time lie dormant and appear to many to be mere empty proclamations. To the wicked and impenitent it may sometimes appear that God is "asleep" with respect to the performance of His word, but God warns that such is not the case, for "when they are saying, Peace and safety, then sudden destruction cometh upon them" (I Thess. 5:3). God is not oblivious to the wickedness of men, nor is He asleep: "Behold, he that keepeth Israel will neither slumber nor sleep" (Ps. 121:4). On the contrary, He continually keeps watch over His word and will "awake" to action in due time. Therefore, God never delays divine judgment beyond its set time. If it seems thus, it is because He has good and sufficient reasons. The Scriptures suggest several:

a. The righteous often do not obtain immediate relief from the distress and affliction caused by the wicked because God may have higher purposes for them in not doing so. Through the trials of faith its genuineness is proved, character is strengthened, and God's confidence in the faithfulness of His children, in spite of calamities and distress, is vindicated as seen in the case of Job (Job 1:20-22).

b. God for His own reasons waits for sin to "ripen" to maturity and the wickedness of man to reach its climax before He acts in judgment (Lev. 18:24-25; Deut. 9:4).

c. God's apparent delay in executing judgment has a redemptive aim in view as the Apostle Peter shows: "The Lord is not slack concerning his promise, as some count slackness; but is long suffering to you-ward, not wishing that any should perish, but that all should come to repentance" (II Peter 3:9). Thus as the harvest which ripens slowly is gathered in haste, the impending judgment of God, while it may seem to delay, nevertheless will come suddenly as in the days of Noah, in the destruction of Sodom and Gomorrah, and in the fall of Jerusalem. When the armies of Nebuchadnezzar assaulted the walls of Jerusalem and overthrew the city, the Jews, apparently secure in their sinful complacency, discovered too late that God had "watched over" the word of His Prophet Jeremiah to perform it at its appointed time.

2. The vision of the boiling pot. "And the word of Yahweh came unto me the second time, saying, What seest thou? And I said, I see a boiling caldron; and the face thereof is from the north. Then Yahweh said unto me, Out of the north evil shall break forth upon all the inhabitants of the land. For, lo, I will call the families of the kingdoms of the north, saith Yahweh; and they shall come, and they shall set every one his throne at the entrance of the gates of Jerusalem, and against all the walls thereof round about, and against all the cities of Judah. And I will utter my judgments against them touching all their wickedness, in that they have forsaken me, and have burned incense unto other gods, and worshipped the works of their own hands" (Jer. 1:13-16).

This second vision, like the first, signifies the word which is about to be performed against Jerusalem and Judah for their iniquities. The boiling pot is an Oriental symbol of raging war, and signifies how God would stir up the warlike spirit of Judah's enemies against her. The figure chosen by God is quite appropriate. The vessel is slowly heated to the boiling point, suddenly spilling over, just as sin and wickedness gradually gain momentum until their consequences suddenly break forth upon the transgressors. The pot was facing

Palestine from the north, overturning so that its boiling contents spilled out southward upon Judah, signifying the destruction that was soon to break forth upon her out of the north at the hands of Babylon. "Then Yahweh said unto me, Out of the north evil shall break forth upon all the inhabitants of the land."

The twofold lesson contained in the vision of the wakeful almond tree and the boiling pot was in reality one; the visions were symbolic of the inevitable accomplishment of the word of God which was to issue in sudden and violent destruction upon the wicked. As swiftly and unexpectedly as a boiling pot overflows, so God, who was watching over His word, would at the proper moment pour forth His wrath upon sinners in a sudden overwhelming flood of punishment.

God then admonishes Jeremiah saying, "Speak unto them all that I command thee: be not dismayed at them, lest I dismay thee before them" (1:17). The prophet is solemnly charged to remain steadfast in the face of all opposition to his message and to proclaim faithfully *all* that God has commanded him to speak. It is sometimes a temptation for a man to proclaim only as much of God's Word as the people will receive without rejecting him and his ministry. But God warns Jeremiah in advance that any failure to proclaim faithfully His whole counsel will result in judgment upon the messenger as well as the people. If he fears the consequences of faithful preaching, then he will face a severer judgment at the hands of the Lord. Fidelity to the Word of God is not merely preaching carefully selected themes in order to please the hearers, nor following some liturgy; it is the proclamation of the whole counsel of God, the threats as well as the promises, the judgments as well as the blessings, the rebukes as well as the condolences, at whatever the personal cost. As it is treason for an ambassador to suppress those elements of his commission that are harsh and severe in order to spare himself unpleasant experiences, so much more treasonous is it for the messenger of the Lord who, through fear, cowardliness and desire for peace at any price, neglects to proclaim *all* that God has spoken.

IV. The Historical Background

Jeremiah was the last of the preexilic prophets. His ministry was primarily to Judah, although he was commissioned to be "a prophet to the nations." He prophesied to the southern kingdom of Judah before the period of the Babylonian exile and during the difficult days of the siege and captivity of Jerusalem. The ministry of Jeremiah attracts attention because of the varied scenes in which it was carried on and the unique nature of his message. The background of

his ministry is set against a constantly changing religious and political situation both nationally and internationally. Preceding the reign
of Josiah, Judah had declined religiously under the apostate reigns of
Manasseh and Amon. Shortly after Jeremiah's call the book of the
law was discovered in the temple in 621 B.C. (II Kings 22-23; Jer.
11:1-8?) which resulted in a sincere, although temporary, religious
reform in Judah. The political vicissitudes of Jeremiah's time were
quite extensive. Five different kings occupied the throne of Judah
during this period, beginning with a flush of religious enthusiasm
under Josiah. The kingdom declined under the reigns of Jehoahaz,
Jehoiakim and Jehoiachin, ending in the defeat and captivity of
Judah under Zedekiah. Nor, as we have seen, was this the limit of
Jeremiah's ministry, for he continued to prophesy under the governorship of Gedaliah and later in Egypt where he had been carried by
the people after Gedaliah's assassination.

On the international scene a threefold contest for world supremacy was being waged during this period between Egypt, Assyria
and Babylonia. For about three hundred years Assyria had dominated the scene through ruthless conquest, and had destroyed the
northern kingdom of Israel in 722 B.C. However, the power of
Assyria was now in decline, while her neighbor to the south, Babylon, presented a new threat. Nabopolassar had rebelled against Assyria in 626 B.C. and established the Neo-Babylonian Empire. This was
only a year after Jeremiah's call in 627 and about fourteen years
before the fall of Nineveh in 612 which resulted from an alliance of
the Medes, Babylonians and Scythians against Assyria. Seven years
after the fall of Nineveh, Babylon under Nebuchadnezzar crushed the
power of Egypt in the famous Battle of Carchemish and for the next
seventy years dominated the Old Testament world, the same seventy
years of Judah's captivity as Jeremiah had prophesied (Jer. 25). In
609 B.C., at the Battle of Megiddo, Josiah, the last faithful king of
Judah, was slain by the Egyptians (II Chron. 35:20-27).

The northern kingdom of Israel had fallen about a century before
Jeremiah's call to the prophetic ministry in 627 B.C. The prophet's
message of a similar fate awaiting Judah because of her idolatry and
wickedness was by no means a popular one, as his book indicates. It
was against such a background that the prophet was called to
preach; his ministry was to be conducted within a constantly changing and rapidly declining religious and political situation.

V. PROBLEMS

The main problem concerning the book of Jeremiah relates to

authorship. Pfeiffer alleges that critical analysis of the book reveals three different groups of writings: (1) the words of Jeremiah, (2) a biography of Jeremiah written by his secretary Baruch, (3) a miscellaneous collection from the hands of redactors and later authors.[6] Passages generally denied to Jeremiah by the critics are: 10:1-16; 17:19-27; 30-33; 50-51; and the historical appendix, chapter 52. Still other passages in addition to these are denied to Jeremiah by some critics. Duhm in his commentary of 1901 suggested the radical position that, with the exception of chapter 29, Jeremiah wrote exclusively in *poetry* (the *qinah* measure; cf. Lamentations), and thus limits his genuine prophecies to 268 verses, the remaining 1,350 verses being assigned to others.

Moreover, the Hebrew text of Jeremiah differs widely from that of the Septuagint, the latter being about one-eighth shorter. Also the prophecies concerning the foreign nations (46-51) are inserted after 25:13 in the LXX. It has been suggested by Driver that the existing Hebrew text and the Hebrew text from which the LXX translation was made, represent two different recensions of Jeremiah's original writings.

In reply to these allegations concerning the genuineness of the prophecies, there is no evidence whatever to refute the authorship of Jeremiah for the book, the presuppositions of the critics being based solely on subjective factors. The apparent composite nature of the book, as Unger rightly suggests, is easily explained by the unique nature of its composition. The prophecy was written in several stages as the book itself indicates. Jeremiah dictated the first twenty-three years of his prophecies which were subsequently destroyed by Jehoiakim, whereupon they were rewritten with additions. Later prophecies were no doubt dictated to Baruch who at the close of Jeremiah's ministry in Egypt probably gathered and edited the entire collection. Chapter 52, which is practically identical to II Kings 24-25, could, if adopted from the historical records in Kings, have been added as a conclusion to the book at the direction of Jeremiah.

As to the divergences between the Hebrew text and that of the LXX, it is quite impossible to know the precise reasons for this. But they certainly do not represent, as Driver contends, two different recensions of Jeremiah's original writings. Whatever the reasons motivating the LXX translators to omit approximately one-eighth of the Hebrew text, its omission cannot reflect upon the authenticity of the present Hebrew Masoretic text. On the contrary, the LXX translators are subject to question inasmuch as elsewhere they are some-

[6]Robert H. Pfeiffer, *Introduction to the Old Testament,* p. 500.

times careless and untrustworthy in the transmission of the Old Testament text. Moreover, many of the omissions are unimportant words that occur repetitiously (e.g., "the prophet," "saith Yahweh," etc.). Other reasons for the omissions may have been theological. Young suggests, for instance, that the LXX translators, being Alexandrian Jews, may have been influenced by Greek philosophical ideas, which caused them to delete certain portions of the Hebrew text.

I Intro - Call of Jeremiah
II Prophecies Against Judah & Jerusalem

Chapter 19

HABAKKUK

I. THE NATURE OF THE BOOK

THE BOOK OF HABAKKUK contains a single prophecy arranged in two parts. In the first division (chaps. 1-2) there is a dialogue between the prophet and God concerning an announcement of judgment upon the kingdom of Judah at the hands of the Chaldeans. The second section (chap. 3) is a poetic prayer and a theophany of God who comes to judge the world and deliver His people as in ancient times. Isaiah had foretold the Babylonian captivity of Judah for her sins over a century earlier; Habakkuk now stands at the threshold of the fulfillment of his predecessor's prediction.

In the first chapter Habakkuk, concerned over the unchecked iniquity and widespread corruption in Judah which seems to go unpunished, is informed by God that the nation's judgment is soon to be accomplished. The instrumentality through whom God will punish their iniquity is to be the Chaldeans, a ruthless, aggressive and warlike nation. This perplexes the prophet even more for he cannot reconcile the problem of how God, in righteousness and holiness, uses such a wicked instrument as the Chaldeans to chasten Judah. Although Judah deserves punishment, her godless executioner is more wicked than she. What is the solution to this dilemma? The prophet presents his problem to the Lord and awaits His answer which is forthcoming (chap. 2).

He learns that the principle upon which God deals with men is that *the just shall live in his faithfulness, whereas the proud and wicked shall perish.* That is, evil is by its very nature self-destructive, whereas the righteous shall live in his faithfulness (Hab. 2:4, 5-20). With blind arrogance and pride the Chaldeans are unmindful of the fact that they are but the rod of God's wrath for the chastisement of a sinful nation, and that on account of their own ruthlessness they too are doomed to destruction. God's reply to Habakkuk implies that the righteous man exercises a continuous and abiding confidence and trust in God in the face of all adversity and trial and under every circumstance of life. To Habakkuk this means that the just live in

251

faithfulness both in time of religious declension, which he is experiencing in Judah, and in time of national calamity, which he is commissioned to foretell.

Hence, the Chaldeans will inevitably receive their punishment also, although they are for the moment, like Assyria who destroyed Israel, God's instrument of chastisement upon His people because of their sins and disobedience. The prophet, now reconciled to the righteousness of God's government over the nations, petitions the Lord on behalf of the people, "O Yahweh, revive thy work in the midst of the years; in the midst of the years make it known; in wrath remember mercy" (3:2).

Habakkuk is concerned with solving a profound theological problem. His message comes as a result of his inquiry and God's answer.

II. THE DATE

Dates ranging from 701 to 330 B.C. have been proposed for the book. Some contend that the oppressors are not the Chaldeans but the Assyrians, who afflicted the Jews during the invasion of Judah by Sennacherib in 701 B.C., and whose overthrow was accomplished by the Chaldeans as later history shows. G. A. Smith proposed Egypt as the oppressor when Necho invaded Judah and slew King Josiah at Megiddo in 609 B.C. and was in turn defeated by the Chaldeans at Carchemish in 605. However, it is sufficient to reply that neither the Assyrians nor Egyptians are mentioned, which is highly unlikely if either of them is the object of judgment instead of Judah. Duhm, on the other hand, makes the hazardous conjecture that the prophet refers to the coming invasion by Alexander the Great. To do this he makes a textual emendation, changing Chaldeans (*Kasdîm*) in 1:6 to Greeks (*Kittîm*). This radical view is disproved by the Dead Sea Scrolls which read "Chaldeans," as does the present Masoretic text.

Other critics, who reject the idea of supernatural revelation, settle the question of the prophet's date by insisting that the book was written after the Chaldean punishment upon Jerusalem, or else was so close to the time previous to the fall of Jerusalem that the prophet's natural astuteness enabled him to foresee the logical consequences of Judah's sinfulness. But this does not dispose of the problem of how the prophet could predict the overthrow of Babylon itself which came within seventy years of its destruction of Jerusalem.

However, the time of the prophecy can be determined within a general period from internal considerations of the book itself, without the need of resorting to unwarranted emendations of the text, or forcing the book into a period more in harmony with a preconceived concept of Old Testament prophecy. There are three views as to the date of the prophecy based upon internal considerations:

1. The book is to be dated during the reign of Jehoiakim (609-597). Assyria is off the historical scene and the Chaldeans seem to be just now rising to power (1:5-6). Nineveh had fallen in 612 and Babylonia was in power from 625-539. The time indicated by the book appears to be after 612 but before the first invasion of the Chaldeans in 605 (cf. II Kings 24). The conditions described by Habakkuk in 1:2-4 indicate that it is a period of corruption and apostasy. The social and moral evils depicted by the prophet are like those of the reign of Jehoiakim (609-597) rather than that of Josiah who preceded him.

2. The book is to be dated, according to Delitzsch, during the reign of Josiah (640-609). However, the description of the moral conditions in Habakkuk 1:2-4 causes many to reject this date as inconsistent with the period of Josiah's reformation, unless it is put into the brief period before his reforms began. Moreover, the phrase "in your days" (1:5) would seem to contradict the prophecy of the Prophetess Huldah, in which she predicted that the calamity (described in Habakkuk) would not fall upon Judah in the lifetime of Josiah (II Kings 22:18 ff.).

3. Keil, following early Hebrew interpreters, suggests that Habakkuk prophesied during the closing days of the reign of Manasseh (686-642). The position of the book in the Hebrew and Greek canon, and social and moral conditions described in 1:2-4, are consistent with this view. The phrase "in your days" could well embrace the period of those addressed, even though it would be approximately forty years from the close of Manasseh's reign to the first invasion and captivity in 605. Advocates of this view also point out that the prophet is told that the work of God is to be an incredible one: "I am working a work in your days, which ye will not believe though it be told you" (1:5). It is expressly stated in II Kings 21:10-16 and II Chronicles 33:10 that God announced through His prophets the coming of such a calamity in the time of Manasseh (viz., the destruction of Jerusalem), and that the ears of all who heard it would tingle. Habakkuk is said to have been one of these prophets. Zephaniah and Jeremiah, who made the same announcement in the period of Josiah which followed, are said to refer to Habakkuk's prophecy (cf. 2:20 with Zeph. 1:7; 1:8 with Jer. 4:13). However, the resemblances in these passages are not too exact, and such resemblances could indicate either a contemporaneous ministry of the prophets or a later reference by Habukkuk to the other two.

Moreover, the period of Manasseh is unlikely for several reasons. Manasseh instituted reforms in the latter part of his reign (II Chron. 33:15-16), which would not seem to fit the corrupt condition of Judah described in Habakkuk 1:2-4. The description of the Chaldeans (1:6-11) would indicate that they are already on the world scene engaged in their swift and ruthless conquests. Judah's foe, Assyria, has been destroyed and the Chaldeans have not yet molested the Jews. The preaching of Jeremiah in the fourth year of Jehoiakim (605 B.C.), in which he warns of the approaching destruction of Jerusalem just a few years hence at the hands of the Babylonians, is still considered impossible and regarded as an act of treason (Jer. 36). Hence, the reference in Habukkuk 1:5-6 that the work which God will perform is to be something incredible could refer to the same thing. Furthermore, such a statement would indicate a time for the prophecy just before the defeat of the Egyptians by the Babylonians in the Battle of Carchemish (605), when it was indeed incredible that the Egyptians, regarded as invincible by Judah since the Battle of Megiddo, should be defeated by the Chaldeans. Had Habakkuk's prophecy (and Jeremiah's in 605) been delivered after the great Babylonian victory at Carchemish, then the Chaldean threat would not have seemed incredible, nor would Jeremiah's prediction of the same have been considered treason.[1]

Hence, all evidence considered, the conditions would seem to place the prophecy early in the reign of Jehoiakim (609-597). J. P. Lange, G. L. Robinson, J. Barton Payne, among others, follow this line. The suggested date is, therefore, 609-605 B.C. While some critical scholars find this date attractive in that it enables them to view the book more from the standpoint of history than prophecy, it by no means discounts the prophetic element in Habakkuk's message. Divine inspiration is not determined by the length of time that must elapse between the event prophesied and its fulfillment. Many instances prove this to be true. Jeremiah also predicted the downfall of Jerusalem up until the actual event occurred. Divine revelation of this act is not to be discounted because of the time element involved. Micah predicted the fall of Samaria as imminent and lived to see its fulfillment. Micaiah ben Imlah predicted the death of Ahab within the week of its accomplishment. Daniel foretold the fall of Babylon the same night in which it occurred (Dan. 5)! On the other hand, Habakkuk had also predicted the fall of Babylon, an event not

[1]John Peter Lange, *Commentary on the Holy Scriptures,* trans. and ed. Philip Schaff, p. 5.

accomplished until almost a century later, which gives conclusive evidence as to the inspired nature of the entire prophecy.

III. THE PROPHET

The name Habakkuk means "embrace." Some of the ancient rabbis, connecting the name with II Kings 4:16, "Thou shalt embrace a son," believed that the prophet was the son of the Shunammite woman in the time of Elisha in the ninth century B.C. The book itself throws little light on the prophet, nevertheless numerous legends and speculations have grown up around his name. The identification of the prophet with the son of the Shunammite woman is one. Another which relates Isaiah 21:6 with Habakkuk 2:1 makes Habakkuk the watchman set by Isaiah to watch for the fall of Babylon. The Apocryphal book *Bel and the Dragon* claims Habakkuk carried pottage and bread to Daniel in the lion's den, having been transported there by an angel. According to another work, he was a man of the tribe of Simeon who died two years before the return of the Jews from exile.[2]

Keil, on the basis of the rubric at the end of the psalm (3:19) in which the prophet directs that the psalm when sung be accompanied by "my" stringed instrument, holds that Habakkuk must have been officially qualified to participate in the temple music, and must therefore have been a Levite.[3] But neither David nor Hezekiah were Levites, and yet they sang in the temple with their stringed instruments (Isa. 38:20). Habakkuk was a contemporary of Zephaniah and Jeremiah who predicted the Babylonian invasion and the destruction of Jerusalem.

IV. THE HISTORICAL BACKGROUND

In earlier times Assyria had extended her control over Mesopotamia, bringing Babylonia into subjection. The Chaldeans, whom Jeremiah called "an ancient nation" (5:15), were a Semitic people who are known from ancient records to have been living in southeastern Babylonia about 1000 B.C. They stirred up dissatisfaction against the Assyrian rule of Babylonia, which was finally to be punished by Sennacherib who destroyed Babylon completely. Esarhaddon (681-669 B.C.) restored Babylon. Shortly after the death of Ashur-

[2]Frederick Carl Eiselen, *The Minor Prophets*, pp. 463-64.
[3]C. F. Keil and F. Delitzsch, *The Twelve Minor Prophets, Biblical Commentary on the Old Testament*, II, 49.

banipal in 633, Nabopolassar, a Chaldean, seized the kingship of Babylon and established an independent Chaldean empire known as the New Babylonian Empire in 625. Nabopolassar joined in the destruction of Nineveh in 612 with Cyaxares the Mede and the king of the Scythians. The Neo-Babylonian Empire was soon challenged by Egypt, and in 605 Pharaoh Necho marched to meet the son of Nabopolassar, Nebuchadnezzar II, in a decisive battle at Carchemish in which Egypt was defeated.[4] Nebuchadnezzar pursued the Egyptians through Syria and Palestine. He advanced against Jerusalem, which was subdued, taking numerous hostages, including Daniel, in 605. Word reached Nebuchadnezzar of the death of his father in the same year and he returned home to ascend the throne.

Previously Josiah had been slain in 609 by Pharaoh Necho on his advance through Palestine to meet the Babylonians. The Jews had made Jehoahaz, Josiah's son, king; but he was deposed after three months by Necho, who installed Jehoahaz' brother Eliakim (Jehoiakim) as king in his stead, the latter becoming vassal to Nebuchadnezzar in 605 upon the defeat of Egypt (II Kings 24:1). When Jehoiakim, three years later, rebelled against his Babylonian overlord against the advice of Jeremiah, the Chaldean armies invaded Judah, and Jehoiakim was killed, perhaps in an uprising at court (cf. Jer. 22:18 f.; 36:30). His son and successor, Jehoiachin, surrendered after a reign of only three months in 597 B.C. He was taken to Babylon with other captives, and Zedekiah was made king in his stead. Enticed by Egyptian support, Zedekiah revolted after ten years. The Babylonians came in strength, burned the city, destroyed the temple and deported its citizens, leaving only a remnant under Gedaliah as governor. The fate of Judah, predicted by Jeremiah and Habakkuk, had been realized.

V. Problems

According to the school of negative criticism, the book is of composite authorship and not a unity. The problem is twofold, the problem of chapters 1-2, and the authenticity of the psalm in chapter 3.

1. The problem of chapters 1-2 is in two parts:

a. The critics say that 1:5-11 is a misplaced passage which should be inserted after 2:4. They argue that in 1:5-11 the Chaldeans are depicted as about to be raised up, whereas in verses 12-17 they appear at the height of power. Thus 1:12 is the true sequel of 1:4.

---

[4]Jack Finegan, *Light from the Ancient Past,* pp. 183-85.

But in reply it is to be noted that there are no internal reasons for separating verses 5-11 from 1-4. The reference in 1:6 is not to the first appearance of the Chaldeans in history, but they are pictured as being already engaged in conquest (as 12-17 confirms) and are to be "raised up" with respect to the punishment of Judah. Furthermore, to remove verses 5-11 from their present position is to destroy the theological as well as logical development of the passage. In 1:1-4 the prophet complains of widespread corruption in Judah. In reply God declares in 1:5-11 that judgment is about to be executed at the hands of the Chaldeans, "that bitter and hasty nation, that march through the breadth of the earth, to possess dwelling-places that are not theirs. They are terrible and dreadful" (1:6-7). This announcement perplexes the prophet who next asks in verses 12-17: How can a holy God look in silence upon the cruelties of the Chaldeans? How can God employ as executioners those who are more wicked than the Jews? The prophet is perplexed, and his faith is taxed; but he will submit the problem to God and await His answer (2:1), which comes speedily (2:2 ff.). If the prophecy is to be interpreted properly there can be no justifiable rejection of verses 5-11. Their obvious connection with the logical and theological movement of the passage cannot be successfully denied.

b. Another problem is concerned with 2:6-20 and the five woes contained therein. Some parts contain citations from other prophets and are considered by critics to be glosses by later scribes. These are viewed as pious reflections thrown carelessly into the text with no logical or metrical connection with the context (cf. 2:12 with Micah 3:10; 2:13 with Jer. 51:58; 2:14 with Isa. 11:9; 2:16*b* with Jer. 25:15-16; 2:18-20 with Isa. 44:9 ff.; 46:6-7; Jer. 10:1-16). However, arguments based upon comparisons are always precarious, and if these resemblances do indicate acquaintance with other prophets, there is no reason why they could not be from the hand of Habakkuk himself, for both Isaiah and Micah preceded him, and Jeremiah was a contemporary.[5]

2. Chapter 3 presents a problem unique in itself. The third chapter, which is a psalm, is denied to Habakkuk and is held to be a separate production by one or more authors after the exile. Driver urges that (1) the title in 3:1 and the musical notations (3, 9, 13, 19) indicate that chapter 3 is a psalm from some liturgical collection and placed here by a later editor. (2) There are no historical allusions to Habakkuk's own age as seen in 1:2—2:8; hence, there can be

[5]Eiselen, p. 472.

found no internal connection between chapters 1-2 and 3. (3) The nation, not the prophet, is the speaker in 3:14, 18-19. (4) There is no specific reference to the Chaldeans.[6] In addition to these arguments contemporary critics cite the fact that the Dead Sea Scroll commentary on the book of Habakkuk ends with chapter 2.

These arguments lose their force when they are carefully evaluated as follows:

a. The objection that chapter 3 is a psalm, and therefore is not the work of Habakkuk, is groundless, since change to poetic form cannot prove that it is not original with the prophet, unless one insists that there was no preexilic psalm literature. Jonah 2 is just such a prayer or psalm. Further, 3:1 definitely states that it is a prayer of *Habakkuk.*

b. In chapter 3 the prophet is quite obviously speaking *for* the nation (vv. 1-2). Jeremiah in the same period speaks for the nation (3:21-24; 8:14-15; 10:23-25, etc.).

c. There is a clear reference to the Chaldean invasion in 3:16.

d. The claim that there is no essential connection with the rest of the book is also groundless. The style, of course, would be expected to be different since chapters 1-2 are prose while chapter 3 is poetry. There is an essential unity, however, to be seen from internal considerations. In both 1:13 and 3:13 the enemy is designated as "wicked." The prophet's plea in 3:2 has a definite relation to chapter 1 and God's declaration that He will punish Judah. The theme of chapters 1-2 is the same as chapter 3. In chapter 3 he delineates the judgment of God upon the ungodly, and through it all runs a stream of consolation to the righteous. Habakkuk closes his prayer by expressing fear of the coming chastisement but hope and confidence in the future salvation. The invaders in 3:16 clearly refer to the invading Chaldeans of chapters 1-2. Moreover, there is a definite connection between 2:1, 3:2 and 3:16. The psalm itself is found in 3:3-15. In 2:1 Habakkuk awaits God's reply, and in 3:2 he makes reference to God's reply: "O Yahweh, I have heard the report of thee, and am afraid." Again in 3:16 the prophet repeats this refrain: "I heard, and my body trembled . . . because I must wait quietly for the day of trouble, for the coming up of the people that invadeth us." Hence, the thoughts of the entire prophecy are so closely related that chapter 3 is seen to be essential to the book.

Finally, the fact that the Qumran commentary on Habakkuk contains no reference to chapter 3 is not so weighty an argument as

[6] S. R. Driver, *An Introduction to the Literature of the Old Testament,* p. 339.

the critics contend. First of all this is another argument from silence, which is never conclusive in itself. But there is no problem really when it is remembered that what was found in the cave at Qumran was not the *book* of Habakkuk, but simply a *commentary* on the book written by the Qumran community. Since the commentary is limited to chapters 1-2 and does not include chapter 3, there must have been a purpose. This is not difficult to discover. Habakkuk 1-2 deals with the Chaldean persecution and their ultimate overthrow, which theme might well have been used by the Qumran community as a means of encouragement during their own trials and persecutions which are known to have come, for example, at the hands of the Romans. Since chapter 3 is a *poetic theophany* there would have been no purpose for including a commentary on the psalm.

A reading of the commentary will quickly indicate its sectarian purpose and character; for their interpretation of Habakkuk was not an exposition of the author's original meaning, but an effort to read elements of the history of the sect back into the text. The following example which is an "interpretation" of Habakkuk 2:17 by the Qumran community indicates this. The American Standard Version reads:

> For the violence done to Lebanon shall cover thee, and the destruction of the beasts, which made them afraid; because of men's blood, and for the violence done to the land, to the city and to all that dwell therein.

The Qumran interpretation is as follows:

> the wicked priest, to repay him for his recompense which he recompensed the poor. For Lebanon is the Council of the Community, and the beasts are the simple ones of Judah, the doer of the Law. . . .[7]

OUTLINE OF HABAKKUK

I. THE PROPHET'S PERPLEXITY AND THE DIVINE SOLUTION   Chapters 1-2
  A. The Prophet's First Perplexity   1:2-11
    1. God's Silence in View of Judah's Iniquities   2-4
    2. The Divine Solution: The Chaldean Invasion   5-11
  B. The Prophet's Second Perplexity   1:12—2:20
    1. God's Employment of the Wicked Chaldeans as
      His Instrument of Chastisement   1:12-17
    2. The Divine Solution: The Chaldeans' Destruction   2:1-20
      a. The prophet's watch for God's answer   1
      b. God's directions in preparation for His reply   2-3

[7]William Sanford LaSor, *Amazing Dead Sea Scrolls*, p. 48.

Chapter 20

DANIEL

I. The Nature of the Book

THE BOOK OF DANIEL has, without question, been the object of more negative criticism than any other book of the Old Testament. Its authenticity was first challenged in the third century A.D. by the Neoplatonist Porphyry, who alleged that the book was a forgery written during the Maccabean period inasmuch as the history of this period is clearly detailed in the book. Modern criticism following this rationalistic conclusion contends that Daniel was composed by an anonymous author during the persecutions of Antiochus Epiphanes (c. 167 B.C.) in an effort to encourage the suffering Jews to remain faithful in the midst of their afflictions. This date for the book is established with such certainty in the minds of the critics that we are repeatedly informed by this school that no Old Testament scholar of any repute now maintains that the book was written by Daniel. That such a conclusion is unwarranted and fallacious is shown in the discussion of the date, authorship and problems of the book.

Furthermore, it should be noted at the outset that the only satisfactory interpretation of the prophecy of Daniel, we believe, is one which is made from the *premillennial* point of view, as a prophecy concerning God's providential dealings with *Israel* from the time of Nebuchadnezzar until the second advent of Christ. Daniel's prophecy portrays the course of Gentile world power, called in Scripture "the times of the Gentiles" (Luke 21:24), in its relation to Israel from the period of the Babylonian exile to its final overthrow by Christ at the second advent and the establishment of the millennial kingdom. In Daniel 2 there is recorded a dream by Nebuchadnezzar, the interpretation of which God revealed to Daniel concerning events of "what shall be in the latter days" (2:28). As the prophet speaks there unfolds a remarkable prophecy concerning the four Gentile kingdoms, Babylon, Medo-Persia, Greece and Rome, which were to rule successively during "the times of the Gentiles" until they had run their course and would finally be destroyed by a fifth kingdom (Messiah's), depicted as a stone cut out without hands (2:38).

Israel, in prophecy, is not merely a type of the church, but a people eternally bound to God in covenant (Rom. 11:27), their national restoration being promised again and again in the Scriptures (cf. Amos 9:11-15; Ezek. 37; Rom. 11:25-29; Luke 19:11 ff.; Acts 1:6-7, etc.). However, Erich Sauer is correct when he cautions that it would be inaccurate to say that the Old Testament kingdom prophecies never speak of the blessings of the present age of the gospel. This would not do justice to the manner in which the New Testament cites the Old Testament prophecies concerning this fact. The New Testament often states that the prophets spoke of "these days" (cf. Acts 4:26-28; 13:33; 2:16-17 with Joel 2:28-29; Acts 3:24; Rom. 1:1-2; cf. Acts 13:47 with Isa. 49:6; Acts 26:22-23; I Peter 1:10-12). Similarly David in Psalm 110 spoke of an age or period to intervene between the ascension of Messiah and His ultimate triumph, in which the Father says to the Son: "Sit thou at my right hand, *until* I make thine enemies thy footstool" (Ps. 110:1).

On the other hand, it would likewise be incorrect to say that because the Old Testament speaks somewhat of the present age there is no further, still larger, fulfillment in the future in which Israel, restored, will realize the innumerable prophecies concerning her future blessings. It is just as one-sided to spiritualize all the Old Testament kingdom prophecies and apply them to the present gospel age and the church as it is to apply them all to the future millennium alone. The term "kingdom of God" consists of more than one aspect; only the context can make clear precisely which aspect is under consideration: whether the Old Testament theocratic kingdom (Matt. 21:43) or the present invisible spiritual kingdom (Luke 17:20-21; Matt. 13:11) or the visible kingdom of the millennium (Luke 19:11 ff.; Acts 1:6; Rev. 20) or the eternal kingdom (I Cor. 15:24-25).

Until the restoration of Israel, the nation as a people is set aside "until the fulness of the Gentiles be come in" (Rom. 11:25), for "Jerusalem shall be trodden down of the Gentiles, until the times of the Gentiles be fulfilled" (Luke 21:24). Then "all Israel shall be saved: even as it is written, There shall come out of Zion the Deliverer; he shall turn away ungodliness from Jacob: and this is my covenant unto them, when I shall take away their sins . . . . As touching the election, they are beloved for the fathers' sake. For the gifts and the calling of God are not repented of" (Rom. 11:26-29; cf. Matt. 19:28; 25:31).[1]

[1]Erich Sauer, *From Eternity to Eternity,* trans. G. H. Lang, pp. 171-76.

The book of Daniel is found, not among the Major Prophets as in the English arrangement, but in the third division of the Hebrew canon called the Writings, which fact the critics cite as proof of its late date since this was the last division of the canon to be completed. However, this is a groundless assumption which, first of all, erroneously presupposes that the threefold division of the canon (Law, Prophets, Writings) indicates three successive stages of collection for the books. Second, it overlooks the unique nature of Daniel's ministry in the heathen court at Babylon. Daniel, while he was a prophet (Matt. 24:15) who exercised the prophetic gift, nevertheless appears as did Joseph, his patriarchal prototype, in the capacity of a Hebrew statesman at the Gentile court. Added to this, the book's internal features, namely, its composition in Hebrew and Aramaic, and its strong historical emphasis, may easily explain its place among the Writings in the Hebrew canon.

The general structure of the book is twofold, and the book is written in two languages, Hebrew and Aramaic. Chapters 1-6 set forth events in the life of Daniel and his role as an interpreter of dreams under the reigns of Nebuchadnezzar, Belshazzar, Darius and Cyrus. Chapters 7-12 consist of prophetic visions which Daniel received during the reigns of Belshazzar, Darius and Cyrus. The book is not in chronological order; hence, two possible methods of outline for the prophecy are possible, one according to content, the other based upon the languages used in Daniel.

Outlined according to its contents the book falls logically into two divisions as previously noted, chapters 1-6 and 7-12. The first six chapters are historical in character (although prediction is not totally absent), relating events in the life of Daniel, whereas the last six chapters consist of visions and predictive prophecy. However, as Culver has shown, the key to the book is its linguistic structure. Hebrew is used in Daniel 1:1—2:4a; 8:1—12:13, while Aramaic is found in 2:4b—7:28. The reason for this peculiarity would seem to stem from the fact that Daniel had two distinct, although related, messages to deliver. One was *a message of judgment* concerning the defeat and final overthrow of the Gentile world powers of whom Nebuchadnezzar, Belshazzar, Darius and Cyrus were at present the chief representatives. The other was *a message of consolation and hope* concerning the future deliverance for God's people, the nation of Israel. The first message in Aramaic, the lingua franca of the Near East, was appropriate for the prophet's message concerning the future history of the Gentile kingdoms. The second message, which is exclusively directed to the Hebrew people, is appropriately in Hebrew.[2] What concerned the Gentiles was written in Aramaic, the commercial and diplomatic language of the time. That which concerned the people of Israel was written in Hebrew, although on the basis of chapter 1, which is an introduction to the book, the entire prophecy would, when written down by Daniel, be addressed to the Jewish people.

Chapter 1, written in Hebrew, is *introductory*, setting forth the account of the deportation of Daniel and his selection and education for service in the Babylonian court, an appointment which was to continue until the first year of Cyrus. The second division of the book, chapters 2-7, is in Aramaic and concerns primarily the *Gentile* nations and rulers. Here revelations are made to the Gentile rulers in the form of dreams and visions, and in one instance by handwriting upon a wall (2:1; 4:5; 5:5). Chapter 3 which relates the fiery furnace incident, and chapter 6 setting forth Daniel's experience in the lions' den, likewise are directly concerned with the Gentile rulers of Babylon. The third division, chapters 8-12, is again in Hebrew, having primary reference to *Israel* in her relationship to the Gentile world kingdoms. In this section it is Daniel who is the recipient of the revelations directed to the people of Israel.

II. THE DATE

The date of the book of Daniel is inseparably bound up with the question of authorship. Modern criticism holds that the book was written by an anonymous author about 167 B.C. during the Maccabean period to encourage Jewish resistance during the persecution by Antiochus Epiphanes. Their reasons for the abandonment of the traditional view, which maintains that the book is the work of the Prophet Daniel in the sixth century B.C., are as follows:

1. The book does not claim to be the work of Daniel. Although the first person "I" frequently occurs, this does not imply that Daniel wrote it any more than the use of "I" by the writer of Ecclesiastes, where he speaks in the character of Solomon ("I the Preacher was king over Israel in Jerusalem," Eccles. 1:12), means that Solomon wrote Ecclesiastes. The use of the first person is a common literary device.

We have here, first of all, a classic example of the inconsistency of modern critical scholarship. Their argument for denial of the authorship of the book of Jonah to the prophet himself (whose existence, like Daniel, as a historical figure the critics admit) is that Jonah is always referred to in the *third* person in the book bearing his name.

[2]Robert D. Culver, *Daniel and the Latter Days,* pp. 95-99.

Hence, an anonymous writer long after the time of Jonah wrote the prophecy using the historical figure of Jonah to teach Israel, by means of an allegory, a spiritual lesson. Had Jonah composed the book he would have written in the *first* person concerning himself. However, in the case of Daniel who does this very thing, rather than its being evidence of Danielic authorship, Daniel's employment of the first person is set aside by the critical school as "a common literary device employed to give vividness to the narrative"![3] Moreover, the comparison of the use of "I" in Daniel to that in Ecclesiastes, and deducing thereby that Daniel could not have written the book bearing his name inasmuch as Solomon did not write Ecclesiastes, is reasoning in a circle. It assumes the truth of one premise (in this case that Solomon is not the author of Ecclesiastes) to prove the validity of another. Since there is much evidence from internal considerations that Solomon was in fact the author of Ecclesiastes, the argument by analogy is not valid.

Furthermore, there is evidence in the book of Daniel that the prophet is its author, and the use of the first person is itself strong support of this fact. Again Danielic authorship is indicated by the command in 12:4, 9 to the prophet: "But thou, O Daniel, shut up the words, and seal the book." We have here an obvious reference to the "words" which have been revealed unto him in the book bearing his name (cf. 8:26), for the term "book" without question signifies the book of Daniel itself.

2. The book is never quoted or alluded to in the intertestamental Jewish literature until after 180 B.C. Ecclesiasticus, for example (*c.* 180), mentions Isaiah, Jeremiah, Ezekiel and the Twelve Minor Prophets, but does not speak of Daniel. Hence, the book of Daniel was not written before the Maccabean period (*c.* 167 B.C.).

However, such an argument from silence cannot disprove the existence of the book of Daniel at this time (180). Moreover, Jesus Ben Sirach, the writer of Ecclesiasticus, is following the Hebrew order of the books in his citation. He does not mention Daniel because his book was not classified with the Prophets, but the Writings.

3. The place which the book occupies in the Hebrew canon is decisive. Daniel is included in the third division of the canon, the Writings. The book therefore was not in existence at the time when the second division of the canon, the Prophets, was closed in the second century B.C.

The reply to this assumption is simply that the threefold division

[3]Arthur S. Peake (ed.), *A Commentary on the Bible,* p. 522.

of the Hebrew canon does not indicate three successive stages of collection, one section being closed before another. Furthermore, Daniel was doubtless placed among the Writings, as has already been shown, because of his status, not because the book was late.

4. The writer's knowledge of the period in which Daniel lived, the sixth century B.C., is imperfect, for the book is filled with historical inaccuracies, whereas his account of the history of the Greek period (at which time the author lived) is remarkably accurate. Some of the most obvious errors are:

a. The statement in Daniel 1:1 that Nebuchadnezzar came to Jerusalem and besieged it "in the third year of the reign of Jehoiakim king of Judah" is incorrect and contradicts Jeremiah 25:1, 9; 46:2 which state that the event occurred in the *fourth* year of Jehoiakim.

One of two solutions is possible, however. Keil, Green, Raven and others suggest that the word translated "he came" in 1:1 can be translated "he set out." Thus the date mentioned by Daniel actually refers to the *starting* of Nebuchadnezzar's expedition from Babylon in Jehoiakim's third year. Before besieging Jerusalem, however, he was engaged in battle at Carchemish (605 B.C.) with Pharaoh Necho (Jer. 46:2), and then proceeded to Judah, arriving the following year. Such usage of the verb *bā'*, "he set out," is found in other Old Testament passages (e.g., Jonah 3:3; II Kings 5:5, etc.). Wiseman, however, believes this attempted solution is countered by the Babylonian chronicle which may indicate that the Babylonian army could not have "set out" for Carchemish in the year preceding its siege of Jerusalem inasmuch as the chronicle shows that it did not return from a prior campaign until Shebat (January-February), 605 B.C., the year of the Battle of Carchemish.[4] A more natural solution, therefore, is that Daniel, living in Babylon, dates Jehoiakim according to the Babylonian method, while Jeremiah in Palestine uses the Palestinian method of dating a king's accession. According to the Babylonian system, the year in which the king ascended the throne was not counted as his first year, but as the "year of accession," the first year of his reign being actually the second year; in Palestine the year of accession was also the first year of the king's reign. Therefore, Jehoiakim's third year according to Daniel would be the same as that king's fourth year according to Jeremiah.

b. The description of Belshazzar as king and the son of Nebuchadnezzar (5:18, 22, 30), when as a matter of fact he was

[4]D. J. Wiseman, "Some Historical Problems in the Book of Daniel," *Notes on Some Problems in the Book of Daniel,* pp. 9-18.

neither, are historical inaccuracies. Belshazzar's father was Nabonidus, who was himself the last king of Babylon (556-539) according to the inscriptions.

However, the discovery of the Chronicles of Nabonidus has authenticated the account in Daniel. These inscriptions show that Nabonidus shared the kingship with his son Belshazzar. In one cuneiform text he states that he entrusted the kingship to his eldest son while he himself undertook a distant campaign after which he established his residence away from Babylon in Tema in Arabia.[5] Hence, Daniel is not incorrect in representing Belshazzar as the last king of Babylon. (Note the probable allusion to Nabonidus in 5:7, 16, 29.) Also the mention of Belshazzar as the son of Nebuchadnezzar, whereas Nabonidus was in fact his father, is in perfect harmony with Semitic usage, the term "son" often referring to a successor in the same office without regard to blood relationship. It doubtless is used here by Daniel in the sense of "successor of" Nebuchadnezzar. In similar fashion Jehu is called the "son of Omri" in the Assyrian inscription. Others suggest that Belshazzar may have been the grandson of Nebuchadnezzar;[6] then as his descendant he would be called his "son."

c. Darius the Mede is represented as receiving the kingdom after the conquest of Babylon and the death of Belshazzar (5:30-31), whereas Cyrus of Persia was the immediate successor of the Babylonian ruler. Moreover, contemporary history knows of no such person as Darius the Mede. Hence, critical scholars such as H. H. Rowley conclude that the Darius of Daniel was fictitious, resulting from the author's confusion of the history of the period of Cyrus with the later reign of Darius Hystaspes (520 B.C.).

However, it should be noted that although the name of Darius the Mede has not been found as yet outside the record in Daniel, the examples of Belshazzar and Sargon (Isa. 20:1), both of whom were formerly unknown in history outside the Old Testament, but whose existence has now been confirmed by extrabiblical history, should be sufficient caution to modern critics against a categorical denial of the historicity of Darius the Mede. One interesting and possible suggestion is the view which identifies Darius the Mede of Daniel with Gubaru, the governor of Babylon under the appointment of Cyrus.[7]

[5]Finegan, *Light from the Ancient Past*, pp. 189-90. See also R. P. Dougherty, *Nabonidus and Belshazzar* (New Haven: 1929), pp. 105-200.

[6]On the assumption that Nabonidus may have married a daughter of Nebuchadnezzar to legitimize his usurpation of the throne in 556 B.C.

[7]John C. Whitcomb, Jr., *Darius the Mede*, p. 24.

In 5:31 Darius is said to have *"received* the kingdom" and in 9:1 he is said to have been *"made* king over the realm of the Chaldeans," indicating perhaps that he was appointed to the kingship by a higher authority. Moreover, W. F. Albright suggests that it is highly probable that the governor assumed the name Darius, it being perhaps an old Iranian royal title of honor, as was "Caesar" in the Roman Empire.[8] (Cf. Pul who after usurping the Assyrian throne took the famous name of Tiglath-pileser, yet was known by both names [II Kings 15:19, 29].)

D. J. Wiseman, on the other hand, proposed the Cyrus theory which identifies Darius the Mede with Cyrus the Persian king on the basis of Daniel 6:28, which can be translated "Daniel prospered in the reign of Darius, even [or i.e.] the reign of Cyrus the Persian." Such a use of the appositional (Hebrew waw) construction is also found in I Chronicles 5:26. Herodotus represents Cyrus as son of a Median princess, and Xenophon speaks of him as heir to the Median throne. The identification of Cyrus with Darius the Mede accords well with Isaiah 13:17 and Jeremiah 51:11, 28 which denote the Medes as the conquerors of Babylon. Wiseman's scholarly and plausible theory, first proposed in 1957, deserves serious consideration in any attempt to solve the problem of Darius the Mede.[9]

d. The reference to a canon of Scripture in 9:2 is an inaccuracy since such a collection of sacred books did not exist at this time.

However, the expression by the prophet, "I, Daniel, understood by the books the number of the years whereof the word of Yahweh came to Jeremiah the prophet, for the accomplishing of the desolations of Jerusalem, even seventy years," does not imply that these books referred to an already formed canon, but rather to the Scriptures generally (including Jeremiah's prophecy) which were then in existence.

e. The critical argument that since chapter 11 sets forth such an accurate detailed history of the Greek period it must therefore have been composed by one living during the time of Antiochus Epiphanes is scarcely tenable unless one has already ruled out the possibility of predictive prophecy. The purpose for the detailed history foretold in this chapter is sufficient to explain its minuteness of detail, for when the record of the history of this period is examined it is apparent that the persecutions during this time presented one of

---

[8]W. F. Albright, "The Date and Personality of the Chronicler," *Journal of Biblical Literature,* XL (1921), 11, n. 2.
  [9]Wiseman, pp. 9-18.

the greatest threats of all time to the survival of Israel and her worship. Moreover, as is shown in the discussion of chapter 11, Antiochus and his persecutions were to serve as types and forerunners of Antichrist and the period of the great tribulation.

5. The language of the book indicates a late date after the Chaldean period. A number of Persian and Greek words are used; the Aramaic used betrays signs of a later date, and the Hebrew is characterized by late forms and constructions.

Since Daniel's ministry continued into the Persian period, the presence of a few Persian words presents no problem. The use of three Greek names of musical instruments does not require a date after the spread of Greek culture by Alexander the Great in the fourth century B.C., inasmuch as Greek influence and culture, through contact with other nations, had taken place by this time (sixth century B.C.). Moreover, as Gleason L. Archer has shown in his discussion on this subject, the presence of Greek loanwords is one of the most compelling evidences that Daniel could not have been composed as late as the Greek period. By 170 B.C. a Greek-speaking government had been in authority over Palestine for one hundred sixty years, and Greek political and administrative terms would have intruded into Palestinian Aramaic (cf. the Aramaic of Daniel which had absorbed fifteen words of Persian origin which relate to government and politics). However, not a single term pertaining to politics or administration had intruded into the Aramaic of the book of Daniel (allegedly composed in Palestine) although Greek had been the language of government for over one hundred sixty years. The same is true of the Hebrew portions of Daniel, which contain some Persian terms but not a single word of Greek origin.[10]

Concerning the Aramaic there is nothing requiring a date later than Daniel. The Aramaic as well as the Hebrew of Daniel could have been modified by Ezra or the scribes to conform to that in current use. Moreover, several grammatical evidences for an early date of Daniel's Aramaic are available. The texts of Ras Shamra, which date from the fifteenth century B.C. and contain Aramaic elements, show in one instance at least an Aramaic peculiarity formerly regarded by critics as evidence for a late date for Daniel (viz., Daniel in certain instances spells words with a *d* instead of *z*, the same phenomenon occurring in the Ras Shamra texts).[11]

[10]Gleason L. Archer, Jr., *A Survey of Old Testament Introduction*, pp. 374-76.
[11]E. J. Young, *Introduction to the Old Testament*, p. 362.

Again, the late Aramaic documents published from the Dead Sea caves do not show some early forms characteristic of Daniel (e.g., fairly frequent internal vowel-change passives). None of the Qumran sectarian documents composed in Hebrew show any distinctive linguistic characteristics in common with Daniel.[12]

Furthermore, K. A. Kitchen has shown in his excellent study on the Aramaic in Daniel that a comparative study of biblical Aramaic with inscriptions and papyri in Old and Imperial Aramaic and cognate West Semitic and Akkadian reveals that nine-tenths of the biblical Aramaic vocabulary is attested in texts of the ninth to the fifth centuries B.C., which would clearly allow a sixth century B.C. date for the Aramaic of Daniel.[13]

6. The theology of the book, critics assert, is too advanced for the period of Daniel, particularly in regard to the doctrines of angels, resurrection, judgment, and the Messiah and His kingdom. Daniel, according to Pfeiffer, represents the latest phase of religious thought in the Old Testament period. Individual angels, Gabriel and Michael, are first named in Daniel, as they are in the intertestamental Apocryphal book of Tobit (*c*. 190-170 B.C.) where Raphael, one of seven holy angels, plays an important role, as do Michael and Gabriel in Daniel (Tobit 5:4; 12:15), and in the pseudepigraphical book of Enoch which mentions four by name (Enoch 9:1). The hierarchy of angelic ministers implied in Daniel is the most advanced in the Old Testament. Again, the doctrine of resurrection is first stated as a dogma in Daniel 12:2, where it occurs in connection with the idea of individual retribution after death, just as it is found in the later Judaism of the Maccabean period (II Macc. 7:9 ff.; 14:46) and in the pseudepigraphical literature (Enoch, Testament of the Twelve Patriarchs, etc.). The concept of the kingdom in conflict with the heathen kingdoms, Babylonian, Median, Persian, and Greek, reaching its apex in the Greek period, indicates a date during the latter era.

The theology of the book is not so advanced, however, that it must be dated as late postexilic in the Greek period. All of the doctrines alleged by the critics to be late concepts appear throughout the Old Testament and not necessarily, as it is asserted, in a more primitive stage of development than that found in Daniel. The book of Zechariah from the same century as the book of Daniel makes a distinction in rank among the three angels who appear in his prophecy, namely, the angel of Yahweh, the "interpreting" angel and one

[12]Archer, pp. 376-79.

[13]K. A. Kitchen, "The Aramaic of Daniel," *Notes on Some Problems in the Book of Daniel*, pp. 31-79.

designated as "another angel" in 2:3, as well as between the angelic messengers (1:8-10). Moreover, angelology is not a late concept, for the angel of the Lord appears as early as Genesis 16:7 in the time of Abraham and frequently thereafter. He appears in company with two other angels in Genesis 18-19 and later gives His name to Manoah, the father of Samson (Judges 13:17-18; cf. Isa. 9:6). As for the doctrine of the resurrection and belief in the afterlife, these truths are taught throughout the Old Testament (e.g., Ps. 16:10; 17:15; 49:15; 73:24-26; Job 14:13-15; 19:25-27; Isa. 26:19; cf. Deut. 32:39; I Sam. 2:6, etc.). The doctrine of judgment is frequently referred to in the Old Testament before the sixth century B.C. (e.g., Obad. 15 ff.; Joel 3:2 ff.; Zeph. 1; Isa. 2:4-22; 66:24; Ps. 9:17; 49:14-15; 69:28; 73; 75:8-10; 96:13; Prov. 14:32, etc.). Abraham recognized Yahweh as "the Judge of all the earth" (Gen. 18:25). The Messianic concept permeates the entire Old Testament (e.g., Gen. 3:15; 9:25-27; 12:1-3; 49:8-12; Num. 24:17-19; Deut. 18:15-19; II Sam. 7:11-16; Ps. 2; 22; etc.).

Therefore, the arguments of the destructive critics in their effort to date the book of Daniel in the period of the persecution under Antiochus Epiphanes, written as an encouragement to the Jewish people to remain faithful through their trials, are fallacious and unconvincing. The contention that the stories of Daniel and his three friends are unhistorical and intended by the writer to convey a message of hope to people who are suffering similar trials is without any evidence whatever. The detailed history of Daniel 11 concerning the Greek period and the persecution under Antiochus Epiphanes is not proof that the book had to be written after these events occurred, unless one reject, as the negative school does, the possibility of predictive prophecy. Christ, however, confirmed the authenticity of the book of Daniel when He referred His disciples to that "which was spoken of through Daniel the prophet" (Matt. 24:15), quoting from that portion of Daniel's prophecy which criticism insists proves the book to be from the Maccabean period (viz., 9:27; 11:31; 12:11). Manuscripts of Daniel have been discovered among the Dead Sea Scrolls used by the Qumran community datable to the second century B.C., the same century in which critics claim the book was composed (167 B.C.)! Moreover, the manuscripts agree with the present Hebrew text, the arrangement of the Hebrew and Aramaic portions being precisely the same. It is quite impossible, in view of the scrupulousness of the Jews concerning the authenticity of the prophetic literature of the Old Testament, that a work of such recent production, previously unknown to Israel and purporting to be by

Daniel, should have been raised to canonical status as soon as it appeared. Moreover, in the Maccabean age the canon was long considered completed, and Jewish works of that very era were rejected as not being divinely authoritative.

III. THE PROPHET

Daniel, whose name means "God is my Judge," was carried captive as a youth to Babylon in the deportation by Nebuchadnezzar in 605 B.C. during the reign of Jehoiakim (1:1-7). Daniel appears to have been of royal blood (1:3) and from the kingdom of Judah (1:6). Along with other youths of noble birth, Daniel was selected for an education in "the learning and the tongue of the Chaldeans" for service at the Babylonian court. Daniel and his three companions, Hananiah, Mishael and Azariah, mindful of the Mosaic requirements concerning food and drink, abstained from partaking of the food from the king's allotment lest they be defiled, and requested a simple fare of vegetables and grain and water. The request was granted and the youths, after ten days' trial, excelled in health and appearance over the others who ate the king's dainties (1:10-16). In addition, they were blessed by divine providence, God endowing them with "knowledge and skill in all learning and wisdom," far exceeding the Chaldean wise men in the entire realm.

Moreover, Daniel was given understanding in all visions and dreams, his reputation extending far and wide, seen in the fact that his contemporary, Ezekiel, makes several references to the younger prophet's righteousness, twice comparing him with Noah and Job (14:14, 16, 18, 20; cf. 28:3). Under Nebuchadnezzar, Belshazzar, Darius the Mede and Cyrus, Daniel exercised his gifts at the Chaldean court until the first year of Cyrus (1:21). His visions doubtless continued until 536 B.C. and the end of the Babylonian exile for Israel, the prophet witnessing the nation's release by Cyrus after his own seventy years' exile at the Chaldean court (539 B.C.; 9:1 ff.).

There is no record of Daniel's prophetic activity during the intervening period between the death of Nebuchadnezzar and Belshazzar. The latter king, alarmed at the inability of the Chaldeans and astrologers to interpret the cryptic handwriting upon the palace wall, is reminded of the wisdom of Daniel who had interpreted the dreams of Nebuchadnezzar. Upon interpreting the writing as predictive of Babylon's overthrow at the hands of the Medes and Persians, Daniel is elevated to the rank of third ruler of the kingdom. Under Darius, Daniel's enemies, moved with envy and taking advantage of his piety and faithfulness to God, successfully conspired against him. Their treachery caused him to be cast in a den of lions from which, however, he was miraculously delivered, his accusers suffering the fate intended for the prophet. "So this Daniel prospered in the reign of Darius, and in the reign of Cyrus the Persian" (6:28). Daniel survived the seventy-year exile of his people in Babylon, where he remained until his death.

IV. THE HISTORICAL BACKGROUND

The Chaldeans, a Semitic people, were living in southeastern Babylonia about 1000 B.C. They were an aggressive and nomadic people who were troublesome to the Babylonians. One of their leaders, Merodachbaladan later ascended the throne and ruled Babylon in the eighth century B.C. Assyria, under Sennacherib, destroyed Babylon because of its rebelliousness, but the city was later restored by Esarhaddon. In 626 B.C. Nabopolassar, a Chaldean, rebelled against Assyria and established the new Babylonian Empire. In 612, together with Cyaxares the Mede and the king of the Scythians, he destroyed the city of Nineveh. In 605 the Neo-Babylonian Empire was challenged by the Egyptians under the leadership of Pharaoh Necho, but the forces of Egypt were decisively defeated in the Battle of Carchemish by Nabopolassar's son and successor, Nebuchadnezzar (605-562). Jehoiakim, whom Necho had placed upon the throne of Judah (II Kings 23:34), became the vassal of Nebuchadnezzar (II Kings 24:1) who now occupied Palestine, deporting hostages of noble blood to Babylon in 605, among whom were Daniel and his three companions (Dan. 1:1-7). Jehoiakim rebelled after three years (II Kings 24:1), whereupon bands of Chaldeans, Syrians, Moabites and Ammonites overran Judah. In 597 Nebuchadnezzar pillaged the temple and carried Jehoiachin, the son and successor of Jehoiakim, to Babylon together with many captives, including Ezekiel, the priest (II Kings 24:13-14; Ezek. 1:1-3). Zedekiah, who became king and subject to Nebuchadnezzar, revolted in the ninth year of his reign, whereupon the Babylonians returned in force and destroyed the city and temple, carrying King Zedekiah and the inhabitants into Babylon in 586.

The Neo-Babylonian Empire was to survive for about seventy years after the first deportation from Judah in 605. Evil-Merodach (562-560) succeeded his father Nebuchadnezzar on the throne. He was slain by his brother-in-law, Neriglisar, who ruled for the next four years (560-556). His successor, Labashi-Marduk, reigned but a few months (556) and was followed by a usurper, Nabonidus (556-539), whose son Belshazzar (Dan. 5) ruled as coregent until the fall of Babylon to the Persians at the hands of Darius the Mede in 539 (Dan. 5:30-31). Daniel's ministry continued until the return of Israel from captivity in 536 (9:1 ff.). Ezekiel's last dated prophecy occurred in 571 (Ezek. 29:17).

V. PROBLEMS

Problems concerning the date and authorship of the book have already been sufficiently examined in discussion of the date. The remaining questions requiring careful consideration involve interpretation of the prophecies and visions of the book. Interpretations of Daniel are so profuse as to practically defy analysis or summary, a situation which is perhaps true of no other book outside the Apocalypse of John. The literature written, for instance, on the prophecy of the seventy weeks (Dan. 9:24-27) consists of scores of volumes, and that on the book of Daniel itself runs into hundreds. The meaning of the dream of Nebuchadnezzar concerning the identification of the four kingdoms has occasioned much controversy. The same is true concerning the four beasts of chapter 7, the chronology of chapter 11, as well as the other visions and prophecies. The great diversity of interpretation is not confined to the irreconcilable differences that exist between conservative interpreters and the school of higher criticism. But among Evangelicals themselves there is no precise agreement, as can be seen, for example, in the disharmony between the views of premillennial and amillennial interpreters. Inasmuch as the scope of this introduction forbids an examination of the numerous interpretations of the prophecies and visions of the book, which would be of doubtful value anyway, the interpretation which the author believes to be most in harmony with the principles of biblical prophecy and eschatology is set forth.

1. The first question concerns the interpretation of Nebuchadnezzar's dream of the *colossal image* in Daniel 2. In the second year of Nebuchadnezzar, the king had a dream which troubled him exceedingly. Upon awaking he was unable to recall the nature of his dream; his wise men also failed in their efforts to give either the dream or its interpretation. The secret was revealed to Daniel in a vision from God, whereupon he made known both the dream and its interpretation to Nebuchadnezzar, who acknowledged Daniel's God as "the God of gods," promoting Daniel to high office in the province of Babylon. The dream, Daniel informed the king, concerned "what shall be in the latter days."

The image represents a prophetic view of "the times of the Gentiles," depicting the four Gentile world kingdoms which were to rule successively from Nebuchadnezzar and the Babylonian Empire to the second advent and establishment of the millennial kingdom. Verses 28-29, 45 give the scope of the prophecy as "what shall be in the latter days" and "what shall come to pass hereafter." The head of gold is identified as the first or *Babylonian kingdom*, for Daniel declares to Nebuchadnezzar, "Thou art the head of gold" (2:38). Hence, "the times of the Gentiles" (i.e., Gentile world dominion, especially as it would relate to Israel) began with Nebuchadnezzar and the Babylonian kingdom.

After the Babylonian kingdom there would arise another kingdom, represented in the image as the breast and arms of silver, identified elsewhere in the prophecy as the *Medo-Persian kingdom* (Dan. 5:28; 8:20; cf. 6:8, 12, 15, 28). The belly and thighs of brass symbolize the *Greek kingdom* which was to overthrow the empire established by Cyrus. In chapter 8 "the king of Greece" is represented as conquering "the kings of Media and Persia" (8:20-21). This was fulfilled in the conquests of Alexander the Great and the subsequent world dominion of the *Greco-Macedonian Empire*. The image had legs of iron and feet part of iron and part of clay, depicting the fourth empire, the *Roman kingdom*, which, although not specifically named in Daniel, history shows succeeded the third or Greco-Macedonian kingdom.

The critical school, assigning a Maccabean date for Daniel and denying the possibility of predictive prophecy, places all four kingdoms prior to the alleged date of the book's composition (*c.* 167 B.C.) and thus identifies them as Babylonian, Median, Persian and Greco-Macedonian. According to this theory, the supposed second century B.C. Jewish author of the book, ignorant of the precise historical succession of kingdoms in the sixth century B.C., erroneously believed the Medes constituted a separate kingdom ("the breast and arms of silver") following the Babylonian. The Persians then supplanted the Medes, which were followed by the fourth and last kingdom of the Greeks. It was during this latter period that the book was composed; therefore, the Roman kingdom could not have been predicted.

However, this erroneous assumption by the critics is disproved by the book itself, which identifies the second kingdom quite specifically as Medo-Persian. These two elements of the one kingdom are seen first of all in Daniel 5:28, 30. Darius the Mede received the kingdom of the Chaldeans (5:30), but as a representative of the Medes and Persians (5:28). In Daniel's interpretation of the word *peres* in the handwriting on the wall, he declared, "Thy kingdom is divided and given unto the Medes and Persians." He gives here an interpretation of the significance of the term *peres* for Belshazzar's kingdom, not a translation of the Aramaic word which means simply "divided," and in its verbal form "to break in two" or "to divide." The application of this meaning to the *division* of the Babylonian kingdom is clear. Moreover, there is an obvious and intended association between the word *peres* and "Persians" (*pāras*) in verse 28. It is also significant that Daniel does not say that the Babylonian kingdom will first be given to the Medes and then the Persians, but "given to the Medes and Persians," the Persians being in fact emphasized in the usage of the word *peres*.

Again in Daniel 6:8, 12, 15 Darius is said to have ruled according to "the law of the Medes and Persians." If Persia constituted a separate kingdom following the alleged Median kingdom, it is obvious that Darius could not have known of, nor been bound by, the laws of the Persians. In addition, Darius seems definitely associated with the reign of Cyrus in Daniel 6:28. Moreover, II Chronicles 36:20 disproves the alleged belief by the Jews of any intermediate Median empire before Persia.

The symbolism of the visions in chapters 7-8 indicates that the author intends that Media and Persia were to be seen as two elements of one realm. There is uniform agreement among interpreters that the first beast like a lion with eagle's wings represents the Babylonian kingdom (7:4). The third beast, like a leopard with four wings and four heads, is an obvious reference to the Greek Empire which, upon the death of Alexander the Great, was divided into four parts (cf. 8:21-22). However, the Persian kingdom was never so divided, thus indicating that the second beast (the bear raised up on one side, signifying Persia's dominant position over Media) symbolizes Medo-Persia (7:5). This is confirmed in chapter 8, which speaks of Media and Persia as parts of one realm (8:20), which was to be followed by the Greek Empire (8:21-22). The two-horned ram is specifically said to be "Media and Persia," and the he-goat (with the great horn which was broken and in its place came up four horns) which succeeded it, is said to be Greece.

It is significant that whereas the other three kingdoms are only mentioned as supplanting one another, the fourth is described in much more detail. Although this kingdom is described as constituting several parts, indicated by the legs, feet and toes, these parts nevertheless signify but one kingdom, the fourth. This is confirmed by the fact that the next kingdom mentioned is the final kingdom, or fifth (2:44-45). The fourth kingdom is described as "strong as iron"

(2:40), certainly descriptive of the Roman Empire, as is the next statement, "as iron breaketh in pieces and subdueth all things." Iron and clay are the material of which the feet and toes are composed, indicating thereby that as iron and clay do not mix, "the kingdom shall be partly strong, and partly broken" (2:42).

In fact, the composition of the image indicates a progressive deterioration in sovereignty. From the most precious metal, gold, each succeeding metal is less valuable: silver, brass, iron, and finally iron and clay. Nebuchadnezzar, an absolute monarch ("whom he would he slew; and whom he would he kept alive," 5:19; "king of kings," 2:37; cf. 2:38), was the head of gold. The kingdom which followed, represented by the breast and arms of silver, was a coalition of Medes and Persians, less autocratic than the Babylonian. Moreover, Darius himself was subject to the laws of the Medes and Persians (6:14-15). The belly and thighs of brass are even more inferior, for we see the Greek kingdom being divided among Alexander's military leaders. The Roman Empire, later torn by internal division into East and West (Constantinople and Rome), is signified by the two legs, ultimately to be further subdivided as indicated by the ten toes, part of iron and part of clay (indicative of inherent weakness), which according to Daniel symbolize ten kings, that is, a tenfold division of the Empire. Daniel interprets the ten toes thus, for in verse 44 he refers to the toes of verse 43 and says, "And in the days of those kings" shall God establish the final kingdom of the Messiah. This is further confirmed in Daniel 7:7-8, 24 where the fourth beast, corresponding in description to the fourth kingdom (Rome) of chapter 2, has ten horns which are identified as ten kings, and again in Revelation 17:12 where the ten horns are called ten kings (cf. Rev. 13:1 ff.).

When are these ten kings to be manifested? The Roman Empire as such does not exist today, but the integral parts remain, although broken up into separate states; and since the fourth kingdom is the last to rise until the advent of the fifth or final kingdom (which destroys it), then it or remnants of it must in some sense still remain, to be more fully manifested in "the latter days." In view of this, and since the ten kings have not appeared as yet upon the stage of history, their appearance must be looked for at some future time. This is precisely what the Scriptures indicate. Daniel 2:44 states that "in the days of those kings shall the God of heaven set up a kingdom which shall never be destroyed," a prediction of the sovereign kingdom of the Messiah, thus signifying the time of their rise as the end of the age. That this is true is seen from chapter 7 where the "little horn" (Antichrist), who does not appear until the close of the present age, uproots three of these horns (7:8; cf. "he shall put down three kings," 7:24). Moreover, the fifth kingdom (Messiah's), described as a stone cut out without hands, smites the image on the *feet* (and toes). These facts concerning the four kingdoms of chapter 2 are further delineated in the discussion of the prophecies and visions which follows.

Amillennialists, on the other hand, interpret the prophecy of the falling stone which smites the image as representing the first advent and the gradual victory of the gospel in the present church age, culminating in the final overthrow of sin in the day of judgment. However, two fallacies are apparent. First, there appears to be in this view an unwarranted identification of the church with the kingdom of God (2:44-45). Second, the graphic description of the stone striking the image on the feet in no sense suggests a gradual extension and growth of the kingdom or church (a progressive destruction of the heathen image). On the contrary, the stone smites the image a single crushing, destructive blow, after which the pulverized image "became like the chaff of the summer threshing-floors; and the wind carried them away, so that no place was found for them" (2:35). Only after the removal of the kingdoms are we told that the stone "became a great mountain, and filled the whole earth." Thus the final kingdom (2:44-45) will not arise until the appearance of the ten kings in the latter days; the overthrow of the fourth kingdom must therefore refer to the time of the second advent and the establishment of the millennial kingdom.

2.   The second significant prophecy about which there are differing opinions of interpretation is Daniel's vision of the *four beasts* and of the *Ancient of days* in Daniel 7.

It is generally acknowledged that chapters 2 and 7 present the same prophecy, with two differences however. In chapter 2 the prophecy in the form of a dream comes to a heathen monarch and is presented under the colossal image of man, stately and majestic. There Gentile world power was seen, apparently from the point of view of the unregenerate world. In chapter 7, however, the vision is given to the prophet of God wherein the Gentile kingdoms are portrayed as four ravenous beasts, thus depicting, it would appear, their inward character as seen by God (cf. Ezek. 29:3 ff.; Isa. 27:1). The second difference between the dream of Nebuchadnezzar in chapter 2 and Daniel's later vision under Belshazzar's reign in•chapter 7 is the fact that there is an elaboration on the details concerning the fourth kingdom (Rome), together with the introduction of the Antichrist

(the "little horn") in chapter 7. A comparison of the two chapters
will indicate the fact that the prophecies deal with the same subject,
except that the latter, which is directed especially to Israel, is ex-
panded and given a more detailed treatment, which was unnecessary
in the prophecy to the heathen monarch in chapter 2. Note the ac-
companying summary comparison of chapters 2 and 7 with their
interpretation.

Chapter 2	Chapter 7	
Dream of the Colossal Image	*Vision of the Four Beasts*	*Interpretation*
The head of gold	The lion with eagle's wings	Babylon
The breast and arms of silver	The bear, raised up on one side (the ram with two horns, chap. 8)	Medo-Persia
The belly and thighs of brass	The leopard with four wings and four heads (the he-goat with a great horn which becomes four horns, chap. 8)	Greece
The legs of iron	The fourth beast with iron teeth	Rome
The feet and ten toes of iron and clay	The ten horns of the fourth beast	**The final stage of the fourth kingdom in the latter days**
(not mentioned)	The "little horn" (the "king of fierce coun- tenance," chap. 8; the "prince that shall come," chap. 9; the "wilful king," chap. 11)	Antichrist
The stone cut with- out hands	The Son of Man	**The kingdom of God established by the Messiah**

In the first year of Belshazzar, Daniel receives a vision in which
the four winds of heaven break forth upon the great sea and four
great beasts are seen emerging from the sea: a lion with eagle's
wings, a bear, a leopard with four wings and four heads, and a fourth
beast "terrible and powerful, and strong exceedingly; and it had
great iron teeth; it devoured and brake in pieces, and stamped the
residue with its feet: and it was diverse from all the beasts that were
before it; and it had ten horns . . . and, behold, there came up among
them another horn, a little one, before which three of the first horns
were plucked up by the roots: and, behold, in this horn were eyes like
the eyes of a man, and a mouth speaking great things" (7:7-8). At
this point Daniel witnesses a great judgment scene: the Ancient of
days, who appears in all His glory and splendor, surrounded by His
angelic hosts, is seen seated upon His throne, whereupon the judgment begins and the books are opened. The beast whose "little horn"
spoke great things is slain and the rest of the beasts have their
dominion taken away, but their lives are prolonged for "a season and
a time." Then One like a son of man comes with the clouds of
heaven unto the Ancient of days "and there was given him dominion,
and glory, and a kingdom, that all the peoples, nations, and languages
should serve him: his dominion is an everlasting dominion, which
shall not pass away, and his kingdom that which shall not be destroyed" (7:14).

What does the vision symbolize? The parallel between chapter 2
and chapter 7 is unmistakable, the symbolism of the fourth kingdom
being more highly developed in chapter 7 however. Daniel beholds
the four beasts arising from the great sea stirred up by the winds of
heaven, signifying the providential agency of God whereby He raises
up the four nations, Babylon, Medo-Persia, Greece and Rome
(7:1-3). Elsewhere the waters symbolize humanity and nations as,
for instance, in Revelation 17:15: "The waters which thou
sawest . . . are peoples, and multitudes, and nations, and tongues" (cf.
21:1; Isa. 17:12-13; Ps. 65:7). Thus out of the tumultuous sea of the
Gentile nations, four are specifically brought into view. This interpretation is confirmed in Daniel 7:17 where the beasts are identified as
such: "These great beasts, which are four, are four kings, that shall
arise out of the earth."

The first beast "was like a lion, and had eagle's wings." This first
beast corresponds to the head of gold in chapter 2 and symbolizes
Babylon. Nebuchadnezzar and Babylon are compared in Scripture to
the lion and eagle (cf. Jer. 4:7; 49:19, 22; Hab. 1:8, etc.). The lion,
as king of the beasts, and the swift, powerful eagle are fitting symbols

of Nebuchadnezzar, the absolute monarch. As Daniel beholds the beast, its swift wings are plucked, depriving it of its power of flight; it proceeds to lose its beastly and ferocious character and is made to stand upon its "two feet as a man; and a man's heart was given to it." This humanizing of the beast signifies Nebuchadnezzar's humiliation in chapter 4 where the great monarch is made to know that he is but flesh, mere *man* under God's sovereign control (7:4).

The second beast, like a bear and inferior to the lion, corresponds to the breast and arms of silver in chapter 2 which signify Medo-Persia. Daniel saw that the bear was raised up on one side, indicating the two-sided nature of the kingdom which overthrew Babylon (i.e., Medo-Persia), the higher side being the kingdom of Persia, the stronger and more dominant side of the double empire. In chapter 8 this twofold nature of the kingdom is represented by the two horns, one being higher than the other (v. 3). The beast had three ribs in its teeth signifying perhaps the conquest of Lydia, Babylon and Egypt (7:5).

After this a third beast like a leopard, having four wings of a bird upon its back and four heads, comes into view, corresponding to the belly and thighs of brass of Nebuchadnezzar's colossal image. The beast, a fleet leopard, which represents Greece who overthrew Medo-Persia, is portrayed with two pairs of wings indicating, as history confirms, the unparalleled swiftness of Alexander the Great's conquests. The beast also had four heads which symbolize the four principal divisions of the Greek Empire upon the death of Alexander to his four generals, Cassander, Seleucus, Lysimachus and Ptolemy (7:6). In chapter 8 Greece is symbolized as a "he-goat" with a great horn (Alexander the Great) which defeated a ram with two horns (Medo-Persia), after which the great horn was broken and replaced by four notable horns (the four generals).

The fourth beast, corresponding to the legs of iron and the feet part of iron and part of clay in chapter 2, is described thus:

> After this I saw in the night-visions, and, behold, a fourth beast, terrible and powerful, and strong exceedingly; and it had great iron teeth; it devoured and brake in pieces, and stamped the residue with its feet: and it was diverse from all the beasts that were before it; and it had ten horns. I considered the horns, and, behold, there came up among them another horn, a little one, before which three of the first horns were plucked up by the roots: and, behold, in this horn were eyes like the eyes of a man, and a mouth speaking great things (Dan. 7:7-8).

This fourth beast with the great iron teeth is clearly to be identified with the iron legs of the colossal image, signifying the Roman Empire. The beast had ten horns which are identified in verse 24 as ten kings (cf. Rev. 13:1 ff.; 17:12) and correspond to the ten toes of the image in chapter 2. From among the horns there arises "a little horn" with the eyes of a man and a mouth speaking great things, whom all interpreters identify as the Antichrist (except the critical school which dates the prophecy in the Maccabean period and equates the little horn with Antiochus Epiphanes). The fourth beast, the Roman kingdom, is judged and destroyed by the Ancient of days, after which the Son of Man is given an everlasting kingdom (7:9-14). This can only mean then that the kingdom of the Messiah *follows a final form* (i.e., the eschatological phase) of the fourth or Roman kingdom.

That this is the case is seen from the following considerations:

a. The Messiah's kingdom is not established until after the fourth beast is judged and slain (7:9-14). This is also true in chapter 2 where the fifth kingdom (the stone) destroys the image, and after it has been blown away the stone fills the earth (2:34-35).

b. The fourth kingdom is still in existence when the Son of Man returns in the clouds of heaven to receive His everlasting kingdom. Moreover, no intervening kingdom is ever mentioned (cf. chap. 2).

c. The ten horns on the fourth beast are identified in Revelation 17:12 (cf. Dan. 7:24) as "ten kings, *who have received no kingdom as yet; but they receive authority as kings, with the beast* [Antichrist], *for one hour.*" This clearly means that they are contemporary with each other and have not appeared as yet.

d. The "little horn," whom all identify as Antichrist, and who all agree does not appear upon the scene of history until the time just preceding the second advent (II Thess. 2:1-9), arises while the ten horns are in existence. This is proved from the fact that the little horn uproots three of the ten horns (7:8, 24). Hence, if Antichrist does not appear until eschatological times and the ten kings are contemporary with him, then they too have not appeared as yet and are not to be identified with ten kings or kingdoms of past history as some interpreters contend (cf. 2:44).

e. Furthermore, the Messianic kingdom in chapters 2 and 7 was not established at the beginning of the church age, but, as chapter 7 proves, will not appear until *after* Antichrist is himself slain (7:11, 21-27).

f. Finally, the overthrow of Antichrist and the destruction of the fourth kingdom are inseparably related to the national restoration of Israel, an event still future to the church age. Three times in chapter 7 it is stated that "the saints shall possess the kingdom" after having suffered at the hands of Antichrist (cf. 7:18, 22, 27). The term "saints" at no time in Daniel refers to the church, but always to the people of Israel as distinguished from the Gentiles (cf. Isa. 62:12). This is confirmed also in chapter 8, a prophecy concerning the conflict of the Jews with the Greek kingdom. Here the Jewish people are called "the holy people" (8:24; ASV margin, "the people of the saints"). In Daniel 12:7 they are again called "the holy people," where they also as in 7:25 are afflicted "for a time, times, and a half." In 12:1 they are designated as "the children of thy [Daniel's] people," the children of Israel.[14]

3. The *vision of the ram and the he-goat* in chapter 8 is the third prophecy requiring consideration. This chapter contains further details about the second and third kingdoms described in chapters 2 and 7, namely, Medo-Persia and Greece. The additional information concerns the career of Alexander the Great and the rise of Antiochus Epiphanes, who typifies Antichrist (cf. 8:23-25), and who was to present one of the greatest threats to the survival of the Hebrew race in all its history.

In the third year of the reign of Belshazzar a vision appeared to Daniel of a ram with two horns, one higher than the other, pushing toward the west, north and south without interference. But finally a he-goat with a great horn between his eyes rushed upon the ram in fury and smote it, breaking its two horns. The he-goat increased in power and ultimately the great horn was broken; in its place there arose four notable horns. Out of one of these horns came forth "a little horn" which extended its power greatly toward the south, east and the holy land. The little horn exalted itself against the host of heaven and against its prince, causing the daily sacrifice to cease for 2,300 days and desecrating the sanctuary.

The interpretation of the vision is given to Daniel by the angel Gabriel: the ram with the two horns is Medo-Persia. One horn "was higher than the other, and the higher came up last," signifying the same thing as the bear raised up on one side in chapter 7, that is, the higher horn represents Persia, who under Cyrus dominated the consolidated kingdoms of the Medes and Persians. The he-goat which came from the west is the Greek Empire and the great horn is its first king, Alexander the Great, who smote the ram and broke its two horns. When the he-goat was strong the great horn was broken and four horns came up in its place. This indicates how Alexander, at the

[14]See Culver, chap. 3, for an excellent discussion of the various views on Daniel 7.

height of his power, died and his empire was divided among his four generals forming four kingdoms: Macedonia under Cassander, Thrace and Asia Minor under Lysimachus, Syria and Babylonia under Seleucus, and Egypt including Palestine under Ptolemy.

Then out of one of them (i.e., these four Greek kingdoms) came forth a "little horn." This horn is not to be identified with the "little horn" of chapter 7 which there symbolizes the Antichrist. That horn uproots three of the ten horns of the fourth or Roman kingdom, whereas this horn grows out of one of the four horns of the third or Greek kingdom and is to be identified with Antiochus Epiphanes, who came out of the kingdom of Syria ruling over the Seleucid kingdom (175-163 B.C.). He was a wicked tyrant who sought to Hellenize the Jews and persecuted them severely. According to I Maccabees he sought to stamp out Judaism altogether, substituting Greek customs and the worship of Zeus and the Greek deities. He abolished the Jewish sacrifices, set up an altar of Zeus in the temple (the abomination of desolation, Dan. 11:31), prohibited circumcision and Sabbath observance, destroyed all copies of the law that could be found, putting their owners to death, polluted the altar by offering swine's flesh thereon, and desecrated the holy temple. His persecution and efforts to destroy the Jewish religion led to the Maccabean revolt under the priest Mattathias in 167. Judas Maccabaeus, his son and successor, defeated the Seleucid army in 165, whereupon he cleansed and rededicated the temple and the sacrifices were resumed (cf. 8:9-14).

In the interpretation Gabriel calls the "little horn" of verse 9 the "king of fierce countenance" in verse 23. Here the description would appear to pass from the literal Antiochus Epiphanes to a representation which only partially applies to him but finds its fullest expression in the Antichrist. Moreover, the repeated phrase "the time of the end" (vv. 17, 19; cf. 23, 26) in reference to this figure indicates that Antiochus is but the forerunner of Antichrist of whom he, in his wickedness, defiance of God (8:25) and persecution of Israel, stands as the type. In Revelation 13:2 Satan is said to give Antichrist his power, and Daniel 8:24 likewise states concerning the king of fierce countenance that "his power shall be mighty, *but not by his own power.*" In verse 25 we are told that "he shall magnify himself in his heart, and . . . he shall also stand up against the prince of princes [Messiah]; but he shall be broken without hand" (cf. v. 11). Such is the description of Antichrist in Scripture: "And he shall speak words against the Most High" (7:25); "and he shall exalt himself, and magnify himself above every god, and shall speak marvellous things

against the God of gods" (11:36); "the man of sin . . . that opposeth
and exalteth himself against all that is called God or that is worshipped" (II Thess. 2:3-4); "and he opened his mouth for blasphem-
ies against God, to blaspheme his name" (Rev. 13:6; cf. Dan. 7:11).
In Daniel 7:11 the fourth beast from which the little horn (Antichrist) comes is said to be "slain," "destroyed," and "burned with
fire" by the Ancient of days. This is the fate of the king of fierce
countenance in 8:25: "he shall be broken without hand," that is, by
supernatural agency as in Revelation 19:19-20.

Hence, "the king of fierce countenance" would appear to describe
not only Antiochus Epiphanes as the type but also his antitype, the
Antichrist. If this were not the case then the vision of chapter 8 alone
among the chapters portraying the future course of the Gentile
world powers (viz., chaps. 2, 7, 8, 9, 11) would contain no reference
either to him personally or to the fourth and final kingdom from
which he arises. In chapter 2 the fourth kingdom is described together with the nature of its final form (feet and toes of iron and clay);
chapter 7 portrays the Antichrist as the "little horn"; in chapter 9 he
is the "prince that shall come"; in chapter 11 he becomes the "wilful
king"; and thus it would follow, in view of the description in 8:23-25,
that the "king of fierce countenance" typifies Antichrist also.

4.   The difficulty of finding precise agreement among interpreters
concerning the *prophecy of the seventy weeks* is evident to anyone
who has attempted even a cursory study of Daniel 9:24-27. In the
first year of Darius the Mede the seventy-year period of Israel's
captivity was drawing to a close as predicted by the Prophet Jeremiah (25:11; 29:10). Daniel, concerned for the restoration of his people, makes supplication to God on their behalf (9:1-19). As he prays,
the angel Gabriel appears, announcing a prophecy of "seventy weeks"
which are to be fulfilled concerning Israel and the holy city "to finish
transgression, and to make an end of sins, and to make reconciliation
for iniquity, and to bring in everlasting righteousness, and to seal up
vision and prophecy, and to anoint the most holy" (9:24).

The interpretations of this difficult passage are legion, and the
only satisfactory solution is that which views the prophecy as relating wholly to Israel from the time of the rebuilding of Jerusalem to
the overthrow of Antichrist at the second advent. The seventy weeks
(as most interpreters agree) refer to weeks of *years*, a period totaling
490 years (Heb. literally "seventy sevens"). This period is then
divided into three periods: "seven weeks" (49 years); "threescore
and two weeks" (434 years); and "one week" (7 years). These three
divisions have reference to three important events:

a. *Seven weeks* (49 years) will elapse from the issuance of the command to restore Jerusalem (the decree of Artaxerxes to Nehemiah) until the completion of the work (9:25).

b. *Sixty-two weeks* (434 years) follow this, from the completion of the work "unto Messiah the prince" (9:25, margin). After these two periods (i.e., 7 plus 62 weeks, 483 years) "shall the Messiah be cut off" (9:26), a clear reference to Christ's crucifixion.

c. *One week* (7 years), the final division of the 490-year period, is known as "Daniel's seventieth week" and is yet future. It is the period of the "great tribulation" which will occur between the translation of the church and the second advent. Hence, the church age, not revealed in Daniel's prophecy, intervenes between the sixty-ninth and seventieth weeks.

Evidence for this has been very carefully set forth by Culver in his work *Daniel and the Latter Days.* The final or seventieth week (v. 27) appears *after* a verse (26) which *describes events not belonging to the previous sixty-nine weeks.* The first sixty-nine weeks came to a conclusion during the lifetime of the Messiah but *before* His crucifixion (see v. 26), and the events of the seventieth week belong to a future seven-year relationship between Antichrist and Israel for the following reasons:

a. The crucifixion and the destruction of Jerusalem are clearly said to occur *after* the sixty-nine weeks (9:25-26).

b. The seventieth week is not mentioned *with* the events of verse 26.

c. Thus verse 26, which predicts the death of Christ and destruction of Jerusalem in A.D. 70, belongs to the period *between* the sixty-ninth and seventieth weeks.

d. The leading protagonist of verse 27 is Antichrist ("the prince that shall come," v. 26), who does not appear until the end-time according to Scripture.

e. The subjects with whom Antichrist deals in verse 27 are Daniel's people Israel. The opening words of Gabriel's prophecy specifically state that the "seventy weeks are decreed upon *thy people* and upon *thy holy city.*"

f. Antichrist is said in chapter 7 to persecute Israel for "a time and times and half a time" (7:25), a period which corresponds to the half week of 9:27, that is, three and one-half years. This period is identical with the "forty and two months" of Revelation 13:5, and with the "thousand two hundred and threescore days" of Revelation 11:3 (cf. Dan. 12:7).

g. The act of desecration of the temple ("the abomination that maketh desolate," cf. 11:31; 12:11; II Thess. 2:4) by Antichrist and his causing the sacrifice and oblation to cease (9:27) presuppose the future existence of another temple in the time of Antichrist, as predicted in Revelation 11:1-2. Added confirmation of this is seen from the fact that the scope of the prophecy of seventy weeks includes end-time events, such as the reestablishment of the temple as indicated in the statement that seventy weeks are decreed "to anoint a most holy place" (9:24, margin).

h. Christ Himself interpreted the offensive event which occurs in the middle of the seventieth week ("the abomination of desolation") as *immediately preceding* His second advent (Matt. 24:15; cf. vv. 21, 27, 29-30). Hence, Jesus located the seventieth week of Daniel in the last seven years of the present dispensation prior to His second advent.[15]

THE PROPHECY OF ISRAEL'S SEVENTY WEEKS

[15]Culver, pp. 135-60.

5. Because of the relevance to the other prophecies of chapters 10-12, which contain the final prophetic vision concerning *Israel and the Gentile nations* from Cyrus until the second advent, the most significant details of this section will be traced. These three chapters are a single prophecy, being the final vision revealed to the prophet. The scope of the prophecy is seen from the words of the angel to Daniel in 10:14: "Now I am come to make thee understand what shall befall thy people in the latter days." Chapter 10 does not contain the prophecy but circumstances concerning the giving of the vision to Daniel. Chapter 11 is especially important and introduces the prophecy which embraces the same prophetic period as chapter 8, from the period of the Persian kingdom until the end of the present age, which carries through chapter 12 of the book. The scope of the prophecy includes the kingdoms of Persia, Greece and Syria, the career of Antiochus Epiphanes, and events of the latter days, such as the appearance of Antichrist, the great tribulation, and resurrection.

a. *Introduction to the prophecy (10:1—11:1)*. In the third year of Cyrus, after having fasted for three weeks, Daniel receives a vision. A man clothed in linen, whose face has the appearance of lightning and whose voice is like the voice of a multitude, appears to Daniel by the Tigris River, and the prophet, terrified by the vision, falls upon his face to the ground.

Daniel's vision of the "man clothed in linen" is doubtless a Christophany on the basis of the majestic description which follows (10:5-9). The vision of the Apostle John on Patmos of the risen Christ is strikingly similar (cf. Rev. 1:10-17; Ezek. 1). The speaker of verses 10-12 is not necessarily the "man" who first appeared in vision to Daniel, but more likely is an angel, inasmuch as the words of verse 13 would suggest another besides the Lord. The angel informs Daniel that his coming with the revelation, in answer to his prayer concerning Israel's restoration (v. 12), was hindered for three weeks by the "prince of Persia." This reference is not to the king of Persia, Cyrus, but to an angelic prince (cf. Isa. 24:21). This is confirmed by the fact that Michael is designated as the prince of Israel in 10:21. Hence, "the prince of Persia," like "the prince of Greece" in 10:20, refers to the satanic guardian spirits of these kingdoms (cf. Eph. 6:12). God's messenger to Daniel was detained by the opposition of these hostile powers of darkness, apparently indicating a celestial struggle on behalf of Israel, the satanic spirit perhaps seeking to influence the Persian king adversely concerning Israel's restoration to her land. This would explain why the messenger with the report to Daniel concerning Israel's deliverance and the ultimate overthrow of the nations is intercepted and delayed until relieved by Michael, Israel's "prince." The angel then informs Daniel that his warfare will be continued with the prince of Persia (concerning the opposition the Jews are still to experience under Persian rule), and after him with the prince of Greece, the hostile world power which succeeded Persia, especially as it is to be manifested under the reign of Antiochus Epiphanes, and later by his antitype, the Antichrist whom Michael will help to overcome (10:20-21; 12:1).

The first verse of chapter 11 belongs with the preceding chapter. The introductory section concludes by the angel's stating how he had previously aided Michael in the first year of Darius, referring no doubt to the overthrow of Babylon by the Medo-Persian kingdom, accomplished through supernatural agency.

b. *The prophecy (11:2—12:4)*. The prophecy divides into two sections: 11:2-35 concerns events already fulfilled in regard to the kings of Persia, Greece, Egypt and Syria with particular emphasis upon the period of Antiochus Epiphanes (11:21-35); 11:36—12:4 is wholly eschatological, concerning the career of Antichrist, the great tribulation of Israel and her deliverance, and the resurrection of the dead. Inasmuch as the scope of this introduction limits a detailed treatment of this prophecy, only a general summary outline of events is presented.

1) *Prophecy concerning the kings of Persia (11:2)*. The "three kings in Persia" are Cambyses, Pseudo-Smerdis and Darius Hystaspes; "the fourth" is Xerxes who was defeated in his campaign against Greece.

2) *Prophecy concerning Greece (11:3-4)*. The prophecy of "a mighty king" describes Alexander the Great; "his kingdom shall be...divided toward the four winds of heaven" predicts the division of his kingdom among his four generals, Cassander, Lysimachus, Seleucus and Ptolemy.

3) *Prophecy of the wars between the kings of the South and the kings of the North (11:5-20)*. The "king of the south" was Ptolemy Soter, "one of his princes" being Seleucus Nicator, a general under Ptolemy who later became king of the powerful Syrian (Seleucid) Empire (v. 5). The "daughter of the king of the south" was Berenice, daughter of Ptolemy Philadelphus who married Antiochus II, "the king of the north," and was later murdered (v. 6). "A shoot from her roots" signifies Ptolemy III, the brother of Berenice, who invaded Syria and prevailed against the king of the North (v. 7), taking much plunder and spoil (v. 8). The king of the North, Seleucus Callinicus, was defeated in a later invasion of Egypt (v. 9). "His sons

shall war" is a reference to Seleucus Ceraunus and Antiochus the Great. Seleucus was slain in Asia Minor in battle; Antiochus invaded Egypt but was defeated by Ptolemy Philopator with great loss in the battle at Raphia (vv. 10-12). Antiochus gathered a larger army and returned later, successfully defeating the Egyptians (vv. 13-15). "The glorious land" (Palestine) was subjected to Antiochus (v. 16). "The daughter of women" was Cleopatra, whom Antiochus gave in marriage to Ptolemy, hoping thereby to gain control of Egypt; but she sided with her husband against her father (v. 17). Antiochus then turned his attention toward "the coastlands" (Asia Minor principally), but was defeated by the Romans under Lucius Scipio Asiaticus and returned to his own land where he was slain (vv. 18-19). "Then shall stand up in his place one," Seleucus Philopator, "but within few days he shall be destroyed." Seleucus was soon removed, possibly poisoned by Heliodorus the prime minister (v. 20).

4) *Prophecy of the career of Antiochus Epiphanes (11:21-35).* "And in his place shall stand up a contemptible person," that is, Antiochus Epiphanes, a type of the Antichrist, who obtained "the kingdom by flatteries." Antiochus was not the rightful heir but gained the throne by intrigue in place of Demetrius Soter the legitimate heir (v. 21). Antiochus was successful against Egypt (v. 22), later deceitfully feigning friendship for selfish advantage (v. 23). He was lavish in his distribution of spoil (v. 24). A second Egyptian campaign led by Antiochus resulted in the defeat of Ptolemy Physcon (or Philometor) aided by treachery by Ptolemy's supporters (vv. 25-26). "Both these kings" signifies the king of Egypt and Antiochus who plotted against each other (v. 27). "Then shall he return into his land with great substance; and his heart shall be against the holy covenant." Antiochus returned from Egypt with great spoil and marched through the holy land, attacking Jerusalem, plundering the temple and making a great massacre of the inhabitants (v. 28; cf. I Macc. 1:16 ff.). Antiochus made another expedition against Egypt but without his former success, and he was forced by the Romans to retire: "For ships of Kittim shall come against him; therefore he shall be grieved, and shall return, and have indignation against the holy covenant" (vv. 29-30*a*). Antiochus, in his anger for being turned from Egypt by the Romans, returned and vented his wrath upon Jerusalem. The city was attacked, women and children taken prisoner, many were slain, and the Jewish religion was suppressed. "And they shall set up the abomination that maketh desolate." An idol altar and image of Jupiter Olympus were erected on the Jewish altar of burnt offering (vv. 30*b*-31). "But the people that

know their God shall be strong, and do exploits." The faithful Jewish remnant, the Maccabees, led a successful revolt against their oppressors, the Syrians, but not without great affliction and suffering (vv. 32-35).

5) *Prophecy of the willful king (11:36—12:1).* In 11:21-35 the wicked exploits and atrocities of Antiochus Epiphanes are set forth. But beginning with verse 36 a figure is introduced who is described as "the king [who] shall do according to his will; and he shall exalt himself, and magnify himself above every god, and shall speak marvellous things against the God of gods" (11:36). In view of the harmony of this description with the scriptural predictions of the Antichrist, together with the testimony of the future events outlined in the succeeding verses, it becomes evident that the career of Antiochus Epiphanes is concluded in verse 35, and that of Antichrist, the willful king, commences with verse 36. That there is no correspondence of the predictions of Daniel 11:36-45 with the events of past history during the period of Antiochus Epiphanes is evident from a careful examination of the passage. The description of the willful king in this passage corresponds so closely with other references in Scripture to Antichrist (viz., the "little horn," Dan. 7; the "man of sin," II Thess. 2; the "beast," Rev. 13) that the identity of the two is unmistakable (here the amillennial school also agrees). (Cf. Dan. 11:36 with 7:25; Rev. 13:6; cf. Dan. 11:37 with II Thess. 2:3 ff.; cf. Dan. 11:45 with 7:11, 26 and Rev. 19:20, etc.) As Culver has correctly observed, the decisive evidence for an eschatological setting for the willful king is the opening phrase of chapter 12: "And at that time" (i.e., the time of the events described in 11:36-45). There then follow three unquestionable eschatological events: the great tribulation for Israel (12:1), the resurrection of the dead (12:2) and the final reward of the righteous (12:3). Moreover, a totally new subject is introduced in 11:36. Verses 21-35 concerned the conflicts between the king of the South (Egypt) and the king of the North (Antiochus Epiphanes). In verses 36-45, however, the willful king is introduced as a *third party* in conflict with both the king of the South and the king of the North.[16]

Briefly summarized, the passage (11:36—12:1) sets forth the following events concerning Israel's conflict with Antichrist just prior to the second advent: A king who shall do according to his own will (11:36) will appear upon the scene in the latter days (8:23; 10:14; 11:40), exalting himself above God (11:36-37; 7:25; 8:25; II Thess. 2:4; Rev. 13:5). At the time of the end, two kings will move against

[16]Culver, pp. 164-68.

him and challenge his authority, the king of the South (11:40) and the king of the North (11:44; Ezek. 38-39). The willful king and his forces will enter "the glorious land" (Palestine) and in the ensuing conflict overcome the adversaries, gaining control over much adjacent territory, Edom, Moab and Ammon alone excepted (11:41-44). His headquarters are established in Jerusalem (11:45), whereupon he proves himself the great adversary of Israel (12:1; 7:21, 25; 8:24; Rev. 13:7). This will begin "the time of Jacob's trouble," the period of the great tribulation upon Israel (9:27; 12:1; Jer. 30:7; Matt. 24:21-22; Rev. 6:15-17), which will culminate in the deliverance of Israel (12:1) and the destruction of Antichrist (7:11, 26; 8:25; 9:27; 11:45).

6) *Prophecy of the resurrection of the dead and reward of the righteous (12:2-3).* "And many of them that sleep in the dust of the earth shall awake, some to everlasting life, and some to shame and everlasting contempt" (12:2). The prediction is of the bodily resurrection of the Israelites at the close of the tribulation at the second advent. The passage does not speak of a general resurrection; on the contrary, the Hebrew quite definitely forbids such an interpretation as it speaks of "many from among those that sleep . . . shall awake." The text states not *all* but *many* from among the dead will be raised. During the great tribulation many Israelites will be slain. From among those that are asleep *many* (i.e., those who were slain in the tribulation) shall rise. According to Tregelles, supported by Jewish commentators, Daniel 12:2 reads: "Many *from among* the sleepers of the dust of the earth shall awake; *these* shall be unto everlasting life; but *those* [the rest of the sleepers who do not awake at this time] shall be unto shame and everlasting contempt."[17] Hence, the verse speaks not of the general resurrection but of those who share in the first resurrection (Rev. 20:3, 5-6).

"And they that are wise shall shine as the brightness of the firmament; and they that turn many to righteousness as the stars for ever and ever" (12:3). Those who during the tribulation point others to the way of righteousness, that is, to the Messiah, will be gloriously rewarded.

7) *The command to seal the book (12:4).* The prophecies being concluded, Daniel is commanded to seal (preserve) the book until the time of the end. "Many shall run to and fro," that is, scrutinize, investigate or study the prophecy, running to and fro in its pages to understand and increase knowledge of its meaning. There is no sig-

[17]Samuel P. Tregelles, *Remarks on the Prophetic Visions in the Book of Daniel,* p. 159.

nificance, in relation to the prophecy as a whole, that the verse is interpreted to mean there will be an increase in travel and education, or of missionaries going about preaching.

c. *The conclusion to the prophecy (12:5-13)*. As the prophecy draws to a close, Daniel sees two angels as well as "the man clothed in linen" (Messiah) who had appeared to him at the beginning of the vision. One of the angels addresses a question to Him: "How long shall it be to the end of these wonders?" (12:6), whereupon He answers: "It shall be for a time, times, and a half" (12:7), three and one-half years, or forty-two months, the duration of the great tribulation. Daniel heard, but did not understand. He asked, "What shall be the issue [end] of these things?" (12:8). The book closes with a further revelation respecting the time of the end:

> And from the time that the continual burnt-offering shall be taken away, and the abomination that maketh desolate set up, there shall be a thousand two hundred and ninety days. Blessed is he that waiteth, and cometh to the thousand three hundred and five and thirty days. But go thou thy way till the end be; for thou shalt rest, and shalt stand in thy lot, at the end of the days (12:11-13).

The passage is difficult. To what do the 1,290 and 1,335 days refer? Gaebelein's suggestion is perhaps the most satisfactory. The days are literal days. The period of tribulation is 1,260 days (three and one-half years) which are included in the 1,290, with thirty days or one month additional. This thirty-day period may be the period required for the judgment of the nations and other events immediately following Armageddon and the overthrow of Antichrist and Gentile world power preceding the millennium. The 1,335 days refer to the same period including an additional forty-five days; 1,335 days after the abomination of desolation has been set up, or seventy-five days after the tribulation and judgment of the nations, the full blessing for Israel will be realized in the establishment of the millennial kingdom. We are not told precisely why there is a seventy-five-day interval between Armageddon and the beginning of the millennium, but that it is necessary is one of the stated facts of the prophecy.

OUTLINE OF DANIEL

I. INTRODUCTION   Chapter 1

II. HISTORICAL EVENTS FROM NEBUCHADNEZZAR TO DARIUS CONCERNING THE CHARACTER, SUCCESSION AND OVERTHROW

Chapter 21

EZEKIEL

I. The Nature of the Book

THE BOOK OF EZEKIEL consists of three divisions, dealing with its three principal subjects: (1) announcement of the approaching fall of Jerusalem (chaps. 1-24); (2) prophecies against the foreign nations (chaps. 25-32); (3) prophecies of Israel's future restoration (chaps. 33-48). One unique feature of Ezekiel's prophecies is the orderly arrangement of the book, giving evidence of a well-considered plan. Moreover, Ezekiel carefully dates his prophecies which are, with minor exceptions, in chronological sequence. They are dated according to the years of Jehoiachin's captivity in which they were delivered.

Ezekiel is the prophet of the exile, having been deported to Babylon in 597 B.C. at the time of the captivity of King Jehoiachin. While Jeremiah, his contemporary, was preaching the imminent fall of Jerusalem in that city, Ezekiel was predicting its fate from his position in Babylon (chaps. 1-24). From a theological standpoint his ministry falls into two periods: (1) from 593-586 B.C., or up to the fall of Jerusalem, the work of the prophet consisted primarily in the preaching of judgment against Judah; (2) from 586-571, after the destruction of Jerusalem and the temple, the ministry of the prophet was one of consolation, predicting the restoration of the nation with its temple and worship.

Ezekiel's message to Judah prior to its downfall contained words of "lamentations, and mourning, and woe" (2:10). His complaints were largely directed against the same evils condemned by Jeremiah, namely, apostasy, foreign alliances and idolatry. He denounced the false prophets who were leading the people astray with deceptive and lying promises concerning the approaching calamity. The people had been deceived by false hopes of peace and the overthrow of their oppressors. Ezekiel's concern was to vindicate God's justice in the punishment and exile of Judah for her sins. There is scarcely a sin of which the nation has not been guilty, or a moral and religious

295

precept the people have not violated, the prophet charges. The allegories of Ezekiel also reveal the moral condition of Judah. The inhabitants of Jerusalem were a worthless vine, suitable only as fuel for the fire (chap. 15). Jerusalem had become a faithless wife, repaying with infidelity the loving-kindness of Yahweh (16:1-43). Again, Ezekiel describes the past history of Samaria and Jerusalem under the figure of two sisters. The first, Samaria, because of her idolatries became intolerable and God rid Himself of her. The other sister, Jerusalem, instead of taking warning by her sister's fate, surpassed her in wickedness by playing the harlot (23:1-49).

Nor do the exiles in Babylon escape the condemnation of Ezekiel. He addresses them repeatedly as a "rebellious house" (2:1 ff.; 12:21 ff.; 14:1 ff.; 20:1 ff.). He is characterized as living among "briers and thorns" and as one who "dwells among scorpions" (2:6). They are "impudent and stiff-hearted" (2:4), and enjoy hearing the words of the prophet but hate to heed his admonitions: "And, lo, thou art unto them as a very lovely song of one that hath a pleasant voice . . . for they hear thy words, but they do them not" (33:32). The spiritual condition of the inhabitants of Judah and that of the exiles showed very little difference; in both instances they were idolatrous, rebellious and infested with iniquity. As their fathers had been, they too were transgressors (2:3) who rejected Yahweh's ordinances and walked not in His statutes (5:6-7). As for the inhabitants of Judah, they defiled His sanctuary with their abominations (5:11); high places, heathen altars and images were conspicuous on "every high hill, on all the tops of the mountains, and under every green tree, and under every thick oak, the places where they offered sweet savor to all their idols" (6:13). The prophet condemns the inhabitants of Judah for idolatry, lewdness, oppression, robbery and adultery, together with the faithlessness of the prophets, priests and princes (chap. 22). Zedekiah and the inhabitants of Jerusalem are given up to destruction since their corruption is incurable (9:9 ff.; 12; 17:1 ff.; 21:25-27).

The second division of the prophecy, however, speaks a message of consolation and hope to the exiles (33-48). The exiles, when purged, would be delivered from their disgrace and affliction, the separated kingdoms of Judah and Israel would be reunited, their enemies overthrown, and their temple and worship restored at the advent of the Messianic kingdom. As Ezekiel's mission in the first section was to justify the divine providence of God for punishing rebellious Judah by exile, so through their affliction and chastisement they would come to know that Yahweh is God. The phrase "they shall know that I am Yahweh" is the dominant theme, occurring over sixty times in the book (cf. 6:7, 10, 13, 14; 7:4; 11:10; 12:15; 22:16; 33:29; 38:23, etc.). The author's purpose throughout the entire prophecy was to keep before the exiles the sins of the nation which were the grounds for her punishment, and to sustain and encourage the faithful remnant concerning future restoration and blessing (cf. 14:21-23). At seven periods during his ministry Ezekiel is given prophetic visions concerning God and His future plans for Israel (1:3; 3:14, 22; 8:1; 33:22; 37:1; 40:1), indicated by the expression "the hand of Yahweh was upon me."

Ezekiel's style of prophetic utterance has many peculiarities, as Keil has noted. The clothing of symbol and allegory prevails in his book to a greater degree than in any of the other prophets; and his symbolism and allegory are not limited just to general outlines, but are elaborated in minute detail, presenting his ideas with boldness surpassing reality. Ezekiel portrays nations under the personification of animals, plants and specific types of people. Jerusalem and Samaria are prostitutes (23:2-3); the house of David is a lion's den (19:1 ff.) or a vine (19:10 ff.; 17:6 ff.) or a cedar (17:3); Egypt is a cedar (31:3 ff.) or a crocodile (32:1 ff.); and the Chaldeans are pictured as an eagle (17:3).

The book of Ezekiel has a definite style of its own. The interrogative sentence is used frequently, for example: "Son of man, seest thou what they do?" (8:6). Ezekiel's most notable modes of expression are the proverb, parable and allegory. Typical of his proverbs are "The fathers have eaten sour grapes, and the children's teeth are set on edge" (18:2); "As is the mother, so is her daughter" (16:44). The use of allegory is displayed in chapter 16 in the allegory of the foundling child. An example of the parable is the Messianic parable of the cedar (17:22-24).

Ezekiel employs allegory and parable regarding not only predictions of the future but also past and contemporary events. Israel is the foundling child, faithless to Him who had made her His wife (16:1 ff.); she is the lioness which reared her whelps only to become the hunter's prey (19:1 ff.); she is the stately cedar which will be destroyed (chap. 17); she is the vine which is doomed to destruction (19:10 ff.; cf. 15:1 ff.; 17:6); Nebuchadnezzar is described as one great eagle, the king of Egypt another (17:3, 7); the city of Tyre is a stately ship which will be sunk (27:5 ff.); and Egypt is a monstrous crocodile that God will slay (32:2 ff.).

An interesting aspect to consider is the question, Why did Ezekiel speak in parable and allegory rather than simply preaching a clear, direct message? Was his purpose to reveal truth or to cloak it in symbolism and mystical figures to all but the initiate? The question is significant when one remembers that Jesus' use of the parable in the New Testament was not always to reveal truth, but sometimes to conceal the inner spiritual meaning from all but the initiate, His disciples, and those who, by asking for an explanation, manifested a desire to know the truth. "Then the disciples came, and said unto him, Why speakest thou to them in parables? And he answered. . . them, Unto you it is given to know the mysteries of the kingdom of heaven, but to them it is not given" (Matt. 13:10-11).

Ezekiel's symbolic acts, for example, obviously were for the purpose of vividly illustrating certain truths. As a sign of famine he lived on loathsome bread. He lay on one side for a long period to depict the discomfort of the siege. He shaved off his hair and beard and destroyed it to show the fate of Jerusalem. He dug through the wall and carried out an exile's baggage, thereby depicting the approaching captivity and exile. A study of the various accounts will show that they were intended to convey a message to be understood. In Ezekiel 4:3 it is said after his symbolic siege of the city, "This shall be a sign to the house of Israel." After each of the symbolic acts the Lord speaking through Ezekiel interprets the meaning of the act. (Note 4:1-3; 4:4-8; 4:9-13; 5:1-12; 12:1-6, etc.)

If we are to find a satisfactory solution to why the prophet used allegory, it will be necessary to define the allegory, which is often confused with the parable. The allegory is a symbolical narrative in which every detail has a figurative meaning as in John Bunyan's *The Pilgrim's Progress*. It is a common error for Christians to attempt to allegorize the parables of Jesus by looking for a meaning in every detail. The word "allegory" is derived from the Greek *állēgoria*, a description of one thing under the image of another.

A clear example of an allegory and how it is developed can be seen in Galatians 4:21-31. Paul intentionally gives an allegorical interpretation to the historical narrative of Hagar and Sarah. He does not mean that the Genesis narrative is an allegory, but draws from it a deeper spiritual meaning than is evident on the surface. He does this by making an allegory out of a historical event. In an allegory the narrative contains some hint of its application, as in the book of Ezekiel; or the allegory and interpretation are combined as in John 15:1-8 in Jesus' discourse on the vine and the branches (cf. John 6; Ps. 80).

The parable, on the other hand, is a simple comparison, true to life with one lesson to teach, and its meaning is left to the hearer to interpret. The allegory is based on metaphors, uses unrealistic imagery, may have many lessons to teach through its details, and the interpretation is either given or clearly implied. The latter characteristic is always evident. Thus, from the nature of the allegory it is evident that Ezekiel's purpose was not to conceal the inner spiritual meaning to all except the initiate, as often was the purpose in the use of the parable. He chose the allegory rather than the parable to delineate graphically the message God wanted to reveal to Israel. This is seen, for example, in chapter 15 in the allegory of the worthless vine, which was not good enough to be used as timber or even as a small peg, but only for the fire. Ezekiel gives the interpretation of its meaning as all true allegories will do.

The Allegory
And the word of Yahweh came unto me, saying, Son of man, what is the vine-tree more than any tree, the vine-branch which is among the trees of the forest? Shall wood be taken thereof to make any work? Or will men take a pin of it to hang any vessel thereon? Behold, it is cast into the fire for fuel; the fire hath devoured both the ends of it, and the midst of it is burned: is it profitable for any work? Behold, when it was whole, it was meet for no work: how much less, when the fire hath devoured it, and it is burned, shall it yet be meet for any work! (15:1-5).

The Interpretation
Therefore thus saith the Lord Yahweh: As the vine-tree among the trees of the forest, which I have given to the fire for fuel, so will I give the inhabitants of Jerusalem. And I will set my face against them; they shall go forth from the fire, but the fire shall devour them; and ye shall know that I am Yahweh, when I set my face against them. And I will make the land desolate, because they have committed a trespass, saith the Lord Yahweh (15:6-8).

II. The Date

The beginning of the ministry of Ezekiel is placed by the book itself in 593 B.C. With the exception of Haggai and Zechariah, no other prophetic book provides such full chronological data as the book of Ezekiel. The prophet was deported to Babylon in 597. In 593, the fifth year of the captivity of King Jehoiachin, Ezekiel received his call to the prophetic office (1:1-3), and continued his ministry for at least twenty-two years. His last dated prophecy was in the twenty-seventh year of his captivity (571) according to 29:17.[1] Including

[1]For an excellent up-to-date study of the date of Ezekiel see Carl Gordon Howie, "The Date and Composition of Ezekiel," *Journal of Biblical Literature,* Monograph Series, Vol. IV (1950).

these two dates (593, 571) there are no less than fourteen exact chronological notices, giving even the day and month, contained in the book.

The chronological arrangement according to the threefold division of the book is as follows:

Chapters 1-24, the denunciation and prediction of the destruction of Jerusalem, *dated 593-588* B.C.

Chapters 25-32, prophecies against foreign nations, *dated 587-585*, with the exception of 29:17-21 which is actually the last dated prophecy of the book (571), occurring sixteen years after the date given in 29:1. It was included here in the prophecy against Egypt because of its relationship to the subject under consideration (cf. 29:1-16; 30:1—32:32).

Chapters 33-48, prophecies of the future restoration of Israel, *dated 585-573* (33:21; 40:1).

The fourteen chronological notices given by the prophet are: 1:1; 1:2; 8:1; 20:1; 24:1; 26:1; 29:1; 29:17; 30:20; 31:1; 32:1; 32:17; 33:21; 40:1. The intervening prophecies between these dates, which give no notice of the time of their delivery, connect themselves closely in content with the dated utterances and doubtless belong to the same period.

Until recent years few Old Testament critics questioned the unity of the book, accepting the dates as accurate and Ezekiel as the author. S. R. Driver wrote: "No critical question arises in connexion with the authorship of the book, the whole from beginning to end bearing unmistakably the stamp of a single mind."[2] In 1900 Kraetzschmar proposed a two-recension theory based on so-called parallel texts and doublets in the book which were later joined by a redactor. Since that time various theories have questioned the integrity of the date and authorship of the book. The most radical theory regarding the date and origin of the book was advanced by C. C. Torrey in 1930 in his work *Pseudo-Ezekiel*. The prophecy was pseudepigraphic and composed in Jerusalem about 230 B.C., purporting to denounce the sins under the reign of Manasseh. The first prophecy, according to 1:1, is said to be dated in "the thirtieth year" of Manasseh, alleges Torrey. He contends that chapters 1-39 are an accurate description of the conditions under Manasseh as recorded in II Kings 21:2-16. Every item given there is utilized by "Ezekiel." The circumstances of that time are perfectly reproduced (cf. 3:5-7; 5:6 ff.; 6:3-6; 13; 16:16, 27, 39, etc.). Moreover, Ezekiel never mentions

[2]S. R. Driver, *An Introduction to the Literature of the Old Testament,* p. 279.

Jeremiah, although they both prophesied concerning the same things regarding Judah, which indicates a period earlier than Jeremiah's arrival upon the scene.[3]

However, Torrey apparently overlooks the fact that the conditions pictured in Ezekiel 1-39 are those which also obtained during the time of Jeremiah and the closing days preceding the fall of Jerusalem. Furthermore, Haggai and Zechariah were contemporaries in Judah, both preached concerning the rebuilding of the temple, and yet neither mentions the other. This is also true of Hosea, Amos, Isaiah and Micah. Ezekiel does, however, mention Daniel, his contemporary in Babylon, confirming the exilic date of the book (14:14); and Jeremiah himself refers to "the priests" taken captive in his letter to the exiles, which in his mind might well have included Ezekiel (29:1-2).

There is some question as to the precise meaning of the phrase in 1:1 "in the thirtieth year." The question is, To what thirtieth year does the prophet refer? Verse 1 reads as follows: "Now it came to pass in the thirtieth year, in the fourth month, in the fifth day of the month, as I was among the captives by the river Chebar, that the heavens were opened, and I saw visions of God." According to the second verse the "thirtieth year" was in "the fifth year of king Jehoiachin's captivity." Various theories as to the meaning of the phrase "in the thirtieth year" have been suggested.

1.   The prophet refers to the thirtieth year after the ascension of Nabopolassar to the throne of Babylon. Since Ezekiel is exiled in Babylon, he refers here to Babylonian chronology. However, the prophet very clearly dates his prophecies in connection with the years of King Jehoiachin's captivity (1:2). Moreover, it is unlikely that he would refer to the reign of the Babylonian monarch without naming him (cf. Dan. 1:1) and expect his readers to know to whom he referred. Nowhere else does he use a double system of chronology.

2.   The reference, according to some Jewish interpreters, is to the thirtieth year from a jubilee (celebrated every fiftieth year), but this is mere conjecture.

3.   The years are reckoned from the discovery of the book of the law under Josiah (II Kings 22:8). However, as in the first view, the same objections apply to the second and third, namely, that the prophet clearly dates his ministry according to the captivity of Jehoiachin, and does not elsewhere use a double chronology. Moreover, this event does not precisely agree chronologically with the fifth year of Jehoiachin in 593 B.C.

[3]C. C. Torrey, *Pseudo-Ezekiel and the Original Prophecy*, pp. 64-70.

4. C. C. Torrey argues that "in the thirtieth year" has reference to Manasseh's long reign; hence, the prophecy is to be placed during his reign, since the contents of the book indicate the circumstances which prevailed at that time. This extreme viewpoint has already been answered.

5. The correct view, following Origen, Hengstenberg, Lange and others, is to apply this reference to the prophet's age at the time of his call to the prophetic ministry. It is a Jewish mode of reckoning, the thirtieth year being the age of full maturity. At that age the Levites entered on their ministries (Num. 4:23, 30, 39, 43, 47), and Ezekiel was a priest (1:3). Also, as in the cases of Jesus (Luke 3:23) and John the Baptist, it seems to have been recognized as the age for the inauguration of a prophet's ministry.

III. THE PROPHET

Ezekiel, whose name in Hebrew signifies "God strengthens," was, like Jeremiah and Zechariah, of priestly descent. His father was Buzi of whom the Scriptures relate nothing more. A groundless Jewish tradition makes Ezekiel the son of Jeremiah, based upon the name Buzi ("the despised one"), since the Prophet Jeremiah, it is said, was called "a despised one." Ezekiel was carried into captivity in 597 B.C., eleven years before the fall of Jerusalem along with King Jehoiachin, many nobles and priests, and the better class of the population (II Kings 24:14 ff.; Jer. 29:1-2). Jeremiah belonged, as a priest, to the line of Ithamar. Ezekiel, as a Zadokite deriving his descent from the line of Eleazar the son of Aaron, was of the priestly aristocracy, which may account for his exile, while Jeremiah was allowed to remain behind in the deportation of the royal house and nobility in 597.

Ezekiel lived in Babylonia among a colony of exiled Jews in a place designated as Tel-abib by the river Chebar (1:1; 3:15; 8:1). He was married (24:18), the prophet's wife dying the same day the siege of Jerusalem began (24:1, 15-18). He had his own house where the elders came to him for counsel and instruction, which may be the prototype of the Jewish synagogue which had its rise after the destruction of the temple and interruption of sacrificial worship (8:1; 14:1; 20:1; 33:30-33). He received his divine call and commission in the form of a majestic theophany when he was thirty years of age (1:1-3) in the fifth year of his exile (593). His ministry extended for at least twenty-two years (593-571), the last dated prophecy being in the twenty-seventh year of his captivity (29:17). Like his contemporary Daniel, the sphere of his labors was in Babylonia, Daniel's at the royal court and Ezekiel's among the exiles where he spent the remainder of his life. Although he never left his place of captivity, he did by virtue of a unique experience visit Jerusalem before its downfall in 586. A year and two months after his call, he was transported in the spirit by vision to Jerusalem where he was shown the abominations and idolatry of the city (chap. 8), the judgment of the inhabitants and the city (chaps. 9-10), and the departure of the glory and presence of the Lord from the city (chaps. 10-11), after which he was carried back in vision by the Spirit to Chaldea (11:24-25). This supernatural experience was repeated in the twenty-fifth year of his captivity when he again was brought in vision to the land of Israel (40:1-2) where he was given revelations concerning the future temple and worship which restored Israel was to enjoy during the millennium.

In the person of Ezekiel there is a synthesis, as it were, of prophet and priest. These two strains are woven together into the character of Ezekiel. The priestly element is seen in his sense of holiness (4:14; 22:26), his familiarity with the various sacrifices and types of offerings (42:13; 43:27; 44:29-31; 45:17; 46:20) and tithes (44:30) and his emphasis upon the priesthood, temple and worship (40-48). Ezekiel's priestly background, as that of Zechariah, was preparatory for the visions he was given respecting the future restoration of the temple and national worship during the millennium. More than the other prophets, Ezekiel and Zechariah stress the importance of the priesthood (cf. Zech. 3; 6:9-15), the future worship and observance of religious ceremonies and festivals (cf. Zech. 7-8; 14:16-19), the new sanctuary (cf. Zech. 1-6) and the need of holiness (cf. Zech. 3; 5; 13:1; 14:20-21). Ezekiel envisions the new temple and the details of its construction; new laws as to sacrifice and festivals are outlined; and the Zadokite priests with the assistance of the Levites are to serve in the restored holy city and the sanctuary. He lays emphasis upon the necessity of the spiritual renewal of the people and the holiness of the kingdom (11:19-20; 36:24-29; 44:1 ff.). But Ezekiel is also a prophet; hence, because God is holy and acutely aware of every detail of the nation's spiritual and moral uncleanness, the prophet, in His name, pronounces judgment. Yahweh, as the holy God of Israel, will punish all iniquity and purge out all uncleanness from His holy land, for "the soul that sinneth, it shall die" (18:4).

The critical contention which follows the errors of Wellhausen, that Ezekiel's emphasis upon ceremonial holiness and ritual makes him thereby "the father of legalistic Judaism" is too innocuous to warrant refutation. Graf surmised that Ezekiel's acquaintance with the Pentateuch and familiarity with sacrificial ritual make him the probable author of the so-called "law of holiness," Leviticus 17-26. However, the affinities of language between Ezekiel and the Pentateuch are what would be expected from one who is of the Zadokite priesthood and familiar with the Mosaic legislation.

IV. THE HISTORICAL BACKGROUND

At the time of Ezekiel's call in 593 B.C. the northern kingdom of Israel had been destroyed for over a century, while the overthrow of Judah was imminent. With the death of Josiah in 609 at Megiddo, a succession of kings antagonistic to the will of Yahweh had hastened the moral and spiritual declension of the nation, which was to lead to its inevitable destruction. On the fall of Nineveh in 612, and with the defeat of Egypt at the decisive Battle of Carchemish in 605, Judah became tributary to Babylon who now occupied Palestine, Nebuchadnezzar in the same year deporting a group of the nobility, including Daniel (Dan. 1:1-3, 6; II Kings 24:1; II Chron. 36:6). From this date, 605 B.C., the Babylonian exile begins.

Jehoiakim, who was king in Judah at this time, ignored Jeremiah's repeated warnings for quiet submission to Babylonia, which alone could avert utter destruction for the nation. After three years of serving Babylon, Jehoiakim revolted in 602 (II Kings 24:1), whereupon Yahweh sent against him bands of the Chaldeans, Syrians, Moabites and Ammonites who overran Judah. Jehoiakim died before the arrival of the main forces of Nebuchadnezzar later in 597, and was succeeded by his son Jehoiachin, who surrendered after a reign of but three months (II Kings 24:8). In 597 Nebuchadnezzar pillaged the temple and carried away Jehoiachin to Babylon, together with "all the princes, and all the mighty men of valor, even ten thousand captives," including Ezekiel the priest (II Kings 24:13-14; Ezek. 1:1-3). Zedekiah (597-586), son of Josiah and uncle of Jehoiachin, was placed on the throne of Judah as a vassal of Nebuchadnezzar. In the fifth year of his reign, Ezekiel received his call in Babylonia to the prophetic ministry. King Zedekiah reigned eleven years as a weak and vacillating ruler, following in the footsteps of his wicked predecessors. In the ninth year of his reign he rebelled against Nebuchadnezzar who laid siege to Jerusalem (cf. Ezek. 24:1-2), which he captured and destroyed in 586, deporting Zedekiah and the population to Babylon.

V. PROBLEMS

1. One of the most discussed problems of the book has to do with the identity of the person described in 28:11-19. It is seriously

questioned by many interpreters whether or not the description in this passage can be limited to the historic king of Tyre inasmuch as the language evidently goes beyond the king and characterizes Satan, as is also the case in Isaiah 14:1-20. A. H. Fausset in his commentary on the Old Testament represents this viewpoint: "The language, though primarily here applied to the king of Tyre, as similar language is to the king of Babylon (Isaiah 14:13, 14), yet has an ulterior and fuller accomplishment in Satan and his embodiment in antichrist."[4] Thus Ezekiel 28 and Isaiah 14 concern the same problem. The passage in Isaiah is addressed to the king of Babylon but the description here also appears inappropriate if limited to that earthly monarch.

The scope of Isaiah's prophecy is future, looking even beyond Israel's return from the Babylonian exile; for as W. E. Vine in his commentary on Isaiah observes, "Chapter 14 introduces the day of Israel's deliverance and Millennial blessing, and it is in the day that the Lord gives them rest."[5] Hence, the ultimate scope of the prophecy is when Israel is restored to her own land (Isa. 14:1), inasmuch as the relative positions of the nations and Israel are reversed (14:2), and Israel has been granted rest by the Lord (14:3). The language in verse 12, which is addressed to the king of Babylon, is used of Satan (Luke 10:18; Rev. 12:7-10) who, as the "prince of this world," was the directing spiritual power behind the king of Babylon. Fausset believes the passage is also descriptive of Antichrist. He writes: "The language is so framed as to apply to the Babylonian king primarily, and at the same time to shadow forth through him, the great final enemy, the man of sin, antichrist. . . ."[6] It is possible in view of the statements concerning Antichrist in Daniel 7:25; 11:36; II Thessalonians 2:4; Revelation 13:5 that the prophecy has reference both to Satan and his embodiment in Antichrist; however, the force of the description ultimately speaks of Satan. Satan was the first to rebel and manifest his sinful will against God. Chafer notes that there are five "I wills" of Satan in this passage which cannot literally be applied to the king of Babylon.[7] Satan said: "I will ascend into heaven"; "I will exalt my throne above the stars of God"; "I will sit upon the mount of congregation"; "I will ascend above the heights of the clouds"; "I will make myself like the Most High" (Isa. 14:13-14). The church Fathers also applied this passage to Satan,

[4]Robert Jamieson *et al., A Commentary, Critical and Explanatory, on the Old and New Testaments,* p. 625.
[5]W. E. Vine, *Isaiah,* p. 53.
[6]Jamieson *et al.,* p. 456.
[7]Lewis Sperry Chafer, *Satan,* pp. 12-13.

translating the Hebrew appellative *hêlēl*, "shining one," as Lucifer (Latin, "light-bearer") in Isaiah 14:12.

This language, like that in Ezekiel 28:11-19, goes beyond the historical king to Satan. Ezekiel 28 describes the original, unfallen state of Satan, whereas Isaiah 14 portrays his fall and ultimate destruction. Why then are these two prophecies addressed to the historical kings of Babylon and of Tyre if they are descriptive of Satan? Primarily because (1) there is to be seen in the characters and careers of these monarchs the wicked character and career of Satan; (2) Satan fulfills himself and his evil administration in and through these earthly kings who rule over his earthly dominions, the heathen world kingdoms; (3) these rulers, like Satan, arrogated to themselves divine honors and prerogatives (cf. Isa. 14:13-14; Ezek. 28:2). Other passages where Satan is addressed indirectly through another, as in Isaiah 14 and Ezekiel 28, are Genesis 3:14-15; Matthew 16:23; John 13:27. In the Messianic psalms David, while he apparently has reference to himself, in reality describes Christ (cf. Ps. 16:10; 22, etc.). So the king of Babylon and the king of Tyre have addressed to them language which, by its very nature, seems descriptive of another than their own persons.

Those who object to the application of these passages to Satan nevertheless labor at great length themselves, and with no little difficulty, in their attempts to relate the unusual language to the historic kings of Babylon and Tyre. This fact is to be seen in the general lack of agreement among the interpreters. In their attempts to relate the description in Ezekiel 28:11-19 to the actual king of Tyre, they say the prophet is here drawing a comparison between Adam in Eden before and after his fall (Keil); or Ezekiel is comparing him to one of the cherubim who guarded the paradise of God (Plumptre); or Ezekiel with sarcastic allusions to the divine pretensions of the Tyrian king (saying "I am a god," 28:2) is merely describing him as a glorious being in the garden of God who will be expelled from his proud position (Driver); or he is illustrating how the pride of Tyre is personified in her king, the city exalting and worshiping her own wisdom and prosperity (McFadyen); or the prophet is giving a sarcastic elegy over the proud king of Tyre, depicting him as a mythological being residing in Eden (Pfeiffer); or Ezekiel is teaching a historical parable, representing the king of Tyre as the "ideal man," complete in all outward excellence and occupying an exalted place in creation from which he, yielding to corruption, falls, as has humanity itself—for man in his best estate has not been perfect before God (Fairbairn); or the language has reference symbolically to the historical relation of Hiram king of Tyre to the building of the temple of Solomon due to his close connection with this work and his consequent association with Jerusalem, "the holy mountain of God" (Lange). There are practically as many interpretations of Ezekiel 28 as there are commentaries. In view of this, and because of the inappropriateness of limiting the unique description in this passage to the historic king of Tyre, it seems quite likely that the language looks beyond the king to another, Satan.

Observe the extraordinary nature of the description in Ezekiel 28:11-19:

a. "Thou sealest up the sum, full of wisdom, and perfect in beauty" (28:12), that is, complete and perfect in these aspects.

b. "Thou wast in Eden, the garden of God" (v. 13), in primeval paradise, not the Eden of Adam, but the garden of God (v. 14, "the holy mountain of God") where he was covered with all imaginable splendor: "every precious stone was thy covering."

c. "In the day that thou wast created" (v. 13). Twice his creation is referred to (cf. v. 15), which is certainly inappropriate when applied to the king of Tyre. The Scriptures speak of Adam's being "created," but not his posterity, who are "born."

d. "Thou wast the anointed cherub that covereth" (v. 14). No amount of spiritualizing has been able to deal satisfactorily with the designation "cherub," outside of its application to a spiritual being. The cherubim in Scripture always appear in the closest relationship to God, bearing the divine throne when He manifests Himself in His glory (Ezek. 1; 9-11; Ps. 18:11), and as guardians of the inaccessibility of His holy presence (Exodus 25:20; I Chron. 28:18; cf. Gen. 3:24). In what sense could such a designation characterize the king of Tyre even symbolically? He was the "anointed cherub," set apart for special responsibility as the following statement indicates.

e. "I set thee, so that thou wast upon the holy mountain of God" (28:14), appointed by God Himself to a position at His eternal throne, "the holy mountain" signifying the center of His divine rule and government (Joel 3:17; Isa. 2:2; 14:13).

f. "Thou hast walked up and down in the midst of the stones of fire" (28:14), doubtless signifying the divine presence of God and His glory around whose feet Ezekiel beheld the "appearance of fire" (1:27), as had Moses earlier: "Under his feet as it were a paved work of sapphire stone. And the appearance of the glory of Yahweh was like a devouring fire" (Exodus 24:10, 17).

g. "Thou wast perfect in thy ways from the day that thou

wast created, till unrighteousness was found in thee" (28:15). Certainly unsuitable and inappropriate when applied to the king of Tyre who was neither originally "perfect" nor "created," later falling from his previous condition of rectitude, this, however, is an accurate description of the career of Satan. Compare Colossians 1:16 with Ephesians 6:12, and John 1:3 with 8:44 which presupposes the fall of Satan from an original state of righteousness. Isaiah 14:13-14, which describes Satan's fall and attempt to usurp the prerogatives of God, should be introduced at Ezekiel 28:15.

h. "Thy heart was lifted up because of thy beauty; thou hast corrupted thy wisdom by reason of thy brightness" (28:17). Satan's fall and condemnation began with pride (I Tim. 3:6; Isa. 14:13-14).

i. "Therefore have I cast thee as profane out of the mountain of God; and I have destroyed thee, O covering cherub, from the midst of the stones of fire. . . . I have cast thee to the ground. . . . I have turned thee to ashes. . . and thou shalt nevermore have any being" (28:16-19). The precise fate predicted for Satan in Revelation (Rev. 12:7-9; 20:10; Isa. 14:12, 15-20) is that which is set forth by the Prophet Ezekiel.

2. The second problem concerns Ezekiel 40-48. The concluding section of the book of Ezekiel, chapters 40-48, is usually designated as the temple vision. The section contains three main divisions however: the temple of the millennium (chaps. 40-43), the worship of the millennium (chaps. 44-46), the boundaries and divisions of the land in the millennium (chaps. 47-48). Due to the unusual nature of these chapters which depict the restoration of the Jewish temple and worship, together with the rearrangement of the Holy Land, many commentators have been led to conclude that any purely literal, material realization of this prophecy is highly improbable. The problem of chapters 40-48 then is concerned with whether or not the nature of these chapters precludes a literal interpretation or whether the particulars described therein are to find actual fulfillment in the millennium.

Basically there are two views of the vision of Ezekiel 40-48, the *literal* and the *symbolical*. The question is, therefore, What significance is to be attached to chapters 40-48? The solution will depend, of course, on what eschatological principle of interpretation is applied. If one's view is in opposition to the millenarian doctrine of Scripture and Israel's restoration in her land, then the symbolical interpretation is the only logical alternative. If, however, the Scriptures justify the expectation of a visible reign of Christ over Israel, redeemed and restored in her own land, at the close of the present age, then the correct interpretation is the literal one[8] which views these chapters as a prophecy yet to be fulfilled in the millennial age.

a. The symbolical interpretation. Those who advocate an allegorical or symbolical interpretation generally interpret the vision as symbolizing the future blessings which God purposed to bestow upon His church. E. J. Young entitles it "The vision of the Church of God upon earth symbolized by the description of the Temple." Objections to a literal interpretation are chiefly twofold: The details of the temple as outlined by Ezekiel are quite impossible of literal fulfillment; and the reinstitution of Levitical sacrifice and worship is in contradiction to the teaching of the epistle to the Hebrews and would constitute a return to the ritualistic elements of Judaism done away with in Christ's atoning work. Those who idealize the prophecy are not in precise agreement as to the *terminus a quo* of these blessings, however.[9]

1) Hengstenberg believes the fulfillment of the vision began with the return from Babylon. The exiles in Babylon were to derive from the symbolism of this prophecy the hope of restoration to their land, the rebuilding of their fallen temple, and reinstitution of their ceremony and worship.

2) Luther, Calvin and the Reformed theologians in general express the amillennial interpretation. The vision symbolizes the church in its origin, development, influence and consequent completion in the hereafter; hence, the fulfillment began with the incarnation. Ezekiel's description of a new temple, a new worship and a new land pointed to a state and condition of things which first began to be realized when the Christian dispensation was instituted by the incarnation of Christ. Ezekiel's vision makes no mention of building materials for the new temple, inasmuch as the church is composed of "living stones," and is a "spiritual house" (I Peter 2:5). The "glory of Yahweh" which departed from the temple at Jerusalem because of the nation's iniquity (chap. 11), and which Ezekiel depicts as returning to the new temple (43:1-6), symbolized the perpetual inhabitation of the church by the Holy Spirit (Eph. 2:21-22). The sanctity with which Ezekiel's temple was surrounded, evidenced by the detailed description of its various divisions—inner and outer courts, ascents, chambers for the ritual and for the priests, the altar with its sacrifices, and the like, the whole surrounded by a wall—fitly symbol-

[8]I.e., literal in the main.

[9]E.g., H. L. Ellison, *Ezekiel: The Man and His Message,* chap. 14, argues that the prophecy of Ezek. 40-48 is symbolic of future millennial conditions.

ized the superior holiness which should belong to the church of God. The absence of the high priest and great Day of Atonement in Ezekiel's vision was predictive of the time when Christ as our High Priest accomplished atonement once for all. The other sacrifices which are mentioned, such as the daily sin offering, meant that in the church of the future there should be a constant remembrance of the atonement of Christ and an ever renewed appropriation of His propitiation by His worshipers. The burnt offerings serve to typify the self-consecration of Christ's worshipers in the new dispensation. The "prince" who presented the offerings for the people foreshadows the offerings of the Christian through Christ. The miraculous river which flows from the temple, increasing as it goes, creating life and beauty wherever it flows, pictures the spiritual influences of the gospel. The introduction of the sons of the stranger to equal privileges with the Israelite and equal division of the land among the tribes foreshadows the time when the distinction between Jew and Gentile would no longer exist in the Body of Christ, and all would share alike in the heavenly inheritance of which Canaan was the earthly symbol.[10] If there are problems in connection with a literal interpretation of Ezekiel 40-48, they certainly are not diminished by such extreme and unwarranted allegorizing as the foregoing amillennial interpretation proves. Only an unjustified equating of the church with Israel could lead to such fanciful and unscriptural allegorizing of this lengthy prophecy concerning Israel in the millennium.

3)   Keil restricts the fulfillment of the vision to the future consummation of the kingdom of God in its perfected or heavenly condition and excludes all allusion to the present or historical state of the church. The vision is a symbolic representation, in Old Testament language, of the introduction of spiritual Israel (the church) into heavenly Canaan and of the perfect service they shall then render to the Lord. He writes:

> The prophetic picture does not furnish a typical exhibition of the church of Christ in its gradual development, but sets forth the kingdom of God established by Christ in its perfect form, and is partly to be regarded as the Old Testament outline of the New Testament picture of the heavenly Jerusalem in Rev. xxi and xxii.[11]

[10]E. H. Plumptre, "The Book of Ezekiel," *The Pulpit Commentary*, XII, 475-77.

[11]C. F. Keil and F. Delitzsch, "The Prophecies of Ezekiel," *Biblical Commentary on the Old Testament*, II, 417.

In reply to the first view of Hengstenberg that the vision was to realize fulfillment after the Babylonian exile in the restoration of Israel and the temple, which hope it symbolized, it must be said that the unusual details of the vision could not in any sense represent symbolically the restoration under Zerubbabel. The extensive nature of the precise details and measurements of the new temple and the numerous regulations concerning the sacrifices, priesthood and worship cannot be satisfied by a merely figurative or symbolical application of these chapters to the temple and worship under Zerubbabel. No reasonable explanation can be given by the advocates of the symbolical view for the immense number of details concerning the temple, worship and reallotment of the land.

These same objections hold true with regard to the other symbolical interpretations which apply the vision allegorically to the present church age or, as Keil does, to the heavenly or final state of the kingdom of God. Ellison explains the details of the vision as signifying symbolically that the people of God, among whom He dwells, cannot be organized haphazardly; hence, in even the smallest details of life and organization the will of God must be done.[12] However, the symbolical and allegorical interpretations of Ezekiel's vision are fraught with innumerable exegetical difficulties. The spiritualization of this prophecy in an effort to apply it to the church is not only hermeneutically unsound, but results in utter confusion when an attempt is made to relate the numerous details concerning construction of the future temple, worship, the allotment of the land, to the church age. The allegorical interpretations of Ezekiel 40-48 are little short of exegetical license, which is all too evident when a comparison is made between the predictions of Ezekiel and these fanciful interpretations.

b. The literal interpretation. Among the advocates of the literal interpretation of Ezekiel 40-48 there are two opinions concerning the *terminus a quo* of its fulfillment: those who maintain the literality of the temple and worship in Ezekiel's vision, but confine its fulfillment to the period of the exiles who returned from Babylon under Zerubbabel; and those who limit its fulfillment to the yet future period of the millennium.

1) The advocates of the first view maintain that the vision was intended to provide literal instructions for the new religious and civil order which was to be established in Palestine upon the return of the exiles. Hengstenberg, it will be recalled, held essentially to the same

[12]Ellison, *Men Spake from God,* p. 114. See also Ellison, *Ezekiel the Man and His Message,* pp. 137-44.

idea concerning the *terminus a quo* of the vision, but denied the literal fulfillment of its details, applying the vision symbolically as a general prediction of the restoration of Israel, the temple and worship after the seventy-year captivity.

The objections to this interpretation of the literal view are significant. First of all, if Ezekiel had intended the vision as a blueprint for the establishment of a new program of worship for Israel, it is quite obvious that it was never realized, nor was there ever the slightest effort on the part of Zerubbabel and the restored exiles to bring it about. They were either unaware of the purpose of the prophecy, or they intentionally ignored the instructions of God revealed through His prophet, both suggestions being too ridiculous to warrant serious consideration. On the contrary, the postexilic leaders purposely restored, as nearly as possible, the conditions and practices which had existed in preexilic times, as the historical accounts in Ezra, Nehemiah and the postexilic prophets clearly indicate. The temple and worship under Zerubbabel do not correspond to the specifications contained in the book of Ezekiel. There are far more points of contrast than agreement. There is an absence in Ezekiel's vision of a high priest and Day of Atonement, as well as other important requirements of the Mosaic legislation, which were to be found in the restored community after the exile under Zerubbabel and Joshua the high priest. Moreover, there are aspects of Ezekiel's vision that the postexilic community could not have fulfilled even if they had so desired, namely, the healing waters which are to flow from the future temple, the return of the "glory of Yahweh" to the temple, the supernatural topographical changes in the land that will be required to resituate enlarged millennial Jerusalem and its temple, the position and duties of "the prince" in the future worship, and the unique allotment of the land among the twelve tribes.

2) It is impossible to maintain seriously the literality of Ezekiel's vision by applying it to the postexilic period of Zerubbabel; the only alternative is to view the vision as a literal prophecy of the future temple and worship to be realized in the millennium. That Ezekiel expected his readers to so view the prophecy is evident from an impartial study of chapters 40-48.

Expositors who spiritualize the prophecy in order to apply it to the church offer several objections to the literal interpretation. The analogy of Ezekiel's vision with the symbolic predictions by the other prophets of Israel's future restoration and blessing in her land is strong evidence for the symbolical interpretation of these chapters also (cf. Zech. 9-14; Jer. 33:17-22; Isa. 2:2-4; 60:1-22, etc.). This objection, however, is reasoning in a circle. The analogy of Ezekiel with other prophets, who foretell a future restoration of the temple, sacrifices and worship, cannot be used to prove that Ezekiel 40-48 is to be interpreted symbolically unless it can first be shown that all these other passages where these things are predicted are to be spiritualized. On the contrary, these analogous predictions by the other prophets confirm the literalness of Ezekiel 40-48. (Cf. Isa. 2:2-4; 60:1-22; Jer. 31: 38-40; 33:17-22; Joel 3:18; Hag. 2:7-9; Amos 9:11; Micah 4:1-4; Zech. 6:9-15; 14:8-21.)

Again it is objected that there is an absence in Ezekiel 40-48 of any command to the prophet, like that given to Moses, to carry out the instructions for building the temple and institute the new system of worship. There is no evidence that the prophet or others were to take the vision literally; hence, it is a symbolical representation of the church. This objection cannot stand in view of the definite statements to the contrary in the prophecy itself whereby specific instructions and commands are given to observe these things:

> Thou, son of man, show the house to the house of Israel, that they may be ashamed of their iniquities; and let them measure the pattern. And if they be ashamed of all that they have done, make known unto them the form of the house, and the fashion thereof, and the egresses thereof, and the entrances thereof, and all the forms thereof, and all the ordinances thereof, and all the forms thereof, and all the laws thereof; and write it in their sight; *that they may keep the whole form thereof, and all the ordinances thereof, and do them.* This is the law of the house: upon the top of the mountain the whole limit thereof round about shall be most holy. Behold, this is the law of the house (Ezek. 43:10-12; cf. 40:4; 44:5 ff.; 45:1 ff.; 46:1 ff.; 47:13 ff., etc.).

It is also objected that it would be geographically impossible to carry out literally the specifications for the city, temple and allotment of the land. The square of the temple in 42:20 is six times as large as the circuit of the wall enclosing the old temple, and, in fact, is larger than the former city itself. The city in Ezekiel has an area of between three and four thousand square miles, including the holy ground set apart for the prince, priests and Levites. Moreover, there is difficulty in the literal distribution of the land of Palestine into equal portions, in parallel sections running east to west, among the twelve tribes, without respect to their relative numbers. However, these objections overlook the predicted supernatural topographical changes that are to be effected at this time:

> And his feet shall stand in that day upon the mount of Olives, which is before Jerusalem on the east; and the mount of Olives shall be cleft in the midst thereof toward the east and toward the

west, and there shall be a very great valley; and half of the
mountain shall remove toward the north, and half of it toward
the south. And it shall come to pass in that day, that there shall
not be light; the bright ones shall withdraw themselves: but it
shall be one day which is known unto Yahweh; not day, and not
night; but it shall come to pass, that at evening time there shall
be light. And it shall come to pass in that day, that living waters
shall go out from Jerusalem; half of them toward the eastern sea,
and half of them toward the western sea: in summer and in
winter shall it be. All the land shall be made like the Arabah,
from Geba to Rimmon south of Jerusalem; and she shall be lifted
up, and shall dwell in her place (Zech. 14:4, 6-8, 10).

These verses clearly indicate significant changes in the topography
of Palestine prior to the millennium sufficient to permit the literal
fulfillment of Ezekiel's prophecy. Zechariah 14:10, for example, indicates how all the district from Geba to Rimmon will be made like the
Arabah, that is, from the north of Judah to its southern boundary the
country will be leveled into a plain, whereas Jerusalem itself "shall be
lifted up," precisely as predicted by Isaiah (2:2); Micah (4:1); and
Ezekiel (40:2).

Finally, it is said that it would be impossible to take literally
Ezekiel's teaching concerning the offering of sacrifices during the
millennium, for such would be a "return to the beggarly elements of
Judaism" which would be in direct conflict with the teaching of the
epistle to the Hebrews which clearly states cessation of all sacrifices
due to their fulfillment in Christ's atoning sacrifice "once for all."
Allis in his work *Prophecy and the Church* cites this as a basic
objection to the literal restoration of the temple and sacrifice since it
would require (1) the restoration of the *Mosaic covenant* with its
institutions and ordinances, and (2) the reinstitution of the Levitical
expiatory sacrifices. However, these conclusions are erroneous. In the
first place, as Pentecost correctly maintains, the kingdom expectation
is based upon the Abrahamic covenant and the Davidic covenant, not
the Mosaic covenant.[13] The former covenants with Abraham and
David, which in reality are one, are eternal and unconditional (Gen.
12:1-3; 15; 17; Ps. 105:9-10; II Sam. 7:12; Jer. 33:19-22; Rom.
11:25-29), whereas the Mosaic covenant was temporal and conditional, governing the nation at the time of the theocracy. As the "old"
covenant, based upon the blood of animal sacrifice (Exodus 24:1-8;
Lev. 16), it was to be superceded by a new covenant in Christ's blood
(Heb. 9:15 ff.). Hence, the two covenants are in a real sense unre-

[13]J. Dwight Pentecost, *Things to Come,* p. 518.

lated, and the fulfillment of the Abrahamic-Davidic covenant and the kingdom prophecies does not necessitate the restoration of the Mosaic covenant with its institutions and regulations.

This does not mean that there will be no similarities between the Mosaic and millennial observances. In the millennial worship, according to Ezekiel, there will be a temple, priests, sacrifices, feast days and the like (this is a strong argument against Ezekiel 40-48 being fulfilled in the church). However, there are many basic and significant differences between the Mosaic and millennial systems, and these differences indicate that the two systems are not to be equated. There are marked differences in the dimensions of the millennial temple from both the temple of Solomon and that of Zerubbabel. There is no mention of an ark of the covenant, golden lampstand, table of shewbread, and veil. The Passover and Feast of Tabernacles are observed but Pentecost is omitted. While the five classes of sacrifices and offerings are cited, the central Levitical sacrifice, the Day of Atonement, is omitted. Likewise while the sons of Zadok serve as priests, there is no high priest himself. The absence of the Day of Atonement together with the sprinkling of the blood upon the mercy seat of the ark by the high priest, which was the most vital element in the Levitical system, is evidence that the millennial practices are not the reinstitution of Judaism. Other notable differences are: the return of the "glory of Yahweh" to Ezekiel's temple; the healing and living waters which flow from the temple; the "prince" who fills a representative position on behalf of the people, not being the same office as formerly occupied by the king in Israel; nor is it Christ, since the prince is said to have sons and to offer a sin offering for himself (46:16; 45:22); the significant topographical changes; and the new allotment of the land among the twelve tribes.[14]

But what of the second contention by Allis that to take literally the prediction by Ezekiel that sacrifices and offerings will be made upon an altar during the millennium is to disregard the teaching of the epistle to the Hebrews? Moreover, Allis states that the sacrifices

> must be expiatory in exactly the same sense as the sacrifices described in Leviticus were expiatory. . . . They were not memorial but efficacious in the days of Moses and of David; and in the Millennium they must be equally efficacious . . . and this cannot be unless the teaching of the Epistle to the Hebrews is completely disregarded. To make use of the "beggarly elements" before the reality had come, and to do this when directly commanded to do

[14]*Ibid.*, pp. 519-23.

so, was one thing. To return to them after the reality has come and when expressly commanded not to do so, would be quite another thing. . . . The thought is abhorrent that after He comes, the memory of His atoning work will be kept alive in the hearts of believers by a return to the animal sacrifices of the Mosaic law. . . . Here is unquestionably the Achilles' heel of the Dispensational system of interpretation.[15]

The problem Allis raises regarding the efficacy of the Old Testament sacrifices is extremely significant in regard to the meaning and purpose of the millennial sacrifices. In the foregoing quotation he states that the millennial sacrifices "must be expiatory in exactly the same sense as the sacrifices described in Leviticus were expiatory." While Allis does not mention it, we might also point out that the identical term translated again and again in Leviticus as "atonement" (*kipper*) is precisely the same word which Ezekiel uses to describe the millennial sacrifices (45:17). Admittedly then, those who interpret Ezekiel 40-48 literally have a crucial problem, for whatever meaning is attached to the Hebrew term *kipper* in Leviticus must also be allowed in the prophecy of Ezekiel. It cannot have one meaning in Leviticus and another in Ezekiel. Allis has stated that the millennial sacrifices must have the same efficacy as the Levitical sacrifices. In what sense then were the Old Testament sacrifices efficacious?[16]

"When the Law itself is consulted as to the effects of these sacrifices upon ceremonial, civil, or moral transgression, it is *always* stated that the effect is the *forgiveness of sins*, with the Israelite restored to both covenant and spiritual standing.

> "And he shall lay his hand upon the head of the sin-offering, and kill it for a sin-offering. . . and the priest shall make atonement for him as touching his sin that he hath sinned, and *he shall be forgiven.* (Lev. 4:33, 35 ASV, Italics mine.)

"The conscience of the pious Israelite, oppressed and burdened with sin, accepted with divine assurance the fact that his sins were forgiven. This is not the same as saying, however, as the writer of Hebrews observes, that the frequent animal sacrifices effected a permanent peace and satisfaction for the conscience, 'Else would they not have ceased to be offered?' (Heb. 10:2). Animal sacrifices were never intended to effect such relief, nor could they, since they did not possess that dynamic operation as the once for all efficacious sacrifice

---

[15]Oswald T. Allis, *Prophecy and the Church,* pp. 247-48.

[16]The following discussion is quoted from the writer's article "The Problem of the Efficacy of Old Testament Sacrifices," *Bulletin of the Evangelical Theological Society,* V (Summer, 1962), 73-79.

of Christ. Animal sacrifices, on the other hand, had to be offered again and again for the atonement of sins.

"But the reality of forgiveness is vouchsafed by the divine promises contained within the Law itself. All sins of weakness and rashness were completely atoned for by the sin-offerings whether done knowingly or unwittingly (Lev. 4-5); by the trespass-offering such sins as lying, theft, fraud, perjury, and debauchery were atoned for (Lev. 6:1-7); and on the Day of Atonement forgiveness was obtained for all the transgressions of Israel, whether people or priests.

. . . .

"Therefore, on the one hand, it seems evident that the Mosaic sacrifices had a certain efficacy ascribed to them in Old Testament Law. It is written again and again in the Book of Leviticus that when the prescribed ritual had been duly performed by the worshipper, the sacrifice offered, and the blood sprinkled, that '. . . it shall be accepted for him to make atonement for him' (Lev. 1:4). On the Day of Atonement complete cleansing and removal of sins is clearly taught in the ritual of the two goats, in which one was slain and his blood sprinkled upon the mercy-seat in the Holy of Holies to propitiate judicial wrath by covering the sins; and the other, after the sins of the people were confessed over it, was sent away into the wilderness bearing the iniquities of the people, thus symbolizing sin's complete removal. It is significant that there is not a word in the ceremony that this great sacrifice made an atonement only with respect to ceremonial sins, but on the contrary, it was an atonement for all the sins of the people. 'And Aaron shall lay both his hands upon the head of the live goat, and confess over him all the iniquities of the children of Israel, and all their transgressions, even all their sins' (Lev. 16:21). In the individual sin-offering it is promised that '. . . the priest shall make atonement for him as touching his sin that he hath sinned, and he shall be forgiven' (Lev. 4:35). From all this it is evident that a real atoning efficacy was in some way related to the Mosaic sacrifices by divine appointment. What the nature of this efficacy was will be demonstrated later.

THE PROBLEM OF THE EPISTLE TO THE HEBREWS

"On the other hand, the New Testament teaching, especially the Epistle to the Hebrews, is very emphatic in its declarations that '. . . the law having a shadow of the good things to come, not the very image of the things, can never with the same sacrifices year by year, which they offer continually, make perfect them that draw nigh' (Heb. 10:11). For they '. . . cannot, as touching the conscience, make the worshipper perfect' (Heb. 9:9), since the blood of goats and bulls availed only to '. . . sanctify unto the cleanness of the flesh' (Heb. 9:13), but 'how much more shall the blood of Christ, who through the eternal spirit offered himself without blemish unto God, cleanse your conscience from dead works . . .' (Heb. 9:14), 'for it is impossible that the blood of bulls and goats should take away sins' (Heb. 10:4).

"Here would appear to be two apparently opposite views of the efficacy of the Levitical sacrifices. But the reconciliation of the difficulty lies, not in a denial of either the Old or New Testament teachings, but in a harmonization of both. This is accomplished through a study of the two different aspects under which sacrifice is regarded in the Mosaic economy and by the Hebrews' Epistle respectively.

RECONCILIATION OF THE PROBLEM

"From the worshipper's standpoint the Levitical sacrifices were, in a sense, efficacious in a two-fold way: (1) they healed the breach of covenant relationship which resulted from either ceremonial or moral transgression, and kept secure their civil and ecclesiastical privileges; and (2) they procured also, when offered with unfeigned penitence and humble faith, actual forgiveness for the sinner in that it is clearly stated the sacrifice '. . . shall make *atonement* for him as touching his sin that he hath sinned, and *he shall be forgiven.*'

"It is dishonoring, it seems, to God's word and promise, which is repeated over and over, to contend that the sins under the first covenant were only symbolically, but never really, forgiven. This is to fail to comprehend the meaning and purpose of Old Testament sacrifice and to reduce it to vague and meaningless ritual. This does not really deal with the problem. It simply raises another one—how can we explain the divine promises of forgiveness in Leviticus?

•　•　•　•　•　•　•　•　•　•　•　•　•　•　•　•　•　•

THE TWO-FOLD DIVINE PURPOSE IN SACRIFICE

"How could God promise the truly repentant worshipper actual forgiveness if the prescribed ritual was properly observed? The solution lies in God's eternal purposes in Old Testament sacrifices. Old Testament ritual and worship may be said to have had a two-fold purpose, one purpose to be revealed and realized in the Old Testament dispensation, the other hidden, and to be realized in the New Testament dispensation.

THE REVEALED AND REALIZED PURPOSE

"The covenant relationship between God and Israel was expressed in ritual worship. Since the aim of the covenant was the process of sanctification expressed by the words in Leviticus 19:2: '. . . ye shall be holy: for I the Lord your God am holy,' the Mosaic ritual was intended as a conscious symbol of this truth. However, the ritual was not simply a system of outward signs of internal truths; but from the standpoint of the worshipper and of the Levitical law, it was the *necessary vehicle* for the actual realization of forgiveness, and for communion and fellowship between God and Israel within the Covenant. This means that a sacrifice did not symbolize forgiveness of sins and propitiation of God apart from the actual realization of these effects. Sacrifice, in the Old Testament, was not *merely* a symbol or type, for this is to rob it of all immediate meaning and purpose; but it expressed the transference of legal guilt to the substitute and the imposition of the capital punishment due the sinner, carried out in the act of sacrifice itself. Thus, from the worshipper's standpoint, and on the basis of God's own promises in Leviticus, the Mosaic sacrifices were efficacious in this two-fold sense; they maintained a covenant relationship between God and Israel, and when offered in humble faith and penitence, they secured for the worshipper a valid atonement and the forgiveness of all sins, moral or ceremonial. It is, however, quite a different matter to view the Levitical sacrifices in the light of New Testament revelation and from the standpoint of God's ultimate and hidden purposes. It must be carefully observed, therefore, that whatever *efficacy* was ascribed to the Levitical sacrifices, it was not *inherent* within the animal itself, and did not, strictly speaking, belong to the sacrifices themselves, which were symbols, from God's viewpoint, of the Lamb of God.

. . . .

THE HIDDEN AND FUTURE PURPOSE

"The direct and immediate efficacy of the sin-offering, on the basis of God's promises, was the securing of forgiveness of sin for the penitent Israelite, and for the entire covenant community on the great Day of Atonement. Atonement was secured, as has been shown, as a result of, and never apart from, the actual ritual sacrifice and death of the animal. Thus the sacrifice itself was the necessary vehicle for securing forgiveness of sins. But it has also been stated that the efficacy did not lie inherently in the animal itself, nor in the Israelite's understanding that the sacrifice he was making was only a shadow and type of the Messiah's sacrifice. How then could God promise the truly penitent worshipper *actual* forgiveness if the prescribed ritual was properly observed? The solution lies in God's eternal purposes in the Old Testament sacrifices and religious institutions. While they truly atoned for the sins of the worshipper, yet the Old Testament sacrifices were validated in the mind of God on the basis of the all-sufficient, truly efficacious sacrifice of *the Lamb of God slain from the foundation of the world* (I Peter 1:20).

"It is categorically true that the blood of bulls and goats could never take away sin; but then the Old Testament *never says that it did*. What God promised to Israel was the *forgiveness of sins* and *restoration to covenant standing* to be accomplished through the death and shedding of the blood of an innocent substitute victim. It was the forfeiting of a life for a life, which was declared in the sprinkling of the blood. 'For the life of the flesh is in the blood; and I have given it to you upon the altar to make atonement for your souls; for it is the blood that maketh atonement by reason of the life.'

"On the basis of the grace shown to Israel in her divine election and the institution of the Covenant, God provided, by His mercy, a means for the sinner to draw near to Him continually. This was the Levitical system of sacrifices. He did not command Moses to tell the children of Israel that a lamb without blemish could *in itself expiate sins*, but He did promise to accept the life of an animal, ceremonially pure, in substitution for the life of the actual transgressor, and in view of this act, would *forgive* his iniquities. It must not be forgotten that it was *God Himself* who instituted sacrifices, specified the procedure, and promised forgiveness.

"Hence, the apparent contradiction between Leviticus and Hebrews 10:4 where we are told that '. . . it is impossible that the blood of bulls and goats should take away sins,' is reconciled in the fact that the Old Testament sacrifices were efficacious only with respect to *God's forgiving grace*, and not with respect to the *final expiation* or *removal* of the sins themselves.

"But forgiveness was promised and guaranteed, according to the Apostle, on the basis of God's future purposes in Christ—the Lamb of God,

"Whom God set forth to be a propitiation, through faith, in his blood, to show his righteousness because of the *passing over* of sins done aforetime, in the forbearance of God. (Rom 3:25, Italics mine.)

"Note also Hebrews 9:15, where the death of Christ, as the Mediator of the new covenant, is said to have been '. . . for the redemption of the transgressions that were under the first covenant . . . ,' the efficacy of His death being regarded by God as retrospective. And again in 9:26 the Apostle states that '. . . now once at the end of the ages hath he been manifested to put away sin by the sacrifice of himself.'

"Through the all sufficient sacrifice of Christ for sins, God's righteousness was at last vindicated. The Apostle in Romans 3:25 and Hebrews 10:4 confirms the fact that while the Old Testament sacrifices provided *forgiveness* for the pious Israelite, yet those sins could never be *purged away* by the blood of bulls and goats, hence they were 'passed over'[17] by the forbearing grace of God until *expiated* by the sacrifice of Christ.

"On account of the eternal purpose of God to punish sin and provide an atonement in His Son, God pardoned the sins of His people under the Old Testament Mosaic dispensation, but they were not actually purged away until covered by the blood of Christ. Owing to the forbearance of His grace He accepted the animal substitutes to make a covering for sin and propitiate His judicial wrath against sin, until in the fulness of time He through His own Lamb would *validate* all forgiveness granted through atonement by animal types. This means that Christ's atonement was made and accepted in God's sovereign counsels and foreknowledge before the foundation of the world (I Pet. 1:20; Rev. 13:8), so that the humble and repentant worshipper with his sacrifices of the Old Testament was accepted on the ground of it."

Therefore, in view of all this it is evident that the Old Testament sacrifices had no intrinsic efficacy whatsoever. The only basis upon which one could maintain, as Allis does, that the sacrifices of the millennium will be expiatory is to contend that the sacrifices of the Old Testament were in themselves efficacious and expiatory, which would be a contradiction of the Scriptures. Sacrifices cannot accomplish in the future that which they could not in the past. Old Testament sacrifices had efficacy only with respect to God's forgiving grace on the ground of His future work in Christ. Their expiatory efficacy was symbolical.

This fact is confirmed by the basic meaning of the Hebrew word *kipper* translated by the English term "atonement." This term does

---

[17]The Greek word is *paresis* meaning "passing by" and is used nowhere else in the New Testament. The term *'aphesis*, usually translated "remission," occurs seventeen times, but is not used here. Quite obviously the apostle would not have used a different word here, unless he intended to express a different sense. The AV is incorrect in rendering *paresis* here in Rom. 3:25 "remission"; the ASV corrects this, however.

not correspond etymologically to, nor convey the exact meaning of, the Hebrew. The Hebrew term *kipper* means "to cover." This usage is seen in Genesis 6:14 where God instructs Noah to "make thee an ark. . . and. . . pitch [*kipper*, literally, 'cover'] it within and without with pitch." When the word is used in a technical sense it can signify the covering over of an offense whereby an offended party could no longer see the offense and was, as a result, pacified or propitiated. This usage of *kipper* is clearly seen in the encounter of Jacob with Esau. Jacob, remembering how he had taken the birthright and blessing from Esau, feared the approaching encounter with his brother. In order to appease his wrath Jacob sent Esau a gift, saying: "I will appease him [literally, 'cover over, or propitiate, his anger,' *kipper*] with the present that goeth before me, and afterward I will see his face; peradventure he will accept me" (Gen. 32:20). This expresses the precise meaning and usage of *kipper* (atonement) in its technical or Levitical employment. In the Old Testament it is always the sin that is covered over by the blood of the sacrifice which hides it from God's view and propitiates His wrath. The Hebrew term never means *expiation* of sins; such a meaning is foreign both to *kipper* and the Greek synonym *hilasmos* in the New Testament. The Hebrew *kipper* means "to cover over" and "to make propitiation." Hence, the blood of the animal sacrifice was to cover over the sins (symbolically) of the offender and thus propitiate the judicial wrath of God. Therefore, this meaning of *kipper* in Leviticus will have the same meaning in Ezekiel and his prophecy of the millennium. *As the Old Testament sacrifices could not expiate sin, but were symbolic of Christ's sacrifice, neither will the sacrifices of the millennium.* Whatever their precise meaning and purpose in the future, this fact will be certain.

As the Old Testament sacrifices symbolically covered over sins and looked forward to the Lamb of Calvary who would effect actual expiation for them, so too the millennial sacrifices which the Prince will provide and offer as the representative of the people will symbolically point back as memorials to the finished work of Calvary. It is important to note in Ezekiel 45 that it is not the people who provide their own sacrifices as in the Old Testament. While they are to make contributions (*terûmâh*) of wheat, barley, oil and animals of the flock to the Prince, it is His responsibility to make provision for the sacrificial worship at stated periods, such as at the religious festivals, new moons and the like, in which the people participate:

> And it shall be the prince's part to give the burnt-offerings, and the meal-offerings, and the drink-offerings, in the feasts, and on

the new moons, and on the sabbaths, in all the appointed feasts of the house of Israel: he shall prepare the sin-offering, and the meal-offering, and the burnt-offering, and the peace-offerings, to make atonement for the house of Israel (Ezek. 45:17).

In all the passages wherein sacrifices are mentioned it is never specifically stated that the individual Israelite himself ever makes a sacrifice, all of which would seem to suggest a different purpose in the sacrificial system of the millennial period (cf. 40:38 ff.; 43:13; 43:18 ff.; 44:11 ff.; 45:13 ff.; 46:2 ff.).

Sacrificial symbols can look back as well as forward. The communion of the bread and cup are literal, material symbols which, as memorials, point back to the redemption already accomplished. So too the sacrifices of the millennium can be commemorative—as the Old Testament sacrifices were anticipative—serving to bring to remembrance the cross of Calvary.

The millennial sacrifices, as Erich Sauer has shown, "will then have an entirely new meaning and an entirely new outlook. In their Mosaic, pre-Christian, Old Testament sense, sacrifices and priesthood will never return. The 'old covenant' is for ever gone and will never again arise and be re-established. Much rather will everything take place in the spirit of the 'new covenant.' The old forms will be filled with a completely new spirit."[18] As the outward rites of Mosaic worship had no intrinsic efficacy, but symbolized great spiritual truths concerning the Messiah and His kingdom, so again literal temple ordinances and service, having no relation to the old dispensation, will set forth symbolically eternal truths of the same realities, perhaps in new and significant ways.

In conclusion, it should not be forgotten that it is *Israel* at worship which the prophet portrays in chapters 40-48, not the church which has put aside the temple, altar, priesthood and sacrificial ritual, as the epistle to the Hebrews teaches (cf. John 4:21-24). However, for national Israel in the new age such is not to be the case, for the Scriptures reiterate again and again that Israel will have these things restored. First, in her apostate condition the old Mosaic rites will be reinstituted (Dan. 9:24, 26-27; Matt. 24:15 ff.; II Thess. 2:4; Rev. 11:1 ff.). And then, during the millennium, after she has been purged and restored, the new temple and worship prophesied by Ezekiel will be realized (Ezek. 40-48; Amos 9:11; Hosea 3:4-5; Isa. 2:2-4; Micah 4:1-4; Zech. 6:9-15; 14:8-21; Dan. 7:22, 27).

Then all which God had originally intended that Israel should be and accomplish nationally upon earth, in regard to both her unique

[18]Erich Sauer, *From Eternity to Eternity,* p. 183.

priesthood and worship, together with her exaltation among the nations in righteousness, will at last be realized. Then the kingdom will be restored to Israel, a fact which the apostles fully expected to be literally fulfilled on the basis of Old Testament prophecy, the exact time of which the Lord declared the Father had Himself determined and would accomplish at its predetermined time and season.

> They therefore, when they were come together, asked him, saying, Lord, dost thou at this time restore the kingdom to Israel? And he said unto them, It is not for you to know times or seasons, which the Father hath set within his own authority (Acts 1:6-7; cf. Rom. 11:25-29).

3. The problem of the alleged nonfulfillment of the prophecy in Ezekiel 26:7-14 (cf. 29:17-20) has already been discussed in Part I of this book, "The Problem of Fulfillment and Nonfulfillment of Prophecy."

OUTLINE OF EZEKIEL

Chapter 22

HAGGAI

I. The Nature of the Book

FROM THE TIME when Habakkuk and Jeremiah prophesied of the Chaldean invasion of Judah until Haggai, the first postexilic prophet, about a century had elapsed. However, during this interval God had not left Himself without a witness; the prophets Jeremiah, Ezekiel and Daniel had continued to proclaim the word of the Lord, emphasizing also how the warnings and predictions of the earlier prophets had come to pass. Israel had fallen to Assyria, and Judah had suffered a similar fate at the hands of Babylon. When the period of judgment came to an end, God directed Cyrus, king of Persia, to allow the Hebrews to return to their homeland in 536 B.C. and rebuild their temple of worship.

During the second year of the reign of Darius Hystaspes, king of Persia (520), the two prophets, Haggai and Zechariah, appeared in Judah, and according to the book of Ezra (5:1 ff.; 6:14; cf. 3:8) the Jews were encouraged in their reestablishment of the temple by their preaching. Haggai's ministry preceded that of Zechariah by a period of two months.

The book of Haggai contains four separate discourses which are easily distinguished and dated. The first (1:1-11) was delivered on the first day of the sixth month of Darius' second regnal year and contains an exhortation to Zerubbabel and the high priest Joshua to undertake the immediate rebuilding of the temple. In this section Haggai reproved the people's unfaithfulness in setting aside their spiritual obligations while they promoted their own prosperity, which, because of their selfishness, never actually materialized. They had deluded themselves into believing that if they first made themselves prosperous and satisfied their own needs, they would then be in a better position to meet their obligations to the Lord. What they failed to see, however, was that when one neglects to discharge his obligations to the Lord first, whatever he does for himself will not prosper. Hence, Israel found to her dismay that when she pleaded exemption from her responsibilities to the Lord on the basis of the severity of the times and lack of resources, her condition grew worse instead of better inasmuch as God withheld the rains and smote them

326

with drought. In spite of God's admonitions, however, this spiritual principle seems lost on every new generation of the people of God and must be relearned by experience. Compare, for example, the same problem about a century later in the day of Malachi (Mal. 3:8-11; cf. II Cor. 9:6). Haggai concluded this address with a historical section (1:12-15) which describes the effects of his first discourse.

The second address (2:1-9), which was delivered the following month, was a message of encouragement to the builders.

The third exhortation (2:10-19) was delivered in the ninth month and describes the infectious nature of sin. By analogy drawn from the law, Haggai shows the people that residence in the Holy Land and the offering of sacrifice do not suffice to make them acceptable to God as long as they themselves remain unclean through neglect of rebuilding the house of the Lord:

> Thus saith Yahweh of hosts: Ask now the priests concerning the law, saying, If one bear holy flesh in the skirt of his garment, and with his skirt do touch bread, or pottage, or wine, or oil, or any food, shall it become holy? And the priests answered and said, No. Then said Haggai, If one that is unclean by reason of a dead body touch any of these, shall it be unclean? And the priests answered and said, It shall be unclean. Then answered Haggai and said, So is this people, and so is this nation before me, saith Yahweh; and so is every work of their hands; and that which they offer there is unclean (2:11-14).

A man who has defiled his life through neglect of his responsibilities to God cannot sanctify himself simply by outward conformity to ritual. Just as the contact with a dead body produced ceremonial uncleanness to the Hebrew until purged by lustrations and other rites, so too the worship and offerings of the disobedient are defiled in the sight of God until purified by total obedience. A disobedient person is defiled in the sight of God, and consequently defiles every work of his hands (v. 14). Limited obedience, in the form of sacrifices, cannot cleanse or make holy one who is disobedient; on the contrary, disobedience infects even that which he offers and renders it unclean.

The fourth utterance (2:20-23) is a Messianic prophecy delivered on the same day as the third discourse.

The messages cover a period of four months and the book, next to Obadiah, is the smallest in the Old Testament, consisting of only thirty-eight verses. It hardly should be supposed that it contains all of the preaching of the prophet, although his ministry was no doubt a limited one and had to do with the restoration of the national life of the Jews in their homeland which centered around the rebuilding of the temple. The style of Haggai is prosaic, which stems no doubt from the practical purpose of his preaching. His message is simple and direct, his short poignant sentences being exactly what his ministry of restoration required.

II. THE DATE

The date of the Prophet Haggai, as well as the exact period of his ministry, is quite easily determined from the text. Haggai appears in 520 B.C., preaches four messages in four months, and disappears from the scene. The first prophetic discourse was delivered August-September, 520; the second, September-October, 520; the third, November-December, 520; and the fourth was delivered in the same period, November-December, 520.

III. THE PROPHET

Scarcely anything is known about the Prophet Haggai. He was the first postexilic prophet of the newly established Jewish community which had returned in 536 B.C. Both in his book and in Ezra 5:1; 6:14 he is designated simply as "Haggai the prophet."

The meaning of the name Haggai is uncertain. It is usually held to mean "festival" or "festive," from ḥag, "a feast," with the adjectival suffix *ai*. From this some infer that the prophet was born on a feast day, while others believe his name to be indicative of the joyful character of his predictions. Still others consider the name an abbreviation for "feast of Yahweh" (cf. I Chron. 6:30) or, taking it literally as it stands, "my feast."

Upon the basis of 2:3, it has been suggested that Haggai was of a small company who had seen the glory of the former temple of Solomon in 586 before its destruction. If so, he would have been an old man over eighty years of age when he prophesied, having returned with Zerubbabel in 536. He seems to have been the senior of Zechariah, for when they are mentioned together Haggai's name always appears first. Some manuscripts of the LXX, as well as the Vulgate and Syriac versions, attribute to Haggai and Zechariah the authorship of certain psalms: 137; 145-48 in the Septuagint; 125; 126; 145-47 in the Syriac; 111; 145 in the Latin. But it is thought by others that these prophets are simply responsible for the arrangement of these psalms for use in the temple services. References to Haggai and his prophecy appear in Hebrews 12:26 (cf. Hag. 2:6); Ecclesiasticus 49:10-11; I Esdras 6:1; 7:3; II Esdras 1:40.

IV. THE HISTORICAL BACKGROUND

The historical situation out of which the prophecies of Haggai and Zechariah developed begins with the first return from exile in 536 B.C. Babylon fell into the hands of Cyrus in 539, and soon after the monarch gave permission to the Jews to return to their homeland. The book of Ezra furnishes most of the details of the history of this period. Under the leadership of Zerubbabel, the civil head of the community, and Joshua, the high priest, 42,360 people, in addition to 7,337 servants, returned to Palestine and settled in Jerusalem and in the neighboring towns of Bethlehem, Bethel, Anathoth, Gibeon and elsewhere (Ezra 2). On reaching Jerusalem they had immediately set up the altar of burnt offering (Ezra 3:2 ff.) and resumed worship. The foundation of the temple was laid in the second year of their return (Ezra 3:8-13).

However, the building enterprise met with unexpected obstacles. The mixed-blooded Samaritans (descendants of the colonists introduced into northern Israel by Sargon in 722 B.C., II Kings 17:24-41) offered to cooperate in the reconstruction of the temple on the basis of brotherhood, but were refused by Zerubbabel. This rejection was bitterly resented and successful efforts were made at the Persian court to discontinue the building; a sixteen-year period of inactivity followed. Other causes contributed to this inactivity: (1) adjustment to worship without the temple during the Babylonian captivity (a new generation had arisen which had never seen the former place of worship); (2) disillusionment upon their return to cities ruined and desolate, hostile neighbors, and scarcity of food and shelter; (3) poverty resulting from failure of crops; (4) the desire to construct their own houses and engage in personal enterprises.

During this period Cyrus died (529). His chosen successor to the Persian throne, and for a short time his coregent, was his son Cambyses (530-522), whose chief exploit was the conquest of Egypt in 525. During his absence there arose an impostor, Gaumata, who pretended to be Smerdis, the younger brother of Cambyses (who had in reality been murdered). Cambyses committed suicide and Gaumata was assassinated after a reign of seven months. Cambyses, who had no son, was succeeded by Darius Hystaspes in 521. The interdict which had stopped the building of the temple was removed by Darius, and the original decree of Cyrus, having been discovered, was reenacted.

At this time Haggai appeared on the scene in the second year of Darius (520) to exhort the people to meet their responsibilities to God, and to encourage their efforts in the completion of the temple. The building of the temple was resumed as a consequence and was completed in 516 at the end of four years. But two things were absent from the second temple that had been present in the first: It was not filled with the cloud of the glory of Yahweh (the Shekinah glory), and the ark of the convenant containing the tables of the law had disappeared in the Babylonian destruction of the city and temple in 586.

The religious and moral conditions in Jerusalem after the return from exile are reflected in the books of Haggai and Zechariah. The one outstanding complaint of Haggai is the religious indifference of the people. The people were neglecting their responsibilities to God and looking after their own interests (1:9), excusing themselves by saying the time for building the temple had not arrived (1:2). They were, however, engaging in some degree of worship and bringing sacrifices (2:14). Zechariah 7-8 shows that both religious feasts and fasts were also being observed. The abuses condemned by Ezra, Nehemiah and Malachi seemed to have developed after the ministries of Haggai and Zechariah.

V. PROBLEMS

The brevity of the book of Haggai (thirty-eight verses) has not prevented the school of negative criticism from challenging its unity. Chapter 2:10-19 is said to present a different point of view from the rest of the prophecy and the vocabulary is dissimilar, hence, it is an interpolation. But these allegations are groundless, being subjective attempts by the critical school to prove composite authorship in every book of the Old Testament Prophets. There are no convincing reasons why the entire book was not written by Haggai. The few attempts to find secondary glosses in Haggai have proved quite unsuccessful, most critics admitting the genuineness of the book. Nevertheless, while admitting that the addresses were originally spoken by Haggai, they deny that the book is from his hand because of the use of the third person throughout. But this contention is never decisive in itself, since use of the third person in Scripture is a common phenomenon; moreover, even the use of an amanuensis is not denial of complete originality (cf. Jeremiah and Baruch).

Another question involves Haggai's meaning in 2:20-23, his last discourse:

> And the word of Yahweh came the second time unto Haggai in the four and twentieth day of the month, saying, Speak to Zerubbabel, governor of Judah, saying, I will shake the heavens and the earth; and I will overthrow the throne of kingdoms; and I will destroy the strength of the kingdoms of the nations; and I will overthrow the chariots, and those that ride in them; and the horses and their riders shall come down, every one by the sword of his brother. In that day, saith Yahweh of hosts, will I take thee, O Zerubbabel, my servant, the son of Shealtiel, saith Yahweh, and will make thee as a signet; for I have chosen thee, saith Yahweh of hosts.

Negative criticism holds that Haggai is here reviving the doctrine of an *ideal king* and has identified *Zerubbabel* as the long-awaited Messiah. It is held that 2:20-23 is Messianic in character and promises the exaltation of Zerubbabel, the prince of David's house. In the second discourse the prophet had announced the shaking of the nations of the earth (2:6-7), and this announcement is now repeated in connection with Zerubbabel (2:20-22). Haggai here promises that this shaking of the thrones of the kingdoms will pave the way for the establishment of the kingdom of God under the rule of the Messianic king, Zerubbabel, the chosen servant of the Lord. Thus Haggai, as subsequent history would prove, erroneously centered his Messianic hopes around this descendant of David, Zerubbabel, who would establish the kingdom of God.

But such a conclusion has no historical basis whatever and is simply another critical illusion superimposed upon the text. The text belongs to Haggai, the interpretation to the school of negative criticism. That the passage is Messianic is evident. Other Messianic passages are also found in the book. Compare "the desire of all nations" (viz., the Messiah, 2:7, margin) and the reference to the future glory of the millennial temple (2:9). What is the true meaning of the passage? Haggai sets forth a message of consolation and hope. The Lord promises to establish Zerubbabel who, as a temporary ruler appointed by Cyrus, was also of the family of David and an ancestor of the true Messiah (Luke 3:27). Hence, the chosen line was restored in Zerubbabel and was to stand secure while the kingdoms of the earth would fall.

This prophecy is similar in some respects to that delivered by Haggai's contemporary Zechariah (4:6-10) in which the hand of Zerubbabel was strengthened and established during this critical period of the postexilic community. Zechariah had no such illusions as to the Messiahship of Zerubbabel, as seen in 6:9-15 of his book where in a symbolic ceremony Joshua, the high priest, is crowned rather than Zerubbabel in an event clearly Messianic. The fact that Zerubbabel is not even mentioned in connection with this symbolic ceremony seems intentional in order to prevent just such a mistake being made. Haggai as Zechariah's contemporary would, without any question, have shared the same understanding concerning Zerubbabel.

Furthermore, no events in the time of Zerubbabel would have satisfied the eschatological predictions of 2:6; 21-22: "I will shake the heavens and the earth; and I will overthrow the throne of the kingdoms; and I will destroy the strength of the kingdoms of the nations." The prophecy is a reference to the future overthrow of

Gentile world power in the Messianic age (Dan. 2). "In that day" has clearly a future reference when the nations of the earth are to be overthrown, and the throne of David, which Zerubbabel represented, will be restored and exalted.

It is a patent fact that Zerubbabel never at any time reigned upon the throne of David in Jerusalem over the subdued kingdoms of the world. Promises are often made to individuals in Scripture which only find actual fulfillment in their descendants. Witness, for example, those promises made to Abraham, the prophecies of Jacob to his twelve sons, and those to David. The promises made to David that his seed should endure upon his throne forever (Ps. 89:36-37; II Sam. 7:16, etc.) were now passed on to Zerubbabel, the first ruler of restored Israel, because from his line would one day come the true Messiah (Matt. 1:12; Luke 1:32-33). Hence, the passage predicts the exaltation of the Messianic line symbolized in Zerubbabel. With the fall of Jerusalem the royal line of David had been cut off. Israel's hope is restored in Zerubbabel as an heir of David.

Chapter 23

ZECHARIAH

I. THE NATURE OF THE BOOK

THE PROPHECY OF ZECHARIAH is, in part, supplementary to that of his contemporary, Haggai. Zechariah's first message was delivered in the eighth month of the second year of Darius (520 B.C.), whereas that of Haggai had begun two months earlier. It was in the midst of the movement to restore the temple, which had been inaugurated by Haggai, that Zechariah received his visions and messages. According to David Baron in his exposition of Zechariah, the difference between the two prophets seems to be that while Haggai's task was chiefly to rouse the people to the *outward* task of building the temple, Zechariah took up the prophetic labors here and sought to lead the people to a complete *spiritual* change.[1] Moreover, the prophecy of Haggai is centered primarily around the local historical situation of the postexilic community in Judah, whereas Zechariah's prophecies are universal in scope and are eschatological and apocalyptic in their outlook.

The book falls into two major divisions, chapters 1-8 and 9-14. The characteristics of the two sections are markedly different from each other. The first division consists chiefly of prophetic *visions;* the remaining chapters are *verbal prophecies* of the future. Chapters 1-8 are dated and were written sometime before chapters 9-14 which are undated. The first eight chapters have, in part at least, more of an immediate reference to the historical situation, whereas the remaining section is clearly eschatological.

There are four logical divisions of the book: (1) the introductory address or call to repentance (1:1-6); (2) a series of eight visions followed by a symbolic transaction, all of which were given to the prophet in one night; and although they have reference to the present historical situation, they extend beyond to the latter days (1:7—6:15); (3) an address in the fourth year of Darius, two years

[1]David Baron, *The Visions and Prophecies of Zechariah*, p. 9.

333

after the first message, in answer to a deputation from Bethel (7-8); (4) a prophecy delivered at a later period which looks beyond the prophet's own time, dealing with the future of Israel, the Gentile world powers and the Messianic kingdom (9-14).

In the latter section (9-14) there are two main divisions, chapters 9-11 and 12-14, each headed with the words "The burden of the word of Yahweh." The two burdens deal with the same subject matter, namely, the future judgment of the world powers and the deliverance of Israel. The second section (12-14) contains a more detailed description of the manner in which the events announced in the first section (9-11) are to take place. All six chapters (9-14) treat of the conflict between the heathen world and Israel, although in different ways. In chapters 9-11 the emphasis is upon the judgment of the *Gentile* world powers in their conflict with Israel; in chapters 12-14 the judgment through which *Israel* is purified and redeemed in her conflict with these Gentile powers is emphasized. The first section is further divided into two sections, chapters 9-10 comprising the first section, chapter 11 the second. Chapters 12-14 form two sections also, 12:1—13:6 and 13:7—14:21.

The connection between chapters 1-8 and 9-14 is such that chapters 9-14 might be called a prophetic description of the future experiences of Israel in her conflict with the kingdoms of the world, her deliverance and cleansing, and the subsequent establishment of the millennial kingdom, as depicted in the eight night visions. These night visions are a sequel to the writings of Haggai, who had predicted two months previously the overthrow of the world kingdoms and the exaltation of the Messianic line, symbolized in Zerubbabel (Hag. 2:20-23).

Zechariah sets forth some of the clearest Messianic teachings in the Old Testament. The principal ones are: (1) Christ as the Branch (3:8); (2) God's Servant (3:8); (3) the Shepherd (9:16; 11:11); the smitten Shepherd (13:7); (4) Christ's entry into Jerusalem on a colt (9:9); (5) betrayal for thirty pieces of silver (11:12-13); (6) the piercing of His hands and feet (12:10); (7) return to the Mount of Olives (14:3-8); (8) the Messiah to remove iniquity (chap. 3); (9) the Messiah to unite the priesthood and kingship in His own person (chap. 6); (10) the Messiah King to be a suffering Servant (chap. 9); (11) the Shepherd to be rejected by Israel (chap. 11); (12) death of the Shepherd (chaps. 12-13); (13) conversion of Israel (chap. 13); (14) the destruction of Israel's enemies, salvation of Jerusalem and the millennial reign of the Messiah over all the world from Zion (chap. 14).

The central purpose of the prophecies of Zechariah is to show that the glorification of Zion, the overthrow of Israel's enemies, and the universal reign of the Messiah—in fact all the promises of Israel's glorious future—would yet be realized in the distant future. The prophecy of Zechariah is to the Old Testament what the book of Revelation is to the New. It is the *Apocalypse* of the Old Testament which portrays God's future dealings with His chosen people Israel. Those interpreters who spiritualize the prophecy and seek to find its fulfillment in the church, instead of in Israel, can do so only by forcing such an unwarranted interpretation upon the book, which results in endless confusion. The nation of Israel is the subject of the prophecy from beginning to end. The book of Zechariah, especially chapter 14, stands as a continual corrective to all those theories that deny the literal, future restoration of Israel, after a period of chastening, in her own land, over whom the Messiah will reign in Zion. The main criticism of the spiritualization method of interpretation of the Old Testament prophecies concerning the future of Israel is that in its effort to explain away even the clearest prophecies about Israel, it applies every promise of *blessing* to the church, while it carefully leaves the *curses* to the Jews! David Baron in his classic work, *The Visions and Prophecies of Zechariah*, points out how the prophecy stresses the momentous events concerning Israel preceding the great and terrible "day of the Lord":

> The presence in Palestine of a representative remnant of the Jewish people in a condition of unbelief; the fiery furnace of suffering into which they are there to be thrown; their great tribulation and anguish occasioned by the final siege of Jerusalem by the confederated Gentile armies under the headship of him in whom both Jewish and Gentile apostasy is to reach its climax; how in the very midst of their final sorrow the spirit of grace and supplication shall be poured upon them, and they shall look upon Him whom they have pierced and mourn; how this blessed One whom they so long rejected shall suddenly appear as their Deliverer, and His feet stand "in that day" on the Mount of Olives, which is before Jerusalem on the east; how God shall again say "Ammi" to the nation which during the long centuries of their unbelief were "Lo-Ammi"—"not My people," and how Israel shall joyously respond, "Jehovah, my God"; how Israel's Messiah shall speak peace to the nations, and Israel himself enter at last on his priestly mission to the peoples for which he was originally destined, and Jerusalem become the centre of God's fear and worship for the whole earth—all these and other solemn events of the time of the end are spoken of in this book with a

clearness and distinctness as if they were occurrences of history instead of prophecies of the future.[2]

II. The Date

Zechariah began his prophetic ministry two months after Haggai in October-November, 520 B.C. (1:1). His last dated prophecy was two years later in 518 (7:1). The last portion of Zechariah's prophecy (9:14) is undated and many feel was written by Zechariah in later life. Due to the fact that chapters 9-14 have been subject to such extensive criticism, some critics assigning this portion of the book to an unknown preexilic author, others to an anonymous author in the postexilic period, the question of the date and integrity of these chapters will be discussed in detail under "Problems of the Book."

III. The Prophet

The name Zechariah which means "Yahweh remembers" is given to more than twenty persons in the Old Testament. Like Jeremiah and Ezekiel he was of priestly descent. Born in Babylonia, Zechariah, under the leadership of Zerubbabel, returned from exile to Palestine in 536. The prophet is mentioned three times outside his own book (Ezra 5:1; 6:14; Neh. 12:16). He is called the son of Berechiah, the son of Iddo (1:1); however, in Ezra 5:1; 6:14 he is simply designated the son of Iddo. Iddo, head of one of the priestly families which returned from Babylon, was the grandfather of the prophet. Berechiah, Zechariah's father, may have died young, or else the name of the better known grandfather was attached by Ezra to that of the prophet, a common practice among Semitic peoples. However, when Joiakim was later high priest, Zechariah himself seems to have succeeded his grandfather Iddo as head of the priestly course (Neh. 12:12-16), from which it is inferred that Berechiah, his father, had died before he was able to succeed to the priesthood.

Zechariah was a young man when he first received the visions contained in chapters 1-6. In 2:4 he is addressed with a Hebrew term meaning "boy, lad or youth," translated "young man" in the American Standard Version. As previously noted he was a contemporary of Haggai, continuing after his predecessor closed his preaching ministry. It is assumed that Zechariah continued his ministry for a longer period than 518 B.C., the date last noted in his book.

IV. The Historical Background

The historical circumstances and conditions under which Zechariah conducted his ministry were in general those of Haggai's time

---

[2]Baron, pp. 6-7.

(Hag. 1:1; Zech. 1:1), since their labors were contemporary (520; see "The Historical Background" under Haggai). Jeremiah's predictions of the seventy-year captivity in Babylon (Jer. 25:11; 29:10) had been fulfilled and the Jews were back in their homeland.

It is at this point that the first vision of Zechariah begins. In 1:11 it is stated that "all the earth sitteth still, and is at rest." This was a description of the Gentile world at the beginning of the reign of Darius Hystaspes as the nations sat in undisturbed complacency and security. There was no sign as yet of the shaking of the nations predicted by Haggai (2:7, 21-22) which was to precede the exaltation of the Messiah and the glorious restoration of Israel. The condition of the Jews was disheartening. The temple was still unbuilt, the walls and city of Jerusalem lay in ruins; the people were constantly exposed to the hostility of their neighbors; there was no sign of the predicted prosperity of Israel; and Judah was still under a foreign yoke.

In the first vision of Zechariah the angel of the Lord interceded for them and cried: "O Yahweh of hosts, how long wilt thou not have mercy on Jerusalem and on the cities of Judah, against which thou hast had indignation these threescore and ten years? And Yahweh answered the angel that talked with me with good words, even comfortable words" (1:12-13). The visions and prophecies of the book of Zechariah concern themselves largely with the messages of *comfort* and *consolation* God gave in answer to the intercession of the angel of the Lord on behalf of the people of Jerusalem and Judah.

V. PROBLEMS

The problem of the book of Zechariah concerns its *unity*. All scholars agree that chapters 1-8 are the work of the Prophet Zechariah since they are ascribed to the prophet by their headings (1:1, 7; 7:1), whereas no statements to this effect are found in chapters 9-14. Because of this, negative criticism has postulated various theories all of which seek to refute the unity of the book. Generally chapters 9-14 of Zechariah are assigned either to the preexilic period or to the postexilic Greek period.

Until the middle of the seventeenth century there was no question over the unity of the book of Zechariah and the genuineness of chapters 9-14. At that time Joseph Mede, in an effort to account for the quotation of Zechariah 11:12-13 in Matthew 27:9-10, where the prophecy is attributed to Jeremiah, suggested that chapters 9-11 were the work of the *preexilic* Prophet Jeremiah. Since that time the question of the unity of the book of Zechariah has received as much

attention as any problem of the Old Testament. Mede's view of
Deutero-Zechariah was adopted in 1700 by Bishop Kidder who extended it to include chapters 12-14. The first to assign chapters 9-14
to the *postexilic* period after Zechariah was Corrodi in 1792. A
similar viewpoint was adopted by Eichhorn in 1824. He assigned
chapters 9-10 to the time of Alexander the Great; 11:1—13:6 he
dated somewhat later; and 13:7—14:21 was assigned to the Maccabean period.

OBJECTIONS TO THE UNITY OF ZECHARIAH

The grounds for the objection to the genuineness of chapters 9-14
are threefold: (1) the problem of Matthew 27:9-10; (2) so-called
inconsistencies of historical and chronological references (presupposed in chaps. 9-14) with the age of Zechariah; (3) differences in
style between the two sections.

1. *The problem of Matthew 27:9-10.* The problem lies in the
fact that Matthew 27:9-10 cites a prophecy from Zechariah
11:12-13, but attributes it to the Prophet Jeremiah. As previously
noted, because of this the integrity of chapters 9-14 was called into
question by Joseph Mede who contended that this section was by the
preexilic Prophet Jeremiah. Mede said:

> It would seem the Evangelist [Matthew] would inform us that
> those later chapters ascribed to Zachary . . . are indeed the
> prophecies of Jeremy, and that the Jews had not rightly at-
> tributed them: . . .there is no scripture saith they are Zachary's,
> but there is a scripture saith they are Jeremy's, as this of the
> Evangelist.[3]

Also he believed he had found internal proof that chapters 9-11
belonged to Jeremiah's day rather than Zechariah's.

2. *Inconsistencies of historical and chronological references in
chapters 9-14 with the age of Zechariah.* Mede contended this section
contains a prophecy of the destruction of Jerusalem which was
fulfilled by Titus, but had no relation to the purpose of Zechariah
whose mission was to console and comfort. Judah and Ephraim are
spoken of together as two distinct kingdoms still in existence, which
was not true after the exile. Assyria and Egypt are seen as formida-
ble powers, which was their preexilic rather than postexilic status,
having been subdued by Persia. Phoenicia, Damascus and Philistia
are mentioned as important foes, but their position had long ago
declined. The false prophets and idolatry are condemned, two evils
which did not exist in postexilic Israel after the captivity. The

---

[3]Baron, p. 263.

representation of the Messiah, in the second part of the book, as rejected and slain is in direct contrast to the first section where He is represented as glorious and blessed.[4]

While early critical scholarship advocated a preexilic date for chapters 9-14, today modern criticism holds that "second Zechariah" (9-14) indicates a complete change in background from the first half of the book and is *postexilic*. Rather than representing the Persian period of Zechariah or earlier, it represents the Greek period following the conquest of Alexander the Great (9:13; 10:10 f.). The Jews of the Diaspora during this period went whenever possible on annual pilgrimages to Jerusalem (14:16). Other facts point to the time of Alexander: the scarcity of true prophets (13:2-6), ritual observances (9:7; 14:19) and the apocalyptic style, typical of this time. The editors of the Minor Prophets took these anonymous prophecies and grouped them in three divisions, each called a "burden" (9:1; 12:1; Mal. 1:1).[5]

3. *Difference in style.* The methodology of the *International Critical Commentary* in dealing with the problem of the authorship of Zechariah 9-14 is to compare the two parts of the book to see if the same features of the one section are reproduced in the second. If not, the unity of the book is to be abandoned. Thus, since there are no dates in the last six chapters as appear in the first section, and since there is no open reference to any person or event that can be accurately dated, Zechariah cannot be the author. Again, the first person is used only once (chap. 11), whereas it occurs frequently in the first eight chapters. Zechariah's fondness for visions seen in the first section is absent in the last. In regard to the literary form, "It is clear" alleges Mitchell, "that, if Zechariah wrote the first eight chapters of the book called by his name, he cannot have written the sections [9:1—11:3]. . . . They constitute an elaborate poem; he in his undoubted writings never attempted to put together a dozen lines."[6]

Concerning the differences in style between the two sections, S. R. Driver bases his conclusions largely on the difference in the "dominant ideas and representations" between the two sections. Similarities are few and insignificant when weighed against the differ-

---

[4]John Peter Lange, "Introduction to the Book of Zechariah," *Minor Prophets, Lange's Commentary on the Holy Scriptures,* trans. Philip Schaff, XIV, 12.

[5]Madeleine S. Miller and J. Lane Miller (eds.), *Harper's Bible Dictionary,* p. 837.

[6]Hinckley G. Mitchell, *Haggai and Zechariah, The International Critical Commentary,* C. A. Briggs *et al.* (eds.), pp. 234-35.

ences in style. In chapters 1-8 the lifetime of Zechariah is pictured, and his interests are the restored community and temple, whereas the distant future is depicted in the second portion. Driver contrasts the different pictures of the Messiah and the Messianic age in the two divisions of the book "(contrast 3:8; 6:12 f. with 9:9 f. and c. 8 with the representation in c. 14)."[7] The prospects of the nation are represented differently in the two sections. "Contrast 1:21; 2:8-11; 8:7 f. with 12:2 ff.; 14:2 f.; and observe that in c. 12-14 the *return* of the Jewish exiles" is not an event looked forward to.[8]

Driver's conclusion as to the authorship of Zechariah 9-14 based upon alleged differences in literary style is: "That the author of Zech. 1-8 should be also the author of either c. 9-11 or c. 12-14 is hardly possible. Zechariah uses a different phraseology, evinces different interests, and moves in a different circle of ideas from those which prevail in c. 9-14."[9]

ARGUMENTS FOR THE UNITY OF ZECHARIAH 9-14

The variation among the critics, wherein some have insisted upon a preexilic date, while others advocate a postexilic date for chapters 9-14, casts suspicion upon their views. The differences which exist between the two sections of Zechariah are not of such a nature as to indicate two or more different authors. While it is true that in chapters 9-14 no visions occur, this does not disprove the unity of the prophecy, since, for example, Amos has visions only in the second part of his book (chaps. 7-9), and not the first (1-6). The absence of dates in the headings of the final chapters may be explained simply by the fact that these are prophecies of the future kingdom which are not as directly associated with Zechariah's own time as, for example, the first vision which describes the conditions of the world in the second year of Darius.

1. *The problem of Matthew 27:9-10.* The prophecy cited in Matthew 27:9-10 is evidently derived from Zechariah 11:12-13, but Matthew attributes it to the Prophet Jeremiah.

> Then was fulfilled that which was spoken through Jeremiah the prophet, saying, And they took the thirty pieces of silver, the price of him that was priced, whom certain of the children of Israel did price; and they gave them for the potter's field, as the Lord appointed me (Matt. 27:9-10).

[7]S. R. Driver, *An Introduction to the Literature of the Old Testament,* pp. 354-55.
[8]*Ibid.*
[9]*Ibid.*

Mede's solution of the difficulty was to assign chapters 9-11 to a preexilic date under the authorship of Jeremiah. The principal theories since that time are as follows:

a. An error on the part of Matthew. This is the questionable solution by Luther, Keil and Wright. Obviously such an explanation as an error of memory is inconsistent with true inspiration.

b. An error by an original copyist was the suggestion of Origen.

c. Jerome (Ewald, *et al.*) conjectures that the reference in Matthew is a quotation from some Apocryphal writing ascribed to Jeremiah.

d. Jeremiah's priority in the Talmud. Lightfoot quotes the Talmud which teaches that in the ancient order of the prophetic books Jeremiah was placed first. Advocates of this view argue that Matthew quoted from this prophetic collection, that is, from the *book* of Jeremiah. Attention is directed to the *Psalms of David* and the *Proverbs of Solomon* in support of this theory. These too are collections consisting of various authors.

e. The reproduction of Jeremiah by Zechariah. This is the view of Grotius, Hengstenberg and others. Hengstenberg holds that later prophets often reproduced earlier prophecies, and that Zechariah is reproducing here Jeremiah 18:2 and 19:2. Matthew intentionally refers to the original source, although adopting mainly the later form. As additional evidence Hengstenberg points out that in the Gospels only Jeremiah, Isaiah and Daniel are quoted by *name* (Jonah is referred to in Matt. 12:39 ff.). Zechariah, on the other hand, is quoted or referred to several times in the Gospels and elsewhere in the New Testament but is *never named.*[10] Matthew, for example, makes two other quotations from Zechariah (21:5; 26:31) without naming the prophet. In 21:5 he combines Isaiah 62:11 and Zechariah 9:9, ascribing both to "the prophet" (i.e., Isaiah). Again, Mark 1:2-3 attributes to Isaiah that which comes partly from Malachi. Since the two prophecies are akin he gives credit for the whole to the earlier noted prophet. Hence, Matthew ascribes the words of Zechariah to Jeremiah to impress upon his readers the fact that Zechariah's prediction was a reiteration of the two solemn prophecies of Jeremiah which would, like them, be accomplished in the rejection and destruction of the Jewish people.

f. David Baron, following Origen, suggests there are strong arguments to show that this is probably a very ancient copyist's error which, however, does not affect the inspiration of the original

[10]John A. Broadus, *Commentary on the Gospel of Matthew, An American Commentary on the New Testament,* ed. Alvah Hovey, I, 558-59.

manuscript. In the original manuscript the name Zechariah, *Zachariou* may have been written in its abbreviated form as *Zriou*, which the copyist could easily have taken for *'Iriou*, the abbreviation of *'Ieremiou*, Jeremiah. Or, in the original text, Matthew may have given no name at all, but simply may have written "as was spoken by the prophet," a formula which he uses often (cf. 1:22; 2:5, 15; 13:35, etc.). And the copyist might have inserted a name, the wrong name, making an error of memory, remembering the purchase of a field in Jeremiah 32:6-12.[11] Again, it is possible Matthew had written "through Zechariah the prophet" and a copyist inadvertently inserted the name of Jeremiah, since he had already written that phrase once before, rightly using Jeremiah's name (Matt. 2:17).

g.   F. F. Bruce suggests that Matthew may have been quoting from a conflation of texts from Jeremiah and Zechariah, a primitive collection of Christian testimonies.[12]

h.   Laetsch, it would appear, presents the most plausible solution to this problem in his commentary *The Minor Prophets*. Matthew combines two prophecies, one from Zechariah and the other from Jeremiah (32:6-8), ascribing them both to the latter prophet. This solution is not to be confused with that of Hengstenberg:

> Matthew here states that a word of Scripture was fulfilled by the purchase of a potter's field for the thirty pieces of silver paid as the price of the Messiah. Zechariah says nothing of the purchase of a field nor of his appointment to buy a field. But Jeremiah, who says nothing of the betrayal, does state that the Lord "appointed him" (Matt. 27:10) to buy a field (Jer. 32:6-8). He was to buy this field as a solemn guarantee by the Lord Himself that fields and vineyards would again be bought and sold in the land (vv. 15, 43 f.).... This potter's field was one of the fields the omniscient Lord (Acts 15:18) had in mind when He spoke to Jeremiah. On the other hand, Jeremiah says nothing of another circumstance closely connected with the purchase of this potter's field, that it was to be bought for the thirty pieces of silver, the price of Him that was valued (Matt. 27:9), nor that this money would be cast into the Temple (Matt. 27:5). These details were added by Zechariah. Matthew combines both prophecies and names Jeremiah, because he was the major prophet and had foretold what Matthew particularly intended to stress, the purchase of the field.[13]

[11]Baron, p. 412.
[12]F. F. Bruce, *Biblical Exegesis in the Qumran Texts*, p. 71.
[13]Theodore Laetsch, *The Minor Prophets*, p. 470.

2. *The alleged discrepancy in the historical period presupposed in chapters 9-14.* Those who reject the traditional view of Zechariah are divided into two groups: those who hold to a preexilic date for chapters 9-14 and those who argue for a postexilic date after Zechariah. Some critics have assigned the date to the time of Uzziah, Jotham, Ahaz or Hezekiah; others contend for the Greek period of Alexander the Great or the Maccabean period.

Mede's contention that the mention of Ephraim (Israel) and Judah implies a preexilic time when these two kingdoms were still in existence infers nothing, since they are used indiscriminately to express the whole people before and after the captivity (cf. Jer. 30:3-4; 31:6, 27, 31; 33:14; Ezek. 37:16; Ezra 1:3; 3:1; 4:1, 3-4). The term Ephraim may designate that part of Israel's population yet existing, as does Malachi 2:11 which is not denied as postexilic. The charge that idolatry is condemned, which would not be the case in postexilic Palestine, is groundless, since very likely Zechariah's reference is to past transgressions; or it could be a warning which would still be needed. While the false prophet and idolatry presented no great postexilic problem, they were not totally absent from Hebrew life (cf. Neh. 6:12-14; Matt. 7:15; 24:11-24). Assyria and Egypt are used as representative of the heathen enemies of the Jews. The name Assyria is used in a loose way for Babylon and Persia in Ezra 6:22; Judith 1:7; 2:1. Phoenicia and the other kingdoms were still in existence in Zechariah's day.

Thus the historical point of view of Zechariah 9-14 can be postexilic. In this section Messiah alone is recognized as King, and there is no allusion to any reigning king of Judah and Israel.[14] Although Judah had partially returned to Jerusalem, there were still "prisoners of hope" awaiting release (cf. 9:11-12 with 2:12), and the house of Joseph (Ephraim) was still to be gathered (10:6-10). God's concern is now with all the tribes of Israel, not just Judah (9:1, 13). The hostile empire is called Javan (from Dan. 8:21, margin), which points to the postexilic period, since Javan (Greece) never appears as a major enemy to Israel before the captivity.

While these facts indicate a postexilic date for chapters 9-14, they do not imply a post-Zecharian date. It cannot be maintained that the composition of chapters 9-11 is to be placed after the invasion of Alexander the Great in 332 B.C. because of the reference to Javan (9:13, margin). The passage is clearly predictive and not contemporary history. Javan was known to Israel before Zechariah's time (Gen. 10:2, 4; Joel 3:6; Isa. 66:19; Ezek. 27:13). The more immedi-

[14]Merrill F. Unger, *Introductory Guide to the Old Testament*, p. 357.

ate future to which chapter 9 as a whole refers is in reference to the future victories of Alexander the Great. The beginnings of the fulfillment of 9:13, as Keil notes, are to be seen in the later wars between the Maccabees and Seleucids or Greek rulers in Syria. However, the prophecy cannot be altogether limited to this struggle, for the passage foreshadows the final conflict and overthrow of Israel's enemies in the day of the Lord.

3. *Differences in style.* The differences in style between chapters 1-8 and 9-14 are explained by the difference in the nature and purpose of these two sections and the probable interval of time which elapsed between their composition. Chapters 9-14 which are apocalyptic, eschatological and prophetic require a different style from 1-8 which consist of visions (1-6) and historical narrative (7-8). The early part of the book is grounded in the immediate historical situation surrounding the returned exiles and the rebuilding of the temple (although it too is predictive). The latter part is clearly eschatological, containing prophetic utterances concerning the judgment of the nations, the deliverance of Israel and establishment of the millennial kingdom. Some difference in style between the two sections is not unusual; on the contrary, it is to be expected.

However, there are sufficient similarities between the two sections to indicate unity of authorship. In both divisions similar and identical expressions are used: The phrase "O daughter of Zion" occurs in 2:10 and 9:9, the thought in both verses being Zion's joy over the coming of the Messiah. The promise in 8:8, "They shall be my people, and I will be their God," is repeated in 13:9. Identical Hebrew expressions are found in 7:14 and 9:8, as well as in 3:4 and 13:2. The phrases "saith the Lord" and "Lord of hosts" are characteristic of both sections. In both portions there are promises of bringing back the exiles (cf. 2:6-13; 8:6-8 with 9:11-12; 10:10-12). The language of both sections is noticeably free from Aramaisms, Messianic hope is strong in both parts, and there is a similar theme and expectation which characterizes both sections: the restoration of Israel, the overthrow of the nations and an expectation of peace and prosperity.

Finally, all admit that chapters 1-8 are postexilic, yet they too represent great diversity of expression. Contrast, for example, the graphic symbolism of the visions (1-6) with the plain, didactic style of chapters 7-8. No one has suggested a different authorship for these two chapters, however. The arguments against the unity of Zechariah are conflicting and inadequate. The critics themselves are hopelessly at variance. The hypothesis of a Deutero-Zechariah has proved, in the final analysis, as unsound as that of a Deutero-Isaiah.

OUTLINE OF ZECHARIAH

Chapter 24

MALACHI
my angel - my messenger

The Prophet Malachi is the last of the series of prophets, beginning with Moses, who for a thousand years had lifted up their voices to the people of God in rebuke and judgment for their transgressions on the one hand, and in the prediction of the future glorious Messianic kingdom on the other. By this time a hundred years had passed since the Jews had returned from their captivity in Babylon to Jerusalem. The early religious enthusiasm after the return had subsided. Following a period of revival (Neh. 10:28-39) the people had again become indifferent religiously and lax morally. The book is a call to repentance and humble obedience, and a stern warning of judgment to the disobedient and rebellious.

The book's three chapters in the Hebrew Bible are divided into four chapters in the English versions, the Septuagint and the Vulgate. The book opens with a declaration of God's love for Israel demonstrated in His choice of her (1:1-5). But Israel has not returned this love which was due. The priests have been foremost in offending Him by polluting His altar and offering unworthy sacrifices (1:6—2:4). Furthermore, they have given the people faulty instruction in the law and have caused many to stumble (2:5-9). The men were likewise profaning the covenant by divorcing their wives and marrying the idolatrous heathen (2:10-17).

Chapter 3 introduces God as coming in judgment. The people have been complacent in their sins, but the Lord shall send His messenger to prepare His way before Him and shall come suddenly and unexpectedly to His temple and shall punish the wicked, executing swift judgment upon the transgressors, delivering the righteous and purifying the land. If the people have complained that God has not yet executed His promises, then let them see the cause in their own transgressions, rebellion and neglect of their responsibilities in the matter of tithes and offerings. However, if they perform their religious obligations God will bless them. There follows a final admonition to obedience before the coming of that great and terrible day of the Lord in which the wicked will be consumed as stubble in the fire, but the righteous will be delivered (chap. 4).

Malachi places considerable emphasis on the "day of the Lord." Six times the prophet announces its approach (1:11, implied; 3:2, 17; 4:1, 3, 5). Thus the Old Testament closes with a final promise of the advent of the Messiah and the day of the Lord. The present interval between the first and second advents was not revealed to Malachi, nor to the other Old Testament prophets. Yet the two aspects are present in their prophecies: those which depict the Messiah as a suffering Servant at His first coming, and those which set forth the Messiah as a reigning King and universal Sovereign at His second coming in glory and judgment.

The appearance of Elijah was to usher in the "day of the Lord" (4:5). There is a real sense in which John the Baptist was Malachi's "Elijah-forerunner" (cf. Mal. 4:5 with Matt. 17:12-13). Yet it is equally clear that as a result of Christ's rejection by Israel there is to be a yet future and final fulfillment of the predictions of Malachi and the day of the Lord. Compare John 1:21 with Matthew 17:11, "Elijah indeed cometh, and shall restore all things," and Acts 3:21; Revelation 11:6. The words in Malachi 4:5, "Behold, I will send you Elijah the prophet before the great and terrible day of Yahweh come," indicate that John the Baptist cannot be exclusively meant, for he came before the final day of the Lord and the restoration of all things.

Malachi's style is prose. It is simple, smooth, concise, and states his message clearly. The expression "saith Yahweh of hosts" occurs twenty times in his little prophecy of fifty-five verses. His style is quite peculiar among the prophets and consists of interrogation and reply which are effective in teaching and preaching. This style is known as the didactic-dialectic method. First he makes a charge or accusation; then the questions or objections of the accused are raised; these are then answered by a withering refutation. Seven distinct examples of this method of (1) affirmation, (2) interrogation and (3) refutation have been noted in his book. (See 1:2-3; 1:6-7; 2:10-16; 2:17; 3:7; 3:8; 3:13-14.) Note the key interrogative phrase "yet ye say."

II. THE DATE

All scholars are in agreement, on the basis of the internal evidence, that the book of Malachi is postexilic. This is seen from the following facts: (1) The Jews were under a governor (1:8). (2) The Edomites had been driven from their old home (1:2-4). The expulsion of the Edomites from their territory by the Nabataean Arabs began during the period of the exile and reached its height during the early part of the fifth century B.C. (3) The date is after Haggai and Zechariah since the temple was completed and Levitical worship was in effect (1:6 ff.; 2:1 ff.; 3:1, 8, 10). (4) The moral and religious offences condemned by Malachi are basically different from those condemned by Haggai and Zechariah who urged the rebuilding of the temple. The sins condemned and reforms urged are those which are found in the books of Ezra and Nehemiah.

Therefore, while the general period of Malachi's prophecies is quite easily determined, the exact date of his appearance is more difficult to ascertain. Two dates have been suggested: (1) after Haggai and Zechariah (520) but before the coming of Ezra (458), or at least before the first arrival of Nehemiah (445); (2) others place it during the period of Nehemiah's visit to Persia and his absence from Jerusalem (after 433). Therefore, the two views usually center around the two dates 458 and 433.

In favor of the 458 date, it is urged that (1) a foreign governor (Persian) was probably ruling when Ezra arrived (1:8). The term used for governor (*peḥâh*) is a foreign word used in Ezra, Nehemiah and Esther to denote a ruler set over a province by the Persian king. (2) Foreign marriages had taken place when Ezra arrived in 458 (cf. Ezra 9 with Mal. 2:14-15). (3) Malachi shows no knowledge of any contemporary or recent reform movement as took place under Nehemiah (Neh. 8:1—13:31), whereas if he would have participated in the reform he probably would have reinforced his words by calling the people's attention to their recent covenant which they had made but were now violating. Hence, the prophecy of Malachi is to be dated immediately before the reform (c. 458) and was instrumental in preparing the way for it.

The date of 433 B.C. for the book has much to recommend it, however. (1) The close agreement between Malachi and Nehemiah. The abuses which Nehemiah sought to correct were (a) the behavior of the priests, (b) the neglect of temple service, (c) the nonpayment of tithes, (d) the desecration of the Sabbath and (e) the mixed marriages. A comparison of Nehemiah and Malachi will indicate the similarity of subject matter, with the exception that Malachi does not refer to the Sabbath (cf. Neh. 13:23 ff. with Mal. 2:10-16; Neh. 13:10-12, 31 with Mal. 1:7 ff.; 3:8-10; Neh. 13:29 with Mal. 2:8). (2) The appeal by Malachi to observe the law of Moses (4:4) presupposes the work of Ezra to restore the law (Neh. 8-10). (3) The condemnation of the unworthy sacrifices (1:7 ff.) and the unfaithfulness in the bringing of tithes (3:7

ff.) presupposes that the people were expected to provide for the sanctuary and priests, whereas in the days of Ezra the government met this expense of the temple (Ezra 7:15-24; cf. 6:9-10). In Nehemiah's day, however (Neh. 10:32 ff.), provision was made for the temple support by the people, and the condemnation by Malachi points to the neglect of these voluntary contributions. (4) While Malachi 1:8 does not exclude the possibility of Nehemiah's being governor, the reference seems to indicate a foreign governor, who was not unwilling to accept gifts from the people (cf. Neh. 5:14 ff.). Nehemiah was absent from Jerusalem at the Persian court in 433 (cf. Neh. 13:6). (5) This interval would likewise explain the prophet's attitude toward heathen marriages and the other abuses mentioned which may have broken out again during Nehemiah's absence. That no attempt was made to abolish mixed marriages until after Nehemiah's second return to Jerusalem supports this. In view of all this, many scholars assign the prophetic ministry of Malachi after 433, probably in connection with Nehemiah's reforms (Neh. 13:6 ff.).

III. THE PROPHET

The name Malachi appears nowhere else in Scripture, and it is seriously questioned by critical scholars whether Malachi is a proper name at all. Inasmuch as the term in Hebrew (*mal'ākî*) means "my angel" or "my messenger," it has been suggested that this is an anonymous prophecy, the term simply designating an office, and verse 1 should be translated "The burden of the word of Yahweh to Israel by [the hand of] *my messenger*."

In support of this theory these facts are suggested: (1) The name occurs nowhere else in the Old Testament. (2) The Septuagint and the Targum, the two oldest translations, did not take Malachi as a proper name but as an office. The LXX translated *mal'ākî* "by the hand of *his messenger*" (or angel). The Targum translated the verse "by the hand of my messenger, whose name is called Ezra the Scribe." (3) The father's name is not mentioned. (4) The similarity of Malachi 1:1 with Zechariah 9:1 and 12:1, the titles of two other alleged anonymous prophecies, is said to favor the view that all three prophecies came without headings to the collector and editor, who then appended the present headings to them. (5) There is no mention of Malachi in the books of Ezra and Nehemiah, whereas the prophets Haggai and Zechariah are both mentioned in Ezra 5:1.

In reply, however, the following should be noted: (1) The first objection is the frequent but inconclusive argument from silence.

There are other Old Testament figures whose names do not occur elsewhere outside the book that mentions them. (2) The uninspired Septuagint *translation* cannot be used as conclusive evidence to decide the problem either way, but it is interesting to note that it does employ the term Malachi as a proper name in the title as *Malachias*. The Targum likewise refers the term to a historical person. (3) The fact that Malachi's parentage is not given is not unique since this omission likewise occurs in the case of Obadiah, Habakkuk and others. (4) The alleged similarity between Malachi 1:1 and Zechariah 9:1 and 12:1 is answered under the discussion of the problems of the book. (5) That the histories of Ezra and Nehemiah contain no reference to Malachi is another argument from silence. Furthermore, it may readily be accounted for by the fact that he exercised his ministry on or before Nehemiah's second visit to Jerusalem of which there is but a brief summary in the last chapter of Nehemiah (Neh. 13:7-31).

If, then, Malachi is a pseudonym for Ezra (Targum), or the title of an office, it is the only exception in all of prophetic literature, since to each of the prophetical books the author's name is attached. Many interpreters believe the prophet's name to be a contracted form of *mal'ākyâh*, meaning "messenger of Yahweh." Such abbreviations are not uncommon. There is, for example, in the Old Testament the name Abi for Abijah (II Kings 18:2; II Chron. 29:1), and Phalti (or Palti) for Phaltiel (I Sam. 25:44; II Sam. 3:15). From his keen remarks to the priesthood some have conjectured that he was a member of the priestly body, but there is no further information to support this. Tradition states, as recorded in the Talmud, that Malachi was a member of the Great Synagogue as Haggai and Zechariah had been. The book has been assigned by other traditions to Mordecai, Haggai, Zerubbabel, Nehemiah and an "angel."

IV. THE HISTORICAL BACKGROUND

The book of Malachi is an important historical source concerning the political and religious state of Judah during the Persian period in the fifth century B.C. Haggai and Zechariah had labored to overcome the religious indifference which had developed in the years immediately following the return from Babylon, and succeeded in arousing the people, who set to work and completed the temple in 516. In Malachi's time the Jews had been home from exile in Babylon about one hundred years. They were cured of their idolatry, but had returned to their former state of indifference and spiritual lethargy. The priests had been lax and degenerate, sacrifices were inferior, tithes and offerings were neglected, divorce and mixed marriage were common (3:9-11).

Still chafing under a foreign yoke, the promises by the prophets concerning Israel's glorious future yet unrealized, many in the nation had begun to ask whether or not God loved Israel (1:2). What had become of divine justice (2:17)? Was it profitable to serve God any longer (3:13-15)? They complained that as God's chosen people they were left in a low estate while the wicked heathen prospered. If God still loved them, where was the promise of the Messiah and His universal kingdom? And where was justice? "Everyone that doeth evil is good in the sight of Yahweh, and he delighteth in them; . . . where is the God of justice?" they cried. Again others lamented, "It is vain to serve God; and what profit is it that we have kept his charge, and that we have walked mournfully before Yahweh of hosts? And now we call the proud happy; yea, they that work wickedness are built up; yea, they tempt God, and escape." Many, therefore, in the face of disappointments, the lack of prosperity, and unscrupulous nobles and priests, turned to sin, religious indifference and skepticism. Thus, the Jews impatiently awaited the Messiah. Malachi assured them He would surely come, but His sudden appearance would only issue in judgment for such as they except they repented and rendered faithful obedience (chaps. 3-4).

V. PROBLEMS

The problems of the date and authorship have already been noted. But closely related to the question of authorship is the problem of the position of the book in the Old Testament canon. To critical interpreters the book of Malachi is an anonymous writing, as are the two final prophecies which constitute chapters 9-14 of Zechariah. Negative criticism holds that the book of the Twelve Prophets contains three independent and anonymous prophecies as its concluding appendix (Zech. 9-11; 12-14; Mal. 1-4). These are said to be clearly distinguished by the unique expression which heads each prophecy: "The burden of the word of the Lord."

In order to make up the sacred number twelve for the books of the Minor Prophets the collector, with the three anonymous prophecies in his possession, added two prophecies, chapters 9-11 and 12-14, to the book of Zechariah, which originally consisted of but eight chapters. The third of these oracles became the book of Malachi, making the total number of prophets twelve. Every test, linguistic, historical and idealogical, gives evidence, it is alleged, that the two oracles attached to Zechariah do not belong to the book.[1] The *International Critical Commentary* on Malachi assumes that the title was attached to the book by a later editor who took the title from 3:1 where the phrase "my messenger" appears.

All this, however, is mere conjecture without a shred of objective evidence to support it. Many factors may be noted that argue against such an unlikely hypothesis. It is alleged, for instance, that a comparison of the titles of Zechariah 9-11, 12-14, and Malachi 1:1 will indicate that when these three anonymous prophecies were added to the collection of prophets the editor then added three identical titles. S. R. Driver states:

> It is a plausible conjecture therefore that, the three prophecies now known as "Zech." 9-11, 12-14 and "Malachi" coming to the compiler's hands with no authors' names prefixed, he attached the first of these at the point which his volume had reached, viz. the end of Zech. 8, arranging the other two so as to follow this, and framing titles for them (Zech. 12:1 and Mal. 1:1) on the model of the opening words of Zech. 9:1.[2]

But a comparison of the three titles in the Hebrew does not indicate such similarity as would be expected if they had all come from the same hand at the same time.

First of all, the titles are not identical, the similarity consisting only in this phrase of each title: "the burden of the word of Yahweh." If one author had compiled them all, why did he use two different prepositions to say the same thing, namely, '*al* in Zechariah 12:1 and '*el* in Malachi 1:1? Furthermore, in Zechariah 9:1 the title forms an integral part of the sentence that follows; in the other two cases they are simply titles as such. If one must accept some critical hypothesis it would appear much more logical to suppose that the present titles were already affixed to the three anonymous prophecies, which would then explain their *differences* rather than their alleged similarity. Also the question might well be asked, If the compiler were trying to convince the readers that these prophecies (9-11 and 12-14) belonged to Zechariah's book, why did he not append Zechariah's name to 9:1 and 12:1?

Old Testament prophecy, moreover, was subjected to a rigorous test by the Hebrews, and the critical school ought not to be expected

[1] R. C. Denton, Introduction to the Book of Zechariah," *The Interpreter's Bible*, ed. Nolan B. Harmon, 1089.

[2] S. R. Driver, *An Introduction to the Literature of the Old Testament*, p. 355.

to be taken seriously when it alleges that three anonymous prophecies were drifting around the nation, were considered to be a part of the inspired literature of Israel, were read, honored and recognized as such, yet without having the names of any authors prefixed. The other fifteen books of the Old Testament prophets state at the beginning the name of the inspired author. Prophecy had its entire value and authority in its divine origin; and its human author, if he expected to be heard by the Hebrew people, must furnish his name and credentials and give evidence that he stood in such a relation to God that he spoke the very word of God! This being the case it is more than unreasonable to suppose that three anonymous documents were quite unceremoniously appended to the biblical text when the Hebrew canon was formed.

On the contrary, in view of the Hebrew concept of prophetic Scripture such nameless works would unquestionably have been rejected as spurious. That this is true is proved by the fact that many prophetic writings were not included in the Hebrew canon which nevertheless had the names of Old Testament personalities attached. Such works were: The Assumption of Moses, the Psalms of Solomon, the Testament of the Twelve Patriarchs, the Testament of Job, among others. The Hebrews were noted for their extreme jealousy for the integrity of their sacred writings. Their absolute silence with respect to the unity of Zechariah and the problem of the three anonymous prophecies is inexplicable if the theories of negative criticism are valid.

In conclusion, the abundance of Messianic prophecies contained in Zechariah 9-14 and the book of Malachi which are quoted repeatedly in the New Testament, many already fulfilled by the first advent of Christ, argue against the theory that these were simply uninspired, anonymous documents which somehow found their way into the Hebrew canon at the hands of a later editor.

OUTLINE OF MALACHI

I. GOD'S LOVE FOR ISRAEL AND HER UNFAITHFUL
RESPONSE   Chapters 1-2; 3:7-15
  A. God's Sovereign Love for Israel   1:1-5
    1. God's Love Declared   1-2
    2. God's Love Demonstrated   3-5
  B. Israel's Unfaithfulness to God   1:6—2:17; 3:7-15
    1. Condemnation of the Unfaithfulness of the Priests   1:6—2:9
      a. Condemnation of their sins of offering unworthy
      sacrifices upon God's altar and showing contempt
      for the temple service   1:6-10

BIBLIOGRAPHY

Aalders, G. C. *The Problem of the Book of Jonah*. London: Tyndale, 1948.

Albright, William Foxwell. *From the Stone Age to Christianity*. Garden City, N. Y.: Doubleday, 1957.

Albright, William Foxwell, and Freedman, David N. (eds.). *The Anchor Bible*. Garden City, N. Y.: Doubleday, 1965.

Alexander, Joseph Addison. *Commentary on the Prophecies of Isaiah*. Grand Rapids: Zondervan, 1953.

Allis, Oswald T. *Prophecy and the Church*. Philadelphia: Presbyterian & Reformed, 1945.

———. *The Five Books of Moses*. Philadelphia: Presbyterian & Reformed, 1949.

———. *The Unity of Isaiah*. Philadelphia: Presbyterian & Reformed, 1950.

Archer, Gleason L., Jr. *A Survey of Old Testament Introduction*. Chicago: Moody, 1965.

Baab, Otto J. *The Theology of the Old Testament*. New York: Abingdon, 1949.

Baillie, John. *The Idea of Revelation in Recent Thought*. New York: Columbia U, 1945.

Baron, David. *The Visions and Prophecies of Zechariah*. London: Hebrew Christian Testimony, 1951.

Batten, L. W. *The Hebrew Prophet*. New York: Macmillan, 1905.

Bentzen, Aage. *Introduction to the Old Testament*. 2 vols. Copenhagen: G. E. C. Gad, 1952.

Berkhof, Louis. *A Summary of Christian Doctrine*. London: Banner of Truth, 1962.

Berkouwer, G. C. *The Providence of God*. Grand Rapids: Eerdmans, 1952.

Briggs, Charles Augustus, *et al.* (eds.). *The International Critical Commentary*. New York: Scribner, 1912.

Brown, Francis; Driver, S. R.; Briggs, Charles A. *A Hebrew and English Lexicon of the Old Testament*. 2d ed., rev. London: Oxford U, 1955.

Bruce, F. F. *Biblical Exegesis in the Qumran Texts*. Grand Rapids: Eerdmans, 1959.

Brunner, Emil. *Revelation and Reason*. Trans. Olive Wyon. Philadelphia: Westminster, 1946.

Burrows, Millar. *What Mean These Stones?* New Haven: American Schools of Oriental Research, 1941.

Buttrick, George A. (ed.). *The Interpreter's Dictionary of the Bible.* 4 vols. New York: Abingdon, 1962.

Calvin, John. *Calvin's Commentaries.* Trans. William Pringle. 30 vols. Grand Rapids: Eerdmans, 1948.

————. *Institutes of the Christian Religion.* Trans. Henry Beveridge. 2 vols. Grand Rapids: Eerdmans, 1953.

Chafer, Lewis Sperry. *Satan.* Chicago: Bible Institute Colportage, 1935.

Cornill, Carl Heinrich. *The Prophets of Israel.* Chicago: Open Court, 1907.

Culver, Robert D. *Daniel and the Latter Days.* Chicago: Moody, 1965.

Davidson, A. B. *Old Testament Prophecy.* Edinburgh: T. & T. Clark, 1903.

————. *The Theology of the Old Testament.* Edinburgh: T. & T. Clark, 1955.

Driver, S. R. *An Introduction to the Literature of the Old Testament.* Edinburgh: T. & T. Clark, 1950.

Driver, S. R., et al. (eds.). *The International Critical Commentary.* Edinburgh: T. & T. Clark, 1959.

Eiselen, Frederick Carl. *Prophecy and the Prophets.* New York: Methodist, 1919.

————. *The Minor Prophets.* New York: Eaton & Mains, 1907.

Ellison, H. L. *Ezekiel: The Man and His Message.* Grand Rapids: Eerdmans, 1959.

————. *Men Spake from God.* Grand Rapids: Eerdmans, 1958.

Ferm, Vergilius (ed.). *An Encyclopedia of Religion.* Paterson: Littlefield, Adams, 1959.

Finegan, Jack. *Light from the Ancient Past.* Princeton: Princeton U, 1954.

Gaebelein, A. C. *The Prophet Joel.* New York: Our Hope, 1909.

Gesenius, Williams. *A Hebrew and English Lexicon of the Old Testament.* Trans. Edward Robinson. 3d. ed. Boston: Crocker & Brewster, 1849.

Girdlestone, Robert Baker. *Synonyms of the Old Testament.* Grand Rapids: Eerdmans, n.d.

————. *The Grammar of Prophecy.* Grand Rapids: Kregel, 1955.

Gottwald, Norman K. *All the Kingdoms of the Earth.* New York: Harper & Row, 1964.

Haldane, Robert. *Exposition of the Epistle to the Romans.* 5 vols. Evansville, Ind.: Sovereign Grace, 1955.

Harmon, Nolan B. (ed.). *The Interpreter's Bible.* 12 vols. New York: Abingdon, 1956.

Hastings, James (ed.). *Encyclopaedia of Religion and Ethics.* 13 vols. New York: Scribner, 1928.

Heinisch, Paul. *Theology of the Old Testament.* Trans. William B. Heidt. St. Paul: Liturgical, 1955.

Heschel, Abraham J. *The Prophets.* New York: Harper & Row, 1962.

Hovey, Alvah (ed.). *An American Commentary on the New Testament.* 7 vols. Philadelphia: American Baptist, 1882.

Jacobus, Melancthon W. (ed.). *A Standard Bible Dictionary.* New York: Funk & Wagnalls, 1909.

Jamieson, Robert, *et al. A Commentary, Critical and Explanatory, on the Old and New Testaments.* 2 vols. Glasgow: Collins, 1873.

Johnson, Aubrey R. *The Cultic Prophet in Ancient Israel.* Cardiff: U of Wales, 1944.

————. *The One and the Many in the Israelite Conception of God.* Cardiff: U of Wales, 1961.

Kaufmann, Yehezkel. *The Religion of Israel.* Trans. Moshe Greenberg. Chicago: U of Chicago, 1960.

Keil, C. F., and Delitzsch, F. *Biblical Commentary on the Old Testament.* Trans. James Martin. 25 vols. Grand Rapids: Eerdmans, 1954.

Kirkpatrick, A. F. *The Doctrine of the Prophets.* London: Macmillan, 1897.

————. (ed.). *The Cambridge Bible for Schools and Colleges.* Cambridge: Cambridge U, 1954.

Koehler, Ludwig, and Baumgartner, Walter (eds.). *Lexicon in Veteris Testamenti Libros.* 2 vols. Grand Rapids: Eerdmans, 1953.

Knudson, Albert C. *The Religious Teachings of the Old Testament.* New York: Abingdon-Cokesbury, 1918.

Laetsch, Theodore, *The Minor Prophets.* St. Louis: Concordia, 1956.

Lange, John Peter. *Commentary on the Holy Scriptures.* Trans. Philip Schaff. Grand Rapids: Zondervan, n.d.

LaSor, William Sanford. *Amazing Dead Sea Scrolls.* Chicago: Moody, 1956.

Lindblom, J. *Prophecy in Ancient Israel.* Philadelphia: Fortress, 1963.

Meek, Theophile James. *Hebrew Origins.* New York: Harper, 1960.

Miller, Madeleine S., and Miller, J. Lane (eds.). *Harper's Bible Dictionary.* New York: Harper, 1952.

Noss, John B. *Man's Religions.* New York: Macmillan, 1956.

Oehler, Gustave Friedrich. *Theology of the Old Testament.* Grand Rapids: Zondervan, n.d.

Oesterley, W. O. E., and Robinson, Theodore H. *An Introduction to the Books of the Old Testament.* Cleveland: World, 1962.

————. *Hebrew Religion: Its Origin and Development.* 2d ed., rev. London: Society for Promoting Christian Knowledge, 1944.

Orelli, C. von. *Old Testament Prophecy.* Edinburgh: T. & T. Clark, 1885.

Orr, James. *Revelation and Inspiration.* Grand Rapids: Eerdmans, 1952.

————. (ed.). *The International Standard Bible Encyclopaedia.* 6 vols. Grand Rapids: Eerdmans, 1946.

Packer, J. I. *Fundamentalism and the Word of God.* London: Inter-Varsity, 1963.

Payne, J. Barton. *An Outline of Hebrew History.* Grand Rapids: Baker, 1954.

————. *The Theology of the Older Testament*. Grand Rapids: Zondervan, 1962.

Peake, Arthur S. (ed.). *A Commentary on the Bible*. London: T. C. & E. C. Jack, 1931.

Pedersen, Johannes. *Israel: Its Life and Culture*. 2 vols. London: Oxford U, 1953.

Pentecost, J. Dwight. *Things to Come*. Findlay, Ohio: Dunham, 1962.

Pfeiffer, Robert H. *Introduction to the Old Testament*. New York: Harper, 1941, rev. ed. 1948.

Pritchard, James B. (ed.). *Ancient Near Eastern Texts*. Princeton: Princeton U, 1950.

Procter, William C. *The Authenticity and Authority of the Old Testament*. London: Thynne & Jarvis, 1925.

Pusey, E. B. *The Minor Prophets*. Grand Rapids: Baker, 1956.

Ramm, Bernard. *Protestant Biblical Interpretation*. Boston: Wilde, 1950.

Raven, John H. *Old Testament Introduction*. New York: Revell, 1910.

Robinson, George L. *The Book of Isaiah*. Rev. ed. Grand Rapids: Baker, 1954.

————. *The Twelve Minor Prophets*. Grand Rapids: Baker, 1962.

Robinson, H. Wheeler. *Inspiration and Revelation in the Old Testament*. London: Oxford U, 1953.

————. *Redemption and Revelation*. London: Nisbet, 1942.

————. *The Old Testament: Its Making and Meaning*. New York: Abingdon-Cokesbury, 1937.

————. *The Religious Ideas of the Old Testament*. 2d ed., rev. London: Duckworth, 1956.

Robinson, Theodore H. *Prophecy and the Prophets in Ancient Israel*. London: Duckworth, 1953.

Rowley, H. H. *The Faith of Israel*. Philadelphia: Westminster, 1956.

————. (ed.). *The Old Testament and Modern Study*. London: Oxford U, 1961.

————. *Prophecy and Religion in Ancient China and Israel*. New York: Harper, 1956.

————. *The Re-discovery of the Old Testament*. Philadelphia: Westminster, 1946.

————. *The Servant of the Lord and Other Essays on the Old Testament*. London: Lutterworth, 1952.

Sauer, Erich. *From Eternity to Eternity*. Trans. G. H. Lang. Grand Rapids: Eerdmans, 1963.

Schultz, Hermann. *Old Testament Theology*. 2 vols. Edinburgh: T. & T. Clark, 1895.

Schultz, Samuel J. *The Old Testament Speaks*. New York: Harper, 1960.

Scott, R. B. Y. *The Relevance of the Prophets*. New York: Macmillan, 1953.

Singer, Isidore (ed.). *The Jewish Encyclopedia*. 12 vols. New York: Funk & Wagnalls, 1905.

Smith, George Adam. *The Book of the Twelve Prophets.* 2 vols. Revised ed. New York: Harper, 1928.

Smith, W. Robertson. *The Prophets of Israel.* London: Black, 1907.

Snaith, Norman H. *The Distinctive Ideas of the Old Testament.* London: Epworth, 1962.

Spence, H. D. M., and Exell, J. S. (eds.). *The Pulpit Commentary.* 23 vols. Grand Rapids: Eerdmans, 1950.

Strong, Augustus Hopkins. *Systematic Theology.* Philadelphia: Judson, 1954.

Tenney, Merrill C. (ed.). *The Zondervan Pictorial Bible Dictionary.* Grand Rapids: Zondervan, 1963.

Terry, Milton S. *Biblical Hermeneutics.* Grand Rapids: Zondervan, 1961.

Thomas, D. Winton (ed.). *Documents from Old Testament Times.* New York: Harper, 1961.

Torrey, C. C. *Pseudo-Ezekiel and the Original Prophecy.* New Haven: Yale U, 1930.

Torrey, R. A. *What the Bible Teaches.* New York: Revell, n.d.

Tregelles, Samuel P. *Remarks on the Prophetic Visions in the Book of Daniel.* London: Bagster, 1883.

Unger, Merrill F. *Introductory Guide to the Old Testament.* Grand Rapids: Zondervan, 1951.

———. *Unger's Bible Dictionary.* Chicago: Moody, 1957.

Vaux, Roland de. *Ancient Israel: Its Life and Institutions.* Trans. John McHugh. London: Darton, Longman & Todd, 1961.

Vine, W. E. *Isaiah.* Grand Rapids: Zondervan, 1961.

Vriezen, T. C. *An Outline of Old Testament Theology.* Oxford: Blackwell, 1958.

Warfield, Benjamin B. *The Inspiration and Authority of the Bible.* Philadelphia: Presbyterian & Reformed, 1948.

Watts, J. Washington. *A Survey of Syntax in the Hebrew Old Testament.* Nashville: Broadman, 1951.

Welch, A. C. *Prophet and Priest in Old Israel.* Oxford: Blackwell, 1953.

Whitcomb, John C., Jr. *Darius the Mede.* Grand Rapids: Eerdmans, 1959.

Wiseman, D. J., et al. *Notes on Some Problems in the Book of Daniel.* London: Tyndale, 1965.

Wright, G. Ernest. *God Who Acts.* London: Student Christian Movement, 1960.

———. *The Old Testament Against Its Environment.* Chicago: Regnery, 1950.

Young, Edward J. *An Introduction to the Old Testament.* Grand Rapids: Eerdmans, 1954.

———. *The Book of Isaiah.* Grand Rapids: Eerdmans, 1965.

———. *My Servants the Prophets.* Grand Rapids: Eerdmans, 1952.

———. *Studies in Isaiah.* Grand Rapids: Eerdmans, 1954.

———. *Thy Word Is Truth.* Grand Rapids: Eerdmans, 1960.

————. *Who Wrote Isaiah?* Grand Rapids: Eerdmans, 1958.

PERIODICALS

Albright, William F. "The Date and Personality of the Chronicler," *Journal of Biblical Literature,* Vol. XL (1921).

Allis, Oswald T. "Nahum, Nineveh, Elkosh," *Evangelical Quarterly,* XXVII, No. 2 (April, 1955), 67-80.

Bowman, John. "Prophets and Prophecy in Talmud and Midrash," *Evangelical Quarterly,* XXII, No. 2 (April, 1950), 107-14.

Culver, Robert D. "The Difficulty of Interpreting Old Testament Prophecy," *Bibliotheca Sacra,* CXIV, No. 455 (July, 1957), 201-5.

Freeman, Hobart E. "The Problem of the Efficacy of Old Testament Sacrifices," *Bulletin of the Evangelical Theological Society,* V (Summer, 1962), 73-79.

Howie, Carl Gordon. "The Date and Composition of Ezekiel," *Journal of Biblical Literature, Monograph Series,* Vol. IV (1950).

Hyatt, J. Philip. "The Date and Background of Zephaniah," *Journal of Near Eastern Studies,* VII, No. 1 (January, 1948), 25-29.

Mowinckel, Sigmund. "The Spirit and the Word in Pre-exilic Reform Prophets," *Journal of Biblical Literature,* LIII (1934), 199-227.

Payne, J. Barton. "The Unity of Isaiah: Evidence from Chapters 36-39," *Bulletin of the Evangelical Theological Society,* VI, No. 2 (May, 1963), 50-56.

Rowley, H. H. "Ritual and the Hebrew Prophets," *Journal of Semitic Studies,* I, No. 4 (October, 1956), 338-60.

Thompson, John A. "Joel's Locusts in the Light of Near Eastern Parallels," *Journal of Near Eastern Studies,* XIV, No. 1 (January, 1955), 52-55.

Tushingham, A. Douglas. "A Reconstruction of Hosea, Chapters 1-3," *Journal of Near Eastern Studies,* XII (July, 1953), 150-59.

SUBJECT INDEX

AUTHOR INDEX

SCRIPTURE INDEX

380   *An Introduction to the Old Testament Prophets*

HABAKKUK   PAGE

2:4	256
2:17	259
2:20	253
3	251, 256-59
3:1	258
3:1-2	73, 258
3:1, 2, 9, 13, 14, 18-19, 19	257
3:2	252, 258
3:3-5, 16	258
3:13	128, 258
3:19	255

ZEPHANIAH

1	271
1-3	12
1:1	233, 234
1:2-3, 14, 15, 17	232
1:3-6, 8-9, 12	233
1:4, 10-11	234
1:7	253
1:14-16, 14-18, 15, 18	146
2-3	147
2:3, 8-11, 11, 15	235
2:13	154, 233
2:13-15	228
2:15	202
3:1-7	233, 235
3:4	104
3:5, 12-13, 14-20	235
3:8, 9-13	232
3:8-20	126, 147
3:9-12	232

HAGGAI

1:1	336
1:1-11	326
1:2, 9	330
1:12-15	327
1:13	41
2:1-9, 11-14, 10-19, 20-23	327
2:3	127, 328
2:6	328
2:6-7, 9, 20-22, 21-22	331
2:7-9	313
2:10-19, 14	330
2:20-23	330-31, 334

ZECHARIAH

1	60
1-6	62, 303, 336, 344
1-8	333, 334, 337, 339, 340, 344
1:1	234, 336, 337
1:1-6	333
1:6	41, 107, 121, 243
1:7, 11, 12-13	337
1:7-17	153
1:7—6:15	333
1:8	180
1:8-10	270
1:12-17	126

ZECHARIAH   PAGE

1:21	340
2:3	270
2:4	336
2:4-13	126
2:6-13	344
2:7, 21-22	337
2:8	238
2:8-11	340
2:10	344
2:12	343
3	303, 334
3:4	344
3:8	26, 206, 334, 340
4:1	62, 180
4:6-10	331
5	303
6	334
6:8	154
6:9-15	205, 303, 313, 323, 331
6:12 f.	340
7-8	303, 344
7:1	336, 337
7:12	40, 57, 71, 72
7:14	344
8	163, 340
8:6-8, 8	344
8:7 f.	340
9-10	338
9-11	334, 338, 340, 343, 352-53
9-14	148, 197, 199, 200, 201, 312, 333, 334, 336-40, 342-44, 352-53, 354
9:1	339, 343, 350, 351, 353
9:1—11:13	339
9:7, 13	339
9:8	344
9:9	334, 341, 344
9:9 ff.	340
9:11-12, 13	343, 344
9:16	334
10:6-10	343
10:10 ff.	339
10:10-12	344
11	339
11:1—13:6	338
11:11	334
11:12-13	334, 337, 338
12-14	12, 147, 334, 340
12:1	339, 350, 351, 353
12:1—13:6	334
12:2 ff.	340
12:10	155
13:1	303
13:2	344
13:2-6	339
13:7	127, 334
13:7—14:21	334, 338
13:9	344
14	128, 147, 163, 335, 340
14:2 f.	340
14:3-8	334

APOCRYPHA INDEX